A Reader and Guide

EYES ON THE PRIZE

America's Civil Rights Years

This book has been developed for general use in American history, Afro-American studies, sociology, political science, law, and religion courses and as the text for a media-based college course. The EYES ON THE PRIZE course consists of six one-hour television programs, ten half-hour audio cassettes, and this text. Also available for course use is EYES ON THE PRIZE America's Civil Rights Years by Juan Williams, a companion book to the PBS television series, published by Viking/Penguin. The series was produced by Blackside, Inc., Boston, Massachusetts. Course materials have been prepared with the assistance of the production staff. Project director and executive producer of EYES ON THE PRIZE is Henry Hampton, president, Blackside, Inc.

* * * *

Special thanks to the Charles H. Revson Foundation for its support of EYES ON THE PRIZE.

* * * *

For further information on telecourse and off-air videotape licensing, contact: PBS Adult Learning Service, 1320 Braddock Road, Alexandria, VA 22314, 1-800-ALS-ALS8 (257-2578); in Virginia, 703-739-5360.

* * * *

For further information on purchase of prerecorded videocassettes, contact: PBS VIDEO, 1320 Braddock Place, Alexandria, VA 22314, 1-800-344-3337; in Virginia, 703-739-5380.

* * * *

A Reader and Guide

EYES ON THE PRIZE

America's Civil Rights Years

General Editors

Clayborne Carson
David J. Garrow
Vincent Harding
Darlene Clark Hine

Managing Editor

Toby Kleban Levine

Research Coordinator
Raynard T. Davis

PENGUIN BOOKS

PENGUIN BOOKS
Viking Penguin Inc., 40 West 23rd Street, New York, New York 10010, U.S.A.
Penguin Books Ltd, Harmondsworth, Middlesex, England
Penguin Books Australia Ltd, Ringwood, Victoria, Australia
Penguin Books Canada Limited, 2801 John Street, Markham, Ontario, Canada L3R 1B4
Penguin Books (N.Z.) Ltd, 182–190 Wairau Road, Auckland 10, New Zealand

First published in Penguin Books 1987
Published simultaneously in Canada

Grateful acknowledgment is made for permission to reprint the following
copyrighted material which appears in the essays in this book:

Page 18: "Let America Be America Again" by Langston Hughes. Copyright 1938 by
Langston Hughes. Copyright renewed in 1965 by Langston Hughes. Used by permission
of Harold Ober Associates.

Page 179: "Our God Is Marching On!" by Martin Luther King, Jr. Copyright 1965 by
Martin Luther King, Jr; 1968 by Estate of Martin Luther King, Jr.; 1986 by
Coretta Scott King, Executrix, Estate of Martiln Luther King, Jr. Used
by permission of Joan Daves.

Page 185: *The Other American Revolution* by Vincent Harding, page 231, UCLA
Center for Afro-American Studies, Publisher. Copyright 1980 by the Regents of
the University of California and the Institute of the Black World.
Used by permission.

Page 186: "Creation-Spell" by Ed Bullins. Copyright by Ed Bullins.
Used by permission of Helen Merrill, Ltd.

All other acknowledgments appear on the first page of text of each selection.

LIBRARY OF CONGRESS CATALOGING IN PUBLICATION DATA
Eyes on the prize.
Text to be used with PBS series, Eyes on the prize.
Includes bibliographies and index.
1. Afro-Americans—Civil rights.   2. United States—
Race relations.   I. Carson, Clayborne, 1944–
II. Eyes on the prize (Television program)
E185.615.E94   1987   973'.0496073   86-22584
ISBN 0 14 00.99981 6

Printed in the United States of America by
R.R. Donnelley and Sons, Harrisonburg, Virginia

The prize was freedom. It was a prize
no American could afford to lose.

But the one thing we did right
Was the day we started to fight
Keep your eyes on the prize
Hold on, hold on.

Traditional
freedom song

CONTENTS

by TOBY KLEBAN LEVINE, Telecourse Director

This section is directed to those individuals who are reading this book as the text for a college credit media-based course. In addition to this Reader and Guide, the course consists of six one-hour television programs and ten half- hour audio cassettes, plus any additional assignments made by your instructor.

The EYES ON THE PRIZE telecourse has a 13-week syllabus divided into four parts.

Part I. **Introduction** (Week 1)
Part II. **The Early Years, 1954–1965** (Weeks 2–7)
Part III. **The Struggle Continues** (Week 8)
Part IV. **The Later Years, 1966–1986** (Weeks 9–13)

WEEK ONE: INTRODUCTION. This week's work consists of an introductory essay that should be read the week before the first television program is broadcast. The essay provides an overview of black American history prior to 1954 and identifies events and themes from the first half of the 20th century that require understanding before one can grasp the full significance of the post-1954 era.

WEEKS TWO-SEVEN: THE EARLY YEARS. This six-week period examines the people, the stories, and the events of the black-led struggle for social justice in America during the period 1954–1965. Among the topics introduced are the social and economic climate of the period, the reaction to and effects of the landmark Supreme Court decision, *Brown* v. *Board of Education of Topeka,* nonviolence as both a life-changing philosophy and a tactic, the struggle for voting rights, the emergence of a mass movement, the effect of mass media on the struggle for social justice, and the emergence of the Southern Christian Leadership Conference and the Student Nonviolent Coordinating Committee. Assignments include text readings and the viewing of the six-hour television series, EYES ON THE PRIZE—America's Civil Rights Years.

WEEK EIGHT: THE STRUGGLE CONTINUES. This week effects a transition from the southern, primarily rural-based movement of the early years to the northern, urban-based struggle that has been more recent. The principal assignment is the reading of an essay in the text that assesses the gains of the previous period and previews the changes in tactics, location, organizations, and style that are paramount in the final part of the course.

WEEKS NINE-THIRTEEN: THE LATER YEARS. This last part of the course covers the period from 1966 to 1986. It differs from the second part of the course in that it is organized thematically, rather than by event or chronological period. Each week's assignment consists of a text chapter and two half-hour audiocassettes. Among the topics introduced in this final part of the course are the black consciousness that emerged with new power in the mid-1960s and was reflected in literature, politics, and education; the revolt and repression that were a part of America in the late 1960s; the new legal battles that emerged in the late 1960s and 1970s regarding affirmative action and school desegregation; the social and economic status of blacks in America after 30 years of concerted civil rights activities; and finally, the political status of blacks as of the 1984 national elections.

By the completion of the course, you should be able to discuss:

the roles individuals, movements, government, and political leaders play in the process of social change;

the ways in which social movements help the United States to ensure that its democratic values are translated into reality;

the impact the media have on the transformation of society;

the effect upheavals in the social order have on the daily lives of individuals;

the relationship between the black freedom movement and all people in the U.S.A.; and

the degrees of effectiveness of different strategies to achieve social justice in America.

THE TELEVISION PROGRAMS

EYES ON THE PRIZE—AMERICA'S CIVIL RIGHTS YEARS consists of six one-hour television programs. These will be broadcast one per week.

001. **AWAKENINGS (1954–1956)** tells the story of two events that helped to focus the nation's attention on the rights of black Americans to life, liberty, and the pursuit of happiness: the 1955 lynching in Mississippi of 14-year-old Emmett Till and the 1955–56 Montgomery, Alabama boycott that forced the desegregation of public buses and opened a new era. The film also shows southern race relations at midcentury and depicts the awakening of individuals to their own courage and power as they began to develop a movement that would challenge America's commitment to justice.

002. **FIGHTING BACK (1957–1962)** examines the law both as a tool for change and resistance to change, particularly as it relates to education. The program covers the court cases of the late 1940s that led to the 1954 Supreme Court *Brown* v. *Board of Education* decision, the stories of nine black teenagers who integrated Little Rock's Central High School in 1957, and James Meredith's 1962 enrollment at The University of Mississippi.

003. **AIN'T SCARED OF YOUR JAILS (1960–1961)** depicts the changing focus of black protest during the early 1960s from legal challenges to specific laws to personal and group challenges to a broad range of racial and economic inequities. The program links four related stories of the period: the lunch counter sit-ins, the formation of SNCC by the students who led the sit-ins, the impact of the sit-ins on the 1960 presidential campaign, and the freedom rides, all of which offered the nation a chance to develop its democracy more fully.

004. **NO EASY WALK (1962–1963)** retells the stories of three cities that are indelibly linked with the civil rights movement: Albany, Georgia, where Police Chief Laurie Pritchett and Martin Luther King, Jr. each tested the strategy of nonviolence in his own way; Birmingham, Alabama, where children marched against Bull Connor's fire hoses and filled the jails; and Washington, D.C., where black and white, young and old, north and south, came together to march in the nation's capital.

005. **MISSISSIPPI: IS THIS AMERICA? (1962–1964)** depicts black citizens who had been denied the right to vote—by law, the weight of history, economic pressure and terror—stepping forward and demanding a place in the political process. Medgar Evers, Michael Schwerner, Andrew Goodman, James Chaney, and others died trying to help them. But before the 1964 Freedom Summer was over a complete delegation from the newly-formed Mississippi Freedom Democratic party had challenged the Democratic party convention—and the American people—in Atlantic City.

006. **BRIDGE TO FREEDOM (1965)** depicts the historic 1965 march from Selma to Montgomery, Alabama in which thousands of blacks and whites came together to march 50 miles for freedom, seeking to establish "a more perfect union." Ten years after Rosa Parks refused to give up her seat to a white man on a Montgomery, Alabama bus and nearly 11 years after the Supreme Court decreed that separate-but-equal was unconstitutional, black Americans were still fighting for equality.

Audio Programs

Ten-half-hour audio programs are part of this course. If they are not in your college bookstore, please contact your instructor. In each of weeks nine through thirteen, you will be expected to listen to two half-hour audio segments. The audio segments provide academic analysis and interpretation of the period 1966–1984 and present dramatic point/counterpoint debates by individuals involved in this period. Some cassettes will feature material from oral history projects; others will include portions of interviews done for the EYES ON THE PRIZE television series, as well as for previously broadcast radio programs from the period.

1A and 1B. **A NEW BLACK CONSCIOUSNESS (1966–1968)**
2A and 2B. **REVOLT AND REPRESSION (1967–1970)**
3A and 3B. **DEFINING EQUALITY: THE NEW LEGAL BATTLES OVER RACE AND CIVIL RIGHTS (1970–1986)**
4A and 4B. **BLACK AMERICA—A BETTER LIFE? (1970–1986)**
5A and 5B. **WHERE DO WE GO FROM HERE? (1984–1986)**

Related Reading

EYES ON THE PRIZE—AMERICA'S CIVIL RIGHTS YEARS is written by Juan Williams and the staff of Eyes on the Prize (Viking/Penguin, 1986). Through dramatic pictures, participant interviews, and an indepth narrative, this companion volume to the television series explores the people, places, and events of the decade 1954–1965. Juan Williams is a national correspondent for *The Washington Post.*

Guidelines For Telecourse Study

No right or wrong way exists to approach EYES ON THE PRIZE as a course; however, a number of suggestions are offered that have worked for other telecourse students.

1. As soon after registration as possible, find out the following:

    • what books are required for the course
    • if and when an orientation has been scheduled
    • when EYES ON THE PRIZE will be broadcast in your area
    • when examinations are scheduled for the course
    • if and when additional on-campus lectures, discussion groups, or review sessions have been scheduled

If more than one public television station exists where you live, several opportunities may be available for you to watch the video assignments during a given week. Further, many public television stations will repeat the program at least once during the week it is first shown. Determine at what time you will watch the program and make this an inviolate part of your schedule.

2. Although you can approach your study assignments in any order, given a choice, it is desirable to skim the text first. On the first page of each text chapter is a list of objectives which will help orient you to those issues that require your concentration. Also, a short narrative overview will suggest some unifying themes that you can be thinking about as you watch or listen to the programs and read the text. A section of questions is at the conclusion of the chapter. These also merit an early review so that your study can be directed to your learning needs.

3. In connection with the viewing and listening assignments, you may find it helpful to refer to Appendix 1—Selected Events in America's Civil Rights History, a chronology that will help place specific events in a broader historical context.

4. When you read the assigned text chapter, read the entire chapter, including the readings. These are a fundamental part of the course and will give you a detailed view of America's civil rights years from individuals who were a part of it. The full bibliographic citation of every reading can be found at the start of the reading. In most cases, what you will be reading is a very small fraction of a much longer work. You are encouraged to seek out the complete works from which these excerpts are taken and to read more. For topics that are especially interesting to you, additional books are recommended at the end of each chapter.

5. Some students have found that notetaking while viewing the television programs is helpful; others find it distracting and prefer to audiotape the programs for later review. It is permissible to videotape the programs off-the-air for your own personal review only. It will probably be helpful for you to view and/or listen to the programs twice whenever possible.

6. After you have completed the media and reading assignments, it probably will be helpful to return to the section in the text labelled Questions for Review. This will help prepare you both for specific, short-answer type questions on examinations and for more wide-ranging short essay questions. In some cases the Questions for Review require that you think about the content of the unit in a context beyond that specifically presented by the readings or programs. They will require you to think about the application of what you have learned to your own life and to America today.

7. Keep up with course assignments on a weekly basis. Some students have found that entering study activities in a log helps them to focus on what assignments require their attention. This is also a good place to note questions for your course instructor and to judge the best order of study and review for you.

8. Keep in touch with your instructor. Know when he or she has call-hours and how to reach him or her by mail. The instructor would like to hear from you and to know how you are doing in the course. You do not need to wait until you have a problem or an assignment due. Call to discuss the content of the course and to obtain clarification of course content. Your instructor may also be able to provide you with names and numbers of the other students registered in this course. While students often enroll in telecourses because of the convenience of independent study, many find informal contact with other students stimulating and helpful. Your instructor might facilitate the formation of an informal study group that can fit in with your schedule.

9. Given the content of this course, it is absolutely essential that you read the newspaper daily. This should be considered an ongoing assignment. Keep a clipping file of all articles that pertain to the struggle for social justice both in America and in other parts of the world. This file will help you analyze the effects of the past 100 years of American civil rights history in the context of the place and time in which you live.

10. Throughout this course, you will be viewing, listening to, and reading about individuals who showed enormous personal courage, who at some point in their lives made a commitment to become involved. While EYES ON THE PRIZE is a history course, the issues that you will read about in this course are ongoing—both in America and throughout the world.

PART I

INTRODUCTION
1850–1954

CHAPTER 1

WE THE PEOPLE: THE LONG JOURNEY TOWARD A MORE PERFECT UNION

by VINCENT HARDING

—Provides an overview of the emergence of the modern civil rights movement during the first half of the 20th century, concentrating on the years between two landmark Supreme Court decisions, *Plessy* v. *Ferguson* in 1896 and *Brown* v. *Board of Education* in 1954

—Discusses the separate-but-equal doctrine, examines its impact on the lives of black Americans, and contrasts the broad significance of the two Supreme Court decisions

—Identifies the national civil rights organizations that emerge during the first half of the 20th century, names their leaders, and examines their principal strategies for achieving social justice

—Analyzes the different social protest strategies of successive generations of black Americans

—Critiques federal social policies of the period and evaluates their impact on the lives of black Americans

—Examines the roles of the black church and religious leaders on the lives of black Americans during this period

—Places the emergence of civil rights activities in the context of the "cold war" and the beginnings of the African independence movement

1

Constitution of the United States

PREAMBLE

We the people of the United States, in order to form a more perfect union, establish justice, insure domestic tranquility, provide for the common defense, promote the general welfare, and secure the blessings of liberty to ourselves and our posterity, do ordain and establish this Constitution for the United States of America.

The images strike us, sometimes touching home at levels deeper than we dare acknowledge. Images: Men and women, many of them still alive in our own time, there on the screen, standing firm, unarmed, facing gun-wielding, menacing police and state troopers, standing their ground, refusing to give in to fears, discovering powerful weapons, old and new, at the center of their lives. Men and women, possessed by new power, determined to be counted as full citizens of this nation, committed to transform this grand and needy country, in search of "a more perfect union."

Images: Women, men, and children, standing, sometimes being smashed down to the ground, paying the price for wanting justice, for believing in a more perfect union. Broken bones, bleeding heads, but spirits undaunted, returning from beds and hospitals and jails to stand and struggle again—for justice, for freedom, for the right to vote, for equal access, for a "domestic tranquility" that we have not yet experienced, for a new society for us all.

Images: Young people, often children, full of life and play and seriousness. Marching, facing dogs and fire hoses, singing freedom songs on the way to jail, rocking the paddy wagons with "Ain't afraid of your jail, 'cause I want my freedom now." Young people, walking the gauntlets of hate, ignorance, and fear, listening to the less-than-human shrieks, just to go to school—really to redefine "the general welfare," to educate America and the world to the meaning of "the blessings of liberty." Teenagers, children, not purposelessly wandering through the fantasy worlds of consumer malls, but sitting in jails, singing in jails, determined to create a land of justice, committed to move with new dignity and hope in their lives.

Images: Black and white women and men, braving the storms of violence and hatred together, marching with King and Fannie Lou Hamer together, taking on the hard, explosive rock of Mississippi together, murdered and hidden underground together, rising as great inspirations and new hope together. Black and white, discovering their common ancestry, their common pain, and their common hope. Unashamed to cry together. Swaying, singing together: "We shall overcome." Singing, "We'll never turn back/Until we've all been freed . . ." Living, arguing, sharing together, "to secure the blessings of liberty to ourselves and our posterity . . ."

Who are these people? Where did they come from, especially these black people, who seemed—at least for a time—to offer direction, purpose and hope to an entire generation of Americans of every racial, social, and religious background? What did they mean then when they spoke of "redeeming the soul of America"? What do they mean now? For us, for black us, for Hispanic us, for Asian us, for white us, for natives of this land? What do they mean for our personal, collective, and national prospects, for our "posterity"?

The images and questions insinuate themselves into our beings and raise fundamental issues about our nation's past and future. They present us with many surprises, not only about the recent similarities between our land and South Africa in 1986, but more importantly they surprise us about humans, ordinary humans like us, whose names we have never learned, whose faces are both familiar and unknown. Ordinary human beings at times acting with extraordinary courage, vision, and hope (at other times stumbling and falling into all the internal and external traps we know so well). Who are they? How are we related to them . . . we the people?

It is often this way: women and men who look carefully, persistently into the face of history are often rewarded with breath-taking surprises—and a host of questions. Of course, in our own time, after the furnaces of Auschwitz and Hiroshima, after the Gulags and the "disappeared," in the midst of South Africa abroad and the human-created epidemics of joblessness, homelessness, and drug addiction at home, some things—unfortunately—do not surprise us. We no longer consider it noteworthy to be confronted with our stunning human capacities for harsh, ruthless, and inhuman oppression. But considerable evidence shows us that we are yet capable of being amazed by unexpected revelations of the great, still largely untapped human potential for resistance and hope, for compassion and grandeur, for courage and visionary self-transcendence—even when pressed against all the walls that oppression has created.

In the annals of our own young nation, no greater repository of such unexpected testimonies to the recreative powers of the human spirit exists than the history of the black struggle for freedom, equality, and social transformation. In the public television series EYES ON THE PRIZE—America's Civil Rights Years, we are drawn into just one generation's experience of that struggle, especially as it developed after World War II. But no human history is rootless, and we see the fullest meaning of the post-1945 events only as we dig deeper.

Such probing work could take us back to the coast of Africa, to the earliest liberation struggles there and on the prison slaveships, and could open up the long, unbroken history of black resistance to slavery and the concomitant movement toward freedom in this country. Digging deep, we might explore the period of great hope and profound betrayal after the Civil War, examining the unpredictable ways in which a people who had been largely defined as humanly inferior, ignorant chattel slaves, came bursting out of the furnaces of the Civil War, bearing the traditions of resistance and hope, to create their own powerful and impressive postwar testimonies to the meaning of freedom, democracy, and justice in America.

Indeed, if we looked closely we would discover that the commitment of these former slaves to the transformation of their own lives and the life of the nation was often so great that it could not be borne by the majority of white America. For this majority was not prepared for fundamental changes toward

3

justice, especially if the changes involved redistribution of landed wealth in the south and the abandonment of white supremacy everywhere, in exchange for a truly shared community, a more perfect union. So we would also need to see the ways in which the postwar black communities and the relatively small band of white allies who offered themselves as full participants in the political, economic, and social/spiritual process to recreate the nation, were effectively, often brutally, driven back from the footholds they had begun to gain. We would see this especially in the political institutions of the postwar south, the region that was home to more than 90 percent of black Americans.

To probe that deeply would bring us to a history of antiblack repression that had possessed the entire south (and too many northern outposts) by the end of the 1870s. We would witness lynchings, ritual burnings, and mutilations, the rise of the Ku Klux Klan (KKK) and other paramilitary organizations, all implicitly or explicitly approved by much southern white leadership, with increasing acquiescence from the northern keepers of power. To dig so deep would reveal to us harsh economic intimidation in the development of a kind of peonage, often called sharecropping. It would recount through much of the 1870s and 1880s the misuses of political, legal, and social systems in a ruthless attempt to deny, subvert, and destroy the power of blackness that had briefly appeared in the land. In other words, we would see the ways in which a nation— led by southern white elites, and often in cooperation with the federal government—sought to create an ersatz "domestic tranquility," by repressing the voices, subverting the power, and destroying the lives of those black people who insisted they were part of "we the people," who dared dream of a just society. For this minority the "manifest destiny" of the United States was something much richer and deeper than "winning the west," destroying the natives of the land, and acquiring material wealth anywhere, and by any means necessary.

Then in 1895, Frederick Douglass died. The great black symbol of the movement from slavery to freedom had not been very active for several years, but he represented something powerful. He bore within himself a history of protest and challenge, a tradition of black determination to claim all the rights and responsibilities of a renewed American citizenship. So it seemed like an even greater loss when, in the same year, the nation's attention was called to Booker T. Washington, head of Tuskegee Institute. Coming to national prominence after more than a dozen years of building an important black educational institution in the heart of Alabama's dangerous white supremacy, Washington's voice carried a different message which seemed to discourage bold, direct, open challenges to white power on behalf of the beleaguered black communities.

It was a hard time, and for many black persons, it seemed as if all the broken promises of Reconstruction were finally, ironically epitomized in the actions of the Supreme Court of the United States. Ever since the 1870s, the Court had been eviscerating the congressional legislation and constitutional amendments which had been established at the height of Reconstruction to protect some of the basic citizenship rights of black people. In 1883, reversing the intentions of the Reconstruction congresses, it had claimed that the Reconstruction-bred Civil Rights Acts did not guarantee black people the same unhampered access to public accommodations that was due to all citizens. Finally, in 1896, the court brought to a climax its thrashing of the hopes of Reconstruction, and essentially gave its blessing to a status of second-class citizenship for

Afro-Americans. The infamous *Plessy* v. *Ferguson* decision ruled that state laws mandating separate facilities for black citizens did not violate the equal protection clause of the 14th Amendment to the Constitution, if the separated facilities were "substantially equal."

With that action, separate-but-equal became both the law of the land and the symbol of the fundamental schizophrenia at the heart of American democracy. But there was more: From that moment on the decision also became the target of a steadily rising, unrelenting black-led attack against the fundamental injustice of the court's action, against its betrayal of the most humane understandings of "we the people of the United States." So, *Plessy* v. *Ferguson* became a stimulus to struggle and defiance, a signal to resistance. It was not surprising, then, that in the same year that the words of the Supreme Court were hurled against black (and white) freedom, it was possible to hear the voices of resistance.

During the 1890s, Nashville, Tennessee (source of much leadership for the continuing freedom movement) was the base of John Hope, a professor at the city's Roger Williams University. Speaking in 1896 to a gathering of black people, immersing himself in the tradition of Douglass, preparing the way for the coming times, Hope urged his audience to resist all temptations to acquiesce and despair. He said,

> Rise, Brothers! Come let us possess this land. Never say 'Let well enough alone.'
> Cease to console yourself with adages that numb the moral sense. Be discontented. Be dissatisfied. . . . Be restless as the tempestuous billows on the boundless sea. Let your dissatisfaction break mountain-high against the walls of prejudice and swamp it to the very foundation. Then we shall not have to plead for justice nor on bended knee crave mercy; for we shall be men. Then and not until then will liberty in its highest sense be the boast of our Republic.[1]

This was a response to oppression, but it was more. Just 30 years after the official end of slavery, here was the articulation of a free people's fierce determination "to possess this land" that had enslaved them, to claim a land they had worked so hard to create. It was an amazing statement of faith in the best possibilities of our republic, and therefore an expression of profound belief in their own capacities—and those of their fellow citizens—to create a more perfect union.

Such a complex, powerful, and explosive cluster of human intentions was at the heart of almost all the struggles for justice, survival, defense, and transformation which were carried on by black people as one century ended and another began. This claiming of the land, this determination to speak the black-envisioned truth and create a new American reality—all these are part of the roots of the struggle that became impossible to hold back.

All these were present in a crusader like Ida B. Wells-Barnett, who was born into the last years of slavery in Mississippi and became another of the living bridges between the black freedom struggles of the 19th and 20th centuries. By the time she was in her late twenties, the articulate and courageous Wells-Barnett had been teacher, newspaper publisher, unrelenting public scourge of injustice, fugitive from southern mob action, and preeminent international lecturer and organizer in the antilynching campaigns of the turning centuries. She spoke and acted in defense of black rights and life, but she always knew that

5

her campaign was for the future of democracy in the United States. That is why, in one of her major speeches (which included a report on her exile from Memphis, Tennessee, because of her bold newspaper attacks on white mob rule) she could say to the nation:

> In one section, at least of our common country, a government of the people, by the people, and for the people means a government by the mob; where the land of the free and the home of the brave means a land of lawlessness, murder, and outrage and where liberty of speech means the license of might to destroy the business and drive from home those who exercise this privilege contrary to the will of the mob.[2]

Although she was describing her own situation and the fate of other outspoken black heralds, the nature of Wells' language made it clear that she was also reaching beyond the personal. For her as for many others, this truth-telling tradition, this protest against injustice, this unrelenting demand for the maturing of American democracy was a part of the larger commitment to possess the land. For them, a necessary part of that process was the action of forcing white America to recognize the degradation of democracy that accompanied all attempts to throttle the voices of black discontent. So the children of the slaves became the major carriers of the dream of freedom, the quintessential visionaries of a more perfect union.

But there was always a tension in the heart of black America, a tension that continues yet, one expressed with typical eloquence by the man who was already becoming the nation's preeminent Afro-American scholar-activist, W.E.B. DuBois. For DuBois, as the 19th century ended, black people could not possess this land unless at the same moment they claimed, nurtured, and possessed their own souls, their African-American heritage, their history, their culture. DuBois, child of the diaspora by birth and by choice, born in the north, educated at Fisk and Harvard, as well as in Berlin, felt this tension at the center of his being.

Later he would speak of it as an "eternal twoness," this life of blackness and of Americanness. But in 1897 he described it less as a tension than as a calling, and he proclaimed, "For the development of Negro genius, of Negro literature and art, of Negro spirit, only Negroes bound and welded together, Negroes inspired by one vast ideal, can work out in its fullness the great message we have for humanity."[3] This audacious young intellectual said he saw black people as "the advanced guard of Negro people" of the world. So he urged his people to see their calling and to recognize that "if they are to take their just place in the vanguard of Pan-Negroism, then their destiny is not absorption by the white Americans . . . not a servile imitation of Anglo-Saxon culture, but a stalwart originality which shall unswervingly serve Negro ideals."[4]

For DuBois, the vision was worldwide. While he agreed on the need for Afro-Americans to lay full claim to the U.S.A., he cautioned against being possessed by America and its worst values. DuBois was setting forth a large, messianic, freedom-fighting, freedom-shaping task for Afro-Americans. So his statement put the community of former slaves in its fullest light, declaring that they "must be inspired with the Divine faith of our black mothers, that out of the blood and dust of battle will march a victorious host, a mighty nation, a peculiar people, to speak to the nations of the earth a Divine truth that shall make them free."[5]

(As his language constantly indicated, while DuBois conscientiously avoided any commitment or conventional religious creeds, he was—like most of his contemporary black colleagues—steeped in the language, literature, and image of the Bible. The Afro-American freedom movement cannot be fully apprehended without that context.)

One of the most fascinating elements of the post-Reconstruction black movement toward new freedom and extended equality was the continuing work of creating independent and semi-independent black institutions. Without them the black community would have been lost. In addition to the central institution of the family, they included schools at every level, churches and other religious institutions, newspapers and other journals, fraternal and sororal organizations, mutual aid societies, women's clubs, banks, insurance companies, unions, farmers' alliances, and emancipation societies.

These were only a portion of the internal, self-claiming, self-defining work that was constantly recreating the black community. Sometimes the institutions were a necessary response to the legal and extra-legal exclusion of black people from most white-dominated American institutions. Just as often, they were expressions of the DuBoisian search "for the development of Negro genius." Often they were both. For many wise men and women clearly understood the paradoxical necessity of developing institutions which would be the grounds for creating and training generations of younger people who would eventually venture out to let their "discontent break mountain-high against the walls of prejudice and swamp it to the very foundation."[6]

At the turn of the century, black people who were committed to challenging the fundamental injustice of the nation's institutions knew that they must always deal with yet another paradox. In a country almost 90 percent white, in a society permeated by conscious and unconscious white supremacist beliefs and social Darwinist assumptions, black people needed dedicated white allies in the struggle for justice. Hope, Wells-Barnett, and DuBois knew this, as did black miners, farmers, forest workers, and many others. As a result, the struggle for, with, and against white allies, was then, as it has always been since then, a crucial element in the black freedom movement.

By the beginning of the 20th century, those battles were carried on in many an arena, among them the Republican party, labor unions, farmers' alliances, populist movements, Christian churches, the world of white philanthropy, and temperance and women's suffrage movements. Almost without exception, the critical issues—sometimes issues of life and death—centered on the willingness of white people to treat black women and men as allies and equals, rather than as wards, pawns, or tools; the willingness of whites occasionally to accept direction and leadership from black people; the readiness of white allies to stand as firmly for the advancement of black-centered concerns as they were asking blacks to stand for other issues; and the determination of whites to pay the psychological, economic, and political costs of black-white solidarity in the midst of an American white supremacy that often turned murderous in its methods. Perhaps all of this was really the willingness of black and white justice-seekers to recognize their own need to become new people in order to create a new society.

To create a new society, a more perfect union. How new? How much more perfect? Afro-Americans, whether in their own organizations and institutions, or banding together with allies, were never monolithic nor dogmatic in response to such questions. The largest agreement among them was that the newness must minimally mean the breaking down of all society. No truly perfect union could even begin to come into being without that—a reality many "progressive" white reformers never recognized.

But then there were the details: Did a new society mean that black farmers or miners should band together with those of their white counterparts who wanted more than a larger income, who envisioned a new social, economic, and political order as the only sound foundation for a society which would accord justice to all its workers? Did it mean creating more truly democratic alternatives to both the Republican and Democratic parties, especially in the light of their different but similar betrayals of black hopes? Did the search for a new society mean that black fathers and sons would no longer have to kill the regularly and variously identified enemies of the American government in order to prove themselves worthy of being men, in order to merit recognition as citizens of a more perfect union? What of those black people who uncritically accepted the nation's destruction of the natives of the land, or entered into the spirit of manifest destiny as it suppressed the revolutions of colored peoples in Cuba and the Philippines? Would they have to take seriously the words of a black socialist who said, "The American Negro cannot become the ally of imperialism without enslaving his own race"?[7] And one of the hardest questions of all, which occasionally surfaced in black debates: Did the creation of a new society require the loss of racial distinctiveness, the disbanding of racially identified institutions, the erosion and deracination of a people's cultural base?

For many persons, of course, these were premature questions. Simply surviving in the midst of a hostile majority was a major focus. For these people, freedom is represented by a name that became almost legendary for a time in part of the black community: Robert Charles.

Robert Charles was one of those people to improvise when pressed against the wall, to define in time of personal crisis what will be necessary for the possession of one's soul. Quiet, intense, in his twenties, a worker at odd jobs, a native of Mississippi, Charles was an agent of an emigration society, a reader of the materials of Bishop Henry McNeal Turner, the brilliant, caustic promoter of African emigration in the black communities of America. Charles apparently did some writing of his own. He also had collected a small arsenal.

Then on a night in July 1900, he is sitting quietly on a front stoop, talking with a male friend. It is near midnight when the almost mythic, tragic encounter begins. Three white policemen appear. The arrogance of race and power is in the air, concretized in the drawn, menacing pistols, the flailing billy clubs, and the unprovoked announcement of arrest. Charles draws a pistol, shoots one of the officers and runs, wounded, from the scene. But he refuses to keep running. He reaches his cache of arms, chooses at least one rifle, and moving from one hiding place to another, kills at least five policemen and wounds a dozen more from the scores who are on his trail. A mob of more than a thousand white men offer their welcome assistance to the police force, periodically pouring their fury and their ammunition into the black community. Finally Charles is burned out, cut down in a hail of bullets, and badly mutilated in death.

But that was not the end. Wells-Barnett almost immediately investigated the incident, and at the end of her report she said, "The white people of this country may charge that he was a desperado, but to the people of his own race Robert Charles will always be regarded as 'the hero of New Orleans.' "[8] This tradition of improvised, life-sacrificing courage, with or without the gun, goes deep into the history of the black struggle to establish justice, to assure domestic tranquility, to possess lives, to claim the land.

Finally, the emergence of the 20th century freedom struggle is not set in proper perspective without remembering what Robert Charles was studying—black emigration. Afro-Americans everywhere, but especially in the south, were always conscious of that option, the possibility of return to Africa. They were stirred by the vision of possessing themselves through reclaiming the motherland, building a new society by returning to the old. Between the crushing of Reconstruction's best hopes and the beginning of the 20th century, thousands of black people returned to Africa. It was so much of a movement and an obsession that it was often called "Africa fever." Indeed, it is likely that tens of thousands more might have tried to go if there had been ships to take them, and if land on which to settle had been available—if European countries had not divided up the African continent among themselves. But the option, at least the dream, was always alive in the heart of black Americans, and in those post-Reconstruction years, thousands of persons were able to follow the dream of possession and renewal at least as far as Kansas and Oklahoma. Others, like their foreparents, the fugitive slaves, were satisfied to create new beginnings in the cities of the north and south.

Now we see. In the roiling, blood-red years of the closing and opening of the centuries, the deeper roots of the 1950s and 1960s were manifest. Many black people had determined that it was not enough for their slavery to be officially ended, and they refused to leave the future definitions of their freedom—and the shaping of this nation—in the hands of white Americans. Rather, by the close of the 19th century, it was clear that some of the most prescient black leaders and seers had declared that it was absolutely necessary for black people to take the initiative. Not only would they defend themselves against the onslaughts of those days, but they would move forward to extend the internal and external limits of their human freedom—and their participation in the recreation of America—as far as was possible, whatever the costs might be.

Often, as the new century began, it seemed that the costs were more than men and women could bear. All the psycho-social anesthesia of avoidance and denial, joined with a crippling array of legalized injustice at local, state, and national levels, backed by every cruel variety of physical force (represented by, but not limited to the KKK) were brought to bear in the struggle against all serious black definitions of a more perfect union. Meanwhile, in almost every public forum, from the halls of Congress to the smallest white churches and newspapers, black people were subjected to a never-ending torrent of racial epithets and public insults attacking their intelligence, the authenticity of their humanity, and their capacities for moral development. But in the midst of all this, the amazingly resilient black thrust toward freedom and justice in America was never destroyed.

Of course, it is constantly necessary to remind ourselves that there were always some whites (and many black people) who understood that the deep issues of the freedom struggle had to do with more than rights for Afro-Americans. They realized that the integrity and future of American democracy were also at stake. In other words, the prize of freedom, justice, and equality for Africa's children in the United States was ultimately a gift for the entire nation. As a result, the central tasks of the 20th century black freedom movement were defined at their best not only as the achievement of rights and justice, but also as transformation of the spirit, consciousness, and heart of a people who had been developed and nurtured on the poisons of white supremacist politics, social philosophy, theology, and history. As Martin Luther King, Jr. would one day put it, achieving the "prize" meant "redeeming the soul of America."

By the beginning of the 20th century many of the essential characteristics of the life of the next period of freedom struggle had already been suggested. Perhaps if we were steeped in Chinese methodology we might summarize them as The Six Claims:

1.   Claiming the right to the land, to full unhindered participation in the life of the nation and in the reshaping of that life

2.   Claiming the right and responsibility to speak the truth from black perspectives and to insist that those truths become part of a new American reality

3.   Claiming the right to possess themselves, their heritage, their Africanness, their souls

4.   Claiming the necessity of building black institutions, as ends in themselves, and as bases for the creation of the women and men who would eventually join others to develop a more perfect union in America

5.   Claiming the right of self-defense against the intrusive and arrogantly destructive forces of white power

6.   Claiming the same right of principled emigration to Africa or elsewhere that brought the pilgrims and subsequent generations of immigrants to these shores

Now, as we move fully into the 20th century and explore some of the more directly connected predecessors of the movements of the 1950s and 1960s, we can trace their root sources to the soil of Afro-American life and struggles. Among the many possible pre-1954 developments, perhaps a dozen briefly sketched, but deeply etched, images will suffice. They help prepare the way. They illuminate the transformations that took us from the time when constitutionally-sanctioned segregation and wide-spread, life-threatening anti-black violence seemed ascendant in the nation to the years when the long, black-led movement toward justice and "a more perfect union" burst to the surface with unparalleled force and creative power.

In 1905 many of the lines of force which moved from the past toward the future were gathered in one place when W.E.B. DuBois sent out a letter to 60 black middle-class professionals, declaring, "The time seems more than ripe for organized, determined, and aggressive action on the part of men who believe in Negro freedom and growth."[9] Standing with DuBois (not always comfortably) was William Monroe Trotter, the outspoken, anti-Booker T. Washington editor of the Boston *Guardian*, like DuBois, a Harvard graduate. Their letter and organizing action led to the formation of the Niagara Movement, a black leadership group. Its first meeting, drawing 29 participants, took place on the Canadian side of Niagara Falls because no unsegregated facilities existed for the meeting in the U.S.A. Niagara's essential focus (apart from its continuing critique of Washington's nonconfrontative leadership and his attempts at censorship and control) was probably best summed up in the words which appeared in the second annual declaration, "We will not be satisfied to take one jot or little less than our full manhood rights . . . . Until we get these rights we will never cease to protest and assail the ears of America."[10]

The Niagara men were responding to the ever-expanding network of legal repression, especially the outpouring of state laws that denied more and more black people access to the vote. They were looking for ways to check the spread of antiblack riots, to call the nation to take a stand against the crime of lynching. They were rebelling against what they considered the dangerous, misleading attempts at sabotage and subversion by Washington. But the Niagara men (and their women's auxiliary, which was the style of the time) had very little money and were not equipped to raise the sums that would match their plans. They did not have the resources to maintain their ground against Washington's divisive and well-financed machinations or to spread their word of protest. In addition, they did not move far enough beyond middle-class protest positions to take on the issue of economic exploitation of the rural majority of the black population, nor did they know how to manage their internal divisions, especially DuBois and Trotter. Within five years after its first meeting at Fort Erie, Niagara had essentially disbanded. But seeds had been sown, a model proposed. The possibility of a 20th century black protest organization undominated by Booker T. Washington was established.

Meanwhile, the scourges of lynchings and antiblack riots continued. At that point in America's history, race riots essentially meant white mobs, on one pretense or another, surging through black communities, battering, burning, killing, raping, and looting, often unhindered by the official forces of the law until it was too late. Black people, hindered by the law (and perhaps by inclination) from organizing local, armed self-defense units, and lacking experience in the development of trained, unarmed corps of protectors, fought back as best they could. In 1908, the black community of Springfield, Illinois was visited with such a burst of armed white hatred. It was Abraham Lincoln's home town, and some members of the mob on their errands of death were heard to shout: "Lincoln freed you—well, we'll show you where you belong." Faced with this bestial denial of their own basic humanity, the small group of Niagara leaders publicly urged black people everywhere to prepare to defend themselves against white mobs with guns.

And yet they knew, as others knew, that defensive action alone was never sufficient. Thus DuBois and some other members of the deteriorating Niagara organization were soon faced with a hard choice, one familiar to the black freedom movement. In 1909, a group of men and women based largely in the white abolitionist tradition was stirred by the Springfield terrorism to call a national "conference on the Negro." It was a white initiative, and the black demand for a larger role in the conference and then in the organization which was created out of it led to harsh debates and crushed feelings.

So when the National Association for the Advancement of Colored People (NAACP) came into existence in 1910 it was immediately heir to much of the ambivalent heritage of such black-white alliances. DuBois was the only black person in a senior staff position when the new organization opened its offices in downtown Manhattan. Stalwarts, like Wells-Barnett and Trotter, believing that they had been shut out of any real power in the organization by a paternalistic, politically moderate-to-liberal white leadership, essentially went their own ways.

Over the next four decades, the conflicts and ambiguities regarding race and power would persist, often with DuBois, founding editor of the association's influential journal, *The Crisis*, at the center of the storm. He and others recognized the elements of a harsh dilemma: In an overwhelmingly white, often murderously supremacist society, it was critical to have relatively friendly white voices raised on behalf of black freedom. It was crucial to have white fund-raisers to gain the trust of white philanthropists. As the association focused on its legal attacks against discrimination, segregation, and white terrorism, it was often necessary to have white allies who had access to the centers of power.

But these were the galling necessities, for black women and men never stopped asking themselves whether it was possible to possess the land if they could not possess themselves and take leadership in the struggle for justice in their own hands. Gradually, this bellweather organization came increasingly under black executive leadership, expanding its unique (but underutilized) membership structure ever more widely throughout the black communities of America, but with white men still in crucial roles on its governing board and in its fund-raising tasks. Meanwhile, the "N double A" developed crucial skills in the tasks of public truth-telling, lobbying for antidiscriminatory and antiterrorist legislation and carrying on the continuing, judicially-based assault on the legal structures of separate-but-equal.

Black leaders like Trotter and Wells-Barnett tried to handle the dilemmas represented by the NAACP in several personal and organizational ways. One was to form new, largely local and regional black organizations for social services and protest actions, centered around their own strong, courageous, but sometimes divisive personalities.

At the same time, other alternatives were constantly being developed out of the desperate creativity of the black community's pre-World War I existence. For instance, Timothy Drew, who had migrated from North Carolina to New Jersey in that period, emerged from his meditations and preaching in the back lots and tenement basements of Newark's black wards to declare his possession of a new name: Noble Drew Ali. Indeed, his vision of possession was for all black people, who he now declared to be Moors in America, a lost-found people whose ancestors, "descendants of the ancient Moabites," had come originally from the area of Morocco. He taught black people that the repossession of their true identity would provide new power for their lives, power eventually to overcome the worst afflictions of this doomed and evil white society.

But neither a relative handful of Moors, a courageous contingent of middle-class leaders, or a fledgling white-dominated association for their "advancement" could affect the emerging black freedom movement of the 20th century in the way that it was cataclysmically moved by the guns of August 1914 and the onset of "the great war."

Some black folk in the United States knew instinctively—as well as through serious study and discussion—that the war was more than a European conflagration. For Europe was much more than a small geographical appendage on the Asian land mass. Ever since the 15th century, its imperial tentacles had gradually reached all over the world of nonwhite peoples, and members of the major body of nonwhite peoples in the U.S.A. sensed that the war—whatever its other issues—was a struggle for international power, for a greater share of the goods of the colonized colored peoples of the globe. Thus the war heightened an international consciousness that had already evolved out of the 19th century, out of "Africa fever," perhaps out of deeply imbedded, often unconscious, longings for "home." So when Hubert Harrison, the brilliant black socialist streetcorner lecturer spoke of his vision of the war on the avenues of Harlem, the crowds cheered, for he was articulating their sense of reality when he said, "As representatives of one of the races constituting the colored majority of the world, we deplore the agony and bloodshed [of the war]; but we find consolation in the hope that when the white world shall have been washed clean by its baptism of blood, the white race will be less able to thrust the strong hand of its sovereign will down the throats of other races."[11]

Based on that set of hopes and assumptions, the self-taught black intellectual declared that as a result of the war he looked for "a free India and an independent Egypt; for nationalities in Africa flying their own flags and dictating their own internal and foreign policies."[12]

Though relatively few persons could know it at the time, this was a prophetic statement; for the "great war" did begin to shake the foundations of Europe's hold on the nonwhite world. But black people, even the most internationally conscious ones, soon saw other, more immediate issues rising out of the fields of war. As with all wars in which the nation became involved, this one served to heighten the already vivid consciousness of Afro-Americans concerning the tragic contradictions endemic to their own native, alien land. Indeed, nothing could have expressed the contradictions more sharply than the April 1917 speech in which a staunchly segregationist president, Woodrow Wilson, called upon a joint session of Congress to enter the war and was interrupted by a Mississippi legislator who led the thunderous applause when Wilson urged them to send American troops "to make the world safe for democracy."

Most Afro-American leaders and spokespersons acceded to the conventional wisdom: It was necessary to go, necessary to send sons, fathers, and husbands to fight overseas for "democracy" in segregated, humiliated military units in order to "prove" to white Americans their worthiness to possess the full rights of first-class citizenship. Of course, according to the conventional wisdom, it was also necessary to go to avoid jail.

Eventually, some 400,000 black men were drafted and served in the war, in spite of the sentiments of A. Philip Randolph, a young black socialist editor, who wrote that those black leaders who supported military participation should "volunteer to go to France, if they are so eager to make the world safe for democracy." As for Randolph and his radical colleagues, he said, "We would rather fight to make Georgia safe for the Negro."[13]

Of course Randolph was essentially right, and every black and every honest white person knew it. And they rediscovered it at excruciatingly deep levels when the word came from East St. Louis, Illinois less than three months after the declaration of the war for democracy, less than a week before the Fourth of July. They knew it when the screams arose and the fires burned, sending signals to the world that another white mob was on the rampage, burning, raping, destroying black women, infants, and old people, as well as armed and unarmed men who were determined to possess their souls. It was one of the most brutal pogroms the nation had known, just when the segregated black servicemen were training to go make the world safe.

The black troops in Houston, Texas, knew Randolph was right when in August 1917, perhaps with the stench and the screams of East St. Louis still filling their being, they made their choice. Goaded by continuous and cruel white civilian attacks and provocations, finding no support from their military superiors, they used their democracy-defending weapons to strike out against those who chose to be their tormentors rather than their fellow Americans. White civilians were killed in a nighttime engagement. The soldiers were imprisoned, secretly tried, and secretly executed. But when the word broke loose, they were applauded by their people as heroes of the long and costly war to make America safe for its black citizens, safe for democracy and justice, safe for its posterity of every color. These were the brothers of Robert Charles.

Of course, the "great war" brought more than consciousness, contradictions, and home front deaths to the struggle for black freedom. It also burst dams and opened up outpourings of human life so vast and roiling that they deeply affected every aspect of the nation's existence, especially its internal struggle to possess its own identity. Within the decade of 1910–1920 a half million black people flooded into the north, breaking like a great tide during the years of the war. For the chaos created by the European-based conflict, and the dangers presented by German submarines operating in the Atlantic Ocean, practically shut down the decades-long surge of European immigrants, just as America's burgeoning war-time industries were expanding in massive proportions. Workers were needed.

The war and the need for workers came at a time of economic depression in the south. It was affected by a disastrous boll weevil epidemic among the cotton crops, along with seasons of devastating floods. Combined with the traditional southern versions of the scourges of lynchings and riots, this concatenation of local, national, and international events unleashed a great black (and white) migration out of the south to the north, out of the rural areas to the cities. Black people began to emerge out of their southernness, their ruralness, their relative hiddenness. They appeared in urban centers all across the country. They showed up at factory gates, in hiring lines for the mines and mills. By their very presence they were placing unprecedented pressure on white America to face critical questions: Who are "we the people of the United States"? Whose country is this? Who are its jobs for? Who are its neighborhoods, its parks, its beaches for? Who are meant to be the creators and benefactors of its justice, its democracy, its future?

Large numbers of white people responded to the expanded black presence and to its insistent questions with fear and rage and great resistance. So the KKK leaped in its membership numbers, and black-white struggles over jobs, over living space, over recreation areas exploded in the north. Then in 1919, shortly after the long and bloody war to make the world safe for democracy had ended, warfare seemed to be erupting on the streets of the United States. In places as apparently disparate as Charleston, South Carolina; Washington, DC; Longview, Texas; and Chicago, Illinois, white mobs attempted many of their familiar tactics of brutal, pogrom-like attacks, often with the assistance of the police forces. But in that Red Summer, as it was called, there was more open, organized, armed black resistance than ever before, and the Afro-American veterans of the "great war" were usually in the forefront of the action. After the Red Summer of 1919 the murderous white civilian-led forays into black communities did not entirely cease, but they clearly became less and less a regular feature of American life.

Many black veterans of World War I were at the core of Marcus Garvey's Universal Negro Improvement Association (UNIA), the largest centralized organization ever created by Afro-Americans. Arriving here in 1916 from his native Jamaica and from travels throughout the Caribbean, Latin America, and England, Garvey stepped into the maelstrom of Afro-American history and attracted major public attention in 1919, the year the war came home.

Sensitive to the pulse of his people, unparalleled in his magnificent capacities to give words to their deepest-felt hurts and their great aspirations, Garvey stood firmly in a rich black tradition. Essentially it was the one that DuBois (his archenemy) had articulated two decades before, a tradition that constantly called for "Negroes bound and welded together, Negroes inspired by one vast ideal [to] work out in its fullness the great message we have for humanity."[14]

Making history, made by history, Garvey came to an aroused people already passing through the travail and transformation of the 20th century. His great gifts of vision, expression, and organization caught the movement of what DuBois had called "the advance guard of Negro People" and urged it forward. Garvey's familiar clarion call became, "UP, up you mighty race! You can accomplish what you will!"[15] And for Garvey there seemed at first to be only one accomplishment worthy of a self-possessed black people, and that was the redemption of Africa from European control.

So in the midst of the struggle in America, Garvey focused the people on a task beyond America. In the heat of that Red Summer of 1919 he dared to announce before cheering black audiences:

> Every American Negro and every West Indian Negro must understand that there is but one fatherland for the Negro, and that is Africa . . . as the Irishman is struggling and fighting for the fatherland of Ireland, so must the new Negro of the world fight for the fatherland of Africa.[16]

Then becoming—or at least it seemed so—much more specific, Garvey hurled out this challenge: "We say to the white man who now dominates Africa, that it is to his interest to clear out of Africa now, because we are coming . . . 400,000,000 strong; and we mean to retake every square inch of the 12,000,000 square miles of African territory that belong to us by right Divine."[17]

In the tradition of self-possession, no one had ever spoken like Garvey. It was an intoxicating vision, this promise of bringing all the scattered and gathered children of Africa into one mighty force (that was the meaning of Garvey's figure of 400,000,000). It was not calling for the return of all black people to Africa, but for the focus of all black energies to be on the struggle to "redeem" Africa. Connected to the bold talk was a vibrant national and international organization, with new chapters developing in many parts of the country and throughout the African diaspora. Its initial focus was on black people

15

possessing themselves, expressing themselves through a variety of commercial enterprises, self-help organizations, religious institutions, publications, including a major newspaper—eventually through the much-heralded, hope-filled Black Star Line, a deeply flawed experiment in developing a pan-African shipping enterprise.

But for those men and women who were committed to redefining the nature of "we the people of the United States," something was amiss—even for those who held great admiration for Garvey (and that was not a universal sentiment in the black freedom-seeking organizations). For Garvey had essentially agreed with white supremacists of this nation, had conceded this to be "a white man's country," and called upon black people to gear themselves toward the redemption of Africa. Only then, he said, could there be any hope of respect and justice here.

As is generally known, the central story did not end well. In spite of tremendous accomplishments, especially where the building of black morale was concerned, in spite of great organizational beginnings, Garvey's summons to Afro-Americans to possess themselves in order to possess Africa had no clear strategic future. And because he conceded this country to its white racist majority, there was no real future here either.

In a sense, the dilemma was epitomized in his own life. As an alien who had now sought American citizenship, who did not choose to be part of "we the people of the United States," he was dangerously vulnerable to deportation actions. The U.S. government held the threat of deportation over Garvey's head. They infiltrated his organization. They connived with his enemies in the black community. They finally brought trumped up charges against him. Then when they ganged up on him and closed off his channels to African contacts and harassed him into a prison sentence, Garvey seemed unprepared to mobilize his followers for any serious resistance. In 1925 he was sent to the federal prison in Atlanta, Georgia. Two years later he was deported to Jamaica.

Garveyism still lives in many forms and places, especially among black men and women who choose its orientation to the absolutely necessary possession of their souls, the affirmation of their Africanness. It lives on in a consciousness, sometimes more or less political, concerning the Afro-American connections to the still beleaguered homeland communities. Through Garvey it was possible to see the dangers inherent in a position where the tradition of profound black self-possession is not connected to a struggle to claim and possess the land that the Afro-Americans have helped to create and fertilize with their blood, spirit, and skills. On the other hand, in their experience with the Communist party in the United States, black people were able to apprehend some of the greatest strengths and weaknesses of black-white alliances in the struggle for justice.

At their best, the white members of the Communist movement in the U.S.A. were among the most courageous and committed of allies. Many risked their lives organizing with and for black people, often exposing themselves to the terrors of the deep south by insisting on interracial organizing and living in Birmingham, in Atlanta, in the rural areas of Alabama and in the small textile towns of North Carolina—in the 1930s! They offered new visions of hope to black men and women like Angelo Herndon, the young southern organizer who became a hero; Richard Wright, who discovered the party in Chicago after a harsh pilgrimage from Mississippi; and Louise Thompson, the well-educated, articulate Harlem social worker and organizer. With a great mixture of motivations the white-dominated party helped to save the lives of a group of southern black teenagers who were headed for a relatively quiet, legal lynching, when they put the Scottsboro Boys into the limelight of the world.

During the depression years the Communists seemed to be one of the few political forces who knew where they were going and were organized to do what they wanted to do. In those years they offered tremendous hope that the black struggle for freedom in the U.S.A. could become part of the forever imminent worldwide revolution of the working classes, and thousands of black people found great resonance with that vision. As a legal party in those days, it became the first significant American political party to nominate a black man—James W. Ford—for vice president.

But the ambiguities of black-white relationships were still present, intensified by a special problem peculiar to the Communist party. Not only did many party members still have hard battles to wage against their paternalism and racism, but they were a predominantly white party and their whiteness and their radicalism made it very difficult for them to have large organizing successes in a black community where the spirit of Marcus Garvey never died. Ultimately, though, what broke the heart of the alliance was the fact that the Communist party, with its black and white members and its ever-widening circle of influence, was not an independent force. It was far too submissive to the strong will of the international center of power in Moscow, a center that was ultimately devoted to the protection of "the mother country" of world communism at any costs.

By the late 1930s, those costs included Russia's selling essential material goods to Italy while it was engaged in its imperialistic war against Ethiopia, a nation considered "the mother country" of the African diaspora. Finally, when Hitler broke a fragile treaty with Stalin and attacked Russia, the word was given throughout the Communist International that all activities which internally challenged the allied, capitalist nations, including the U.S.A., needed to be curtailed. They were now allies of mother Russia in her desperate war against Hitler, and the black vision that demanded an incessant attempt to "swamp . . . the very foundations"[18] of American racism and injustice was no longer convenient. So it was betrayed, as the party withdrew from the frontlines of black challenges to America.

Another high hope was lost; another set of white allies found wanting. But women and men who had seen new visions of a world transformed by the actions of common people, who had caught a glimpse of the possibilities of a more perfect union in which poverty and exploitation would also be overcome, could never be quite the same again. Indeed, it was toward the end of this period of great expectations and soaring vision that Langston Hughes, who was closely allied with the communist forces in the 1930s, wrote one of his most prophetic poems, "Let America Be America Again," closing it with a series of announcements, perhaps predictions:

O, yes,
I say it plain,
America never was America to me,
And yet I swear this oath—
America will be!
An ever-living seed,
Its dream
Lies deep in the heart of me.
We, the people, must redeem
Our land, the mines, the plants, the rivers,
The mountains and the endless plains—
All, all the stretch of these great green states—
And make America again.

Visions were needed in those days. For the realities of separate-but-equal (better known as Jim Crow) were harsh and often seemed immovable. Wherever black people travelled or lived in the south, and in too many parts of the north, they were faced with the humiliation of seeing doors that were open to white citizens legally closed to them: restaurant and motel doors, movie house doors, skilled employment doors, Marine Corps and Air Force doors, the large doors to public parks, pools, beaches, entire neighborhoods, the doors to public service were all closed. Or they would find two sets of doors, two kinds of facilities, from ticket lines to water fountains, from waiting rooms to public schools. One white, one colored, one reasonably clean, well-cared for, well supplied, the other usually broken, neglected by the white authorities, shamefully unequal.

And often in the north, the trouble was that there were too many times when you couldn't tell which doors were which before being shocked by the cruel humiliation of rejection or bodily harm. Of course, it was especially cruel to have to explain these visible and invisible doors, signs and dangers, to young black children who tugged innocently at hands and hearts, eager to be taken in. Only men and women of vision were ready to break the barriers and open the way for the children.

Yes, in the 1930s visions were certainly needed, not only to break open the brutal circle of Jim Crow, but for more as well. The nation was in the grip of the most extended and grueling economic depression it had ever known, one that was being experienced in many parts of the industrialized world. As usual, black people were feeling it in an especially acute way; and, as usual, there were a variety of creative responses to the crisis, many of them based in the religious genius of Afro-Americans.

It was the time when Father Divine rose out of southern black obscurity to great prominence in the communities of black America. Here was a phenomenon to challenge every deeply-held American belief. According to Father and his followers of the Peace Mission, here was God, manifesting himself among humans as a short, ebulient, balding black man. Here was his Kingdom, scattered in Peace Mission centers across the country, populated with black and white "angels" with new names (like Precious Faith, Heavenly Joy, and Patient Bliss), many of whom had contributed all of their earthly goods to the new Kingdom of Peace. Here was a divine being who provided ample feasts, adequate shelter, and a joyful community of singing and spiritual dancing—and celibacy—for all who wanted to share their lives. Here was a religious leader who forbade his followers to resort to violence and who taught them to refuse to take up arms against other humans and to work for justice in the land.

For those who did not choose the way of Father Divine, the dynamic young associate pastor of Harlem's massive Abyssinian Baptist Church provided another alternative. Adam Clayton Powell, Jr. worked with other organizations to struggle for jobs, for government services, for justice. Through effective organizing, he and his coworkers put picket lines on the streets, demanded that white-owned stores in Harlem hire black employees, and offered active, confrontative ways for women and men to carry on a daily struggle to challenge the authorities, to redefine justice, and to possess the land, or at least some part of it. Here again, leadership developed and honed by the black church was moving out of the pulpits into the streets on behalf of a just society. It was an old tradition, and even with the charismatic, academically trained Powell, its fullest moment had not yet arrived.

Meanwhile, in those depression years, other forms of black religion were also creating amazing new and old possibilities out of the cauldron of suffering. In Detroit, the children of Noble Drew Ali and the children of Garvey were melding. Elijah Poole, who had been a part of the Garvey movement, had also known the forces of Ali. But in 1930 he met a man who appeared to be an itinerant peddler of clothes, but who announced, "My name is W.D. Fard, and I come from the Holy City of Mecca." Later there would be disagreement about whether Mr. Fard was a messenger of Allah or a human manifestation of the divine; however, there was no essential disagreement about what he taught and what it meant for black people. One testimony was that Fard taught that "the black men in North America are not Negroes, but members of the lost tribe of Shebazz, stolen by traders from the Holy city of Mecca 379 years ago. The prophet came to America to find and to bring life to his long-lost brethren, from whom the Caucasians had taken away their language, their nation, and their religion."[19]

So the process of repossession involved regaining the religion of Islam, the Arabic language, and "their culture, which is astronomy and higher mathematics, especially calculus."[20] Through strict dietary and moral laws, the lost and found black people were told they must "clean themselves up—both their bodies and their houses,"[21] to be prepared for their deliverance by Allah who would return them to Mecca.

This, too, was black religion, providing a path for the repossession of a people. Eventually, when Mr. Fard mysteriously disappeared, Elijah Poole, whom he had renamed Elijah Kerriem, became the Honorable Elijah Muhammad. Under his guidance the Temple people emerged, soon to be known as the Nation of Islam, the Black Muslims, carrying new names, new histories, new creation myths and cosmologies, attempting to create a new people to serve Allah in the wilderness of North America.

Ever since their first enchained contacts with the terrifying and beautiful land, the children of Africa in America had understood how crucial it was to possess—and repossess—their souls, to define and redefine their own identity, to create—and re-create—their own purpose and direction. So all through slavery and the postslavery decades they fought to protect, maintain, and reshape their basic institutions, especially the family, the centers of worship and spiritual renewal, and the schools. Whether faced toward redemption of Africa or committed to the humanizing transformation of the United States of America—or both—the people knew that they needed solid ground, protected space, to create the soul-full men, women, and children who would catch the vision and do the work, immediate work, generational work.

As the depression years produced their havoc and their many creative responses, nowhere did the potential creative power of black institutions become more evident than in the rather inelegant collection of buildings and often brilliant collection of men and women called Howard University in Washington, DC. Established in the post-Civil War years by benevolent and often committed white and black educators, Howard had finally found its first black president, the Reverend Mordecai Johnson, in 1926. The dynamic, authoritarian leader breathed new life and fire into the federally-funded institution, demanding and receiving more funds and respect than it had ever had before.

Howard's faculty included some of the best minds in America, among them Ralph Bunche, E. Franklin Frazier, Abram Harris, and John Hope. Kenneth Clark, the eminent psychologist who would play a central role in the *Brown* v. *Board of Education of Topeka* decision, at one point reminisced concerning his student days at Howard in the 1930s. He said "there was a great ferment" at the university in those days. Everyone, Clark said, felt the "enormous drive and purpose"[22] of preparing themselves to participate in a movement toward a society of justice and opportunity.

Perhaps the place where this was most evident was at the university's small law school. In 1929 Johnson had convinced Charles Hamilton Houston, a native Washingtonian and graduate of Harvard Law School, to come and transform the mediocre institution. In the course of six years, this brilliant, unyielding and magnificently obsessed black man had created a law school whose central, relentless purpose was to develop the highly trained cadre of lawyers who would lead the next great assault against the legal foundations which supported America's structures of racial injustice. Led by Thurgood Marshall, the most famous graduate of Houston's training ground, they seemed to hear again John Hope's call from 1896: "Let your discontent break mountain-high against the wall of prejudice and swamp it to the very foundation."

Using the laws and the courts of the land, working largely within the structures of the NAACP, undergirded by a generation of unsung and courageous black plaintiffs, they headed toward the foundation. In the midst of the depression, they decided to take on the segregated public school systems as the central support of the entire structure of legalized injustice. Within 20 years, *Plessy* v. *Ferguson* was undone. Using the base of their own institutions, the grandchildren of slaves were creating a more perfect order, redefining the general welfare.

It was only two decades after the armistice which halted "the war to end all wars," that World War II began. Viewed from the perspective of the black struggle for freedom and justice in the United States, much of the wartime drama seemed like a *déjà vu,* a reenactment of all the tendencies of "the war to make the world safe for democracy," with many elements now intensified and magnified.

Before December 7, 1941, the debates over black participation were sharp and the issue of color had been heightened by Japan's involvement. After Pearl Harbor, holding such a position became much more difficult. Still, the old contradictions were present. For instance, when the nation's leaders began to mobilize public opinion against the "racism" of Hitler's "Aryan" forces, or when Franklin Roosevelt stood with leaders of the French and English imperialist nations and invited Afro-Americans into the struggle for freedom, the contradictions were sharp.

Meanwhile, black soldiers were again segregated, harassed, sometimes killed, even before a half million of them left the United States for the official war zones. Black newspapers in this country were so vociferous in their protests against the contradictions inherent in the situation that they were threatened with censorship and with the loss of access to rationed newsprint. Aside from the newspapers, black people were organizing, threatening to march on Washington (under A. Philip Randolph's eloquent leadership) unless a presidential order forced the defense industries to end their shameful discrimination against black workers, unless black soldiers could find safety and justice in their own country. The liberal president finally relented under the pressures of possible international embarrassment and internal discord. He made a move toward breaking down the discriminatory defense industry hiring, but little was done to improve the conditions of black men and women in the military.

All the old ironies were present. In response to another massive, wartime migration of black people out of the south into the coastal cities of the west and southwest, into the heartland of industrial centers, white violence was explosive. In 1943, black and white warfare broke out in Detroit. By the time the war ended in 1945, it was clear to some sensitive observers that nothing at home or overseas would ever be quite the same again where the black struggle for freedom and justice was concerned. The momentum that had been building in the courts, on the streets, in churches, temples and mosques, in the minds and hearts of marching men and women, on battlegrounds at home and overseas, could not be denied.

Besides, the war had helped to transform the world itself, even beyond all the blood and death and terrible grieving. For the colonial foundations which World War I had shaken were now being irremediably torn asunder. The earlier Harlem vision of Hubert Harrison was now being realized. In India, China, all over Africa, Southeast Asia, and the Caribbean, the power of European domination was being challenged and undermined by the rising revolutionary forces of the colonized colored people who were determined to be free, to repossess themselves.

Nothing would ever be the same again, neither within the Afro-American movement for freedom and transformation, nor in the far-scattered confrontations between Europe (and Euro-Americans) and the colonized peoples, confrontations in which many black Americans somehow felt themselves apart. So, some black people looked closely at Gandhi's nonviolent revolutionary movement in India and, while recognizing important differences, saw a possible source of hope. Others were encouraged by China's great movement away from its feudal and European-dominated past. Most black Americans caught the quickening sounds of rebellion rising beneath the surface of Africa and recognized a message there. Nothing would ever be the same again.

Adam Clayton Powell, Jr. knew this. In 1945 he published *Marching Blacks*, an account of the awakening in the postdepression black community, a statement of the domestic meaning of the new international situation. Closing the work, he quoted at length from a statement by one of the black movement's most highly prized white allies, Edwin Embree. In the last year of the war, Embree said,

> The white man of the western world is offered his last chance for equal status in world society. If he accepts equality, he can hold a self-respecting place—maybe a leading place in the new order. And he may continue to contribute much in science, in industry, and in political maturity. But if the western white man persists in trying to run the show, in exploiting the whole earth, in treating the hundreds of millions of his neighbors as inferiors, then the fresh might of the billion and half nonwhite, nonwestern people may in a surging rebellion smash him to nonentity.[23]

Powell agreed and said, "[White] America is not ready for the postwar world," but concluded that "the black man" was. According to Powell "The black man . . . plods wearily no longer—he is striding Freedom Road . . . He is ready to throw himself into the struggle to make the dream of America become flesh and blood, bread and butter, freedom and equality."[24] This was the dream of John Hope in 1896 and of his enslaved foreparents before him. It was Langston Hughes' dream, and in Powell's own lifetime the dream would burst forth again into powerful reality, as the great grandchildren of the slaves kept their eyes on the prize.

After World War II, it was somewhat easier to see what was happening in the United States. From 1941, when Roosevelt was pressured into his executive order on fair employment, there was no single year that did not produce at least one new positive reaction to the black movement from the executive or judicial branches. For instance, in the years from 1944 to 1950, white primaries were struck down in the courts, President Truman formed the first presidential civil rights commission, segregation in interstate bus travel was legally denied, segregation in the army was attacked, literacy tests for voting were declared unconstitutional, and the border states began token desegregation of the graduate schools of their universities.

Then, in 1950, as the international power struggle between Russia and the U.S. developed into its first major armed conflict in Korea, the courts seemed to open like a burst dam. In separate decisions, cases involving five state universities were decided in favor of token black petitioners. Railroad dining car segregation was struck down. Finally, with a group of courageous black families as plaintiffs, the NAACP decided to make a frontal attack on the basic principle of separate-but-equal education. Houston's cadre was striking home.

Why did it happen with such momentum in those years? Part of the answer surely rests with the veterans who came home from the war, determined to create freedom in America, veterans like Amzie Moore and Medgar Evers of Mississippi, like Harry Briggs of Clarendon County, South Carolina, and Oliver Brown of Topeka, Kansas.

Why?

Part of the reason may have been the moral passion and tough, loving courage of the men like Bayard Rustin and Bill Sutherland who had been conscientious objectors during the war and who had fought disciplined, costly battles against the racism of the federal prisons. Part of it was the women, like Ella Baker and Grace Boggs who developed their skills to high levels during the wartime years, working with old campaigners like A. Philip Randolph in the March on Washington movement and with C.L.R. James, the great black Trotskyite intellectual. Of course, much of the answer is wrapped up in the history of the NAACP, continuing to keep the faith, finally zeroing in on the heart of the system of segregation, challenging the idea of the existence of any true equality when forced segregation exists.

Why did it happen with such momentum in those years? Because there were black churches, often built in the hard, post-Reconstruction days, where rallies, mobilizing, and planning could take place. Because black (and a few white) ministers were willing to stand firm on the front lines against the moral evil of segregation and call their people to do the same, regardless of the cost.

It happened because white American leaders knew the cold war-conscious world was watching a nation that dared call itself "the leader of the free world" to see how it would deal with its own citizens who had so long clamored for freedom.

It happened because the post-World War II generation of men and women were the first Afro-Americans who grew to their maturity in a world where the power, hegemony, and wisdom of the European world were everywhere being publicly questioned, rejected, and attacked. They knew a new time had come, was coming, all over the nonwhite world, and that they were related to it all. At great personal costs, DuBois, Paul Robeson, Lena Horne, and others kept reminding black people of their relationship to this vaster world of men and women struggling for transformation.

It happened because the great migrations out of the south had continued and had thrust new millions of black voters into the precincts of urban politics all over the north, many of them into the company of the Democratic party. Their strength could not be ignored. The party could no longer allow its southern white racist firebrands to shape its racial policies. The black presence and its insistent questions about "we the people of the United States" were part of the reason for the momentum.

It happened because the Nation of Islam was quietly rising, gaining power, calling attention to the hypocrisy of white America. It happened because some white people really decided that they must have a more perfect union, must secure the blessing of liberty for themselves and their posterity. And they finally understood that such things were impossible without the establishment of justice for black people. It happened because some white people and their children were ready to pay the price for freedom.

Of course, no one knows all the answers to such a question as why. That's one of the surprises of history—how little we know about so much. But one thing is clear. It happened with such momentum because a people had kept their eyes on the prize, had persisted in a vision of a more perfect union, had waded through rivers of blood to keep promises to their foreparents and to their children. Such unyielding commitment and action eventually builds its own momentum, creates new, surprising realities, beginning deep within individual lives, opening up to the re-creation of a society.

Notes

1. Ridgley Torrence, *The Story of John Hope* (New York: MacMillan, 1948), pages 114–115.
2. Ida B. Wells-Barnett, "Lynch Law in All Its Phases," *Our Day*, Vol. II (1893), pages 333–335.
3. W.E.B. DuBois, *The Conservation of Races* (Washington, D.C: American Negro Academy, Occasional Papers No. II, 1897), pages 487–489.
4. Ibid.
5. Ibid.
6. Torrence, loc. cit.
7. *The Richmond Planet* (July 30, 1898). Also quoted in: Herbert Aptheker, ed., *A Documentary History of the Negro People in the United States*, Vol II (New York: Citadel Press, 1951), page 824.
8. Ida B. Wells-Barnett, *On Lynchings* (New York: Arno Press, 1969), page 42.
9. Herbert Aptheker, ed., *A Documentary History of the Negro People in the United States*, Vol II (New York: Citadel Press, 1951), page 824.
10. Ibid.
11. Hubert Harrison, *When Africa Awakes* (New York: The Porro Press, 1920), pages 96–97.
12. Ibid.
13. John Hope Franklin and August Meier, eds., *Black Leaders of the 20th Century* (Champaign: University of Illinois Press, 1982), page 143.
14. Edmund Cronon, *Black Moses* (Madison: University of Wisconsin Press,1955), page 66.
15. Ibid.
16. Ibid.
17. Ibid.
18. Torrence, loc. cit.
19. Clifton Marsh, *From Black Muslims to Muslims* (Metuchen, NJ: Scarecrow Press, 1984), pages 52–54.
20. Ibid. page 52.
21. Ibid. pages 58–59.
22. Richard Kluger, *Simple Justice* (New York: Knopf, 1976), page 496.
23. Adam Clayton Powell, Jr., *Marching Blacks*, Second edition (New York: Dial Press, 1973), page 206.
24. Ibid.

QUESTIONS FOR REVIEW

1. Do people take the Preamble to the Constitution seriously? How would you express the purposes of the Constitution—according to the Preamble—in your own words? What would you say if someone suggested that these should be the purposes of our nation itself?

2. What significance does the black-led freedom movement have for white people and other nonblacks in our country?

3. What is meant by the statement that during the post-Reconstruction period "the nation . . . sought to create an ersatz 'domestic tranquility . . . '"?

4. What was the significance of the *Plessy* v. *Ferguson* Supreme Court decision of 1896? How did it affect our country as a whole? Why does the introduction describe it as "a stimulus to resistance"?

5. How would you put the essence of W.E.B. DuBois' 1897 statement in your own words? Does any aspect of it still apply in the late 20th century?

6. What kinds of independent black institutions were created in the post-Civil War period? What importance did they have for the black community in its struggle for freedom? Are any such institutions still needed? Why or why not?

7. Why might members of black and white communities in the United States have disagreed in 1900 on how to describe Robert Charles? How do you think Americans would describe Charles today?

8. Why in the early part of this century did major sections of the white population have serious difficulties in defining black Americans as a part of "we the people of the United States"? Do some of those difficulties still exist? Are there other groups now who are not included, or only with great difficulty?

9. How do you account for the fact that in every generation some whites understood that the deep issues of the freedom struggle had to do with more than rights for Afro-Americans? How and why were these people different from the white mainstream? Do you think they had to pay a price for being different?

10. For each of the six claims of the black freedom struggle, identify one way in which black people attempted to live out that claim.

11. Considering such matters as origins, purposes, membership, and leadership, what were some of the similarities and differences between the Niagara Movement and the NAACP?

12. How would you compare the roles of Ida B. Wells-Barnett, Timothy Drew, Marcus Garvey, and W.E.B. DuBois in the pre-World War II struggle for freedom?

13. What were some of the major effects of World War I on the development of the black-led movement for justice in America?

14. What was the significance of the new names that members received in organizations like the Moors, the Nation of Islam, and Father Divine's Kingdom? In what other western religious groups do individuals receive new names?

15. Analyze the major strengths and weaknesses of Marcus Garvey and the UNIA.

16. The introduction claims that the experience of black people with the pre-World War II Communist party of the United States of America revealed some of its greatest strengths and weaknesses. What were these?

17. What is the meaning of the line in Langston Hughes' poem "America never was America to me"? What does he mean by saying "we the people must redeem our land"?

18. What was the role of black religion in the freedom movement prior to 1955?

19. From the 1930s through the 1960s Howard University in Washington, DC provided some of the major leaders and workers in the black-led movement for justice and transformation in America. Is there still a role for such a predominantly black institution? Why or why not?

20. What were the major similarities and differences in the effects of World War I and World War II on the black freedom movement? How did overseas movements for freedom and independence affect the black movement in the United States?

21. Was Adam Clayton Powell, Jr. right when he said, "White America is not ready for the postwar world?" What did he mean? Did black people in America have anything to do with getting the nation ready?

RECOMMENDED READINGS

Aptheker, Herbert. *A Documentary History of the Negro People in the United States*. 3 vols. New York: Citadel Press, 1951–1974. A collection of documents on the period 1896–1910, with strong emphasis on the freedom struggle in that period.

Bennett, Lerone. *Black Power U.S.A.* Chicago: Johnson Publishing Company, 1967. A popular and dramatic account of the black struggle for a new social order during the Reconstruction period.

Berry, Mary Francis. *Black Resistance/White Law*. New York: Appleton-Century-Crofts, 1971. A stimulating discussion of the uses of law against the struggle for justice in the American context.

Clarke, John H., ed. *Marcus Garvey and the Vision of Africa*. New York: Vintage 1974. A good introductory collection of documents and testimonies edited by an activist-historian of Africa and Afro-America.

Cronon, Edmund D. *Black Moses*. Madison: University of Wisconsin Press, 1955. The first major scholarly biography of Marcus Garvey. Although aspects of it are superceded by later studies, it is still valuable.

Duster, Alfreda M., ed. *Crusade for Justice*. Chicago: University of Chicago Press, 1970. Ida B. Well's unfortunately unfinished autobiography as edited by one of her daughters.

Fox, Steven R. *The Guardian of Boston*. New York: Atheneum, 1970. A helpful biography of Monroe Trotter and his important role as a leader of the black freedom movement in the north in the late 19th and early 20th centuries.

Franklin, John Hope. *Reconstruction After the Civil War*. Chicago: University of Chicago Press, 1961. An introduction to the issues, events, and persons who created the crucial period after the Civil War.

Franklin, John Hope and August Meier, eds. *Black Leaders of the 20th Century*. Champaign: University of Illinois Press, 1982. A collection of essays on such persons as Ida B. Wells-Barnett, W.E.B. DuBois, Marcus Garvey, Charles H. Huston, A. Philip Randolph, Martin Luther King, Jr., and others.

Grant, Joanne, ed. *Black Protest*. New York: Fawcett World Library, 1968. A helpful, sometimes uneven collection of documents illustrating the black thrust toward freedom and justice in America since the 18th century.

Harding, Vincent. *There is a River*. New York: Harcourt Brace Jovanovich, 1981. The first of a more detailed trilogy of the history of the black freedom movement. This volume carries the story to the end of the Civil War and the passage of the 13th amendment outlawing slavery in the United States of America.

Henri, Florette. *Black Migration*. New York: Anchor, 1975. An exploration of the nature of the first major black migration from the south to the north that took place from 1900 to 1920.

Hier, William I. *Carnival of Fury*. Baton Rouge: Louisiana State University Press, 1976. The only full length modern treatment of Robert Charles and his life and death in New Orleans.

Hill, Robert. *The Marcus Garvey and UNIA Papers*, 6 vols. Berkeley: University of California Press. 1982. This series will stand as the definitive gathering of the crucial written materials produced by and about Garvey and his movement.

Hughes, Langston. *Fight for Freedom*. New York: W. W. Norton, 1962. Hughes' readable summary of the history of the NAACP up to the early 1960s.

Naison, Mark. *Communists in Harlem During the Depression*. Champaign: University of Illinois Press, 1983. The title adequately describes the thrust of this excellent history of one of the most important black-white alliances in the freedom movement.

Powell, Adam Clayton, Jr. *Marching Blacks*. Second edition. New York: Dial Press, 1973. An early work by the Baptist minister who became the most powerful and controversial black congressman in history, primarily on the black freedom struggle in the New York City area during the 1930s and World War II period.

Rudwick, Elliott. *Race Riot at East St. Louis*. Champaign: University of Illinois Press, 1982. A scholar's telling of the harsh story of one of the nation's most cruel and influential race riots.

Weisbrot, Robert. *Father Divine*. Champaign: University of Illinois Press, 1983. The most recent and most helpful study of the charismatic religious leader, with special emphasis on his concerns for social justice.

Part II

THE EARLY YEARS
1954–1965

Chapter 2 — Awakenings (1954–1956)

by Vincent Harding

RELATED MEDIA:
EYES ON THE PRIZE
Television Program 1
"Awakenings"

—Concentrates on the period 1954–1956 and the growing involvement of existing orgainzations, local leaders, and ordinary citizens in the black freedom struggle

—Illustrates patterns of racial discrimination that prevailed at the beginning of the modern black freedom struggle

—Analyzes the significance of the Emmett Till murder trial on the involvement of the national media in the civil rights movement

—Discusses the key issues and leaders that led to the Montgomery, Alabama bus boycott and assesses the factors that contributed to its success

—Describes the formation and significance of the Southern Christian Leadership Conference (SCLC) and examines the resistance of white southerners to the burgeoning black rights movement

OVERVIEW

"Another man done gone" was the painfully ambiguous, often bitter cry that was so familiar to the black community of the United States in the 1950s. Thus, many persons would not have been surprised if the inhuman, atavistic (but terribly recognizable) murder of a young Chicago-based teenager in Mississippi, and the predictable legal exoneration of his murderers, had led to nothing more than tears, burning, bottled-up rage, and a great outpouring of indignant words from the relatively safe north.

But 1955 was a new time, and more than tears and words were needed. Now, even though the newness of the time was only dimly perceived in that brutally familiar summer, some things were known. Just about everyone who was black and alive at the time realized that the long, hard struggles, led by the National Association for the Advancement of Colored People (NAACP), its often brilliant and courageous lawyers, and its lengthening line of risk-taking black plaintiffs, had forced the Supreme Court to take a major stand on the side of justice in the *Brown* v. *Board of Education of Topeka* decision. A young black man who had been in the Marine Corps at the time of the Court's decision spoke for many black people when he later remembered how he felt when he heard about the 1954 decision:

> My inner emotions must have been approximate to the Negro slaves' when they first heard about the Emancipation Proclamation. Elation took hold of me so strongly that I found it very difficult to refrain from yielding to an urge of jubilation . . . On this momentous night of May 17, 1954, I felt that at last the government was willing to assert itself on behalf of first-class citizenship, even for Negroes. I experienced a sense of loyalty that I had never felt before. I was sure that this was the beginning of a new era of American democracy.

Robert Williams, who shared those memories, in *Negroes With Guns* (Marzani Munsall, 1962), soon after became a fugitive from America's justice.

Yes, it seemed clear that 1955 was different. By then a rising tide of the nonwhite peoples of the globe had gathered at Bandung, Indonesia to demand that the western world hear their determined pronouncements that the old white-dominated colonial order was a dying way of life. And many Afro-Americans understood that they were somehow part of this reemerging contingent of the world's most ancient peoples. They felt a fundamental agreement with Adam Clayton Powell, Jr., the audacious preacher-politician from Harlem who came back from Bandung to announce that the revolutions of the nonwhite world had brought us all to a new point in history with new responsibilities for justice and freedom. Of course, a similarity existed between Powell's sentiments and those of the thousands of black veterans of World War II who had returned home determined to carry on the struggle for democracy. It was they, too, who helped to make it a different time.

In 1955 the nation was deeply involved in what it chose to call a "cold war" with a Russian-led, anticapitalist network of nations. The United States was proclaiming itself "the leader of the free world," and many of its white leaders especially wanted to demonstrate to the raw materials-rich nations of the nonwhite world that the U.S.A. did not deserve their acerbic taunts concerning the apparently unfree condition of this nation's own major, nonwhite community. In a variety of ways, the new international situation put the black community in the United States in its best bargaining position since the end of the Civil War.

Finally, if anyone had any doubts that 1955 was a new time, they needed only to pay close attention to what was developing in Montgomery, Alabama by the end of the year. There, in the old capital of the Confederacy, inspired by one woman's courage; mobilized and organized by scores of grass-roots leaders in churches, community organizations, and political clubs; called to new visions of their best possibilities by a young black preacher named Martin Luther King, Jr., a people was reawakening to its destiny.

By the end of the following year, after a long, hard, and dangerous struggle, it was clear that the events that transpired in Montgomery, Alabama marked a unique, mass-based new beginning in a struggle that had been going on in this land since the first slaveships denied the colonists' claims to be democratic, since the first enslaved Africans demanded through their words and their deeds that this new nation be faithful to its own best vision. Montgomery was the newest manifestation of the embattled black dream, the latest coming of the vision-based people determined to create a new reality for themselves and all Americans, beginning with a chance to sit in peace and dignity on a Montgomery city bus.

READINGS

1. *B*rown v. *Board of Education of Topeka* is the legal term by which the landmark Supreme Court decision has come to be known. But any full appreciation of the historic struggle which finally forced the nation's highest court to face the fundamental contradiction of constitutionally approved segregation in the heart of "the leader of the free world" must go beyond such legalities. To sense the deepest meaning of the event, it is necessary to search out the great personal and collective courage, the terrifying risks, and the often brutal costs paid by the rising number of persons who challenged the violently defended southern white *status quo* of the 1940s.

No one exemplifies the risks, the courage, or the costs more precisely than the Reverend Joseph Albert DeLaine of Clarenden County, South Carolina. It was DeLaine, proud black native of Clarendon County and pastor and teacher in his local community, who provided the initial inspiration and leadership for the quietly audacious group of black plaintiffs who in 1947 had a simple plea—to have one school bus for their children. The brusque rejection of this plea by the white school board eventually became known as the case of *Briggs* v. *Elliott*. This crucial engagement formed the base of the group of cases which eventually became identified as *Brown* v. *Board of Education of Topeka*. The story of DeLaine, his people, and their costly struggle is best told by Richard Kluger in his book *Simple Justice*.

From: *Simple Justice: The History of Brown v. Board of Education and Black America's Struggle for Equality* by Richard Kluger (New York: Vintage Books, 1975), pages 3–4. Copyright 1976 by Richard Kluger. Used by permission of Alfred A. Knopf, Inc.

Before it was over, they fired him from the little schoolhouse at which he had taught devotedly for ten years. And they fired his wife and two of his sisters and a niece. And they threatened him with bodily harm. And they sued him on trumped-up charges and convicted him in a kangaroo court and left him with a judgment that denied him credit from any bank. And they burned his house to the ground while the fire department stood around watching the flames consume the night. And they stoned the church at which he pastored. And fired shotguns at him out of the dark. But he was not Job, and so he fired back and called the police, who did not come and kept not coming. Then he fled, driving north at eighty-five miles an hour over country roads, until he was across the state line. Soon after, they burned his church to the ground and charged him, for having shot back that night, with felonious assault with a deadly weapon, and so he became an official fugitive from justice. In time, the governor of his state announced they would not pursue this minister who had caused all the trouble, and said of him: Good riddance.

All of this happened because he was black and brave. And because others followed when he had decided the time had come to lead.

At first, he acted gingerly. Not quite six feet tall, on the slender side, with a straight-back bearing that seemed to add inches to his height and miles to his dignity, he was no candidate for martyrdom. In his fiftieth year, he had not enjoyed good health for some time. A nearly fatal bite from a black-widow spider—they could find no medical help for him for fifteen hours—and recurring bouts with influenza had drained his constitution, and the emotional demands of teaching and preaching all over the county had taken their toll as well. It was therefore natural that when he began the activities that, a few years later, were to become the profound business of the Supreme Court of the United States, he would begin in a small way.

His name was Joseph Albert DeLaine. His skin was a medium shade of brown, and his friends described him as "handsome" and "clean-cut." Ceremonial photographs in the late Forties and early Fifties show him in a well-worn black suit with a black vest, looking bright-eyed and attentive behind austere glasses. His hair was short and beginning to gray. He was convinced that it grayed rapidly after they decided to ask for the bus.

A school bus. There were thirty school buses for the white children. There was none for the black children. A muscular, soft-spoken farmer named James Gibson remembers what the chairman of the school board said when they asked for the bus. His name was Elliott, R.W. Elliott, he ran a sawmill, and he was white. Everyone who ran anything in the county was white. What he said was: "We ain't got no money to buy a bus for your nigger children." But there was always money for buses for the white children. . . .

And so a lawsuit was filed. A black man sued white officials who he claimed were denying him and his three children the equal protection of the law as guaranteed by the Fourteenth Amendment of the Constitution of the United States. No such thing had happened before in the memory of living men in Clarendon County, South Carolina. For if you set out to find the place in America in the year 1947 where life among black folk had changed least since the end of slavery, Clarendon County is where you might have come. . . . ■

2. **T**he death of Emmett Till, the 14-year-old, Chicago-bred manchild who was brutally murdered in Mississippi in 1955 for purportedly whistling at—or speaking disrespectfully to—a white woman, became a critical experience in the life of this nation's Afro-American community. On one level, it was an overwhelmingly public event, illustrated by the excerpts from the *Chicago Defender*, which are typical of the widespread, often sensational, coverage given by the black press to the murder and the ensuing, justice-mocking trial.

On another level, it was far more personal, experienced by many in the most private and peculiar ways. For Anne Moody, so close to Till in age, and in the frighteningly shared space of Mississippi's stifling realm, the delayed knowledge of the death of Emmett Till exploded in her life like a depth charge, transforming her vision of herself and other black people, opening up to her consciousness a deep hatred and fear of Mississippi's white people. Her autobiography tells the story in a very different way than the *Defender*.

From: Chicago Defender, Chicago, IL (October 1, 1955). Used by permission.

The mother of Emmett Louis Till has accused Tallahatchie County Sheriff H.C. Strider of hiding two key witnesses who possibly would have given explosive testimony in the trial of two white men cleared by an all-white [jury of the] slaying of her 14-year-old son.

* * * *

Meanwhile, Mrs. Bradley announced through her attorney, William Henry Huff of Chicago, that she will file suits totaling at least $200,000 on civil charges with malice counts against persons involved in the kidnap-slaying of her son. Huff said the suits will be filed in U.S. District Court in Mississippi.

Congressman Charles Diggs, Jr., of Detroit, joined Mrs. Bradley in blasting Sheriff Strider, charging that two "very important witnesses" are being held in the Charleston, Miss. jail. Diggs flew to Sumner last week to observe the trial.

The prisoners in question were identified as LeRoy (Too Tight) Collins and Henry Lee Loggins, both in their late teens, who reportedly worked as truck drivers on the Leslie Milam farm. Leslie is a half-brother of J.W. Milam [a defendant].

Sheriff Strider reportedly denied that either boy was being held and claimed he couldn't find them to serve trial subpoenas.

The youths are said to have washed blood from Milam's truck shortly after Till was kidnapped from his uncle's farm the night of August 28. Milam was quoted as saying the blood was from a deer he had shot. (Deer hunting season is closed in Mississippi.)

Congressman Diggs flew to Chicago early Saturday from Mississippi. With him was Willie Reed, 18, of Drew, Miss., one of the prosecution's surprise witnesses. Reed is believed to be the last person, not involved in the brutal slaying, to see Emmett Till alive. . . .

A second surprise witness, Mrs. Mary (Amanda) Bradley, has also arrived in Chicago, where she will reside.

* * * *

During a brief stop-over enroute to Detroit, Diggs said, "I am disappointed, I went to Sumner, with the hope that the Till trial would result in a conviction."

When asked if he planned to propose any legislation as a result of what he observed at the trial, the Congressman replied: "I have some legislation already to give the Justice Department the right to intervene in Civil Rights Cases and from this new experience I hope to strengthen our case for legislation that would have more than the presently casual regard for Negroes trying to participate in the elections."

He continued: "I am interested in something that would assure the right to vote to all citizens. The basis of the selection of the jury is the voter [rolls] and the public officials are elected by the voters. An anti-lynch bill and legislation to eliminate the poll tax are the basic solutions I believe for this. I still have hope that the people will wake up to the international significance of this."

What You Can Do About The Disgrace in Sumner
[An Editorial]

How long must we wait for the Federal Government to act? Whenever a crisis arises involving our lives or our rights we look to Washington hopefully for help. It seldom comes.

For too long it has been the device, as it was in the Till case, for the President to refer such matters to the Department of Justice.

And usually, the Department of Justice seems more devoted to exploring its lawbooks for reasons why it can't offer protection of a Negro's life or rights.

In the current case, the Department of Justice hastily issued a statement declaring that it was making a thorough investigation to determine if young Till's civil rights had been violated.

The Department evidently concluded that the kidnapping and lynching of a Negro boy in Mississippi are not violations of his rights.

This sounds just like both the defense and the prosecution as they concluded their arguments by urging the jury to "uphold our way of life."

The trial is over, and this miscarriage of justice must not be left unavenged. The Defender will continue its investigations, which helped uncover new witnesses in the case, to find other Negroes who actually witnessed the lynching, before they too are found in the Tallahatchie river.

At this point we can only conclude that the administration and the justice department have decided to uphold the way of life of Mississippi and the South. Not only have they been inactive on the Till case, but they have yet to take positive action in the kidnapping of Mutt Jones in Alabama, who was taken across the state line into Mississippi and brutally beaten. And as yet the recent lynchings of Rev. [George] Lee and LaMarr Smith in Mississippi have gone unchallenged by our government.

The citizens councils, the interstate conspiracy to whip the Negro in line with economic reins, open defiance to the Supreme Court's school decision—none of these seem to be violations of rights that concern the federal government.

And congress isn't concerned either. There has never been a congressional investigation of lynching, or of any of the other abuses and humiliations suffered by Negroes.

And the inactivity of congress is all the more pointed when we consider that there are three Negroes in congress, any one of whom could at least propose such.

The President has steadfastly considered any effort to protect the Negro in the United States from those who would ignore him as a citizen as "extraneous."

The appointment of a Morrow, Wilkins, a Davis or a Mahoney [black Eisenhower administration appointees] is significant and is rightfully applauded, but it means little to the millions of Mose Wrights throughout the South.

For the Mose Wrights are born with low ceilings over their heads. They're denied an education, they're denied a fair return for their labor; they're denied the right to participate in their government; they're denied a chance to walk in the sun and frequently denied the right to live until they're sixty-five, as Milam reminded Mose Wright.

In the midst of this frustration, it appears that the Negro in the South as well as the North, has but one way to go. That is to the ballot box.

One of the most important factors accounting for the difference between the Negro in Chicago and the Negro in Money, Miss., is that the Negro in Chicago can and does vote.

And the Negro in Money can and must register and vote. And the federal government, starting with the White House that has been so negligent in the past in these matters, must be prodded into making it possible for the Negro to exercise this one right—the right to vote.

Yes, the Till trial is over, but the Till case cannot be closed until Negroes are voting in Tallahatchie and LeFlore counties and throughout the South. ■

From: Coming of Age in Mississippi by Anne Moody, pages 121–129. Copyright 1968 by Anne Moody. Used by permission of Doubleday & Company, Inc.

. . . I was now working for one of the meanest white women in town, and a week before school started Emmett Till was killed.

Up until his death, I had heard of Negroes found floating in a river or dead somewhere with their bodies riddled with bullets. But I didn't know the mystery behind these killings then. . . .

* * * *

That evening when I stopped off at the house on my way to Mrs. Burke's, Mama was singing. . . . I wondered if she knew about Emmett Till. The way she was singing she had something on her mind and it wasn't pleasant either.

* * * *

Ralph, the baby, started crying, and she went in the bedroom to give him his bottle. I got up and followed her.

"Mama, did you hear about that fourteen-year-old Negro boy who was killed a little over a week ago by some white men?" I asked her.

"Where did you hear that?" she said angrily.

"Boy, everybody really thinks I am dumb or deaf or something. I heard Eddie them talking about it this evening coming from school."

"Eddie them better watch how they go around here talking. These white folks git a hold of it they gonna be in trouble," she said.

"What are they gonna be in trouble about, Mama? People got a right to talk, ain't they?"

"You go on to work before you is late. And don't you let on like you know nothing about that boy being killed before Miss Burke them. Just do your work like you don't know nothing," she said. "That boy's a lot better off in heaven than he is here," she continued and then started singing again.

On my way to Mrs. Burke's that evening, Mama's words kept running through my mind. "Just do your work like you don't know nothing." "Why is Mama acting so scared?" I thought. "And what if Mrs. Burke knew we knew? Why must I pretend I don't know? Why are these people killing Negroes? What did Emmett Till do besides whistle at that woman?"

By the time I got to work, I had worked up my nerves some. I was shaking as I walked up on the porch. "Do your work like you don't know nothing." But once I got inside, I couldn't have acted normal if Mrs. Burke were paying me to be myself.

* * * *

When they had finished [dinner] and gone into the living room as usual to watch TV, Mrs. Burke called me to eat. I took a clean plate out of the cabinet and sat down. Just as I was putting the first forkful of food in my mouth, Mrs. Burke entered the kitchen.

"Essie, did you hear about that fourteen-year-old boy who was killed in Green-wood?" she asked me, sitting down in one of the chairs opposite me.

"No, I didn't hear that," I answered, almost choking on the food.

"Do you know why he was killed?" she asked and I didn't answer.

"He was killed because he got out of his place with a white woman. A boy from Mississippi would have known better than that. This boy was from Chicago. Negroes up North have no respect for people. They think they can get away with anything. He just came to Mississippi and put a whole lot of notions in the boys' heads here and stirred up a lot of trouble," she said passionately.

"How old are you, Essie?" she asked me after a pause.

"Fourteen, I will soon be fifteen though," I said.

"See, that boy was just fourteen too. It's a shame he had to die so soon." She was red in the face, she looked as if she was on fire.

When she left the kitchen I sat there with my mouth open and my food untouched. I couldn't have eaten now if I were starving. "Just do your work like you don't know nothing" ran through my mind again and I began washing the dishes.

I went home shaking like a leaf on a tree. For the first time out of all her trying, Mrs. Burke had made me feel like rotten garbage. Many times she had tried to instill fear within me and subdue me and had given up. But when she talked about Emmett Till there was something in her voice that sent chills and fear all over me.

Before Emmett Till's murder, I had known the fear of hunger, hell, and the Devil. But now there was a new fear known to me—the fear of being killed just because I was black. This was the worst of my fears. I knew once I got food, the fear of starving to death would leave. I also was told that if I were a good girl, I wouldn't have to fear the Devil or hell. But I didn't know what one had to do or not do as a Negro not to be killed. Probably just being a Negro period was enough, I thought.

* * * *

I was fifteen years old when I began to hate people. I hated the white men who murdered Emmett Till and I hated all the other whites who were responsible for the countless murders Mrs. Rice [my homeroom teacher] had told me about and those I vaguely remembered from childhood. But I also hated Negroes. I hated them for not standing up and doing something about the murders. In fact, I think I had a stronger resentment toward Negroes for letting the whites kill them than toward the whites. Anyway, it was at this stage in my life that I began to look upon Negro men as cowards. I could not respect them for smiling in a white man's face, addressing him as Mr. So-and-So, saying yessuh and nossuh when after they were home behind closed doors that same white man was a son of a bitch, a bastard, or any other name more suitable than mister. ■

3. The Montgomery bus boycott of 1955–56 was one of the truly momentous events in the course of this nation's centuries-long struggle with itself for truth, justice, and democracy. Now that we are more than three decades removed from the event and its surrounding circumstances, it is not surprising that important interpretations and revisions of information on its sources, its meanings, and its key participants are emerging in the literature of history and the social sciences.

Among the most perceptive approaches to the Montgomery experience is the study of Aldon Morris, a young, Mississippi-born black sociologist. He invites his readers to see Montgomery in a rich, historically and politically sophisticated social context, one which calls special attention to the role of the local black community's long-term, grass-roots leaders and their organizations. For Morris these women, men, and structures were critical in setting the stage for and grasping the opportunity presented by Rosa Parks' courageous, ultimately interdependent decision to assert her humanity.

From: The Origins of the Civil Rights Movement: Black Communities Organizing for Change by Aldon Morris, pages 51–54. Used by permission of The Free Press, a division of Macmillan, Inc. Copyright 1984 by The Free Press.

The Montgomery boycott was the watershed of the modern civil rights movement for several reasons. Even though it was the second mass bus boycott of the modern civil rights movement [the first was June 19–25, 1953 in Baton Rouge, LA], among blacks and whites across the United States and the world, Montgomery was thought to be the first. The Montgomery protest earned this recognition because it was launched on such a massive scale and lasted more than a year. Its contributions to the emerging civil rights movement were the MIA [Montgomery Improvement Association], the Reverend Martin Luther King, Jr., the nonviolent method, and success.

Mobilization occurred in Montgomery three days before the mass movement. On December 1, 1955, Mrs. Rosa Parks refused to give her bus seat to a white man in defiance of local segregation laws. Who was Rosa Parks? Most accounts, consistent with the view that social movements arise spontaneously, describe Mrs. Parks as a quiet, dignified older lady who, on that fateful day, spontaneously refused to move from her seat because she "had had enough" and was tired after a long, hard day at work. This account is as mistaken as it is popular. Mrs. Parks was deeply rooted in the black protest tradition. Indeed, in the 1940s Mrs. Parks had refused several times to comply with segregation rules on the buses. In the early 1940s Mrs. Parks was ejected from a bus for failing to comply. The very same bus driver who ejected her that time was the one who had her arrested on December 1, 1955. In Mrs. Parks's words, "My resistance to being mistreated on the buses and anywhere else was just a regular thing with me and not just that day."

Thesis- the trajectory & eventual success of the Mon bus boycott was more than the result of a spontaneous act of resistance to ongoing discrimination

Mrs. Parks, like others steeped in the protest tradition, had a long history of involvement with protest organizations. She began serving as secretary for the local NAACP in 1943 and still held that post when arrested in 1955. In the late 1940s the Alabama State Conference of NAACP branches was organized, and Mrs. Parks served as the first secretary for this body. That position brought her into contact with such activists operating on the national level as Ella Baker, A. Philip Randolph, and Roy Wilkins. In the early 1940s Mrs. Parks organized the local NAACP Youth Council, which fizzled out after a few years. However, she and other local women reorganized the Council in 1954–55, with Mrs. Parks as its adult advisor. During the 1950s the youth in this organization attempted to borrow books from a white library. They also took rides and sat in the front seats of segregated buses, then returned to the Youth Council to discuss their acts of defiance with Mrs. Parks. Mrs. Parks had scheduled a NAACP Youth Council workshop to be held on December 4, 1955, but her arrest on December 1 canceled that function.

Clearly, then, Mrs. Parks's arrest triggered the mass movement not only because she was a quiet, dignified woman of high morals but also because she was an integral member of those organizational forces capable of mobilizing a social movement. Importantly, Mrs. Parks was also anchored in the church community of Montgomery, where she belonged to the St. Paul AME Church and served as a stewardess.

The charismatic leader—Dr. Martin Luther King, Jr.—did not formulate the plan for a mass bus boycott in Montgomery. E.D. Nixon, a longtime resident of the city, who had only a grammar school education, and members of the Women's Political Council [WPC] led by Jo Ann Robinson, an English teacher at Alabama State College, were the ones primarily responsible for planning the boycott. Mrs. Parks and Nixon had an organizational association of more than a decade's standing. During most of the years that Mrs. Parks worked as secretary for the local NAACP, Nixon served as its president. She traveled throughout the years with Nixon, assisting him in his work with various organizations. Nixon was an "organization man" in the full sense of the term. By 1955 he had headed the local Brotherhood of Sleeping Car Porters for more than fifteen years. He was also president of the Progressive Democrats, a local political organization.

In the black community E.D. Nixon was considered a militant and the person to see whenever blacks encountered trouble with whites or wanted to fight against racial domination. Three times in 1955, prior to Mrs. Parks's arrest, women had approached Nixon in reference to harsh treatment they had received on the buses. Nixon and other community leaders had discussed those incidents and even entertained the possibility of a bus boycott. It was decided, however, that those cases were not the ideal occasions for such an undertaking.

* * * *

On the evening of Mrs. Parks's arrest a bus boycott was also being discussed and planned by a group of black women who belonged to the WPC. The WPC was organized by professional black women of Montgomery in 1949 for the purpose of registering black women to vote. Shortly after its inception it became a political force in Montgomery. Members of the WPC were especially prepared to play a leadership role in organizing the bus boycott . . .

* * * *

A number of women in the WPC had worked with both Mrs. Parks and E.D. Nixon several times. Members of this organization spoke with Nixon and agreed that a boycott should be initiated. These women immediately activated their organizational and personal networks and spread the word that a boycott was necessary to protest the arrest and challenge the Jim Crow bus laws. On the morning of December 2, Mrs. Robinson and Mrs. Mary Fair Burks of the WPC informed students and teachers at Alabama State College of the pending bus boycott. Mrs. Robinson composed a leaflet, which described the Parks incident and called for community action. Members of the WPC mobilized students and faculty, who immediately assisted them in mimeographing leaflets and distributing them throughout the black community. Hence, the organizational forces of the black community that represented the protest tradition had begun to mobilize in support of one of their own, Mrs. Rosa Parks.

Meanwhile, on December 2 Nixon was busy compiling a list of ministers and asking them to support the boycott. When asked why he started with the ministers Nixon replied, "because they had their hands on the black masses." Some of the "progressive" ministers, including Ralph Abernathy and E.N. French, agreed that a boycott was needed. On Monday, December 5, Abernathy, French, and Nixon met and formulated the demands to be presented to the bus company. They decided that it was essential to form a new organization to lead the protest. Because all three were closely associated with the NAACP, Nixon was asked why they did not organize the boycott through the NAACP. Nixon stated that he explored the idea with the local NAACP, and

> . . . the man who was the president of NAACP at that time said, "Bro. Nixon, I'll have to wait until I talk to New York [NAACP headquarters] to find out what they think about it." I said, man, we ain't got time for that. He believed in doing everything by the book. And the book stated that you were supposed to notify New York before you take a step like that.

Here is a concrete example of how a bureaucratized organization was inappropriate in the early mobilization stage of a mass protest. The group proceeded to form an "organization of organizations," and Abernathy named it the Montgomery Improvement Association. ■

4. **J**o Ann Robinson's letter to the mayor of Montgomery, which was delivered more than six months *before* the Rosa Parks' incident, is an early sign of things to come, a testimony to the ongoing role of the Women's Political Council. Of course, it is also an indication of what can happen when committed individuals and groups—even in apparently unpromising situations—begin to sense their capacity to create new realities and are willing to experiment toward that goal. Mrs. Parks' own recollections, included in an oral history collected by Howell Raines, further exemplifies the power, courage, and spirit of individual action.

Source: A letter from the Women's Political Council to the mayor of Montgomery, Alabama, May 21, 1954. Used by permission of the University of Tennessee Press.

Dear Sir:

The Women's Political Council is very grateful to you and the City Commissioners for the hearing you allowed our representatives during the month of March, 1954, when the "city-bus-fare-increase case" was being reviewed. There were several things the Council asked for:

1. A city law that would make it possible for Negroes to sit from back toward front, and whites from front toward back until all the seats are taken;

2. That Negroes not be asked or forced to pay fare at front and go to the rear of the bus to enter;

3. That busses stop at every corner in residential sections occupied by Negroes as they do in communities where whites reside.

We are happy to report that busses have been stopping at more corners now in some sections where Negroes live than previously. However, the same practices in seating and boarding the bus continue.

Mayor [W.A.] Gayle, three-fourths of the riders of these public conveyances are Negroes. If Negroes did not patronize them, they could not possibly operate.

More and more of our people are already arranging with neighbors and friends to ride to keep from being insulted and humiliated by bus drivers.

There has been talk from twenty-five or more local organizations of planning a city-wide boycott of busses. We, sir, do not feel that forceful measures are necessary in bargaining for a convenience which is right for all bus passengers. We, the Council, believe that when this matter has been put before you and the Commissioners, that agreeable terms can be met in a quiet and unostensible manner to the satisfaction of all concerned.

Many of our Southern cities in neighboring states have practiced the policies we seek without incident whatsoever. Atlanta, Macon and Savannah in Georgia have done this for years. Even Mobile, in our own state, does this and all the passengers are satisfied.

Please consider this plea, and if possible, act favorably upon it, for even now plans are being made to ride less, or not at all, on our busses. We do not want this.

Respectfully yours,
The Women's Political Council
Jo Ann Robinson, President

From: "The Beginning: Montgomery, 1955–56" [Interview with Rosa L. Parks] by Howell Raines in *My Soul Is Rested: Movement Days in the Deep South Remembered*, pages 40–41. Copyright 1977 by Howell Raines. Used by permission of the Putnam Publishing Group.

I had left my work at the men's alteration shop, a tailor shop in the Montgomery Fair department store, and as I left work, I crossed the street to a drugstore to pick up a few items instead of trying to go directly to the bus stop. And when I had finished this, I came across the street and looked for a Cleveland Avenue bus that apparently had some seats on it. At that time it was a little hard to get a seat on the bus. But when I did get to the entrance of the bus, I got in line with a number of other people who were getting on the same bus.

As I got up on the bus and walked to the seat I saw there was only one vacancy that was just back of where it was considered the white section. So this was the seat that I took, next to the aisle, and a man was sitting next to me. Across the aisle there were two women, and there were a few seats at this point in the very front of the bus that was called the white section. I went on to one stop and I didn't particularly notice who was getting on the bus, didn't particularly notice the other people getting on. And on the third stop there were some people getting on, and at this point all of the front seats were taken. Now in the beginning, at the very first stop I had got on the bus, the back of the bus was filled up with people standing in the aisle and I don't know why this one vacancy that I took was left, because there were quite a few people already standing toward the back of the bus. The third stop is when all the front seats were taken, and this one man was standing and when the driver looked around and saw he was standing, he asked the four of us, the man in the seat with me and the two women across the aisle, to let him have those front seats.

At his first request, didn't any of us move. Then he spoke again and said, "You'd better make it light on yourselves and let me have those seats." At this point, of course, the passenger who would have taken the seat hadn't said anything. In fact, he never did speak to my knowledge. When the three people, the man who was in the seat with me and the two women, stood up and moved into the aisle, I remained where I was. When the driver saw that I was still sitting there, he asked if I was going to stand up. I told him, no, I wasn't. He said, "Well, if you don't stand up, I'm going to have you arrested." I told him to go on and have me arrested.

He got off the bus and came back shortly. A few minutes later, two policemen got on the bus, and they approached me and asked if the driver had asked me to stand up, and I said yes, and they wanted to know why I didn't. I told them I didn't think I should have to stand up. . . . They placed me under arrest then and had me to get in the police car, and I was taken to jail and booked on suspicion, I believe. . . . They had to determine whether or not the driver wanted to press charges or swear out a warrant, which he did. Then they took me to jail and I was placed in a cell. In a little while I was taken from the cell, and my picture was made and fingerprints taken. I went back to the cell then, and a few minutes later I was called back again, and when this happened I found out that Mr. E.D. Nixon and Attorney and Mrs. Clifford Durr had come to make bond for me. ■

Durr.

5. **M**artin Luther King, Jr. emerged as a forceful and charismatic leader during the Montgomery bus boycott. It is here that his deep philosophical commitment to nonviolence and his ability to convey his commitment in a manner that caused thousands of blacks in Montgomery to stand with him took root. In the selection from *Stride Toward Freedom* that follows, King recalls his own role in the mass meeting held at the Holt Street Baptist Church on Monday evening, December 5, 1955. A substantial portion of the speech King gave that night follows this reading.

From: *Stride Toward Freedom: The Montgomery Story* by Martin Luther King, Jr. (New York: Harper & Row, 1958), pages 60–61. Copyright 1958 by Martin Luther King, Jr. Used by permission of Harper & Row, Inc.

Within five blocks of the church I noticed a traffic jam. Cars were lined up as far as I could see on both sides of the street. It was a moment before it occurred to me that all of these cars were headed for the mass meeting. I had to park at least four blocks from the church, and as I started walking I noticed that hundreds of people were standing outside. In the dark night, police cars circled slowly around the area, surveying the orderly, patient, and good-humored crowd. The three or four thousand people who could not get into the church were to stand cheerfully throughout the evening listening to the proceedings on the loudspeakers that had been set up outside for their benefit. And when, near the end of the meeting, these speakers were silenced at the request of white people in surrounding neighborhoods, the crowd would still remain quietly, content simply to be present.

It took fully fifteen minutes to push my way through to the pastor's study, where Dr. Wilson told me that the church had been packed since five o'clock. By now my doubts concerning the success of our venture were dispelled. The question of calling off the protest was now academic. The enthusiasm of these thousands of people swept everything along like an onrushing tidal wave.

It was some time before the remaining speakers could push their way to the rostrum through the tightly packed church. When the meeting began it was almost half an hour late. The opening hymn was the old familiar "Onward Christian Soldiers," and when that mammoth audience stood to sing, the voices outside swelling the chorus in the church, there was a mighty ring like the glad echo of heaven itself.

Rev. W.F. Alford, minister of the Beulah Baptist Church, led the congregation in prayer, followed by a reading of the Scripture by Rev. U.J. Fields, minister of the Bell Street Baptist Church. Then the chairman introduced me. As the audience applauded, I rose and stood before the pulpit. Television cameras began to shoot from all sides. The crowd grew quiet. ■

From: Speech by Martin Luther King, Jr. at Holt Street Baptist Church, Montgomery, Alabama, December 5, 1955. Copyright 1955, 1968 by Martin Luther King, Jr. and the Estate of Martin Luther King, Jr. Used by permission of Joan Daves.

"We are here this evening for serious business. We are here in a general sense because first and foremost we are American citizens, and we are determined to apply our citizenship to the fullness of its means. We are here because of our love for democracy, because of our deep-seated belief that democracy transformed from thin paper to thick action is the greatest form of government on earth. But we are here in a specific sense, because of the bus situation in Montgomery. We are here because we are determined to get the situation corrected.

"This situation is not at all new. The problem has existed over endless years. For many years now Negroes in Montgomery and so many other areas have been inflicted with the paralysis of crippling fear on buses in our community. On so many occasions, Negroes have been intimidated and humiliated and oppressed because of the sheer fact that they were Negroes. I don't have time this evening to go into the history of these numerous cases. . . . But at least one stands before us now with glaring dimensions. Just the other day, just last Thursday to be exact, one of the finest citizens in Montgomery—not one of the finest Negro citizens but one of the finest citizens in Montgomery—was taken from a bus and carried to jail and arrested because she refused to get up to give her seat to a white person. . . . Mrs. Rosa Parks is a fine person. And since it had to happen I'm happy it happened to a person like Mrs. Parks, for nobody can doubt the boundless outreach of her integrity. Nobody can doubt the height of her character, nobody can doubt the depth of her Christian commitment and devotion to the teachings of Jesus. . . .

"And just because she refused to get up, she was arrested. . . . you know my friends there comes a time when people get tired of being trampled over by the iron feet of oppression. There comes a time my friends when people get tired of being flung across the abyss of humiliation where they experience the bleakness of nagging despair. There comes a time when people get tired of being pushed out of the glittering sunlight of life's July and left standing amidst the piercing chill of an Alpine November.

"We are here, we are here this evening because we're tired now. Now let us say that we are not here advocating violence. We have overcome that. I want it to be known throughout Montgomery and throughout this nation that we are Christian people. We believe in the Christian religion. We believe in the teachings of Jesus. The only weapon that we have in our hands this evening is the weapon of protest. And secondly, this is the glory of America, with all of its faults. This is the glory of our democracy. If we were incarcerated behind the iron curtains of a Communistic nation we couldn't do this. If we were trapped in the dungeon of a totalitarian regime we couldn't do this. But the great glory of American democracy is the right to protest for right.

"My friends, don't let anybody make us feel that we ought to be compared in our actions with the Ku Klux Klan or with the White Citizens' Councils. There will be no crosses burned at any bus stops in Montgomery. There will be no white persons pulled out of their homes and taken out to some distant road and murdered. There will be nobody among us who will stand up and defy the Constitution of this nation. We only assemble here because of our desire to see right exist.

"My friends I want it to be known that we're going to work with grim and firm determination to gain justice on the buses in this city. And we are not wrong, we are not wrong in what we are doing. If we are wrong, then the Supreme Court of this Nation is wrong. If we are wrong, the Constitution of the United States is wrong. If we are wrong, God Almighty is wrong. If we are wrong, Jesus of Nazareth was merely a utopian dreamer and never came down to earth. If we are wrong, justice is a lie. And we are determined here in Montgomery to work and fight until justice runs down like water and righteousness like a mighty stream.

"I want to say that with all of our actions we must stick together. Unity is the great need of the hour. And if we are united, we can get many of the things that we not only desire but which we justly deserve. And don't let anybody frighten you. We are not afraid of what we are doing, because we are doing it within the law. There is never a time in our American democracy that we must ever think we're wrong when we protest. We reserve that right. . . .

"We, the disinherited of this land, we who have been oppressed so long are tired of going through the long night of captivity. And we are reaching out for the daybreak of freedom and justice and equality. . . . In all of our doings, in all of our deliberations . . . whatever we do, we must keep God in the forefront. Let us be Christian in all of our action. And I want to tell you this evening that it is not enough for us to talk about love. Love is one of the pinnacle parts of the Christian faith. There is another side called justice. And justice is really love in [application]. Justice is love correcting that which would work against love. . . . Standing beside love is always justice. And we are only using the tools of justice. Not only are we using the tools of persuasion but we've got to use the tools of coercion. Not only is this thing a process of education but it is also a process of legislation.

"And as we stand and sit here this evening, and as we prepare ourselves for what lies ahead, let us go out with a grim and bold determination that we are going to stick together. We are going to work together. Right here in Montgomery when the history books are written in the future, somebody will have to say 'There lived a race of people, black people, fleecy locks and black complexion, of people who had the moral courage to stand up for their rights.' And thereby they injected a new meaning into the veins of history and of civilization. And we're gonna do that. God grant that we will do it before it's too late." ■

6. **O**ne of the most important testimonies to emerge from the first days of the Montgomery bus boycott came from an outsider to the movement, Joe Azbell, city editor of the local white daily newspaper, *The Advertiser*. When Azbell attended the founding mass meeting of the MIA on December 5, 1955, he did not even know the names of the speakers; however, he immediately recognized two crucial elements which became central to the entire southern freedom movement of the 1950s and 1960s. One was the awesome combination of firm determination, powerfully expressed emotions, and "almost a military discipline" that he saw and felt in the electric crowd of black people who packed the church and poured over into the surrounding streets. The other element grasped by Azbell was the willingness of the people to accept gracefully the presence of a white man who came in peace among them.

The official business of the first mass meeting at Holt Street Baptist Church was to have the people hear and vote on a series of resolutions related to the continuation of the bus boycott. These resolutions, with their preamble, were unanimously and loudly approved. Their text was carried in the December 13, 1955 issue of the *Birmingham World*, the major regional black weekly newspaper, and follows Azbell's article here.

From: "At Holt Street Baptist Church, Deeply Stirred Throng of Colored Citizens Protests Bus Segregation" by Joe Azbell in *The Advertiser* (December 7, 1955). Used by permission of *The Advertiser*, Montgomery, Alabama.

As I drove along Cleveland Avenue en route to the Holt Street Baptist Church Monday night, I could see Negroes by the dozens forming a file, almost soldierly, on the sidewalk. They were going to the Rosa Parks protest meeting at the church.

They were silent people, bundled in overcoats, performing what appeared to be a ritual. I parked my automobile a block from the church and noticed the time was 6:45. Already cars were strung out for six or seven blocks in each direction. In fact, the area around the church looked like Cramton Bowl at an Alabama State-Tuskegee football game. Except for one thing: these people were stony silent.

The Negroes eyed me and one inquired if I was a policeman. He turned to his three companions: "He says he ain't the law." I walked up to the steps of the church and two Negro policemen were standing there chatting. Both were courteous when I introduced myself and one went inside and found out about the seating arrangement for the press. Chairs were placed down front for the reporters. The TV cameraman from WSFA-TV and the United Press reporter later took these seats. I stood in the rear of the church during the meeting while Reporter Steve Lesher anchored himself in a chair near the church's pulpit.

* * * *

I went inside the church and stood at the front for a few minutes. The two rear doors were jammed with people and a long aisle was crammed with human forms like a frozen food package. I went to the rear of the church and it was the same. The Negro policemen pleaded with the Negroes to keep the aisles free so people could get out. In the end the policemen gave up in despair of correcting the safety hazard. Bodies at the front were packed one against the other. It required five minutes for a photographer to move eight feet among these people. . . .

The purpose of this meeting was to give "further instructions" on the boycott of city buses which had been started as a protest of the Negroes against the arrest, trial and conviction of Rosa Parks, 42-year-old seamstress, on a charge of violating segregation laws. . . .

There were four white reporters or photographers at the meeting. Only one other white person attended. He appeared to be a young college student or airman and he came with a Negro and left with a Negro. He sat in the group of Negroes in the balcony.

The meeting was started in a most unusual fashion. A Negro speaker—apparently a minister—came to the microphone. He did not introduce himself but apparently most of the Negroes knew him. He said there were microphones on the outside and in the basement, and there were three times as many people outside as on the inside. There was an anonymity throughout the meeting of the speakers. None of the white reporters could identify the speakers. Most of the Negroes did. . . .

The passion that fired the meeting was seen as the thousands of voices joined in singing. . . . The voices thundered through the church.

Then there followed a prayer by a minister. It was prayer interrupted a hundred times by "yeas" and "uh-huhs" and "that's right." The minister spoke of God as the Master and the brotherhood of man. He repeated in a different way that God would protect the righteous.

As the other speakers came on the platform urging "freedom and equality" for Negroes "who are Americans and proud of this democracy," the frenzy of the audience mounted. There was a volume of clapping that seemed to boom through the walls. Outside the loudspeakers were blaring the message for blocks. White people stopped blocks away and listened to the loudspeakers' messages.

The newspapers were criticized for quoting police authorities on reports of intimidation of Negroes who attempted to ride buses and for comparing the Negro boycott with the economic reprisals of White Citizens groups.

The remark which drew the most applause was: "We will not retreat one inch in our fight to secure and hold our American citizenship." Second was a statement: "And the history book will write of us as a race of people who in Montgomery County, State of Alabama, Country of the United States, stood up for and fought for their rights as American citizens, as citizens of democracy."

Outside the audience listened as more and more cars continued to arrive. Streets became Dexter traffic snarls. There was hymn singing between speeches. In the end there was the passing of the hats and Negroes dropped in dollar bills, $5 bills and $10 bills. It was not passive giving but active giving. Negroes called to the hat passers outside—"Here, let me give."

When the resolution on continuing the boycott of the bus was read, there came a wild whoop of delight. Many said they would never ride the bus again. Negroes turned to each other and compared past incidents on the buses.

At several points there was an emotionalism that the ministers on the platform recognized could get out of control and at various intervals they repeated again and again what "we are seeking is by peaceful means."

"There will be no violence or intimidation. We are seeking things in a democratic way and we are using the weapon of protest," the speakers declared.

* * * *

The meeting was much like an old-fashioned revival with loud applause added. It proved beyond any doubt that there was a discipline among Negroes that many whites had doubted. It was almost a military discipline combined with emotion. ■

From: Resolution of the Citizens' Mass Meeting, December 5, 1955.

"WHEREAS, there are thousands of Negroes in the city and county of Montgomery who ride busses owned and operated by the Montgomery City Lines, Incorporated, and

"WHEREAS, said citizens have been riding busses owned and operated by said company over a number of years, and

"WHEREAS, said citizens, over a number of years, and on many occasions have been insulted, embarrassed and have been made to suffer great fear of bodily harm by drivers of busses owned and operated by said bus company, and

"WHEREAS, the drivers of said busses have never requested a white passenger riding on any of its busses to relinquish his seat and stand so that a Negro may take his seat; however, said drivers have on many occasions too numerous to mention requested Negro passengers on said busses to relinquish their seats and stand so that white passengers may take their seats, and

"WHEREAS, said citizens of Montgomery city and county pay their fares just as all other persons who are passengers on said busses, and are entitled to fair and equal treatment, and

"WHEREAS, there has been any number of arrests of Negroes caused by drivers of said busses and they are constantly put in jail for refusing to give white passengers their seats and stand.

"WHEREAS, in March of 1955, a committee of citizens did have a conference with one of the officials of said bus line; at which time said official arranged a meeting between attorneys representing the Negro citizens of this city and attorneys representing the Montgomery City Lines, Incorporated and the city of Montgomery, and

"WHEREAS, the official of the bus line promised that as a result of the meeting between said attorneys, he would issue a statement of policy clarifying the law with reference to the seating of Negro passengers on the bus, and

"WHEREAS, said attorneys did have a meeting and did discuss the matter of clarifying the law, however, the official said bus lines did not make public statements as to its policy with reference to the seating of passengers on its busses, and

"WHEREAS, since that time, at least two ladies have been arrested for an alleged violation of the city segregation law with reference to bus travel, and

"WHEREAS, said citizens of Montgomery city and county believe that they have been grossly mistreated as passengers on the busses owned and operated by said bus company in spite of the fact that they are in the majority with reference to the number of passengers riding on said busses.

"Be It Resolved As Follows:

"1.   That the citizens of Montgomery are requesting that every citizen in Montgomery, regardless of race, color or creed, to refrain from riding busses owned and operated in the city of Montgomery by the Montgomery City Lines, Incorporated until some arrangement has been worked out between said company and the Montgomery City Lines, Incorporated.

"2.   That every person owning or who has access to automobiles use their automobiles in assisting other persons to get to work without charge.

"3.   That the employers of persons whose employees live a . . . distance from them, as much as possible afford transportation to your own employees.

"4.   That the Negro citizens of Montgomery are ready and willing to send a delegation of citizens to the Montgomery City Lines to discuss their grievances and to work out a solution for the same.

"Be it further resolved that we have not, are not, and have no intentions of using an unlawful means or any intimidation to persuade persons not to ride the Montgomery City Lines' busses. However, we call upon your consciences, both moral and spiritual, to give your whole-hearted support to this undertaking. We believe we have [a just] complaint and we are willing to discuss this matter with the proper officials." ■

7. **S**even weeks later, King experienced how seriously his commitment to nonviolence in the face of violence would be tested. This selection which, like the beginning of Reading 5, comes from King's own writing, also shows how ably King convinced black Montgomerians to maintain their faith and to continue the nonviolent boycott.

From: *Stride Toward Freedom: The Montgomery Story* by Martin Luther King, Jr., (New York: Harper & Row, 1958), pages 135–138. Copyright 1958 by Martin Luther King, Jr. Used by permission of Harper & Row, Inc.

. . . on January 30, [1956] I left home a little before seven to attend our Monday evening mass meeting at the First Baptist Church. A member of my congregation, Mrs. Mary Lucy Williams, had come to the parsonage to keep my wife company in my absence. After putting the baby to bed, Coretta and Mrs. Williams went to the living room to look at television. About nine-thirty they heard a noise in front that sounded as though someone had thrown a brick. In a matter of seconds an explosion rocked the house. A bomb had gone off on the porch.

* * * *

. . . I interrupted the collection and asked all present to give me their undivided attention. After telling them why I had to leave, I urged each person to go straight home after the meeting and adhere strictly to our philosophy of nonviolence. . . .

I was immediately driven home. As we neared the scene I noticed hundreds of people with angry faces in front of the house. The policemen were trying, in their usual rough manner, to clear the streets, but they were ignored by the crowd. One Negro was saying to a policeman, who was attempting to push him aside: "I ain't gonna move nowhere. That's the trouble now; you white folks is always pushin' us around. Now you got your .38 and I got mine; so let's battle it out." As I walked toward the front of the porch I realized that many people were armed. Nonviolent resistance was on the verge of being transformed into violence.

* * * *

In this atmosphere I walked out to the porch and asked the crowd to come to order. In less than a moment there was complete silence. Quietly I told them that I was all right and that my wife and baby were all right. "Now let's not become panicky," I continued. "If you have weapons, take them home; if you do not have them, please do not seek to get them. We cannot solve this problem through retaliatory violence. We must meet violence with nonviolence. Remember the words of Jesus: 'He who lives by the sword will perish by the sword.' " I then urged them to leave peacefully. "We must love our white brothers," I said, "no matter what they do to us. We must make them know that we love them. Jesus still cries out in words that echo across the centuries: 'Love your enemies; bless them that curse you; pray for them that despitefully use you.' This is what we must live by. We must meet hate with love. Remember," I ended, "if I am stopped, this movement will not stop, because God is with the movement. Go home with this glowing faith and this radiant assurance." ■

QUESTIONS FOR REVIEW

1. Clarendon County, South Carolina was a rigidly segregated deep southern community where its white leadership had exerted powerful political, economic, and social control—backed up by legal and extralegal force—for decades. Why would a group of black people in such a setting decide to challenge the power holders, even when they knew the personal risks were very high?

2. The unpunished murder of black people by whites in Mississippi and other southern (and northern) states was still not unusual in 1955. Why did the Emmett Till case arouse such a furor, especially in the black community, but not there alone? What effect did the murder have on Anne Moody in Mississippi?

3. In 1955 the *Chicago Defender* assumed that the primary initiative for bringing racial justice in America would have to come from "the administration in Washington." How did the events in Montgomery later that year begin to challenge and change such an assumption? How do you think the Montgomery bus boycott and the freedom movement that developed over the next decade in the south might have changed Anne Moody?

4. Rosa Parks and Jo Ann Robinson, two black women in Montgomery, played crucial roles in the development of the boycott movement. What were those roles? Why do you think these women—and their friends—were ready for such roles in December 1955?

5. At first, Martin Luther King, Jr. and most of the other original leaders of the Montgomery bus boycott were not certain that it could succeed. What finally convinced them of its possibilities for real success? What does this experience suggest about the role of "leaders" and "followers" in such social justice movements?

6.   The boycott participants strengthened King's faith in the movement. What did King's first speech do for the Montgomery bus boycott? What did he see as the significance of the Montgomery movement—beyond the issue of seating on the buses? What do you think he meant when he predicted that historians would eventually say that through their freedom struggle Afro-Americans had "injected a new meaning into the veins of history and of civilization"? Do you think he was right or wrong? Why?

7.   How did the bombing of King's house affect his developing commitment to nonviolence?

8.   As a white Montgomery reporter, Joe Azbell had never been to a meeting like the one at Holt Street Church on December 5, 1955. What seemed to impress him the most about the gathering?

9.   What is the special significance of the fact that the meeting was held in a church? Why do you think it was held there? What does it say about the role of religion in the Afro-American struggle for "a more perfect union"?

ADDITIONAL RECOMMENDED READINGS

King, Martin Luther, Jr. *Stride Toward Freedom*. New York: Harper & Row, 1958. A classic statement of King's vision of the Montgomery bus boycott, his role in that movement, and the larger meaning of the black struggle for this nation.

Miller, William R. *Martin Luther King, Jr.* New York: Weybright & Talley, 1968. The first biography published after King's death and one of the most sensitive to the meaning of his nonviolence.

Moody, Anne. *Coming of Age in Mississippi*. New York: Dial, 1968. A young black Mississippian skillfully and painfully tells the story of her early life and times in Mississippi and her entry into the black freedom movement.

Morris, Aldon. *The Origins of the Civil Rights Movement: Black Communities Organizing for Change*. New York: The Free Press, 1984. Concentrates on the early development of black civil rights organizations and tactics, the development of black unity, the importance of black communities organizing to bring about change, and the role of the black church.

CHAPTER 3 · FIGHTING BACK (1957–1962)

by DARLENE CLARK HINE

RELATED MEDIA:
EYES ON THE PRIZE
Television Program 2
"Fighting Back"

—Concentrates on issues relating to the black attack on school segregation during the period 1949–1962

—Identifies the national civil rights organizations involved in the struggle to desegregate schools, names their leaders, and describes the strategies that they favored

—Analyzes the psychological and sociological effects of segregation on blacks and whites

—Describes major state and federal roles *vis à vis* school desegregation laws

—Presents the issues involved in lawsuits brought by parents on behalf of their children during the period 1947–1954, with special emphasis on the critical features of the Supreme Court's *Brown* v. *Board of Education of Topeka* decision

—Defines and gives examples of *federalism, resistance,* and *interposition*

—Contrasts the desegregation of public schools with the desegregation of colleges and universities

—Relates issues and activities of the school desegregation movement to the other parts of the modern black freedom struggle during the period

OVERVIEW

During the 1930s National Association for the Advancement of Colored People (NAACP) attorneys Charles H. Houston, William Hastie, James M. Nabrit, Leon Ransom, and Thurgood Marshall charted a legal strategy designed to end segregation in education. They developed a series of legal cases challenging segregation in graduate and professional schools. Houston believed that the battle against segregation had to begin at the highest academic level in order to mitigate fear of race mixing that could create even greater hostility and reluctance on the part of white judges. After establishing a series of favorable legal precedents in higher education, NAACP attorneys planned to launch an all-out attack against the separate-but-equal doctrine in primary and secondary schools. The strategy proved successful. In four major United States Supreme Court decisions precedents were established that would enable the NAACP to construct a solid legal foundation upon which the Brown case could rest: *Missouri ex rel. Gaines* v. *Canada,* Registrar of the University of Missouri (1938); *Sipuel* v. *Board of Regents of the University of Oklahoma* (1948); *McLaurin* v. *Oklahoma State Regents for Higher Education* (1950); and *Sweatt* v. *Painter* (1950).

In the Oklahoma case, the Supreme Court held that the plaintiff was entitled to enroll in the University. The Oklahoma Regents responded by separating black and white students in cafeterias and classrooms. The 1950 McLaurin decision ruled that such internal separation was unconstitutional. In the Sweatt ruling, delivered on the same day, the Supreme Court held that the maintenance of separate law schools for whites and blacks was unconstitutional. A year after Heman Sweatt entered the University of Texas law school, desegregation cases were filed in the states of Kansas, South Carolina, Virginia, and Delaware, and in the District of Columbia asking the courts to apply the qualitative test of the Sweatt case to the elementary and secondary schools and to declare the separate-but-equal doctrine invalid in the area of public education.

The 1954 *Brown* v. *Board of Education* decision declared that a classification based solely on race violated the 14th Amendment to the United States Constitution. The decision reversed the 1896 *Plessy* v. *Ferguson* ruling which had established the separate-but-equal doctrine. The *Brown* decision is a landmark in American legal and political history. It, more than any other case, launched the "equalitarian revolution" in American jurisprudence and signalled the emerging primacy of equality as a guide to constitutional decisions; nevertheless, the decision did not end state sanctioned segregation. Indeed, the second *Brown* decision, known as *Brown II* and delivered a year later, played a decisive role in limiting the effectiveness and impact of the 1954 case by providing southern states with the opportunity to delay the implementation of desegregation.

The intervention of the federal government and the deployment of the National Guard in the 1954 Little Rock crisis, and again in 1963 when the enrollment of James Meredith desegregated the University of Mississippi, highlights the role of federal power in promoting social change during this era. While black local and national leaders organized and orchestrated the legal struggles, and students joined in freedom rides and staged sit-ins, another equally important dimension of the rights quest took shape: the battle between federal and state authority and the evolution of the doctrine of federalism. The fact remains that the United States Supreme Court lacked the power to enforce its decisions. President Dwight D. Eisenhower's use of federal troops in Little Rock was a major departure from the reluctance of past presidents to display federal power in the south, especially to protect the lives and rights of black citizens.

Black Americans had joyfully applauded the *Brown* decision, equating it with the Emancipation Proclamation. White southerners, on the other hand, almost universally denounced the ruling and even questioned the right of the Supreme Court to deliver such a blow to their way of life. It is possible to decipher two interlocking, mutually reinforcing strands in the southern reaction to Brown: massive resistance and interposition.

Massive resistance assumed many forms. In hundreds of communities local businessmen and social and political leaders organized White Citizens' Councils to undermine black pressure for desegregation of schools and civil rights. Council leaders employed economic sanctions, held rallies, and used intimidating rhetoric to instill fear in local blacks. Prominent southern politicians also demonstrated their displeasure. On March 12, 1956, 100 southern senators and congressmen signed a defiant manifesto vowing noncompliance with court-ordered desegregation. Following the lead of Virginia's Prince Edward County school board, which closed its public school system for almost a decade rather than comply with even token integration, other communities throughout the south established thousands of white private academies.

An array of southern governors, such as Orval Faubus of Arkansas, Ross Barnett of Mississippi, and George Wallace of Alabama, acquired national notoriety in their public displays of defiance to court-ordered desegregation of secondary schools and state universities. It was their obstinate challenge and adherence to the doctrine of interposition which provoked the confrontation between state and federal authority. This doctrine holds that a state may reject a federal mandate it considers to be an encroachment upon a state's rights. But this is only half of the explanation of how the confrontations originated, especially in the Meredith episode. The other half involves the protracted delays, futile negotiations, and considerable vacillation of the Kennedy administration before it finally began to act decisively to protect Meredith's life and right to attend 'Ole Miss.' These power plays revealed a less than noble commitment to impartial justice for all American citizens.

READINGS

1. The 1954 *Brown* decision negated public school segregation and held that a classification based solely on race was prohibited by the 14th Amendment to the United States Constitution. All would agree that the *Brown* decision is a landmark in American legal and political history. The decision launched the "equalitarian revolution" in American jurisprudence and signalled the emerging primacy of equality as a guide to constitutional decision. This is not to claim, however, that the decision in fact dismantled the dual educational system in this country nor did it end state sanctioned segregation.

The Supreme Court's unanimous decision in the *Brown* case relied quite heavily on the research findings of social scientists. Among the seven scholarly works cited in the opinion were the studies completed by psychologist Kenneth Clark on the effects of prejudice and discrimination on personality development. A portion of one of Dr. Clark's books follows the decision. While this particular paper was published after 1954, it summarizes one of the studies that was presented to the Supreme Court.

From: *Oliver Brown* et al. v. *Board of Education of Topeka.* Decided May 17, 1954.

Mr. Chief Justice Warren delivered the opinion of the Court.

These cases come to us from the States of Kansas, South Carolina, Virginia, and Delaware. They are premised on different facts and different local conditions, but a common legal question justifies their consideration together in this consolidated opinion.[1]

In each of the cases, minors of the Negro race, through their legal representatives, seek the aid of the courts in obtaining admission to the public schools of their community on a nonsegregated basis. In each instance, they have been denied admission to schools attended by white children under laws requiring or permitting segregation according to race. This segregation was alleged to deprive the plaintiffs of the equal protection of the laws under the Fourteenth Amendment. In each of the cases other than the Delaware case, a three-judge federal district court denied relief to the plaintiffs on the so-called "separate but equal" doctrine announced by this Court in Plessy v. Ferguson, 163 U.S. 537. . . . Under that doctrine, equality of treatment is accorded when the races are provided substantially equal facilities, even though these facilities be separate. In the Delaware case, the Supreme Court of Delaware adhered to that doctrine, but ordered that the plaintiffs be admitted to the white schools because of their superiority to the Negro schools.

The plaintiffs contend that segregated public schools are not "equal" and cannot be made "equal," and that hence they are deprived of the equal protection of the laws. Because of the obvious importance of the question presented, the Court took jurisdiction. Argument was heard in the 1952 Term, and reargument was heard this Term on certain questions propounded by the Court.

* * * *

In the first cases in this Court construing the Fourteenth Amendment, decided shortly after its adoption, the Court interpreted it as proscribing all state-imposed discriminations against the Negro race. The doctrine of "separate but equal" did not make its appearance in this Court until 1896 in the case of Plessy v. Ferguson (US), supra, involving not education but transportation. American courts have since labored with the doctrine for over half a century. . . .

* * * *

In approaching this problem, we cannot turn the clock back to 1868 when the Amendment was adopted, or even to 1896 when Plessy v. Ferguson was written. We must consider public education in the light of its full development and its present place in American life throughout the Nation. Only in this way can it be determined if segregation in public schools deprives these plaintiffs of the equal protection of the laws.

Today, education is perhaps the most important function of state and local governments. Compulsory school attendance laws and the great expenditures for education both demonstrate our recognition of the importance of education to our democratic society. It is required in the performance of our most basic public responsibilities, even service in the armed forces. It is the very foundation of good citizenship. Today it is a principal instrument in awakening the child to cultural values, in preparing him for later professional training, and in helping him to adjust normally to his environment. In these days, it is doubtful that any child may reasonably be expected to succeed in life if he is denied the opportunity of an education. Such an opportunity, where the state has undertaken to provide it, is a right which must be made available to all on equal terms.

We come then to the question presented: Does segregation of children in public schools solely on the basis of race, even though the physical facilities and other "tangible" factors may be equal, deprive the children of the minority group of equal educational opportunities? We believe that it does.

* * * *

. . . To separate them from others of similar age and qualifications solely because of their race generates a feeling of inferiority as to their status in the community that may affect their hearts and minds in a way unlikely ever to be undone. . . .

* * * *

We conclude that in the field of public education the doctrine of "separate but equal" has no place. Separate educational facilities are inherently unequal. Therefore, we hold that the plaintiffs and others similarly situated for whom the actions have been brought are, by reason of the segregation complained of, deprived of the equal protection of the laws guaranteed by the Fourteenth Amendment. This disposition makes unnecessary any discussion whether such segregation also violates the Due Process Clause of the Fourteenth Amendment.

Because these are class actions, because of the wide applicability of this decision, and because of the great variety of local conditions, the formulation of decrees in these cases presents problems of considerable complexity. On reargument, the consideration of appropriate relief was necessarily subordinated to the primary question—the constitutionality of segregation in public education. We have now announced that such segregation is a denial of the equal protection of the laws. . . .

Note

[1] In the Kansas case, *Brown* v. *Board of Education*, the plaintiffs are Negro children of elementary school age residing in Topeka. They brought this action in the United States District Court for the District of Kansas to enjoin enforcement of a Kansas statute which permits, but does not require, cities of more than 15,000 population to maintain separate school facilities for Negro and white students. . . . Pursuant to that authority, the Topeka Board of Education elected to establish segregated elementary schools. Other public schools in the community, however, are operated on a nonsegregated basis. The three-judge District Court . . . found that segregation in public education has a detrimental effect upon Negro children, but denied relief on the ground that the Negro and white schools were substantially equal with respect to buildings, transportation, curricula, and educational qualifications of teachers. . . .

In the South Carolina case, *Briggs* v. *Elliott*, the plaintiffs are Negro children of both elementary and high school age residing in Clarendon County. They brought this action in the United States District Court for the Eastern District of South Carolina to enjoin enforcement of provisions in the state constitution and statutory code which require the segregation of Negroes and whites in public schools. . . . The three-judge District Court . . . denied the requested relief. The court found that the Negro schools were inferior to the white schools and ordered the defendants to begin immediately to equalize the facilities. But the court sustained the validity of the contested provisions and denied the plaintiffs admission to the white schools during the equalization program. . . . This Court vacated the District Court's judgment and remanded the case for the purpose of obtaining the court's views on a report filed by the defendants concerning the progress made in the equalization program. . . . On remand, the District Court found that substantial equality had been achieved except for buildings and that the defendants were proceeding to rectify this inequality as well. . . .

In the Virginia case, *Davis* v. *County School Board*, the plaintiffs are Negro children of high school age residing in Prince Edward County. They brought this action in the United States District Court for the Eastern District of Virginia to enjoin enforcement of provisions in the state constitution and statutory code which require segregation of Negroes and whites in public schools. . . . The three-judge District Court . . . denied the requested relief. The court found the Negro school inferior in physical plant, curricula, and transportation, and ordered the defendants forthwith to provide substantially equal curricula and transportation and to "proceed with all reasonable diligence and dispatch to remove" the inequality in physical plant. But, as in the South Carolina case, the court sustained the validity of the contested provisions and denied the plaintiffs admission to the white schools during the equalization program. . . .

In the Delaware case, *Gebhart* v. *Belton*, the plaintiffs are Negro children of both elementary and high school age residing in New Castle County. They brought this action in the Delaware Court of Chancery to enjoin enforcement of provisions in the state constitution and statutory code which require the segregation of Negroes and whites in public schools. . . . The Chancellor gave judgment for the plaintiffs and ordered their immediate admission to schools previously attended only by white children, on the ground that the Negro schools were inferior with respect to teacher training, pupil-teacher ratio, extracurricular activities, physical plant, and time and distance involved in travel. . . . The Chancellor also found that segregation itself results in an inferior education for Negro children . . . but did not rest his decision on that ground. . . . The Chancellor's decree was affirmed by the Supreme Court of Delaware, which intimated, however, that the defendants might be able to obtain a modification of the decree after equalization of the Negro and white schools had been accomplished. . . . ■

The measure of a social injustice is its consequences in the lives of human beings. Over and above the political, economic, sociological, and international implications of racial prejudices, their major significance is that they place unnecessary burdens upon human beings, sometimes even distorting and damaging the individual personality.

* * * *

Two researchers, Deutscher and Chein, questioned more than five hundred social scientists in anthropology, sociology, and social psychology who had done work and published scientific articles in the field of race relations. The investigators found that 90 per cent of the social scientists who replied believed that segregation has bad psychological effects on members of the segregated group, even if equal facilities are provided. The majority based their opinion either upon their own professional experience or on the research of other scholars. They said these were the detrimental effects on members of the minority group.

1. Segregation puts special burdens upon members of a minority group by the clear discrepancy between democratic ideals and the actual practice of enforced segregation.
2. Segregation is a special source of frustration for persons who are segregated.
3. Segregation leads to feelings of inferiority and of not being wanted.
4. Segregation leads to feelings of submissiveness, martyrdom, aggressiveness, withdrawal tendencies, and conflicts about the individual's worth.
5. Segregation leads to a distortion in the sense of what is real.

Some of these social scientists said that segregation leads to a vicious cycle: the harmful personality patterns arising from segregation are in their turn used to support arguments for further segregation. A few said that some individuals could be helped by being members of the segregated group; but most of these social scientists maintained that segregated individuals suffer from being segregated.

What of the persons who impose the segregation? What happens, for instance, to whites when they discriminate against Negroes? Of the social scientists who replied to the questions of Deutscher and Chein, 83 per cent maintained that racial segregation has detrimental psychological effects on members of the privileged group. A number of the scholars maintained that segregation harms those who enforce segregation even more than the victims. Although there was less certainty about these results, they may be summarized as follows:

1. Segregation is a symptom of some psychological maladjustment in those who demand segregation.
2. There are pervasive and elusive harmful effects of segregation on members of the majority group—increased hostility, deterioration of moral values, the hardening of social sensitivity, conflict between

ideology and practices, the development of rationalizations and other techniques for protecting one's self.
3. Segregation results in inner conflicts and guilt feelings among members of the group enforcing segregation.
4. Segregation leads to disturbances in the individual's sense of reality and the relation of the individual to the world around him.

This study by Deutscher and Chein has had considerable influence. Its findings were cited in a brief presented to the Supreme Court by the Solicitor General and the Assistant Attorney General of the United States in a case involving the segregation of a Negro in interstate transportation on a railroad. The study was also cited in the social-science appendix submitted to the United States Supreme Court in the segregated-school cases. In addition this was one of the studies cited by the Supreme Court itself. . . . ■

2. **T**he *Brown* decision produced varied responses, two of which follow. Two days after the *Brown* decision was handed down, an NAACP conference was held in Atlanta, Georgia in which the organization expressed complete confidence in rapid compliance to court-ordered desegregation. The reading that follows is a press release from this conference. Black people across the country shared this joy and conviction that the most significant decree since the Emancipation Proclamation would result in radical changes in their lives and bring new opportunities for equal education.

Two months after the 1954 school segregation decision, a small group of men met in Indianola, in Sunflower County, Mississippi to form the first Citizens' Council. Determined to fight desegregation, the Citizens' Councils attracted support from the upper and middle classes. Eschewing Ku Klux Klan-type tactics, the Citizens' Councils employed sophisticated strategies of economic harassment, political pressure, and propaganda to preserve white supremacy and the segregation of the races.

From: "The NAACP Greets the New 'Law of the Land'" in *The Crisis*. Copyright 1954. Used by permission of the NAACP.

All Americans are now relieved to have the law of the land declare in the clearest language: " . . . in the field of public education the doctrine of 'separate but equal' has no place. Separate educational facilities are inherently unequal." Segregation in public education is now not only unlawful; it is un-American. True Americans are grateful for this decision. Now that the law is made clear, we look to the future. Having canvassed the situation in each of our states, we approach the future with the utmost confidence. . . .

We stand ready to work with other law abiding citizens who are anxious to translate this decision into a program of action to eradicate racial segregation in public education as speedily as possible. . . .

While we recognize that school officials will have certain administrative problems in transferring from a segregated to a nonsegregated system, we will resist the use of any tactics contrived for the sole purpose of delaying desegregation. . . .

We insist that there should be integration at all levels, including the assignment of teacher-personnel on a nondiscriminatory basis. . . .

We look upon this memorable decision not as a victory for Negroes alone, but for the whole American people and as a vindication of America's leadership of the free world.

Lest there be any misunderstanding of our position, we here rededicate ourselves to the removal of all racial segregation in public education and reiterate our determination to achieve this goal without compromise of principle. ■

From: The Deep South Says Never by John Bartlow Martin, pages 1–37. Copyright 1957 by John Bartlow Martin. Renewed 1985. Used by permission of Harold Ober Associates, Inc.

One November day in 1953 in the little Mississippi Delta town of Indianola a husky young white man named Robert Patterson, the father of two girls, having nothing better to do, went to a meeting at the school. There he heard a legislator say that soon the Supreme Court might order the schools desegregated and nothing could be done about it. Most of the parents merely nodded. But one old man said, "You mean I have to send my grandchildren to school with niggers after we built that good nigger high school?" Patterson has recalled, "I just sat there like the rest of them, like a bump on a log. But I couldn't sleep that night. I got up out of bed and went into the bathroom and turned on the light and started writing a letter to the editor. Then I wrote to everybody I could think of."

* * * *

He [Patterson] had one letter printed for distribution. It said in part:

> Dear Fellow Americans, . . . It seems a great danger is hanging over the heads of our children—mongrelization. . . . A lot of people are resigning themselves to seeing their children crammed into schools and churches with children of other races and being taught the Communist theme of all races and mongrelization. . . . I gathered my children and promised them that they would never have to go to school with children of other races against their will, and this is my solemn vow and pledge. If every Southerner who feels as I do, and they are in the vast majority, will make this vow, we will defeat this communistic disease that is being thrust upon us. . . .

* * * *

D. H. Hawkins, a stocky man with a hard mouth who manages the compress [the warehouse where cotton is compressed into tight bales and stored] and is at least as rabid on "mongrelization" as Patterson, called a meeting at his home. . . . Fourteen men met there that night of July 11, 1954, two months after the Court decision—a planter, a farmer, a dentist, the mayor, the sheriff, a lawyer, a ginner, a farm implement dealer, two auto dealers, the town banker, a druggist, a hardware dealer.

* * * *

"We just felt," Patterson has said, "like integration would utterly destroy every-thing that we valued. We don't consider ourselves hate-mongers and racists and bigots. We were faced with integration in a town where there are twenty-one hundred Negro students and seven hundred white. We didn't feel the Supreme Court had the right to come into the state and forcibly cause the schools which were supported by the taxpayers of Mississippi to be integrated and therefore destroyed. . . . "

. . . [Patterson and Hawkins] called a public meeting a week later in the city hall. About 100 townsfolk attended. They voted to form the Indianola Citizens' Council. They elected the banker president, the city attorney vice-president, Hawkins treasurer, and Patterson secretary. . . . Thus was formed the first Citizens' Council, a movement that in a few months swept the South and gave loud voice to the Southern resistance to school desegregation. . . .

* * * *

Patterson wrote: "If we are bigoted, prejudiced, un-American, etc., so were George Washington, Thomas Jefferson, Abraham Lincoln and our other il-lustrious forebears who believed in segregation." Patterson's leaflet went on, "The fate of our great nation may well rest in the hands of the Southern white people today. If we submit to this unconstitutional, judge-made integration law, the malignant powers of atheism, communism and mongrelization will surely follow, not only in our Southland but throughout our nation. . . . "

* * * *

How, he asked, would the Councils "roll back the dark cloud of integration?" And replied: By mobilizing public opinion, by organizing white men and women in "every town and county in our state and then every state in the South." He quoted Edmund Burke: "All that is necessary for the triumph of evil is that good men do nothing," and said, "We need every patriotic white Southerner, rich or poor, high or low, who is proud of being a white American. . . . "

* * * *

During 1954 and early in 1955 other groups with similar purposes were springing up all over the South. Some, indeed, had preceded the organization of the first Council at Indianola, such as the American States' Rights Association in Birmingham and the National Association for the Advancement of White Peo-ple. . . . But during 1955 the Citizens' Council movement absorbed some of the other groups and emerged as the dominant force in most of the Deep South. . . .

* * * *

The year-long period of waiting for the Supreme Court's final decree came to a close at the end of May, 1955: The Court ordered schools desegregated "with all deliberate speed." The South heaved mightily. . . . In Alabama, 5,000 persons attending a Citizens' Council rally at which former governor Herman Talmadge of Georgia was present, heard Judge [Tom P.] Brady (intellectual leader of the Council movement) say that the "Supreme Court refuses to recognize that it cannot by a mandate shrink the size of a Negro's skull which is one eighth of an inch thicker than a white man's." Talmadge urged the abolition of the public schools and recommended a social and economic boycott against "scalawags and carpetbaggers" who refused to fight for segregation—"Anyone who sells the South down the river, don't let him eat at your table, don't let him trade at your filling station and don't let him trade at your store."

* * * *

. . . By the end of 1955, one survey showed, there were at least 568 local pro-segregation organizations in the South, claiming membership of 208,000, nearly all of it in a few major organizations of which the Citizens' Councils were by far the largest. . . . ■

3. **Court-ordered desegregation initially met with total resistance across the south. One hundred southern congressmen signed a defiant manifesto on March 12, 1956 urging resistance to integration and denouncing the Supreme Court. Among the southern senators, only Lyndon B. Johnson of Texas and Albert Gore and Estes Kefauver of Tennessee declined to sign. Several southern states adopted the policy of interposition (the doctrine that a state may reject a federal mandate that it considers to encroach on its rights). Virginia's white leaders embarked upon a course of "massive resistance" that for almost a decade shut down the public school system in Prince Edward County rather than accept even token integration. Actually, compliance with the _Brown_ decision was only orderly and meaningful in the border states and in northern and western states with more permissive segregation statutes. The integration plan proposed by the St. Louis Board of Education is an example of a creative and encouraging plan for desegregation.**

From: Official Proceedings of the Board of Education of St. Louis (1953–1954), 1084.

The following statement, outlining the program for desegregation in the Public Schools of the City of St. Louis, was read by the Secretary [on] June 22, 1954. . . .

Neither the Constitution nor the Statutes of Missouri were the specific object of the recent United States Supreme Court decisions against separate public schools for white and Negro children. These documents do, however, stand counter to those decisions and it may be safely presumed that in due course the Missouri Constitution and Statutes will be modified to harmonize with these decisions. In agreement with the spirit of these decisions, therefore, the members of the St. Louis Board of Education, the Superintendent of Instruction, and other executive officers of the St. Louis Public Schools have adopted the following program for the elimination of separate educational facilities for white and Negro children.

It is the general policy of the Board of Education of the City of St. Louis to begin the integration process in September, 1954, and to complete it by the opening day of school in September, 1955.

* * * *

We therefore present the following schedule for the integration process.

I. By the opening of schools next September, we shall have taken two steps:

   (a) Integration at the Junior College and Teachers College level. . . .
   (b) Integration of Special Schools that provide their services on a city-wide rather than on a school district basis. . . .

II. At the beginning of the second semester, February 1, 1955, we will take another step:

   (a) Integration of all the high schools under the Board's control except the technical high schools. New high school district lines will be drawn and published by November 15, 1954.
   (b) Integration of the Adult Education program which is conducted in the high schools and other buildings.

III. At the opening of schools in September, 1955, we will complete the process of integration. At that time, the following steps will be taken:

   (a) Integration of the technical high schools.
   (b) Integration of all regular elementary schools.

We will publish new elementary school district boundary lines by February 1, 1955.

We believe that this schedule will secure for every public school child full, equal and impartial use of our school facilities as rapidly as is practicable.

In devising this schedule, we have been influenced by a number of reasons which make a more rapid unification program questionable.

1. Our staff, the school administrators, must deal with many administrative problems in bringing about integration. There are problems of new boundary lines, student and teacher assignment, and moving supplies and equipment to be faced. . . .

2. The school administrators and the Board must establish new regulations and policies to govern the operation of a unified school system. These regulations and policies must be made clear to the parents. Clarification and explana-

tion, in many instances, will require discussion with parent groups, meetings with our personnel, explanations to individuals. . . .

3. Parents and students will inevitably be confused by a simultaneous city-wide revision of boundary lines. We would find it virtually impossible to establish direct communication with parents and 90,000 children before the students are back in the schools.

4. Our data show that the city population is shifting daily, and we expect unusually heavy population movement during the coming summer. Our tentative school district boundary lines for an integrated school system have already undergone several revisions. We need additional data which we normally secure from the annual fall block report of students' residences.

5. Finally, there is evidence that the best way to integrate a large public school system is in orderly steps. President Eisenhower has suggested that the integration program in Washington, D.C. public schools serve as a model for other public school systems. We have studied the Washington, D.C. plan carefully. It has guided the formation of our own step-by-step program paced over a period of about fifteen months.

The following general principles will govern the integration process for students:

1. The areas to be served by each elementary and each secondary school will be established by new boundaries. In drawing these boundaries, the purpose will be to provide the best use of the facilities of a given school by the students living in the area of that school.

2. These boundaries will provide each school with a district which it will serve. Students must attend the school in the district in which they live, with the following exceptions:

> (a) The proper school authorities may transfer students from one district to another to relieve overcrowding.

> (b) Students already enrolled in a school, but not resident in its new district, may, but are not required to continue at that school until they graduate. . . .

* * * *

We believe that this program will expeditiously and wisely secure for every public school child full, equal, and impartial use of our school facilities and services and will assure our employees fair and impartial treatment. To achieve these ends, we petition the help, the cooperation, and the good will of all of the citizens of our community. ■

4. In its 1954 opinion the Supreme Court invited the attorney generals of the states involved in the school segregation cases to prepare arguments concerning implementation methods for desegregation. After considering the various suggestions and plans, the Court handed down a supplementary ruling on May 31, 1955 establishing guidelines for the lower courts to follow. The decision let it be known that the court expected prompt and reasonable steps towards compliance with the 1954 decision. While the *Brown I* decision was a great decision, the *Brown II* decision and its "deliberate-speed" formula asked blacks that they defer the exercise of a constitutional right and gave southern states time to hold fast to the practice and doctrine of segregation.

From: Oliver Brown et al. v. *Board of Education of Topeka.* Decided May 31, 1955.

Mr. Chief Justice Warren delivered the opinion of the Court.

These cases were decided on May 17, 1954. The opinions of that date, declaring the fundamental principle that racial discrimination in public education is unconstitutional, are incorporated herein by reference. All provisions of federal, state, or local law requiring or permitting such discrimination must yield to this principle. There remains for consideration the manner in which relief is to be accorded. . . .

Full implementation of these constitutional principles may require solution of varied local school problems. School authorities have the primary responsibility for elucidating, assessing, and solving these problems; courts will have to consider whether the action of school authorities constitutes good faith implementation of the governing constitutional principles. Because of their proximity to local conditions and the possible need for further hearings, the courts which originally heard these cases can best perform this judicial appraisal. Accordingly, we believe it appropriate to remand the cases to those courts.

In fashioning and effectuating the decrees, the courts will be guided by equitable principles. Traditionally, equity has been characterized by a practical flexibility in shaping its remedies and by a facility for adjusting and reconciling public and private needs. These cases call for the exercise of these traditional attributes of equity power. At stake is the personal interest of the plaintiffs in admission to public schools as soon as practicable on a nondiscriminatory basis. To effectuate this interest may call for elimination of a variety of obstacles in making the transition to school systems operated in accordance with the constitutional principles set forth in our May 17, 1954, decision. Courts of equity may properly take into account the public interest in the elimination of such obstacles in a systematic and effective manner. But it should go without saying that the vitality of these constitutional principles cannot be allowed to yield simply because of disagreement with them.

While giving weight to these public and private considerations, the courts will require that the defendants make a prompt and reasonable start toward full compliance with our May 17, 1954, ruling. Once such a start has been made, the courts may find that additional time is necessary to carry out the ruling in an effective manner. The burden rests upon the defendants to establish that such time is necessary in the public interest and is consistent with good faith compliance at the earliest practicable date. To that end, the courts may consider problems related to administration, arising from the physical condition of the school plant, the school transportation system, personnel, revision of school districts and attendance areas into compact units to achieve a system of determining admission to the public schools on a nonracial basis, and revision of local laws and regulations which may be necessary in solving the foregoing problems. They will also consider the adequacy of any plans the defendants may propose to meet these problems and to effectuate a transition to a racially nondiscriminatory school system. During this period of transition, the courts will retain jurisdiction of these cases. The . . . [cases, except Delaware, are remanded to the lower courts] to take such proceedings and enter such orders and decrees consistent with this opinion as are necessary and proper to admit to public schools on a racially nondiscriminatory basis with all deliberate speed the parties to these cases. . . . ■

5. The first serious confrontation between federal authority and southern resistance to school desegregation occurred in Little Rock, Arkansas. In this excerpt Daisy Bates describes her role in holding fast to black determination to integrate Central High School in spite of the concerted opposition of Governor Orval Faubus.

According to a plan adopted by the Little Rock school board, nine black students were to begin classes on September 2, 1957 at the previously all-white Central High School. On the evening of September 1, Faubus declared a state of emergency and called out the National Guard to maintain order against imminent racial strife and turmoil. But, when Faubus' troops prevented the entrance of the nine black students into Central High on September 3, the issue of state versus federal authority was joined. On September 20, a federal district judge issued an injunction against Faubus' interference, and Faubus withdrew the troops. By this time Little Rock was filled with segregationists from around the state and the south. The appearance of the nine black students at Central High on Monday, September 23, unleashed a full-scale riot. The next day, President Eisenhower dispatched a thousand paratroopers to Little Rock and augmented their numbers by nationalizing ten thousand members of the Arkansas National Guard. This was the first time since Reconstruction that federal troops had been deployed to protect black citizens.

One of the most moving of all the media images of the civil rights movement was the picture of Elizabeth Eckford sitting alone on a bench in front of the Little Rock Central High School, surrounded by an angry segregationist mob. Her ordeal and solitary encounter with the hostile white mob was blazed across the wire services that evening, and the world's attention was riveted to Little Rock.

It was Labor Day, September 2, 1957. The nine pupils who had been selected by the school authorities to enter Central High School—Carlotta Walls, Jefferson Thomas, Elizabeth Eckford, Thelma Mothershed, Melba Pattillo, Ernest Green, Terrance Roberts, Gloria Ray, and Minnijean Brown—were enjoying the last day of their summer vacation. . . . About mid-afternoon young Jefferson Thomas was on his way home from the pool and stopped at my house for a brief visit. While Jeff was raiding the refrigerator, a news flash came over the radio that the Governor would address the citizens of Arkansas that night.

"I wonder what he's going to talk about," said Jeff. The youngster then turned to me and asked, "Is there anything they can do—now that they lost in court? Is there any way they can stop us from entering Central tomorrow morning?"

"I don't think so," I said.

About seven o'clock that night a local newspaper reporter rang my doorbell. "Mrs. Bates, do you know that national guardsmen are surrounding Central High?"

L.C. [Bates] and I stared at him incredulously for a moment. A friend who was visiting us volunteered to guard the house while we drove out to Central. L.C. gave him the shotgun. We jumped into our car and drove to Central High. . . . Men in full battle dress—helmets, boots, and bayonets—were piling out of the trucks and lining up in front of the school.

As we watched, L.C. switched on the car radio. A newscaster was saying, "National guardsmen are surrounding Central High School. No one is certain what this means. Governor Faubus will speak later this evening." . . .

* * * *

I don't recall all the details of what Governor Faubus said that night. But his words electrified Little Rock. By morning they shocked the United States. By noon the next day his message horrified the world.

Faubus' alleged reason for calling out the troops was that he had received information that caravans of automobiles filled with white supremacists were heading toward Little Rock from all over the state. He therefore declared Central High School off limits to Negroes. For some inexplicable reason he added that Horace Mann, a Negro high school, would be off limits to whites.

Then, from the chair of the highest office of the State of Arkansas, Governor Orval Eugene Faubus delivered the infamous words, "blood will run in the streets" if Negro pupils should attempt to enter Central High School.

In a half dozen ill-chosen words, Faubus made his contribution to the mass hysteria that was to grip the city of Little Rock for several months.

The citizens of Little Rock gathered on September 3 to gaze upon the incredible spectacle of an empty school building surrounded by 250 National Guard troops. At about eight fifteen in the morning, Central students started passing through the line of national guardsmen—all but the nine Negro students.

I had been in touch with their parents throughout the day. They were confused, and they were frightened. As the parents voiced their fears, they kept repeating Governor Faubus' words that "blood would run in the streets of Little Rock" should their teen-age children try to attend Central—the school to which they had been assigned by the school board.

* * * *

On the afternoon of the same day, September 3, when the school was scheduled to open, Superintendent [Virgil] Blossom called a meeting of leading Negro citizens and the parents of the nine children . . . [and] instructed the parents *not* to accompany their children the next morning when they were scheduled to enter Central. "If violence breaks out," the Superintendent told them, "it will be easier to protect the children if the adults aren't there."

During the conference Superintendent Blossom had given us little assurance that the children would be adequately protected. As we left the building, I was aware of how deeply worried the parents were, although they did not voice their fears.

About ten o'clock that night I was alone in the downstairs recreation room. . . .

* * * *

. . . I sat huddled in my chair, dazed, trying to think, yet not knowing what to do. I don't recall how much time went by . . . before some neighbors entered. One of them was the Reverend J.C. Crenshaw, President of the Little Rock branch of the NAACP.

* * * *

"Maybe," I said, "maybe we could round up a few ministers to go with the children tomorrow. Maybe then the mob wouldn't attack them. Maybe with the ministers by their side—"

* * * *

I called a white minister, Rev. Dunbar Ogden, Jr., President of the Interracial Ministerial Alliance. I did not know Mr. Ogden. I explained the situation, then asked if he thought he could get some ministers to go with the children to school the next morning.

* * * *

. . . Tensely I waited for his return call. When it came, he sounded apologetic. The white ministers he had talked to had questioned whether it was the thing to do. Some of the Negro ministers had pointed out that the Superintendent of Schools had asked that no Negro adults go with the children, and that in view of this they felt they shouldn't go. Then he added gently, "I'll keep trying—and, God willing, I'll be there."

Next I called the city police. I explained to the officer in charge that we were concerned about the safety of the children and that we were trying to get ministers to accompany them to school the next morning. I said that the children would assemble at eight thirty at Twelfth Street and Park Avenue. I asked whether a police car could be stationed there to protect the children until the ministers arrived.

The police officer promised to have a squad car there at eight o'clock. "But you realize," he warned, "that our men cannot go any closer than that to the school. The school is off limits to the city police while it's 'occupied' by the Arkansas National Guardsmen."

By now it was two thirty in the morning. Still, the parents had to be called about the change in plan. At three o'clock I completed my last call, explaining to the parents where the children were to assemble and the plan about the ministers. Suddenly I remembered Elizabeth Eckford. Her family had no telephone. Should I go to the Union Station and search for her father? Someone had once told me that he had a night job there. Tired in mind and body, I decided to handle the matter early in the morning. I stumbled into bed.

A few hours later, at about eight fifteen in the morning, L.C. and I started driving to Twelfth Street and Park Avenue. On the way I checked out in my mind the possibilities that awaited us. . . .

The bulletin over the car radio interrupted. The voice announced: "A Negro girl is being mobbed at Central High. . . . "

"Oh, my God!" I cried. "It must be Elizabeth! I forgot to notify her where to meet us!"

L.C. jumped out of the car and rushed to find her. I drove on to Twelfth Street. There were the ministers—two white—Mr. Ogden and Rev. Will Campbell, of the National Council of Churches, Nashville, Tennessee—and two colored—the Reverend Z. Z. Driver, of the African Methodist Episcopal Church, and the Reverend Harry Bass, of the Methodist Church. With them also was Mr. Ogden's twenty-one-year-old son, David. The children were already there. And, yes, the police had come as promised. All of the children were there—all except Elizabeth.

* * * *

Elizabeth, whose dignity and control in the face of jeering mobsters had been filmed by television cameras and recorded in pictures flashed to newspapers over the world, had overnight become a national heroine. . . . The first day that her parents agreed she might come out of seclusion, she came to my house, where the reporters awaited her. Elizabeth was very quiet, speaking only when spoken to. I took her to my bedroom to talk before I let the reporters see her. I asked her how she felt now. Suddenly all her pent-up emotion flared.

"Why am I here?" she said, turning blazing eyes on me. "Why are you so interested in my welfare now? You didn't care enough to notify me of the change of plans—"

* * * *

Little by little Elizabeth came out of her shell. Up to now she had never talked about what happened to her at Central. Once when we were alone in the downstairs recreation room of my house, I asked her simply, "Elizabeth, do you think you can talk about it now?"

She remained quiet for a long time. Then she began to speak.

"You remember the day before we were to go in, we met Superintendent Blossom at the school board office. He told us what the mob might say and do but he never told us we wouldn't have any protection. He told our parents not to come because he wouldn't be able to protect the children if they did.

"That night I was so excited I couldn't sleep. The next morning I was about the first one up. While I was pressing my black-and-white dress—I had made it to wear on the first day of school—my little brother turned on the TV set. They started telling about a large crowd gathered at the school. The man on TV said he wondered if we were going to show up that morning. . . .

* * * *

"Before I left home Mother called us into the living room. She said we should have a word of prayer. Then I caught the bus and got off a block from the school. I saw a large crowd of people standing across the street from the soldiers guarding Central. As I walked on, the crowd suddenly got quiet. Superintendent Blossom had told us to enter by the front door. I looked at all the people and thought, 'Maybe I will be safer if I walk down the block to the front entrance behind the guards.'

"At the corner I tried to pass through the long line of guards around the school so as to enter the grounds behind them. One of the guards pointed across the street. So I pointed in the same direction and asked whether he meant for me to cross the street and walk   down. He nodded 'yes.' So, I walked across the street conscious of the crowd that stood there, but they moved away from me.

"For a moment all I could hear was the shuffling of their feet. Then someone shouted, 'Here she comes, get ready!' I moved away from the crowd on the sidewalk and into the street. If the mob came at me I could then cross back over so the guards could protect me.

"The crowd moved in closer and then began to follow me, calling me names. I still wasn't afraid. Just a little bit nervous. Then my knees started to shake all of a sudden and I wondered whether I could make it to the center entrance a block away. It was the longest block I ever walked in my whole life.

"Even so, I still wasn't too scared because all the time I kept thinking that the guards would protect me.

"When I got in front of the school, I went up to a guard again. But this time he just looked straight ahead and didn't move to let me pass him. I didn't know what to do. Then I looked and saw the path leading to the front entrance was a little further ahead. So I walked until I was right in front of the path to the front door.

"I stood looking at the school—it looked so big! Just then the guards let some white students through.

"The crowd was quiet. I guess they were waiting to see what was going to happen. When I was able to steady my knees, I walked up to the guard who had let the white students in. He too didn't move. When I tried to squeeze past him, he raised his bayonet and then the other guards moved in and they raised their bayonets.

"They glared at me with a mean look and I was very frightened and didn't know what to do. I turned around and the crowd came toward me.

"They moved closer and closer. Somebody started yelling, 'Lynch her! Lynch her!'

"I tried to see a friendly face somewhere in the mob—someone who maybe would help. I looked into the face of an old woman and it seemed a kind face, but when I looked at her again, she spat on me.

"They came closer, shouting, 'No nigger bitch is going to get in our school. Get out of here!'

"I turned back to the guards but their faces told me I wouldn't get any help from them. Then I looked down the block and saw a bench at the bus stop. I thought, 'If I can only get there I will be safe.' I don't know why the bench seemed a safe place to me, but I started walking toward it. I tried to close my mind to what they were shouting, and kept saying to myself, 'If I can only make it to the bench I will be safe.'

"When I finally got there, I don't think I could have gone another step. I sat down and the mob crowded up and began shouting all over again. Someone hollered, 'Drag her over to this tree! Let's take care of that nigger.' Just then a white man sat down beside me, put his arm around me and patted my shoulder. He raised my chin and said, 'Don't let them see you cry.'

"Then, a white lady—she was very nice—she came over to me on the bench. She spoke to me but I don't remember what she said. She put me on the bus and sat next to me. She asked my name and tried to talk to me but I don't think I answered. I can't remember much about the bus ride, but the next thing I remember I was standing in front of the School for the Blind, where Mother works." ■

6. **T**hirty years after the momentous *Brown* decision, black scholars and citizens surveyed the lack of progress in desegregation with dismay. All agreed that change had occurred but that the dream of a fully integrated, racially balanced educational system remained still a dream. The following articles summarize the situation in elementary and secondary education and postsecondary education respectively.

From: "Brown v. *Board of Education:* Uneven Results 30 Years Later" by Walter Goodman, *The New York Times* (May 17, 1984). Copyright 1984 by The New York Times Company. Used with permission.

In 1968, more than a decade after the Supreme Court's decision in Brown v. Board of Education, two-thirds of black students were in virtually all-black schools. Today, after 15 years of earnest efforts at desegregation, that figure is down to one-third.

On this 30th anniversary of the Supreme Court decision barring segregated public schools, its effects seem at once more striking than some expected at the time, yet less thorough than many hoped.

The one-third figure, for example, means that millions of school children continue to attend predominantly black or Hispanic classrooms. The pace of desegregation has slowed in the past few years, perhaps inevitably after so much progress, and in hundreds of places desegregation plans are still laboring through the courts and tensions aroused by court-ordered busing remains high. In Northeastern cities, the number of minority students in segregated schools has been increasing.

Nevertheless, the dual school system based on race that prevailed in the South in 1954 has been dismantled. And there are success stories, like those cited in a report to be released today by the National Education Association naming Charlotte, N.C., Austin, Tex., and Seattle as examples of progress.

* * * *

The mixed picture reflects the profound social changes that have been at work in American society since the case of Linda Brown came to the attention of the Supreme Court and opened an era of civil rights protests and legislation, of accomplishment and disarray.

The black-white alliance built at lunch-counter sit-ins produced laws that transformed the society. But in recent years, that alliance has foundered over such issues as affirmative action. And even as a newly assertive black middle class is making itself felt in every aspect of American life, the urban ghettos continue to be centers of poverty and what has been called a "pathology" that seems immune to social programs. Under the Presidency of Ronald Reagan, the Federal Government has stepped back from its role of leadership in the civil rights movement.

* * * *

So the Browns won, but as Linda Brown Smith recalls, "It was not the quick fix we thought it would be."

* * * *

... In 1954, 99 percent of black students in the South attended all-black schools. Twenty years later, fewer than a quarter of the South's black students were in schools with more than 90 percent black enrollment. The figure remains at about that level.

As the South was accommodating to desegregation, resistance was growing in the North. With the sharp increase of blacks in the nation's inner cities, Northern whites, who had been generally sympathetic onlookers at desegregation efforts in the South, found themselves embroiled in a turbulent controversy of their own over busing students to desegregate schools that were segregated not by law but by income and tradition.

* * * *

By any accounting, the movement that began with Brown v. Board of Education touched off a continuing social revolution in America. In 1950, only 13 percent of black youths were completing high school; in 1982, according to the Commerce Department, that figure was up to more than 58 percent. In 1982, 12.4 percent of blacks had gone through college, as against 2.2 percent in 1950.

At a meeting at Rhode Island College this month to mark the anniversary, Dr. [Charles] Willie, the Harvard professor who has served as an expert in many desegregation cases, acknowledged the problems of enforcement but concluded, "School desegregation has worked."

"Busing has been effective," he said. "All of the methods and techniques for bringing the races together in our schools have enhanced the education of students."

* * * *

Back in Topeka, where the case of Brown v. Board of Education continues as a lawsuit seeking racial balance in the public schools, Charles Henson, the school board attorney, observes of the continuing dispute, "I don't expect it to end in my lifetime." ■

From: "Promise of the Landmark 'Brown' Decision Is Unfulfilled" by Charles S. Farrell in *Chronicle of Higher Education* (May 16, 1984). Used by permission.

... ironically, say many educators and legal experts, the promise of the Court's landmark decision has been least fulfilled in the very area it was aimed at equalizing—education—and particularly at many of the nation's public colleges and universities and in Northern public schools.

* * * *

Jack Greenberg, director and chief counsel of the NAACP Legal Defense and Education Fund and the lawyer who argued *Brown* before the Supreme Court, said that while carrying out the directive of the decision was unfinished in higher education, it had had an "inspirational effect," because most colleges established affirmative-action programs that have led to larger enrollments of black and Hispanic students and to better minority-group representation on faculties, staffs, and boards of trustees. "Without a doubt," he said, "the process has begun to dismantle segregated systems."

But college desegregation is still in its infancy, even though 30 years have passed since the concept of "separate but equal" was obliterated by the Supreme Court. . . .

* * * *

Among the many barriers remaining, according to Mary F. Berry, a professor of history and law at Howard University and a member of the U.S. Commission on Civil Rights, is an erosion of national commitment to desegregation, an erosion demonstrated by the Reagan Administration's conservative civil-rights policy as it relates to education. A renewed national commitment is needed "to achieve the promises of *Brown*," she said. "Without a commitment, we still drag the chains and shackles of the past toward the twenty-first century."

One barrier impeding further desegregation of colleges is the continued threat to cut federal aid to students, Ms. Berry said. Even when the threats are not carried out, she said, many blacks do not apply to college because they believe they cannot get financial aid.

While the number of black students in higher education has increased, she said, blacks are still underrepresented in fields that promise the best opportunities for the future. Black enrollment in graduate and professional schools reached a peak several years ago, she said, and is now falling. ■

QUESTIONS FOR REVIEW

1. Imagine that you were NAACP attorneys Charles Houston or Thurgood Marshall. How would you mastermind a legal strategy to end educational segregation?

2. Why did the NAACP legal effort attack segregation in higher education first?

3. How did social science research on racism help inform the Supreme Court decision in *Brown* v. *Board of Education*?

4. In what ways did the second *Brown* decision impede or hinder the process of desegregation?

5. What are some psychological effects of segregation on blacks and whites?

6.   Identify and assess the significance of Daisy Bates, Elizabeth Eckford, and James Meredith.

7.   Define and give examples of *massive resistance* and *interposition*.

8.   Compare the Ku Klux Klan and white Citizens' Councils in terms of composition, tactics, and objectives.

9.   Explain the concept of *federalism* as it relates to school desegregation. What were some of the limitations of judicial authority?

10.   Analyze the role played by the federal government in the quest for racial equality and social change. Compare and contrast the performance of the Eisenhower and Kennedy administrations.

11.   What were/are some of the benefits that Americans derived from the 1954–1963 phase of the civil rights movement?

ADDITIONAL RECOMMENDED READINGS

Bartley, Numan V. *The Rise of Massive Resistance: Race and Politics in the South During the 1950's*. Baton Rouge: Louisiana State University Press, 1969. This is one of the best treatments of the white reaction to the forces of social change unleashed by the U.S. Supreme Court in the *Brown* decision. The author describes and evaluates the rise of white massive resistance to public school desegregation. It is clearly written and based upon thorough research.

Kluger, Richard. *Simple Justice: The History of Brown v. Board of Education and Black America's Struggle for Equality*. New York: A.A. Knopf, 1976. A comprehensive, single volume treatment of the school desegregation decision. It includes an historical overview of the forces and personalities which made up the entire battle against the separate-but-equal doctrine.

Sitkoff, Harvard. *The Struggle for Black Equality, 1954–1980*. New York: Hill and Wang, 1981. A sound, readable synthesis of the civil rights movement. It is especially recommended for undergraduate students who desire concise narrative and provocative interpretation of the events, organizations, and individuals who led and were transformed by the struggle for black rights.

CHAPTER 4

AIN'T SCARED OF YOUR JAILS (1960–1961)

by CLAYBORNE CARSON

—Concentrates on the 1960–1961 period of the civil rights movement

—Examines the emerging role of college students and other young people in the civil rights movement

—Compares and contrasts the techniques of sit-ins and freedom rides with previously used civil rights tactics with respect to their goals, participants, and the responses of local and federal officials

—Discusses why sit-ins and the freedom rides are considered nonviolent direct action techniques

—Assesses the role of national and international media in drawing attention to movement activities of the period

—Identifies major civil rights organizations, names their principal leaders during this period, and discusses the major differences between them with respect to their use of nonviolent direct action

OVERVIEW

The years 1960 and 1961 were a time of profound change, growth, and development in the civil rights movement. Although the Supreme Court *Brown* v. *Board of Education* decision had outlawed school segregation in 1954, few changes in discriminatory practices had occurred. But there was a restlessness that was slowly building within the black community, particularly among the youth. Many had been profoundly influenced by memories of Emmett Till's brutal killing in 1955 and of Elizabeth Eckford walking alone to Little Rock's Central High School. They were impatient, angry, and unwilling to suffer the racist indignities inflicted on their parents' lives. It was out of this discontent and the legacy of earlier protests that the sit-ins of 1960 were born. Though few realized it when the sit-ins began, they would generate mass student support for the civil rights movement, galvanize established organizations, attract national media attention, and eventually precipitate federal intervention in the south.

The first sit-in occurred in Greensboro, North Carolina on February 1, 1960. The four North Carolina Agricultural and Technical College students who initiated this wave of protests had acted on their own, although they were members of a National Association for the Advancement of Colored People (NAACP) youth chapter. The sit-ins would spread rapidly throughout the south, with over 70,000 participants and 3,000 arrests by August 1961. The sit-ins provided an important model for protest and showed students that they could affect the political process. They also encouraged liberal white students to work together with blacks for social change. The increasing confidence of the student activists was evident in a new organization, the Student Nonviolent Coordinating Committee (SNCC), and in a new wave of protests called freedom rides.

The formation of SNCC followed the sit-ins by only a few months and not only solidified student involvement in the movement but placed them in leadership roles. SNCC was established at the Southwide Student Leadership Conference held at Shaw University in Raleigh, North Carolina on April 15–17, 1960. The conference was called by Ella J. Baker of the Southern Christian Leadership Conference (SCLC) who became an important advisor to the students. Influenced by James Lawson, a divinity student at Vanderbilt University with a philosophical commitment to nonviolent direct action, the students began to develop an organization that would channel their concerns and energy. What emerged was a coordinating committee that operated independently of other established civil rights organizations and relied on strong local leadership. The formation of SNCC helped transform the student movement from one that emphasized small scale protests to a sustained force that would challenge racism throughout American society.

The growth, spread, and intensity of movement activities had a major effect on the presidential election contest of 1960 between John F.

Kennedy and Richard M. Nixon. The tactic of mass, nonviolent sit-ins brought the civil rights agenda to national prominence and caused both candidates to pay at least lip service to the movement. John F. Kennedy's phone call to Coretta Scott King in October 1960 following Martin Luther King, Jr.'s arrest at an Atlanta sit-in had a dramatic impact on the 1960 presidential campaign. While his actions were politically motivated, Kennedy's pressure to help secure King's release was appreciated in the black community and prompted a large black voter turnout. Kennedy won the election by the narrowest of margins and the black vote was acknowledged as an important factor in his victory. In spite of this, however, Kennedy ruled out adopting a major civil rights legislative agenda, opting for a less controversial plan that focused on investigating voting rights violations. Only later, after numerous movement activities, would his administration push for the strengthening of federal civil rights laws.

Of all the tactics utilized during this period, the one that most galvanized national attention was the freedom rides. When they were announced by the Congress of Racial Equality (CORE) in 1961, the goal was to challenge segregation on interstate buses and in terminals. When the freedom riders were brutally attacked in Alabama, however, it initiated a new phase of the movement. As CORE was preparing to call off the rides because of the fear of violence, the original group of freedom riders flew to New Orleans. Diane Nash, a sit-in leader in Nashville, called James Farmer, the executive director of CORE, to insist that the rides not be stopped. She announced that volunteers from Nashville would continue the rides. The ensuing confrontation in Mississippi forced the federal government to take action to protect the freedom riders, thus supporting desegregation. The freedom rides also solidified support for CORE, marked the emergence of SNCC, and caused the nation to focus on the civil rights movement.

In summary, the development of nonviolent tactics, intergenerational conflicts between students, parents, and established organizations, and an increasing involvement of young white activists in the civil rights struggle all helped take the movement to a new level. More importantly, the expansion of protest activity caused youth and elders alike to think about the realities of the prevailing American value system and what it would take to achieve the type of society they wanted to live in.

READINGS

1. Although The Rev. Martin Luther King, Jr. served as a role model for many southern black student protesters of the 1960s, his philosophy of nonviolence was not universally accepted. Robert F. Williams of Monroe, North Carolina, was one of the few civil rights activists who openly challenged the idea that blacks should rely on nonviolent tactics. In 1959 Williams' position had prompted the national office of the NAACP to suspend him as head of its Monroe chapter. In the following selections, Williams expresses his doubt about the effectiveness of nonviolent tactics as a means of overcoming black oppression, while King reaffirms his reasons for advocating nonviolence as an alternative to armed self-defense.

From: "Is Violence Necessary to Combat Injustice? For the Positive: Williams Says 'We Must Fight Back' " by Robert F. Williams in *Liberation* (September 1959). Used with permission of Robert F. Williams.

In 1954, I was an enlisted man in the United States Marine Corps. I shall never forget the evening we (heard) the historic Supreme Court decision that segregation in the public schools is unconstitutional.

At last I felt that I was a part of America and that I belonged. That was what I had always wanted, even as a child.

I returned to civilian life in 1955 and the hope I had for Negro liberation faltered. Acts of violence and words and deeds of hate and spite rose from every quarter. There is open defiance to law and order throughout the South today. I have become disillusioned.

Laws serve to deter crime and protect the weak from the strong in civilized society. Where there is a breakdown of law, where is the force of deterrent? Only highly civilized and moral individuals respect the rights of others. The Southern brute respects only force. Nonviolence is a very potent weapon when the opponent is civilized, but nonviolence is no repellent for a sadist.

I have great respect for the pacifist, that is for the pure pacifist. I am not a pacifist and I am sure I may safely say most of my people are not. Passive resistance is a powerful weapon in gaining concessions from oppressors, but I venture to say that if Mack Parker [a black man lynched in 1959] had had an automatic shotgun at his disposal, he could have served as a great deterrent against lynching.

In 1957 the Klan moved into Monroe and Union County (N.C.). Their numbers steadily increased to the point wherein the local press reported 7500 at one rally. They became so brazen that mile-long motorcades started invading the Negro community.

These hooded thugs fired pistols from car windows. On one occasion they caught a Negro woman on the street and tried to force her to dance for them at gun point. Drivers of cars tried to run Negroes down. Lawlessness was rampant. Instead of cowing, we organized an armed guard. On one occasion, we had to exchange gunfire with the Klan.

Each time the Klan came on a raid they were led by police cars. We appealed to the President of the United States to have the Justice Department investigate the police. We appealed to Governor Luther Hodges. All our appeals to constituted law were in vain.

A group of nonviolent ministers met the City Board of Alderman and pleaded with them to restrict the Klan from the colored community. The city fathers advised these cringing, begging Negro ministers that the Klan had constitutional rights to meet and organize the same way as the NAACP.

Not having been infected by turn-the-other-cheekism, a group of Negroes who showed a willingness to fight caused the city officials to deprive the Klan of its constitutional rights after local papers told of dangerous incidents between Klansmen and armed Negroes. Klan motorcades have been legally banned from the City of Monroe.

On May 5, 1959, while president of the Union County branch of the NAACP, I made a statement to the United Press International after a trial wherein a white man was supposed to have been tried for kicking a Negro maid down a flight of stairs in a local white hotel. In spite of the fact that there was an eyewitness, the defendant failed to show up for his trial, and was completely exonerated.

Another case in the same court involved a white man who had come to a pregnant Negro mother's home and attempted to rape her. In recorder's court the only defense offered for the defendant was that "he's not guilty. He was just drunk and having a little fun." A white woman neighbor testified that the woman had come to her house excited, her clothes torn, her feet bare and begging her for assistance; the court was unmoved.

This great miscarriage of justice left me sick inside, and I said then what I say now. I believe Negroes must be willing to defend themselves, their women, their children and their homes. They must be willing to die and to kill in repelling their assailants. Negroes *must* protect themselves, it is obvious that the federal government will not put an end to lynching; therefore it becomes necessary for us to stop lynching with violence.

Some Negroes leaders have cautioned me that if Negroes fight back, the racist will have cause to exterminate the race.

This government is in no position to allow mass violence to erupt, let alone allow twenty million Negroes to be exterminated.

It is instilled at an early age that men who violently and swiftly rise to oppose tyranny are virtuous examples to emulate. I have been taught by my government to fight. Nowhere in the annals of history does the record show a people delivered from bondage by patience alone. ■

From: "The Social Organization of Non-Violence" by Martin Luther King, Jr. Copyright 1959. Originally appeared in *Liberation* (October 1959). Reprinted by permission of Joan Daves.

Here one must be clear that there are three different views on the subject of violence. One is the approach of pure nonviolence, which cannot readily or easily attract large masses, for it requires extraordinary discipline and courage. The second is violence exercised in self-defense, which all societies, from the most primitive to the most cultured and civilized, accept as moral and legal. The principle of self-defense, even involving weapons and bloodshed, has never been condemned, even by Gandhi, who sanctioned it for those unable to master pure nonviolence. The third is the advocacy of violence as a tool of advancement, organized as in warfare, deliberately and consciously. To this tendency many Negroes are being tempted today. There are incalculable perils in this approach. It is not the danger or sacrifice of physical being which is primary, though it cannot be contemplated without a sense of deep concern for human life. The greatest danger is that it will fail to attract Negroes to a real collective struggle, and will confuse the large uncommitted middle group, which as yet has not supported either side. Further, it will mislead Negroes into the belief that this is the only path and place them as a minority in a position where they confront a far larger adversary than it is possible to defeat in this form of combat. When the Negro uses force in self-defense he does not forfeit support—he may even win it, by the courage and self-respect it reflects. When he seeks to initiate violence he provokes questions about the necessity for it, and inevitably is blamed for its consequences. It is unfortunately true that however the Negro acts, his struggle will not be free of violence initiated by his enemies, and he will need ample courage and willingness to sacrifice to defeat this manifestation of violence. But if he seeks it and organizes it, he cannot win. . . .

The Negro people can organize socially to initiate many forms of struggle which can drive their enemies back without resort to futile and harmful violence. In the history of the movement, . . . many creative forms have been developed— the mass boycott, sitdown protests and strikes, sit-ins—refusal to pay fines and bail for unjust arrests—mass marches—mass meetings—prayer pilgrimages, etc.

There is more power in socially organized masses on the march than there is in guns in the hands of a few desperate men. Our enemies would prefer to deal with a small armed group rather than with a huge, unarmed but resolute mass of people. However, it is necessary that the mass-action method be persistent and unyielding. Gandhi said the Indian people must "never let them rest," referring to the British. He urged them to keep protesting daily and weekly, in a variety of ways. This method inspired and organized the Indian masses and disorganized and demobilized the British. It educates its myriad participants, socially and morally. All history teaches us that like a turbulent ocean beating great cliffs into fragments of rock, the determined movement of people incessantly demanding their rights always disintegrates the old order. ■

2. Though first of a wave of lunch counter sit-ins occurred on February 1, 1960 in Greensboro, North Carolina. Although this was not the first desegregation sit-in, the protest in Greensboro had special significance because it was initiated by black college students who would serve as a model for discontented black students in other southern black colleges. Franklin McCain, David Richmond, Joseph McNeil, and Ezell Blair, Jr. were students at North Carolina A&T when they developed their plan for the initial sit-in at the Woolworth's lunch counter. Despite the fact that they had been affiliated with NAACP youth chapters, they planned their protest on their own during extended discussion sessions in their dormitory rooms.

From: "The South's First Sit-in" [Interview with Franklin McCain on February 1, 1960] by Howell Raines in *My Soul Is Rested,* pages 78–79. Copyright 1977 by Howell Raines. Used by permission of the Putnam Publishing Group.

The planning process was on a Sunday night, I remember it quite well. I think it was Joseph who said. "It's time that we take some action now. We've been getting together, and we've been, up to this point, still like most people we've talked about for the past few weeks or so—that is, people who talk a lot but, in fact, make very little action." After selecting the technique, then we said, "Let's go down and just ask for service." It certainly wasn't titled a "sit-in" or "sit-down" at that time. "Let's just go down to Woolworth's tomorrow and ask for service, and the tactic is going to be simply this: we'll just stay there." We never anticipated being served, certainly, the first day anyway. "We'll stay until we get served." And I think Ezell said, "Well, you know that might be weeks, that might be months, that might be never." And I think it was the consensus of the group, we said, "Well, that's just the chance we'll have to take."

* * * *

Once getting there . . . we did make purchases of school supplies and took the patience and time to get receipts for our purchases, and Joseph and myself went over to the counter and asked to be served coffee and doughnuts. As anticipated, the reply was, "I'm sorry, we don't serve you here." And of course we said, "We just beg to disagree with you. We've in fact already been served. . . . The attendant or waitress was a little bit dumbfounded, just didn't know what to say under circumstances like that. And we said, "We wonder why you'd invite us in to serve us at one counter and deny service at another. If this is a private club or private concern, then we believe you ought to sell membership cards. . . . That didn't go over too well, simply because I don't really think she understood what we were talking about, and for the second reason, she had no logical response to a statement like that. . . .

. . . At that point there was a policeman who had walked in off the street, who was pacing the aisle . . . behind us, where we were seated, with his club in his hand, just sort of knocking it in his hand, and just looking mean and red and a little bit upset and a little bit disgusted. And you had the feeling that he didn't know what the hell to do. You had the feeling that this is the first time that this big bad man with the gun and the club has been pushed in a corner, and he's got absolutely no defense, and the thing that's killing him more than anything else—he doesn't know what he can or what he cannot do. He's defenseless. Usually his defense is offense, and we've provoked him, yes, but we haven't provoked him outwardly enough for him to resort to violence. And I think this is just killing him; you can see it all over him.

* * * *

. . . If it's possible to know what it means to have your soul cleansed—I felt pretty clean at that time. I probably felt better on that day than I've ever felt in my life. Seems like a lot of feelings of guilt or what-have-you suddenly left me, and I felt as though I had gained my manhood, so to speak, and not only gained it, but had developed quite a lot of respect for it. Not Franklin McCain only as an individual, but I felt as though the manhood of a number of other black persons had been restored and had gotten some respect from just that one day. . . .

* * * *

The movement started out as a movement of nonviolence and as a Christian movement, and we wanted to make that very clear to everybody, that it was a movement that was seeking justice more than anything else and not a movement to start a war. . . . We knew that probably the most powerful and potent weapon that people have literally no defense for is love, kindness. That is, whip the enemy with something that he doesn't understand.

. . . The individual who had probably the most influence on us was Gandhi, more than any single individual. During the time that the Montgomery Bus Boycott was in effect, we were tots for the most part, and we barely heard of Martin Luther King. Yes, Martin Luther King's name was well-known when the sit-in movement was in effect, but to pick out Martin Luther King as a hero . . . I don't want you to misunderstand what I'm about to say: Yes, Martin Luther King was a hero. . . . No, he was not the individual that we had upmost in mind when we started the sit-in movement. . . .

* * * *

Credit for the initiation of the sit-in movement has been granted to one or two ministers, the NAACP, Ralph Johns, CORE, at least a dozen people, and it's rather amusing when you do read some of these articles. I think it's a game. The same type tactic that has been used over and over and over by the white news media and the white press to discredit blacks with particular types of achievement. . . .

* * * *

. . . Remember, too, you had four guys who were pretty strong-willed, pretty bull-headed, and who were keenly aware that people would rush in and try to take over the Movement, so to speak. And we were quite aware of that, and we felt—not felt—*were* very independent. . . . As a matter of fact, we were criticized on several occasions for being too damned independent. But I still don't regret it. ■

3. In each city where sit-ins occurred student protest groups produced leaders with unique qualities and distinctive long-range goals. Thus, the national student leaders, influenced by James Lawson, were noted for their firm commitment to the philosophy of nonviolent direct action. Student activists elsewhere, however, were more likely to view nonviolence as an appropriate strategy but not as a philosophy of life. Some students had a narrow conception of their goals; others believed that the lunch counter sit-ins were only the first stage of a struggle to bring about far-reaching reforms. The Atlanta Committee on Appeal for Human Rights launched their sit-in movement with a statement that expressed the broad range of social concerns that produced black student discontent.

From: "An Appeal for Human Rights," a paid advertisement appearing in *The Atlanta Constitution*, Wednesday, March 9, 1960.

We, the students of the six affiliated institutions forming the Atlanta University Center—Clark, Morehouse, Morris Brown, and Spelman Colleges, Atlanta University, and the Interdenominational Theological Center—have joined our hearts, minds, and bodies in the cause of gaining those rights which are inherently ours as members of the human race and as citizens of these United States.

* * * *

. . . We want to state clearly and unequivocally that we cannot tolerate, in a nation professing democracy and among people professing Christianity, the discriminatory conditions under which the Negro is living today in Atlanta, Georgia—supposedly one of the most progressive cities in the South.

Among the inequalities and injustices in Atlanta and in Georgia against which we protest, the following are outstanding examples:

(1) Education: In the Public School System, facilities for Negroes and whites are separate and unequal. Double sessions continue in about half of the Negro Public Schools, and many Negro children travel ten miles a day in order to reach a school that will admit them.

* * * *

(2) Jobs: Negroes are denied employment in the majority of city, state, and federal governmental jobs, except in the most menial capacities.

(3) Housing: While Negroes constitute 32% of the population of Atlanta, they are forced to live within 16% of the area of the city.

* * * *

(4) Voting: Contrary to statements made in Congress recently by several Southern Senators, we know that in many counties in Georgia and other southern states, Negro college graduates are declared unqualified to vote and are not permitted to register.

(5) Hospitals: Compared with facilities for other people in Atlanta and Georgia, those for Negroes are unequal and totally inadequate.

* * * *

(6) Movies, Concerts, Restaurants: Negroes are barred from most downtown movies and segregated in the rest. Negroes must even sit in a segregated section of the Municipal Auditorium. If a Negro is hungry, his hunger must wait until he comes to a "colored" restaurant, and even his thirst must await its quenching at a "colored" water fountain.

(7) Law Enforcement: There are grave inequalities in the area of law enforcement. Too often, Negroes are maltreated by officers of the law. An insufficient number of Negroes is employed in the law-enforcing agencies. They are seldom, if ever promoted. Of 830 policemen in Atlanta only 35 are Negroes. ■

4. **On the weekend of April 15, 1960 student leaders of the southern sit-in movement met at Shaw University in Raleigh, North Carolina. The meeting, held at the initiative of SCLC leader Ella Baker, attracted 126 student delegates from 56 colleges in 12 southern states. In addition, 19 northern schools were represented, along with 13 organizations and 57 students and observers. Marion Barry, a Nashville student leader, was elected chairman of the temporary coordinating body that formed during the meeting. This body eventually became the Student Nonviolent Coordinating Committee.**

SCLC's president, Martin Luther King, Jr., spoke to the gathering, but many accounts suggest that the students were more strongly influenced by the speech given by Rev. James Lawson, who had been expelled from Vanderbilt Divinity School because of his refusal to withdraw from the Nashville protest movement. Lawson drafted SNCC's statement of purpose, which expressed the religious idealism that underlay the nonviolent activism of black students, especially those from Nashville.

"Student Nonviolent Coordinating Committee Statement of Purpose," drafted by Rev. James Lawson for the Temporary Student Nonviolent Coordinating Committee, May 14, 1960.

Carrying out the mandate of the Raleigh Conference to write a statement of purpose for the movement, the Temporary Student Nonviolent Coordinating Committee submits for careful consideration the following draft. We urge all local, state or regional groups to examine it closely. Each member of our movement must work diligently to understand the depths of nonviolence.

We affirm the philosophical or religious ideal of nonviolence as the foundation of our purpose, the pre-supposition of our faith, and the manner of our action. Nonviolence as it grows from Judaic-Christian traditions seeks a social order of justice permeated by love. Integration of human endeavor represents the crucial first step towards such a society.

Through nonviolence, courage displaces fear; love transforms hate. Acceptance dissipates prejudice; hope ends despair. Peace dominates war; faith reconciles doubt. Mutual regard cancels enmity. Justice for all overthrows injustice. The redemptive community supersedes systems of gross social immorality.

Love is the central motif of nonviolence. Love is the force by which God binds man to himself and man to man. Such love goes to the extreme; it remains loving and forgiving even in the midst of hostility. It matches the capacity of evil to inflict suffering with an even more enduring capacity to absorb evil, all the while persisting in love.

By appealing to conscience and standing on the moral nature of human existence, nonviolence nurtures the atmosphere in which reconciliation and justice become actual possibilities. ■

5. **W**hen she wrote "Bigger Than a Hamburger," Ella Baker was planning to leave her post as executive director of the Southern Christian Leadership Conference to accept a post with the YWCA, a job which allowed her to remain in close touch with the student activities in SNCC. Although she was 55 at the time of SNCC's founding, student protesters accepted her advice which was based on her long experience in movements to bring about social change. After her graduation from Shaw University in the 1920s, she had been a community activist in Harlem—she was a founder of the Young Negroes' Cooperative League—before becoming a member of the NAACP's field staff. Her growing disenchantment with the cautiousness of the established civil rights groups led her to encourage black students to form their own independent organization that would emphasize "group-centered leadership" rather than the "leader-oriented pattern of organization" found in the SCLC.

"Bigger Than a Hamburger" by Ella J. Baker in *The Southern Patriot*, (June 1960). Used by permission of Anne Braden.

RALEIGH, N.C.—The Student Leadership Conference made it crystal clear that current sit-ins and other demonstrations are concerned with something much bigger than a hamburger or even a giant-sized coke.

Whatever may be the difference in approach to their goal, the Negro and white students, North and South, are seeking to rid America of the scourge of racial segregation and discrimination—not only at lunch counters, but in every aspect of life.

In reports, casual conversations, discussion groups, and speeches, the sense and the spirit of the following statement that appeared in the initial newsletter of the students at Barber-Scotia College, Concord, N.C., were re-echoed time and again:

> "We want the world to know that we no longer accept the inferior position of second-class citizenship. We are willing to go to jail, be ridiculed, spat upon and even suffer physical violence to obtain First Class Citizenship."

By and large, this feeling that they have a destined date with freedom, was not limited to a drive for personal freedom, or even freedom for the Negro in the South. Repeatedly it was emphasized that the movement was concerned with the moral implications of racial discrimination for the "whole world" and the "Human Race."

This universality of approach was linked with a perceptive recognition that "it is important to keep the movement democratic and to avoid struggles for personal leadership."

It was further evident that desire for supportive cooperation from adult leaders and the adult community was also tempered by apprehension that adults might try to "capture" the student movement. The students showed willingness to be met on the basis of equality, but were intolerant of anything that smacked of manipulation or domination.

This inclination toward *group-centered leadership,* rather than toward a *leader-centered group pattern of organization,* was refreshing indeed to those of the older group who bear the scars of the battle, the frustrations and the disillusionment that come when the prophetic leader turns out to have heavy feet of clay.

However hopeful might be the signs in the direction of group-centeredness, the fact that many schools and communities, especially in the South, have not provided adequate experience for young Negroes to assume initiative and think and act independently accentuated the need for guarding the student movement against well-meaning, but nevertheless unhealthy, over-protectiveness.

Here is an opportunity for adult and youth to work together and provide genuine leadership—the development of the individual to his highest potential for the benefit of the group.

Many adults and youth characterized the Raleigh meeting as the greatest or most significant conference of our period.

Whether it lives up to this high evaluation or not will, in a large measure, be determined by the extent to which there is more effective training in and understanding of non-violent principles and practices, in group dynamics, and in the re-direction into creative channels of the normal frustrations and hostilities that result from second-class citizenship. ■

6. **P**rotest activity among white college students was uncommon during the 1950s, for college campuses were affected by the McCarthy era's suppression of vigorous political dissent. Thus, for the small population of white student activists, the sit-ins led by southern black students were a source of encouragement. Although few black student protesters held radical political views when they joined the sit-in movement, their increasing tactical sophistication and elan greatly influenced the subsequent emergence of a student-led new left that would revive activism among white students and ultimately provide many new recruits for the southern black struggle. The following selection discusses the attitudes of northern white students during the late 1950s and the reactions of these students to the southern sit-in movement. Its author was a student at the University of Chicago during the period.

From: "Conference on the Sit-ins," by Ted Dienstfrey in *Commentary* (June 29, 1960). Used by permission; all rights reserved.

It is with a desire to do *something* that many Northern white college students look at the sit-in movement of their Southern Negro counterparts. . . . That the Northern response has been almost unanimously favorable is no surprise: of all the current social and political issues—the cold war, disarmament, the draft, planned obsolescence, the double standard—integration is the only one which does not have to be discussed. We all agree that segregation must end; we only disagree on when it will end, on what will end it, and who is responsible for ending it.

* * * *

We have had our student government pass resolutions decrying the present situation, and we have sent many telegrams stating our position. Several times we have tried unsuccessfully to pressure the University into enforcing desegregation on its off-campus real estate holdings. We have circulated and signed petitions addressed to city, state, and national legislatures and executives asking them to pass and *enforce* various anti-segregation ordinances and laws.

* * * *

In April 1959, we participated enthusiastically along with 25,000 other students in the Youth March for Integration. (Reverend Martin Luther King, Jr., in the May *Progressive,* claims that there were 40,000 in the march; 25,000 was the figure the police reported.) With the backing of the NAACP, labor unions, Reverend King, and various other notables, the students of the country were to demonstrate in Washington—to Congress, to the people, and to ourselves—that the youth wanted segregation to end *now.* But when we went to Washington, we found ourselves walking down four back streets to the rear of the Washington Monument, and listening there to an endless number of self-righteous speeches by labor leaders and Congressmen who told us what we already knew—that integration was better than segregation. The newspapers gave us only minimal coverage, and many of us—the white Northerners, I mean—felt very little enthusiasm over attending another such event, and giving our energy and support to what seemed a kind of betrayal.

Yet in February 1960 we began hearing about the Southern sit-in demonstrations, and by March we had set up sympathetic picket lines in front of Chicago's Woolworth stores. Our reasons for picketing were, as usual, mixed. We were picketing to demonstrate sympathetic support, to arouse Northern interest, to pressure Woolworth, to be part of the movement. Few of us thought we would go to jail. (One of my friends brought his schoolbooks to the picket line just in case.) But mixed as they were, our feelings must have been duplicated throughout the North. The spread of similar picket lines to other cities was in no way coordinated, and they seem to have been as spontaneous as the sit-ins themselves.

* * * *

The only heated discussion of the entire meeting came on Sunday: were Northerners to be represented on the temporary planning committee of the not yet established organization? Lawson and the other leaders felt that whatever ideology and/or momentum the group now had would be dissipated by Northern intervention. But to the Northerners and to many Southern participants, such "second class membership" was unacceptable. A compromise set up a de facto all-Southern planning committee which Northerners could *earn* the right to join by participating in non-violent demonstrations against segregation in the North. Sympathetic Woolworth picketing did not count as such a demonstration. . . .

* * * *

What did the weekend mean? That with or without the help of Northern students, the South is changing. Soon Negroes will be able to eat at most restaurants, and their friends will not have to pack big lunches for traveling. And schools will be integrated, and the Negro will vote. All this will change, but— and this is what no one at the Southern conference wanted to discuss—very much in American society will not change. ■

7. **W**illiam Mahoney was one of hundreds of student activists who continued the freedom rides after the initial CORE-sponsored group was attacked by segregationists at Anniston, Birmingham, and Montgomery, Alabama. The new recruits to the freedom rides were characterized by youthful idealism and a determination to extend the rides into the stronghold of segregation—Mississippi. Mahoney and other students were arrested on breach of the peace charges soon after their arrival in Jackson. Rather than becoming discouraged after they were imprisoned in Parchman Penitentiary, their idealism and militancy became stronger as the result of their prison experience.

From: "In Pursuit of Freedom" by William Mahoney in *Liberation* (September 1961).

In early May I heard from fellow Howard University students that the Congress of Racial Equality was looking for volunteers to ride from Washington, D.C. to New Orleans by bus to determine whether bus station facilities were integrated in compliance with Supreme Court rulings. I was sympathetic to the idea, but approaching final examinations. . . .

I forgot about the CORE-sponsored trip, known as the Freedom Ride, until Monday, May 15th, when the morning papers were delivered to the dormitory desk at which I was working and I saw pictures of a fellow Howard student with whom I had participated the past year and a half in the Non-Violent Action Group (N.A.G.) of Washington, leaving a flaming bus on the outskirts of Anniston, Alabama. The caption said that the student . . . had been struck on the head as he left the bus. I was infuriated.

* * * *

At 11 p.m. on Friday, May 26th . . . I boarded a Greyhound bus in Washington with tickets for Montgomery. . . .

At our first stop in Virginia . . . I [was] confronted with what the Southern white has called "separate but equal." A modern rest station with gleaming counters and picture windows was labelled "White," and a small wooden shack beside it was tagged "Colored." The colored waiting room was filthy, in need of repair, and overcrowded. When we entered the white waiting room Frank [Hunt] was promptly but courteously, in the Southern manner, asked to leave. Because I am a fair-skinned Negro I was waited upon. I walked back to the bus through the cool night trembling and perspiring. . . .

The Montgomery bus station was surrounded by Army jeeps, trucks, and the National Guard in battle gear. . . . We found the people from the Christian Leadership Council who had been sent to meet us and drove away cautiously, realizing that the least traffic violation would be an excuse for our arrest. . . .

* * * *

Once across the [Mississippi] state line we passed a couple of police cars, which began to follow us. At our first stop the station was cordoned off a block in every direction. A police officer jumped on the bus and forbade anyone to move. One woman, who was a regular passenger, frantically tried to convince the police that she was not involved with us. After checking her ticket the police let her get off.

As we rolled toward Jackson, every blocked-off street, every back road taken, every change in speed caused our hearts to leap. Our arrival and speedy arrest in the white bus station in Jackson, when we refused to obey a policeman's order to move on, was a relief. . . .

* * * *

At 2 p.m. on May 29th, after spending the night in a barracks-like room of which I can only remember, with trepidation, a one-foot-high sign written on the wall in blood, "I love Sylvia," our group joined nine other Freedom Riders in court. . . .

We were charged with a breach of the peace and then the tall, wiry state prosecutor examined Police Chief Wray, the only witness called to the stand. Chief Wray said that we had been orderly but had refused to move on when ordered to do so by his men. . . .

* * * *

The thirty or more of us occupied five cells and a dining hall on the top floor. At night we slept on lumpy bags of cotton and were locked in small, dirty, blood-spattered, roach-infested cells. Days were passed in the hot, overcrowded dining room playing cards, reading, praying and, as was almost inevitable, fighting among ourselves over the most petty things. . . .

Time crawled painfully, 15 days becoming 45 meals, 360 hours, 100 card games or 3 letters from home. The killing of a roach or the taking of a shower became major events, the subjects of lengthy debate. But morale remained high; insults and brutality became the subject of jokes and skits. The jailers' initial hostility was broken down by responding to it with respect and with good humor. . . .

* * * *

The jails began to bulge as even Mississippi Negroes, who according to Southern whites are happy, began to join in the protest. To relieve the crowding, about fifty of us were piled into trucks at 2 a.m. June 15th and sped off into the night. It was rumored that in spite of a law against putting persons convicted of misdemeanors into a penitentiary, we were going to the state penitentiary.

* * * *

Questions have been raised as to the character of the people who willingly withstand such punishment. . . .

In cell 14 was a middle-aged art dealer from Minneapolis who had three dollars his name and had come . . . "because it is one way of fighting a system which not only hurts the Negro but is a threat to world peace and prosperity." . . .

My cellmate, a Negro worker, came because he had been chased home by white toughs once too often, because his sister was determined to come, and because a friend of his, William Barbee, had been almost killed by a mob while on a Freedom Ride. He admits that his behavior is not ordinarily disciplined, but he readily accepted any restrictions required of him by the movement. . . .

On my right, in cell 12, was the son of a well-to-do business man who had come because it was his moral duty. His aim was to "change the hearts of my persecutors through the sympathy and understanding to be gained by non-violent resistance." He spoke proudly of his father who had fought hard and "made it," and was constantly defending North America's economic and political system from the attacks made upon it by myself and the art dealer. We never changed each other's views but the arguments passed time and gave us mental exercise.

These three philosophies—political, emotional, and moralist—represent the three major viewpoints I found while spending forty days in various Mississippi prisons. ■

8. **T**he protest movement led by southern black students had a dramatic impact on white college students, for it offered them new and appealing models for political activism. Young white activists were particularly attracted to SNCC's brash militancy and its distinctive style of organizing communities "from the bottom up." SNCC's example contributed to the emergence of a youthful new left and to the rapid growth of the largest student leftist group, Students for a Democratic Society (SDS). SDS's 1962 manifesto, the Port Huron Statement, acknowledged that the southern struggle had "compelled" white students to move "from silence to activism." Robert Zellner, a native white southerner who joined the black protest movement, was one of a number of white students who played significant roles in SNCC and in SDS and conveyed SNCC's radical ideas to northern students engaged in campus political activism and the antiwar movement.

From: Interview with Robert Zellner by Clayborne Carson (September 19, 1978). Copyright 1978 by Robert Zellner. Used by permission.

My father's father was a Klansman and my father's father's father might have been a Klansman . . . but I do know my grandfather was a Klansman, and he was in Birmingham, Alabama. So my father grew up in Birmingham which . . . is [a] very rough kind of town [with] a terrorist conservative tradition. . . . He went to Bob Jones College . . . [a] very reactionary fundamentalist institution . . . I think, and my mother also graduated from Bob Jones College. . . . But dad was also a thinking person and [a] real dedicated Christian and as he got older he just could not . . . make his Klanism and his Christianity jive. . . .

One of the reasons . . . I was a little bit different from my peers [is] we were poor. Now my mother was a school teacher and my father was a preacher and there were five boys in the family. [But] my daddy never was a first church minister. He was always the circuit rider preacher with six, seven, sometimes twelve churches, mostly in the country and always in small towns.

When I was in 10th grade we moved to Mobile [Alabama] where I got my first taste of big city life and I graduated high school there in '57 and went to Huntington College in Montgomery, Alabama. It was while I was in college in Montgomery that I first got involved in the civil rights movement.

In my senior year, which was '60 and '61, in a sociology class I was assigned . . . to study the racial problem and write a paper presenting my ideas of solutions to the problem. Now this was in Montgomery, Alabama—the heart of the Confederacy, heart of Dixie—but it was an academic thing, and you are supposed to have enough sense to know that you looked in the books and stuff like that, and I did all that. And then some of the students went to the Klan headquarters, and they came back with literally wheelbarrows full of Klan literature. So I said o.k., we'll do that, too. So we went and got our Klan literature, too, and the Citizens' Council's. We said, "Well what about the Montgomery Improvement Association?" That was the other side of the question. Being good academicians we figured [we] should check that out, too.

Anyway, to make a long story short, we did go to the Montgomery Improvement Association and we went to a federal court hearing in Montgomery where Dr. King, Rev. [Ralph] Abernathy, and Rev. [Solomon] Seay, and many other local and national leaders had been charged with libel of the Montgomery city commissioners and the county commissioners and so forth. . . . Four or five of us from campus went there and in the process we met Dr. King and Reverend Abernathy and . . . we asked them if it was possible for us to maybe meet with some students from Alabama State, which was a black campus near our campus. In the back of our minds this was in keeping with our assignment. They gave us the names of students and we just went over there and met with them. By this time the police got interested, and they were following us; it became sort of an adventure thing. Eventually it wound up that a nonviolence workshop was to be held at the . . . Baptist Church.

So right after the workshop . . . we told Rev. Abernathy and the other ministers that we wanted to come to the meetings and they said, "Well, we'd like you to come, too, but you will be arrested if you come."

We said, "Oh, we don't believe it. We have a right to come. We know the constitution and everything." They said, "Well, we want you to come, but we want you to know what's going to happen."

We'd come to the meetings after they started, and the people would take us to the balcony, or they would hide us out at the corner somewhere because state investigators were in the meetings. . . . By the end of the week they knew who we all were and after the Saturday workshop the whole church was surrounded by police. There were five of us in the church—five white students—and the Rev. Abernathy told us that the police were going to arrest us when we left and that the police told him that we would be placed under arrest. So we said, "Well, you know we're willing to be arrested," but we said that it's important to make an attempt to escape. . . . This seemed important at the time. It's ridiculous now. We went to the back door. All the police were up in the front. Sure enough we got back to campus and after we were on campus for about an hour the administration came and collected all of us and said, "The police think you are still trapped in the . . . church." So there was a big meeting with the administration, and we were asked to resign from the school on the grounds [that] what we were doing [was illegal].

So out of the five guys involved in that particular incident, I was the only person out of the five that graduated. One attempted suicide. [The others] got tremendous pressure from their families. Mine was the only family that backed me up in the whole thing. In a sense . . . they gave no white southerner of that period any choice. If you backed the system at all you had two choices: you either capitulated absolutely and completely, or you became a rebel, a complete outlaw, and that's the way I went because I was contrary enough and had backing from my family which was very important.

* * * *

[In the] early spring of '61, SNCC was looking for someone to do white campus travelling. I had already met some of the SNCC people at the nonviolence workshop and SNCC already had a name and an image before it was even basically an organization. One thing that had gotten me involved in this whole thing was the whole p.r. thing of the sit-ins [in] the spring of '60, actually the end of my junior year in college. So here were all these students. They all wore trench coats and suits and ties. They never went to a sit-in without their books. . . . I know they're studying biology and sociology and psychology and everything like I'm studying and . . . going out and going up against this authority. That was exciting to me, because I was in an authoritarian state, and I was in an authoritarian college. And, here these guys sit down and say, "If you don't feed me I'm going to tie up your place of business. And if you're going to haul me to jail, then let's go on to jail, and we'll sing and everything." That was really inspiring.

. . . Spring of '61 was the end of my senior year in college. Here I am in Montgomery, and the buses are coming. They leave Atlanta. They come to Anniston. And, the mob bust them up and burned the bus and everything. They go to Birmingham. It looks like it's all over. You know the Klan has won, and then a new shipment of blood comes from Nashville, and the guys say they are going on. Here they are. I am in Montgomery. I'm in the direct path of all this and still I'm a civilian. The freedom rides are coming through. They eventually get to Montgomery, and here is a riot going on in my own city, and people are getting stoned. I'm here. I'm seeing this. I'm hearing it on the radio so I go down to the city to see if I could put my body between some Klansmen and some freedom rider. And cars are being burned up, and churches are being torn and everything. How could you fail to get involved? ■

9. A**lthough** the proponents of nonviolent direct action were often described in press reports as less militant than such self-defense advocates as Robert F. Williams, they often saw themselves as the true revolutionaries of the black struggle. James Lawson, for example, insisted that violent revolution was "counterfeit," because it sought only to destroy an evil regime without creating anything better in its place. By the end of 1961, it had become clear to nonviolent radicals such as Lawson that the nonviolent struggle could succeed only if a sufficient number of nonviolent "warriors" were recruited who were courageous, committed to nonviolence, and determined and willing to confront injustice in all its forms. Lawson's article outlines his plan for a nonviolent campaign to bring about a "total" revolution that would question all existing social institutions.

From: "Eve of Nonviolent Revolution?" by James M. Lawson, Jr. in *The Southern Patriot* (November 1961). Used by permission of Anne Braden.

Nonviolent revolution is always a real, serious revolution. It seeks to transform human life in both private and public forms . . . involves the whole man in his whole existence . . . maintains balance between tearing down and building up, destroying and planting.

* * * *

It is interesting to notice that while we recognize segregation as harmful to the whole nation and the South, we rarely blame this on the system and the structure of our institutions. Most of us work simply for concessions from the system, not for transforming the system.

But if after over 300 years, segregation (slavery) is still a basic pattern rather than a peripheral custom, should we not question the American way of life which allows segregation so much structural support?

Does not our political system encourage segregation? Is it not just the lack of Negro voting, but the failure of systems to provide real choices for voters? . . .

* * * *

We must recognize that we are merely in the prelude to revolution, the beginning, not the end, not even the middle. . . . I do not wish to minimize the gains we have made thus far. . . . But it would be well to recognize that we have been receiving concessions, not real changes. The sit-ins won concessions, not structural changes; the Freedom Rides won great concessions, but not real change.

There will be no revolution until we see Negro faces in all positions that help to mold public opinion, help to shape policy for America. . . .

. . . One federal judge in Mississippi will do more to bring revolution than sending 600 marshals to Alabama. We must never allow the President to substitute marshals for putting people into positions where they can affect public policy. . . .

Remember that the way to get this revolution off the ground is to forge the moral, spiritual and political pressure which the President, the nation and the world cannot ignore. . . .

How can we do this? I propose a very concrete way. The only way is through a nonviolent army. Let SCLC, in concert with other groups committed to nonviolence begin to plan, recruit, organize and discipline a nonviolent corps. . . . Let us call for from 2000 to 7 or 8 thousand nonviolent volunteers.

Let us work out with them a private discipline, reconciliation in personal life. Let us establish work camps for training, study, reading, meditation and constructive work in voting, repairing neighborhood slums, community centers.

Let us prepare these people for mass nonviolent action in the Deep South. Let us recruit people who will be willing to go at a given moment and stay in jail indefinitely; the Freedom Rides were a start at this, but they involved too many people for a court test and too few for a jail-in.

Imagine, if you can, what would happen in the next 12 months if we had such an army ready. The whole nation would know that we meant serious business. The Deep South would begin to realize that . . . the moment of truth is not far off.

A campaign with such an army would cause world-wide crisis, on a scale unknown in the western world except for actual war; not even a Berlin crisis could be used as an excuse for America to escape its cancer at home. . . .

We would lay this issue on the soul of the nation and perhaps cause the nation . . . to adjust to the world by beginning a revolutionary change at home. . . . The womb of revolution is the nonviolent movement. . . . ■

1.   Compare and contrast the tactics of the sit-ins and freedom rides. Where did these tactics develop and how did people respond to them? How did they differ from civil rights tactics of earlier years?

2.   What factors motivated students to become heavily involved in the civil rights movement during this period? To what extent was their discontent motivated by factors other than segregation in eating places?

3.   What national and international events of the late 1950s and early 1960s affected the growth of the civil rights movement during this period?

4.   What was the role of Ella Baker in the formation of the Student Nonviolent Coordinating Committee?

5.   How did the activities and values of SNCC activists differ from those activists associated with SCLC and NAACP?

6.   What impact did the lunch counter sit-ins of 1960 have on the outcome of that year's presidential election?

7.   What was the origin of the use of nonviolence in the civil rights movement? What are the differences between nonviolence as a philosophy of life and nonviolence as a tactic?

8.   Define *mass movement* and discuss why it begins to be used to describe the modern black freedom struggle during this period.

9.   How did the increasing media attention brought on by nonviolent direct action tactics advance the cause of civil rights? How did these methods heighten awareness of racial segregation, particularly in the south?

10.   As proponents of nonviolent action developed their tactics, how important were the training workshops given by such groups as CORE and SCLC? To what degree was this learning process effective in unifying people and breaking down old stereotypes? How were white students like Robert Zellner influenced by this experience?

11.   What, for James Lawson, was the key to success of nonviolent activism? Why did he consider many of the changes gained as a result of the sit-ins and freedom rides "concessions?"

12.   Why did Robert F. Williams feel that blacks needed to adopt a strategy that promoted self-defense? What deficiencies does he point out in the dispensation of American justice toward black Americans?

ADDITIONAL RECOMMENDED READINGS

Carson, Clayborne. *In Struggle: SNCC and the Black Awakening of the 1960s.* Boston: Harvard University Press, 1981. This is the most comprehensive look at the development, personalities, and achievements of SNCC. Carson explores the development of a social movement and the effects it had on both whites and blacks during that time and describes the history of what was one of the most influential of the civil rights organizations of the 1960s.

Chafe, William. *Civilities and Civil Rights: Greensboro, NC and the Black Struggle for Freedom.* New York: Oxford University Press, 1980. An informative book in the development in the south of the civil rights movement, particularly the importance of student and community activity. The book concentrates on Greensboro, North Carolina, a center of organization and enlightened black activism prior to the 1960s. Chafe looks carefully at the people who were involved in these early efforts and at what factors motivated them to act against the powerful system of racism and discrimination operating in the south. Chafe also examines the background and impact of the 1960 Woolworth's sit-in.

Meier, August and Elliott Rudwick. *CORE: A Study in the Civil Rights Movement, 1942–1968.* New York: Oxford University Press, 1980. An important work that examines the development of the Congress of Racial Equality. It is particularly valuable in showing the early growth of ideas and strategies that became the backbone of the civil rights movement. It also points out the important connections between the early CORE activists and the American left and pacifist movement, which was central to the notion of nonviolent direct action that became so important in the 1960s.

Zinn, Howard. *SNCC: The New Abolitionists.* Boston: Beacon Press, 1965. The first book to examine the development of SNCC. Zinn, a former professor at Spelman College and SNCC adviser, writes from a first-hand perspective. Provides an excellent complement to the Carson book.

CHAPTER 5 — NO EASY WALK (1962–1963)

by David J. Garrow

—Examines the further development of the civil rights mass movement

—Describes the growing commitment of movement activists to the tactic of nonviolence and contrasts the effect of the use of this tactic on desegregation efforts in Albany, Georgia and Birmingham, Alabama

—Identifies the major civil rights organizations involved in the freedom struggle during this period, names their leaders, and compares their approaches

—Discusses the growing role of the national media in the spread of the civil rights movement

—Analyzes the impact of national and international media attention on federal policy and involvement and looks at the effect of the expanding African independence movement on the American black rights struggle

OVERVIEW

In August 1961, the Student Nonviolent Coordinating Committee (SNCC), the group of young college student activists who had emerged from the 1960 sit-ins as the new shock troops of the black freedom struggle in the south, made a decision that represented a crucial turning point in the civil rights movement. A number of SNCC activists decided that rather than return to college that fall, they would move into rural areas of the deep south and become full-time organizers, seeking to stimulate new black initiatives in thoroughly-segregated and often Klan-dominated local communities.

One group of young SNCC workers went into the small city of McComb in southwest Mississippi and persevered in its efforts despite heavy white harassment. Another youthful SNCC activist, Charles Sherrod, later to be joined by Cordell Reagon and Charles Jones, made initial contacts in and around the city of Albany—ALL-BENNY, residents pronounced it—in southwest Georgia.

In both towns the SNCC workers found some black adults, often middle-class professional men who had served abroad in the U.S. military, who already were trying to pursue modest, local-level civil rights initiatives despite white opposition and hostility. Over time, the local civil rights movements that emerged in towns like McComb and Albany owed their strength and resilience to the combination of both the SNCC workers' outside organizational ties and the long-term commitment and dedication of local activists whose names often have gone largely unrecorded.

Although McComb and southwest Mississippi became an intense civil rights battleground in the fall of 1961, it was Albany that emerged as America's first nationally-covered civil rights struggle since the freedom rides crisis in May 1961. Like the freedom rides, the initial focus was transportation. While the Interstate Commerce Commission (ICC) order, stemming from the freedom rides, mandated the desegregation of all interstate transportation facilities—such as train stations and bus terminals—on November 1, 1961, Albany was one city where local officials had no interest in complying with that ruling. When both SNCC and Albany's branch of the National Association for the Advancement of Colored People (NAACP) organized "tests" of those facilities, Albany Police Chief Laurie Pritchett had the participants, often young black students recruited by SNCC workers from Albany State College or local high schools, arrested for attempting to desegregate the terminals. Those arrests mobilized the local black community into peaceful mass prayer marches that resulted in hundreds of further arrests. The local black adult leadership, which had banded together into the Albany Movement to give direction to the new civil rights efforts, called Dr. Martin Luther King, Jr. in Atlanta to seek his assistance and involvement.

The arrival of King and several aides from the Southern Christian Leadership Conference (SCLC) gave a boost to the mass demonstrations but further intensified the organizational tension and conflict between the representatives of SNCC, the NAACP, the Albany Movement, and the SCLC, all of which wanted at least a degree of primacy in the daily news stories about Albany's demonstrations that now were being featured on network television news and the front pages of major national newspapers.

On December 18, the protests ended when the Albany Movement leadership reached what they believed was a negotiated desegregation accord with representatives of the city government. King left town, but over the next few weeks it became increasingly clear that the whites would not make good on their promises, which they had voiced simply to end the demonstrations and remove Albany from the national headlines. When Albany Movement representatives appeared before the City Commission on January 23, 1962, to ask that the city not renege on its promises, white officials curtly dismissed them and asserted that no binding agreement had ever taken place.

Throughout the spring and early summer of 1962 the Albany Movement and the small band of SNCC workers kept up their efforts, focusing much energy on an economic boycott of white Albany businesses. Many white business leaders were angered when the City Commission allowed the city bus company to go out of business rather than permit the company to desegregate bus seating as the Movement had demanded and the company had agreed. The business leaders lobbied without success for the city officials to place Albany's economic well-being ahead of a hard-line defense of rigid segregation. The Commission held its ground, and when protests resumed in mid-July, the city fathers instructed Police Chief Pritchett to continue with a policy of mass arrests rather than give into King's and the Albany Movement's request that the city sanction some desegregation efforts and open official biracial discussions with its own black citizens.

Laurie Pritchett's peaceful defense of segregation led not to national criticism but to widespread news media praise of his professionalism and strategic sagacity. Without any incidents of mass violence akin to the attacks on the freedom riders, neither the American public nor the Kennedy administration paid much heed to Albany's successful repression of the black demonstrations. By the end of August both the Albany Movement and King's SCLC had concluded that any further protests and arrests served no strategic purpose. Albany activists shifted their efforts to voter registration and attempted to rebut press claims that Albany had been a civil rights "failure" and "defeat." SNCC turned its attention to the rural counties around Albany, and King and his SCLC colleagues pondered how a more successful mass protest campaign might be launched in some other southern city.

That next city would be Birmingham, Alabama, where King's long-time SCLC colleague, Rev. Fred Shuttlesworth, had headed up an aggressive local civil rights organization, the Alabama Christian Movement for Human Rights (ACMHR), ever since state authorities had forced the NAACP out of business in Alabama in 1956. Shuttlesworth was eager for King and the SCLC to help him mount a full-scale protest campaign against Birmingham's rigid segregation and the man who aggressively led its defense, infamous Public Safety Commissioner Eugene "Bull" Connor. Although some Birmingham merchants, much like Albany's business-men, had told Shuttlesworth they would rather desegregate than pay the economic price that would result from mass demonstrations, they re-fused to act in the face of Connor's forceful championing of total segrega-tion. King and the SCLC weighed a number of factors including the ACMHR's commitment, the economic vulnerability of the white mer-chants, Connor's quick-tempered penchant for violent responses to black activism, and the 1961–1962 lesson that the Kennedys would respond to violent civil rights repression with direct federal intervention while largely ignoring Pritchett-style repression. They decided that Connor and Birmingham might well be just the tonic that the southern movement needed after the disappointments and frustrations of Albany.

The SCLC and the ACMHR launched their Birmingham demon-strations in April 1963. After a slow start, King intentionally chose to submit to arrest, hoping his incarceration might spark the campaign into greater action and win it more national—and federal—attention. When Connor's jailers placed King in solitary confinement, King's friends and aides became deeply concerned and persuaded his wife, Coretta Scott King, to phone the Kennedy White House to seek federal reassurance of her husband's safety. Both Attorney General Robert Kennedy and Presi-dent John Kennedy responded with personal calls to Mrs. King, and King's jailing did help spark an intensification of the movement's Bir-mingham protests. "Bull" Connor employed both snarling police attack dogs and high-powered fire hoses to drive back black demonstrators who sought to march into downtown Birmingham. National and international outrage resulted as graphic photos and television footage of the police violence were printed and shown across the country and around the world. The Kennedy administration sprang into action and successfully lobbied Birmingham's economic leadership into reaching a desegrega-tion accord with King and Shuttlesworth before the police violence and resulting black anger got totally out of hand.

Coverage of the Birmingham protests made Americans more profoundly aware of the obstacles and opposition facing the southern black freedom struggle than any events from preceding years. Several weeks later, as smaller demonstrations spread across the south and Alabama Governor George C. Wallace sought unsuccessfully to block the court-ordered integration of the University of Alabama, President Ken-nedy went on television to declare, in words far stronger than he or any previous president had ever used, that racial discrimination and injustice was a serious and profound moral evil that American society had to confront and strive to eliminate. For the first time in his presidency, Kennedy committed himself to aggressively championing federal legislation that would mandate public desegregation and racial nondiscrimination in many facets of American life.

Although Kennedy's declaration of support for far-reaching civil rights legislation was greeted enthusiastically by civil rights proponents, Kennedy and his administration at first openly opposed black leaders' announcement of a late-August March on Washington which would seek to highlight the economic disadvantages experienced by black America as well as call upon the Congress to pass Kennedy's civil rights bill. The long-time dean of black American leaders, A. Philip Randolph, president of the Brotherhood of Sleeping Car Porters (BSCP) and the Negro American Labor Council (NALC), was the major proponent of the march and its economic focus. The Kennedys, plus some civil rights supporters, feared that any such mass demonstration might harm rather than help the congressional prospects of the civil rights bill. Only after some hesitation did NAACP executive secretary Roy Wilkins and National Urban League (NUL) chief Whitney Young endorse and join in the march.

Throughout the weeks leading up to the August 28th March on Washington, Kennedy administration officials and such civil rights leaders as Wilkins, did all they could to ensure that the tone of the march and the content of its leaders' speeches at the climactic Lincoln Memorial rally would do everything possible to aid Kennedy's legislation. In the process, Randolph's original economic focus became largely invisible, and administration loyalists became extremely concerned when the advance text of SNCC chairman John Lewis' speech called the Kennedy bill "too little, and too late." Under great pressure that continued up until just a few moments before the rally itself got underway, Lewis, a veteran of both the sit-ins and the freedom rides, finally was convinced to delete the language that the Kennedys and some of their civil rights allies found offensive.

Notwithstanding the serious private controversy over Lewis' text, the March on Washington, which drew over 200,000 participants and climaxed with Martin Luther King, Jr.'s famous "I Have A Dream" oration, represented a new high-water mark for the black freedom struggle. Even more so than in the wake of the Birmingham protests, America seemed to manifest a new and greater level of support for fundamental improvements in the lives of black citizens. Nonetheless, the march was only a one-day event, and when it concluded, as Martin Luther King, Jr. stated that afternoon, "it was time once again for the movement to 'return to the valley' "—the harshly segregated valley of the American south, exemplified best—or worst—by Mississippi and the deadly obstacles that movement workers continued to encounter in that most southern of southern states.

READINGS

1. Charles Sherrod was a twenty-two-year-old SNCC worker from Petersburg, Virginia when he became the first "outside agitator" for civil rights to go into Albany and southwest Georgia in 1961. In this excerpt from an untitled and undated account of his work that Sherrod wrote just a year or two later, he recounts the earliest experiences that he and his first SNCC partner, Cordell Reagon, encountered in Albany. Even after the most heavily-publicized civil rights organizing of 1961–1963 in Albany was succeeded by different efforts, Sherrod remained there and continued to do civil rights work in southwest Georgia, except for several years in divinity school at New York's Union Theological Seminary. More than twenty years after he first arrived in Albany, in the 1980s Sherrod serves as an elected member of the Albany City Commission.

From: An untitled essay by Charles Sherrod. Used by permission of Charles Sherrod.

Cordell Reagon of Nashville, and Charles Sherrod of Petersburg, Virginia, arrived in Albany by bus in early October, after having been "railroaded" out of McComb, Mississippi where we had been engaged in a voter-registration campaign that erupted into a significant move on the part of the populace which has won the attention of the nation.

The population of Albany was in the first days of our stay here, very apprehensive. We had told many that our intention was to organize a voter-registration campaign, the first step of which was to establish an office. At the same time, it was known that we had little or no money. Further, there was doubt in the minds of many people as to who we really were.

The first obstacle to remove was the mental block in the minds of those who wanted to move but were unable for fear that we were not who we said we were. But when people began to hear us in churches, social meetings, on the streets, in the pool halls, lunch rooms, night clubs, and other places where people gather, they began to open up a bit. We would tell them of how it feels to be in prison, what it means to be behind bars, in jail for the cause. We explained to them that we had stopped school because we felt compelled to do so since so many of us were in chains. We explained further that there were worse chains than jail and prison. We referred to the system that imprisons men's minds and robs them of creativity. We mocked the system that teaches men to be good Negroes instead of good men. We gave an account of the many resistances [to] injustice in the courts, in employment, registration, and voting. The people knew that such evils existed but when we pointed them out time and time again and emphasized the need for concerted action against them, the people began to think. At this point, we started to illustrate what had happened in Montgomery, Macon, Nashville, Charlotte, Atlanta, Savannah, Richmond, Petersburg, and many other cities where people came together and protested against an evil system.

This placed us near November 1st, the date when the Interstate Commerce Commission had issued its ultimatum for all interstate facilities to be desegregated. . . . ■

2. **I**n Albany, civil rights proponents from a variety of organizations—SNCC, the SCLC, and the NAACP—banded together in one comprehensive organization (much like the Montgomery Improvement Association) called the Albany Movement. Despite the fact that white city officials reneged on the verbal accord that had brought the mass demonstrations of December 1961 to a halt, Albany Movement leaders continued to hope, up until their January 23, 1962 appearance before the Albany City Commission, that the city would live up to its promises. In this document, the statement of its history and purposes that the Albany Movement presented to the Commission that evening, the black leaders recount their experiences and hopes. The City Commission, however, rejected their statements out of hand, and Albany experienced a renewed round of mass civil rights protests during the summer of 1962.

Source: Letter from the Albany Movement to the Albany City Commission, January 23, 1962.

Gentlemen:

The Albany Movement came into being as a result of repeated denials of redress for inadequacies and wrongs, and finally, for the refusal to even consider petitions which have been presented to your group from as far back as 1957.

The first request was for sewage and paving relief in the Lincoln Heights area—nothing done. Next, the stoning of Negro ministers' houses, following an inflammatory editorial in the local press, caused a request to be sent by registered mail to the Mayor that a joint group try to stop the worsening conditions—no official acknowledgement of this request has ever been received by us. Again, a request that segregated polling places, which we felt were used to counteract the effect of our vote, was made from the top to the bottom—the refusal to attempt any kind of redress necessitated a successful suit to be waged in the Federal Court by us. Finally, it was the refusal of Albany officials, through its police department, to comply with the ICC regulation which became effective last November 1, that made the creation of this body a necessity. Test rides were conducted throughout the entire state of Georgia. Atlanta, Savannah, Augusta, Macon, Columbus, Valdosta and Waycross all complied. Only Albany resisted.

Accordingly we staged further tests on November 22, which resulted in the initial arrests, trials, convictions and appeals. The cases were headed for higher courts and things would have proceeded in an orderly fashion to its conclusion, but for the arrests of the so-called "Freedom Riders."

This testing of the railroad's compliance with another ICC directive has been laid at our doors. Actually, we had absolutely nothing to do with this. It was the elaborately staged "infraction" and arrests of those people that caused us to rush to their defense. They were fighting for the same purpose as we and we could not abandon them to the wolves.

The mockery of fair play and justice which followed, in turn, caused the first planned "Marching Protest." The harsh, repressive measures employed caused further protests and further arrests. By now, the whole country, and the world for that matter, were aware of the unyielding, cruelly repressive measures used to combat our use of that First Amendment to the United States Constitution, "Freedom of Speech" through peaceful protest.

When an agreement was reached on December 18, one of the cardinal points was the privilege of substituting signature bonds in lieu of cash bonds. This agreement has not been kept by the city of Albany. Another agreement was that the police department would not interfere with the compliance of the bus company to the ICC order. This agreement has been only partly kept by the city of Albany.

The Albany Movement wishes to go on record, without reservation, of requesting the city of Albany to keep the faith by honoring its commitments.

We the members of the Albany Movement, with the realization that ultimately the people of Albany, Negro and white, will have to solve our difficulties; realizing full well that racial hostility can be the downfall of our city; realizing that what happens in Albany, as well as what does *NOT* happen in Albany, affects the whole free world, call upon you tonight to hear our position.

It is our belief that discrimination based on race, color or religion is fundamentally wrong and contrary to the letter and intent of the Constitution of the United States. It is our aim in the Albany Movement to seek means of ending discriminatory practices in public facilities, both in employment and in use. Further, it is our aim to encourage private businesses to offer equal opportunity for all persons in employment and in service.

Some of these ideals which are inherent in the Constitution of the United States of America are:

1. Equal opportunity to improve one's self by good education.

2. Equal opportunity to exercise freedom and responsibility through the vote and participation in governmental processes.

3. Equal opportunity to work and advance economically.

4. Equal protection under the law.

5. The creation of a climate in which the talents and abilities of the entire community may be used for the good of all, unfettered by considerations of race or class.

Before going into plans for implementation of these goals, we wish to ask of you, gentlemen, tonight to reaffirm in writing your oral agreement of December 18, 1961, that, (1) the bus and train station will be open at all times without interference from the police; (2) the cash bonds will be refunded in exchange for security bonds, at an early date, the date to be set tonight.

We submit as the next step the creation of a biracial planning committee . . . [to] be composed of 6 members, 3 of which shall be appointed by the Albany Movement and 3 by the City Commission. Because of the tremendous responsibilities that will be invested in this committee, we pledge ourselves, as we also urge the commission, to choose men of the highest integrity, good will and sincerity.

It is our hope that through negotiations and arbitrations, through listening and learning from each other, that we can achieve the purposes that will benefit the total community.

The problem of human rights belongs to us all, therefore, let us not falter in seizing the opportunity which almighty God has given to create a new order of freedom and human dignity. What is your pleasure gentlemen, in proceeding with the negotiations?

Respectfully Submitted,
For The Albany Movement

W.G. Anderson, President
M.S. Page, Executive Secretary

■

3. **W**hen a second round of mass protests took place in Albany during July and August 1962, many white businessmen and merchants unsuccessfully lobbied the City Commission to reach some sort of accord with the Albany Movement. The merchants' unhappiness with the Commission's hard-line, no-negotiations position was in large part a product of the very successful economic boycott that black Albany had mounted against many downtown white businesses in the hope that pressure on the pocketbook would achieve what appeals to whites' consciences had not produced. Despite the boycott's success, the Commission paid little more heed to white appeals for a more moderate stance than it had to black pleas. At the end of the summer, mass protests ended and the movement rechanneled its efforts into voter registration drives.

Source: Letter from Albany merchant Leonard Gilberg to Albany Police Chief Laurie Pritchett, July 23, 1962. Used by permission of Leonard Gilberg.

Dear Chief Pritchett:

In order to inform you as to the situation business-wise for myself and other merchants with whom I have spoken, I am sure you will find the following to be true.

At least 90 to 95% of all the negro business I have enjoyed in past years has been lacking for the last 7 months due to an obvious boycott on the part of the negroes and threats and coercion toward other negroes not in sympathy with the movement to keep them from shopping downtown in Albany.

Now to top all this off, their constant harassment, sit-ins, demonstrations, marching, etc. are keeping all people both white and negro from Albany. Many customers have told me direct that they would not come to Albany from out of town due to fear of demonstrations in Albany and local people have said that they ask their wives and children to stay out of town for the same reason.

Our business is at present suffering an approximate 50% decrease due to lack of customer traffic in Albany and it is an intolerable situation. This fear of mob violence and demonstration has made our situation a dire one. Any aid you can give us in the matter will be greatly appreciated and our thanks to you for the wonderful manner in which you have handled these past events.

Very truly yours,

GILBERG's

Leonard Gilberg

■

4. **I**n Birmingham, Alabama, where Martin Luther King, Jr. and the SCLC mounted an extremely successful campaign of mass protests in April and May of 1963, the core of the movement's support was the ACMHR, led by the diminutive but courageous Rev. Fred L. Shuttlesworth, one of King's cofounders of the SCLC. This reading, from a pamphlet first published in 1966, recounts some of the often-unheralded pre-1963 efforts of Shuttlesworth and the ACMHR to fight segregation in Birmingham.

From: Birmingham: People in Motion (Birmingham: ACMHR, 1966).

It was in December, 1956 that the U.S. Supreme Court ruled that bus segregation in Montgomery was illegal. This was a climax to the historic yearlong Montgomery bus protest.

Immediately, the ACMHR announced that a group of its members would test segregation laws in their city by attempting to integrate Birmingham buses. The protest was scheduled for December 26.

But Christmas night, the night before the protest, the home of Rev. Shuttlesworth was bombed. The bed in which he was sleeping was directly over the spot where the bomb went off. The bed was blown to bits, but he escaped unhurt. Members of the ACMHR say he was saved to lead the movement.

Shuttlesworth took a neighbor who was hurt in the explosion to the hospital. Then he took a bus home—and he rode in front. The bombing strengthened the determination of his followers in the same way.

"On the 25th day of December, that's when they blew up Rev. Shuttlesworth's house," says Mrs. Walker. "And when I went to the meeting the next morning Rev. Shuttlesworth was the first thing I saw. And I knowed as how their house was blowed up, and I couldn't figure out how he was there. And I said then, that I'm going into it. And I went into it on that day."

More than 250 others "went into it" with Mrs. Walker. Twenty-one of them were arrested that day, one the following day. They were convicted and fined, and they then filed suit in federal court, in January, 1957.

The new organization's first efforts were directed toward getting the City of Birmingham to hire Negroes as policemen. When petitions and delegations failed, a suit was filed against the Personnel Board, demanding the right of Negroes to take examinations for all civil service jobs. But it was not to be until ten years later, after months of picketing and marching outside city hall and the county courthouse, that the first four Negro policemen were hired.

In its first year, the movement also filed suit in federal court on behalf of a Milwaukee couple arrested because they sat in the "white" waiting room in the city's railway station.

Both these actions followed the pattern of court action established by the NAACP, and indeed, suits have always been one of the ACMHR's most effective weapons. But in December 1956 the movement entered a new phase, and took on the character it was to retain—of a movement of people putting their bodies into a challenge to the system.

In May 1956 Alabama politicians "stood on the beach of history and tried to hold back the tide." They outlawed the National Association for the Advancement of Colored People, in a desperate attempt to halt the movement for Negro equality. But their action had precisely the opposite effect. For almost immediately the Negroes of Birmingham came together to form a movement which during the last ten years has transformed life in Birmingham—which has shaken America.

"They could outlaw an organization, but they couldn't outlaw the movement of a people determined to be free," said the Rev. Fred L. Shuttlesworth, president of the new group. And at a mass meeting called by a committee of Negro ministers, the Alabama Christian Movement for Human Rights (ACMHR) was born. Many Negroes in "the Johannesburg of North America" were afraid to join. But many others echoed the sentiments of Mrs. Rosa Walker, one of the first members: "I was frightened, but I figured we needed help to get us more jobs and better education. And we had the man here to help us."

In its original statement of principles, the ACMHR stated:

> As free and independent citizens of the United States of America, we express publicly our determination to press forward persistently for freedom and democracy, and the removal from our society of any forms of second-class citizenship . . . We Negroes shall never become enemies of the white people. But America was born in the struggle for Freedom from Tyranny and Oppression. We shall never bomb any homes or lynch any persons; but we must, because of history and the future, march to complete freedom with unbowed heads, praying hearts, and an unyielding determination.

* * * *

The question of desegregating the buses wasn't over until late 1959. At that time, federal court rulings held the police were wrong in arresting Negroes who rode the buses integrated in 1958 and the Milwaukee couple who sat in the railroad station in 1959. But the segregation signs were still up, and by now ACMHR people knew that court rulings only come to life when people put their bodies on the line in a challenge to the old ways.

* * * *

The victories were important and gave people the knowledge that they do have strength, but as yet life in Birmingham had not really changed. Ever since the movement began leaders had received threats of death over the telephone and through the mail. Phones rang all night and strange cars circled the blocks where leaders of the movement lived. Every night after the first bombing in December, 1956 volunteer guards sat all night watching the Shuttlesworth house and church.

Police joined in the harassment. They tapped the telephones and searched and arrested guards at the Shuttlesworth home. Every non-white who came through his street was stopped and questioned. One man was arrested for distributing literature in alleged violation of Alabama's anti-boycott law. Each week city detectives attended the ACMHR mass meetings. They stopped and searched members leaving the meetings and charged them with blocking traffic. One man, the Rev. Charles Billups, was arrested on a charge of interfering with the entrance of a detective at a meeting; it was said he "touched the officer's coat." Later he was tied to a tree and beaten by the Ku Klux Klan. Other ACMHR members were threatened with loss of their jobs, and some were actually fired.

* * * *

During 1960 and 1961 the ACMHR filed a variety of suits—to desegregate the parks and schools, open airport eating facilities, and to stop the police from attending ACMHR meetings. . . .

* * * *

1961 ended with victories in the courts.

A federal court ruled that the ordinance forbidding whites and Negroes to play any games together—baseball, checkers, or dominoes—was unconstitutional. Shuttlesworth described the ordinance as "the backbone of Birmingham segregation" and noted that it was the first time a local federal judge had ruled against segregation without a higher court order. "Even here, the light appears," he said.

But a court ruling ordering the desegregation of public parks was turned to defeat for both Negro and white citizens of Birmingham when the city commissioners closed down the parks. . . .

* * * *

It was early in 1962 that the pressure which finally cracked the solid white wall of opposition of the city's power structure began to build up. . . .

In the spring, Birmingham Negro college students and the ACMHR put on an effective selective buying campaign against the downtown stores. Their demands were desegregation of public accommodations and hiring of Negro clerks. Newspapers ignored the boycott but business leaders admitted privately it hurt them badly. Negro leaders claimed it was eighty per cent effective. Connor retaliated by cutting off the city relief payments, most of which go to Negroes. . . .

* * * *

The break came when the Rev. Martin Luther King, Jr. announced plans to hold SCLC's 1962 convention in Birmingham . . . [In] order to avert demonstrations . . . Birmingham business leaders sent delegates to confer with SCLC. SCLC replied that whether there would be demonstrations in Birmingham was a matter for local civil rights leaders to decide. So Birmingham business leaders were forced to talk to Shuttlesworth for the first time. . . .

Business leaders had decided that some changes would have to be made if the city's economy was to avoid drastic damage. They found themselves pitted against the city's political leaders, who were unbending in their extreme segregationist position. ■

5. **W**hen Martin Luther King, Jr. and the SCLC joined with Shuttlesworth and ACMHR early in April 1963 to launch a campaign of mass demonstrations against Birmingham's segregation, one of King's foremost hopes was to use the Birmingham protests to win a far greater level of national outrage and federal intervention against southern racism than had occurred in re-

sponse to the Albany protests of 1961–1962. After King intentionally allowed himself to be arrested and jailed for leading a Birmingham demonstration on Good Friday, April 12, King's aides, particularly the SCLC Executive Director Wyatt T. Walker, encouraged his wife, Coretta Scott King, to phone President Kennedy to seek federal reassurance concerning her husband's safety. When President Kennedy returned Mrs. King's call on Monday, April 15, he informed her that federal inquiries were being made and that King's jailers had told the FBI that they would allow him to phone his wife. When he did call, the Birmingham police recorded and transcribed the Kings' conversation. In this edited version of their phone call, King reassures his wife about his spirits, expresses his pleasure at the presidential initiative, and strongly encourages his wife to tell Walker about Kennedy's call so that the news media can be alerted to this important development.

Following the transcript is a portion of King's now famous "Letter from Birmingham City Jail," dated the day after the phone call, in which he explains his purpose for being in Birmingham, the strategies employed, and his general disappointment in the responses of many so-called white moderates.

From: Wiretap transcript of Martin Luther King, Jr.'s and Mrs. King's phone conversation, Birmingham Police Department, April 15, 1963. Used by permission of the Martin Luther King, Jr. Center for Social Change through the Joan Daves office.

Mr. King: I just read your lovely letter.

Mrs. King: You just got it?

Mr. King: Yes.

Mrs. King: I just got a call from the President and he told me you were going to call me in a few minutes.

Mr. King: Who was that? (At this point King talked with his two children, Marty and Yoki.)

Mrs. King: Are you being guarded?

Mr. King: Yes.

Mrs. King: Did they give you a time limit?

Mr. King: Not exactly, but [they] hear everything, you know. Who did you say called you?

Mrs. King: Kennedy, the President.

Mr. King: Did he call you direct?

Mrs. King: Yes, and he told me you were going to call in a few minutes. It was about thirty minutes ago. He called from Palm Beach. I tried to phone him yesterday.

Mr. King: Is that known?

Mrs. King: It's known here; I just got it.

Mr. King: Let Wyatt know.

Mrs. King: The Executive in Birmingham?

Mr. King: Yes, do that right now.

* * * *

Mrs. King: Is your spirit all right?

Mr. King: Yes. I've been alone, you know.

Mrs. King: Yes, I know that. Are things pretty good?

Mr. King: Uh huh.

Mrs. King: Now, he told me the F.B.I. talked with you last night, is that right?

Mr. King: No. No.

Mrs. King: They sent them in there, they must have talked with some of the others. They sent them in last night. I talked with Bobby last night. He called twice and told me he would call me today, and it was the President, himself, and he assured me of his concern. He asked if we had any complaints and said if we did to be sure and let them know.

Mr. King: Be sure and get that to the Reverend. I think it will make a very good statement.

Mrs. King: He's very sympathetic and kept saying, "How are you, I understand you have a little baby." He said things might get better with the new administration. This is a problem.

Mr. King: Is it being carried well?

Mrs. King: Not too well here, still not too well. There was a good program today with Dick . . . Arnell. . . .

Mr. King: What about the *Constitution*—that's not important, it's what they say.

Mrs. King: They have been carrying articles. Yesterday they had something about the sixty. The [Atlanta Daily] *World* has had front page about every day recently, but it was not accurate. They said the boycott was not effective. There was something this morning about yesterday. It's been carried pretty good. They had a picture last night, of A.D. [King—Martin's brother]. I think with the *National* it's been pretty good; it's been pretty good today.

Mr. King: When you get this over it will help.

Mrs. King: Yes.

* * * *

Mr. King: . . . I'll probably come out in the next day or so. Be sure to get in touch with the Reverend. I think this gives it a new dimension.

Mrs. King: I just thought about it yesterday, and I told the Reverend and he tried to get to you, but there was no choice. . . . ■

From: "Letter from Birmingham City Jail" by Martin Luther King, Jr., April 16, 1963. Copyright 1963, 1964 by Martin Luther King, Jr. Used by permission of Joan Daves.

MY DEAR FELLOW CLERGYMEN,

While confined here in the Birmingham City Jail, I came across your recent statement calling our present activities "unwise and untimely." Seldom, if ever, do I pause to answer criticism of my work and ideas. . . . But since I feel that you are men of genuine good will and your criticisms are sincerely set forth, I would like to answer your statement in what I hope will be patient and reasonable terms.

I think I should give the reason for my being in Birmingham, since you have been influenced by the argument of "outsiders coming in." I have the honor of serving as president of the Southern Christian Leadership Conference, an organization operating in every Southern state with headquarters in Atlanta, Georgia. We have some 85 affiliate organizations all across the South. . . . Several months ago our local affiliate here in Birmingham invited us to be on call to engage in a nonviolent direct action program if such were deemed necessary. We readily consented and when the hour came we lived up to our promises. . . .

* * * *

In any nonviolent campaign there are four basic steps: 1) collection of the facts to determine whether injustices are alive; 2) negotiation; 3) self-purification; and 4) direct action. We have gone through all of these steps in Birmingham. . . . Birmingham is probably the most thoroughly segregated city in the United States. Its ugly record of police brutality is known in every section of the country. Its unjust treatment of Negroes in the courts is a notorious reality. There have been more unsolved bombings of Negro homes and churches in Birmingham than in any city in this nation. These are the hard, brutal, and unbelievable facts. On the basis of these conditions Negro leaders sought to negotiate with the city fathers. But the political leaders consistently refused to engage in good faith negotiation.

Then came the opportunity last September to talk with some of the leaders of the economic community. In these negotiating sessions certain promises were made by the merchants—such as the promise to remove the humiliating racial signs from the stores. On the basis of these promises Reverend Shuttlesworth and the leaders of the Alabama Christian Movement for Human Rights agreed to call a moratorium on any type of demonstrations. As the weeks and months unfolded we realized that we were the victims of a broken promise. The signs remained. As in so many experiences of the past, we were confronted with blasted hopes, and the dark shadow of a deep disappointment settled upon us. So we had no alternative except that of preparing for direct action, whereby we would present our very bodies as a means of laying our case before the conscience of the local and national community. We were not unmindful of the difficulties involved. So we decided to go through a process of self-purification. We started having workshops on nonviolence and repeatedly asked ourselves the questions, "Are you able to accept the blows without retaliating?" "Are you able to endure the ordeals of jail?"

* * * *

You may well ask, "Why direct action? Why sit-ins, marches, etc.? Isn't negotiation a better path?" You are exactly right in your call for negotiation. Indeed, this is the purpose of direct action. Nonviolent direct action seeks to create such a crisis and establish such creative tension that a community that has constantly refused to negotiate is forced to confront the issue.

* * * *

My friends, I must say to you that we have not made a single gain in civil rights without determined legal and nonviolent pressure. History is the long and tragic story of the fact that privileged groups seldom give up their priv-

115

ileges voluntarily. Individuals may see the moral light and give up their unjust posture; but as Reinhold Niebuhr has reminded us, groups are more immoral than individuals.

We know through painful experience that freedom is never voluntarily given by the oppressor; it must be demanded by the oppressed. Frankly I have never yet engaged in a direct action movement that was "well timed," according to the timetable of those who have not suffered unduly from the disease of segregation. For years now I have heard the word "Wait!" It rings in the ear of every Negro with a piercing familiarity. This "wait" has almost always meant "never." It has been a tranquilizing Thalidomide, relieving the emotional stress for a moment, only to give birth to an ill-formed infant of frustration. We must come to see with the distinguished jurist of yesterday that "justice too long delayed is justice denied." We have waited for more than 340 years for our constitutional and God-given rights. The nations of Asia and Africa are moving with jetlike speed toward the goal of political independence, and we still creep at horse and buggy pace toward the gaining of a cup of coffee at a lunch counter.

I guess it is easy for those who have never felt the stinging darts of segregation to say wait. But when you have seen vicious mobs lynch your mothers and fathers at will and drown your sisters and brothers at whim; when you have seen hate-filled policemen curse, kick, brutalize, and even kill your black brothers and sisters with impunity; when you see the vast majority of your 20 million Negro brothers smothering in an airtight cage of poverty in the midst of an affluent society; when you suddenly find your tongue twisted and your speech stammering as you seek to explain to your six-year-old daughter why she can't go to the public amusement park that has just been advertised on television, and see the tears welling up in her little eyes when she is told that Funtown is closed to colored children, and see the depressing clouds of inferiority begin to form in her little mental sky, and see her begin to distort her little personality by unconsciously developing a bitterness toward white people; when you have to concoct an answer for a five-year-old son who is asking in agonizing pathos: "Daddy, why do white people treat colored people so mean?"; when you take a cross country drive and find it necessary to sleep night after night in the uncomfortable corners of your automobile because no motel will accept you; when you are humiliated day in and day out by nagging signs reading "white" men and "colored"; when your first name becomes "nigger" and your middle name becomes "boy" (however old you are) and your last name becomes "John," and when your wife and mother are never given the respected title of "Mrs."; when you are harried by day and haunted by night by the fact that you are a Negro, living constantly at tip-toe stance, never quite knowing what to expect next, and plagued with inner fears and outer resentments; when you are forever fighting a degenerating sense of "nobodiness"—then you will understand why we find it difficult to wait. There comes a time when the cup of endurance runs over, and men are no longer willing to be plunged into an abyss of injustice where they experience the bleakness of corroding despair. I hope, sirs, you can understand our legitimate and unavoidable impatience.

* * * *

I must make two honest confessions to you, my Christian and Jewish brothers. First, I must confess that over the last few years I have been gravely disappointed with the white moderate. I have almost reached the regrettable conclusion that the Negroes' great stumbling block in the stride toward freedom is not the White Citizens' "Counciler" or the Ku Klux Klanner, but the white moderate who is more devoted to "order" than to justice; who prefers a negative peace which is the absence of tension to a positive peace which is the presence of justice; who constantly says "I agree with you in the goal you seek, but I can't agree with your methods of direct action"; who paternalistically feels that he can set the timetable for another man's freedom; who lives by the myth of time and who constantly advises the Negro to wait until a "more convenient season." Shallow understanding from people of good will is more frustrating than absolute misunderstanding from people of ill will. Lukewarm acceptance is much more bewildering than outright rejection.

* * * *

You spoke of our activity in Birmingham as extreme. At first I was rather disappointed that fellow clergymen would see my nonviolent efforts as those of the extremist. I started thinking about the fact that I stand in the middle of two opposing forces in the Negro community. One is a force of complacency made up of Negroes who, as a result of long years of oppression, have been so completely drained of self-respect and a sense of "somebodiness" that they have adjusted to segregation, and of a few Negroes in the middle class who, because of a degree of academic and economic security, and because at points they profit by segregation, have unconsciously become insensitive to the problems of the masses. The other force is one of bitterness and hatred and comes perilously close to advocating violence. It is expressed in the various black nationalist groups that are springing up over the nation, the largest and best known being Elijah Muhammad's Muslim movement. This movement is nourished by the contemporary frustration over the continued existence of racial discrimination. It is made up of people who have lost faith in America, who have absolutely repudiated Christianity, and who have concluded that the white man is an incurable "devil."

* * * *

The Negro has many pent-up resentments and latent frustrations. He has to get them out. So let him march sometime; let him have his prayer pilgrimages to the city hall; understand why he must have sit-ins and freedom rides. If his repressed emotions do not come out in these nonviolent ways, they will come out in ominous expressions of violence. This is not a threat; it is a fact of history. So I have not said to my people, "Get rid of your discontent." But I have tried to say that this normal and healthy discontent can be channeled through the creative outlet of nonviolent direct action. . . .

* * * *

In spite of my shattered dreams of the past, I came to Birmingham with the hope that the white religious leadership of this community would see the justice of our cause and, with deep moral concern, serve as the channel through which our just grievances could get to the power structure. I had

117

hoped that each of you would understand. But again I have been disappointed.

I have heard numerous religious leaders of the South call upon their worshippers to comply with a desegregation decision because it is the law, but I have longed to hear white ministers say follow this decree because integration is morally right and the Negro is your brother. In the midst of blatant injustices inflicted upon the Negro, I have watched white churches stand on the sideline and merely mouth pious irrelevancies and sanctimonious trivialities. In the midst of a mighty struggle to rid our nation of racial and economic injustice, I have heard so many ministers say, "Those are social issues with which the Gospel has no real concern," and I have watched so many churches commit themselves to a completely other-worldly religion which made a strange distinction between body and soul, the sacred and the secular.

* * * *

I hope this letter finds you strong in the faith. I also hope that circumstances will soon make it possible for me to meet each of you, not as an integrationist or a civil rights leader, but as a fellow clergyman and a Christian brother. Let us all hope that the dark clouds of racial prejudice will soon pass away and the deep fog of misunderstanding will be lifted from our fear-drenched communities and in some not too distant tomorrow the radiant stars of love and brotherhood will shine over our great nation with all of their scintillating beauty.

Yours for the cause of Peace and Brotherhood,

M.L. King, Jr.
■

6. On May 10, 1963, after a week of intensive negotiations, the SCLC and the ACMHR reached a written agreement with representatives of Birmingham's business leaders and merchants on halting demonstrations in exchange for certain beginnings of racial change. The settlement accord, energetically encouraged by the presence in Birmingham of U.S. Assistant Attorney General Burke Marshall, a close advisor to both Robert and John Kennedy, was, relative to existing conditions in Birmingham, a significant step forward. Nonetheless, as the text of the agreement indicates, the settlement was a

very modest set of particulars, and it ended up taking several years, rather than several months, for the city of Birmingham to move forward in any meaningful fashion with regard to nondiscriminatory job opportunities—both public and private—for its black citizens.

Source: Burke Marshall Papers, John F. Kennedy Library, Boston, Massachusetts.

The Birmingham Truce Agreement

1. Within 3 days after close of demonstrations, fitting rooms will be desegregated.

2. Within 30 days after the city government is established by court order, signs on wash rooms, rest rooms and drinking fountains will be removed.

3. Within 60 days after the city government is established by court order, a program of lunchroom counter desegregation will be commenced.

4. When the city government is established by court order, a program of up-grading Negro employment will be continued and there will be meetings with responsible local leadership to consider further steps.

Within 60 days from the court order determining Birmingham's city government, the employment program will include at least one sales person or cashier.

Within 15 days from the cessation of demonstrations, a Committee on Racial Problems and Employment composed of members of the Senior Citizens' Committee will be established, with a membership made public and the publicly announced purpose of establishing liaison with members of the Negro community to carry out a program of up-grading and improving employment opportunities with the Negro citizens of the Birmingham community. ■

7. The greatest impact of the Birmingham demonstrations was national rather than local. Similar protests against racially discriminatory public accommodations spread across the south, and large sympathy demonstrations in support of the Birmingham campaign and the broader southern movement took place in many cities all across America. Several weeks after the climax and settlement of the Birmingham protests, Alabama Governor George C. Wallace unsuccessfully sought to block the desegregation of the University of Alabama by obstructing the registration of two black students whom a

federal court had ordered admitted to the university. Only President Kennedy's deployment of federalized National Guard troops insured the peaceful admission of the two young people into the university. That evening the President went on nationwide television to comment on his actions and offer a ringing endorsement of the black civil rights activism which Birmingham demonstrated. Within hours after Kennedy's important address, Mississippi NAACP leader Medgar Evers was shot from ambush and killed outside his home in Jackson.

From: President John F. Kennedy's nationally televised speech, June 11, 1963.

This nation was founded by men of many nations and backgrounds. It was founded on the principle that all men are created equal; and that the rights of every man are diminished when the rights of one man are threatened.

It ought to be possible, therefore, for American students of any color to attend any public institution they select without having to be backed up by troops. It ought to be possible for American consumers of any color to receive equal service in places of public accommodation, such as hotels and restaurants, and theaters and retail stores without being forced to resort to demonstrations in the street.

And it ought to be possible for American citizens of any color to register and to vote in a free election without interference or fear of reprisal.

It ought to be possible, in short, for every American to enjoy the privileges of being American without regard to his race or his color.

This is not a sectional issue. Difficulties over segregation and discrimination exist in every city, in every state of the Union, producing in many cities a rising tide of discontent that threatens the public safety.

Nor is this a partisan issue. In a time of domestic crisis, men of goodwill and generosity should be able to unite regardless of party or politics.

This is not even a legal or legislative issue alone. It is better to settle these matters in the courts than on the streets, and new laws are needed at every level. But law alone cannot make men see right.

We are confronted primarily with a moral issue. It is as old as the Scriptures and is as clear as the American Constitution. The heart of the question is whether all Americans are to be afforded equal rights and equal opportunities; whether we are going to treat our fellow Americans as we want to be treated.

If an American, because his skin is dark, cannot eat lunch in a restaurant open to the public; if he cannot send his children to the best public schools available; if he cannot vote for the public officials who represent him; if, in short, he cannot enjoy the full and free life which all of us want, then who among us would be content to have the color of his skin changed and stand in his place?

Who among us would then be content with the counsels of patience and delay. One hundred years of delay have passed since President Lincoln freed the slaves, yet their heirs, their grandsons, are not fully free. They are not yet freed from the bonds of injustice; they are not yet freed from social and economic oppression.

And this nation, for all its hopes and all its boasts, will not be fully free until all its citizens are free.

Now the time has come for this nation to fulfill its promise. The events in Birmingham and elsewhere have so increased the cries for equality that no city or state or legislative body can prudently choose to ignore them.

The fires of frustration and discord are burning in every city, North and South. Where legal remedies are not at hand, redress is sought in the streets in demonstrations, parades and protests, which create tensions and threaten violence—and threaten lives.

We face, therefore, a moral crisis as a country and a people. It cannot be met by repressive police action. It cannot be left to increased demonstrations in the streets. It cannot be quieted by token moves or talk. It is a time to act in the Congress, in your state and local legislative body, and, above all, in all of our daily lives.

I am, therefore, asking the Congress to enact legislation giving all Americans the right to be served in facilities which are open to the public—hotels, restaurants and theaters, retail stores and similar establishments. This seems to me to be an elementary right.

I'm also asking Congress to authorize the Federal Government to participate more fully in lawsuits designed to end segregation in public education. We have succeeded in persuading many districts to desegregate voluntarily. Dozens have admitted Negroes without violence.

Other features will also be requested, including greater protection for the right to vote.

But legislation, I repeat, cannot solve this problem alone. It must be solved in the homes of every American in every community across our country.

In this respect, I want to pay tribute to those citizens, North and South, who've been working in their communities to make life better for all.

They are acting not out of a sense of legal duty but out of a sense of human decency. Like our soldiers and sailors in all parts of the world, they are meeting freedom's challenge on the firing line, and I salute them for their honor—their courage. ■

8. The August 28, 1963 March on Washington, which had originated in the minds of black leaders as a protest against the federal government's relative disinterest in the economic plight of black Americans, was transformed by the time of its occurrence into a rally of support for the civil rights legislation President Kennedy had sent to the Congress after his televised speech of June 11.

SNCC Chairman John Lewis, however, in the advance text of his prepared remarks for the march's climactic rally at the Lincoln Memorial, strongly dissented from any endorsement of the Kennedy administration's new stance towards civil rights in the wake of Birmingham. Calling the president's legislative package "too little, and too late," Lewis harshly condemned both the Democratic and Republican parties' toleration of extreme segregationists in their ranks and pointed out that the Kennedy Justice Department which had failed to intervene in several instances of white brutality against Albany civil rights activists, nonetheless had found the time to indict nine Albany Movement workers on federal criminal charges for picketing a grocery store whose owner had served on a federal grand jury.

Last minute pressure from other civil rights leaders reluctantly convinced Lewis to tone down several of the strongest statements in his text; this excerpt from his *original* version, however, strongly reveals how for SNCC, the federal government's ambivalent support of civil rights in the south was increasing its distaste and distrust for the nation's political leaders.

From: Original text of speech by John Lewis, SNCC Chairman, that was altered before delivery at the Lincoln Memorial during the March on Washington, August 28, 1963.

We march today for jobs and freedom, but we have nothing to be proud of. For hundreds and thousands of our brothers are not here. They have no money for their transportation, for they are receiving starvation wages . . . or no wages, at all.

In good conscience, we cannot support the administration's civil rights bill, for it is too little, and too late. There's not one thing in the bill that will protect our people from police brutality.

This bill will not protect young children and old women from police dogs and fire hoses, [from] engaging in peaceful demonstrations. . . .

The voting section of this bill will not help thousands of black citizens who want to vote. It will not help the citizens of Mississippi, of Alabama, and Georgia, who are qualified to vote, but lack a 6th Grade education. "One man, one vote," is the African cry. It is ours, too. (It must be ours.)

* * * *

We are now involved in . . . revolution. This nation is still a place of cheap
political leaders who build their careers on immoral compromise and ally

themselves with open forms of political, economic and social exploitation. What political leader here can stand up and say, "My party is the party of principles"? The party of Kennedy is also the party of Eastland. The party of Javits is also the party of Goldwater. Where is *our* party?

In some parts of the South we work in the fields from sun-up to sun-down for $12 a week. In Albany, Georgia, nine of our leaders have been indicted not by Dixiecrats but by the Federal Government for peaceful protest. But what did the Federal Government do when Albany's Deputy Sheriff beat Attorney C.B. King and left him half dead? What did the Federal Government do when local police officials kicked and assaulted the pregnant wife of Slater King, and she lost her baby?

It seems to me that the Albany indictment is part of a conspiracy on the part of the Federal Government and local politicians in the interest of expediency.

I want to know, which side is the Federal Government on?

The revolution is at hand, and we must free ourselves of the chains of political and economic slavery. The non-violent revolution is saying, "We will not wait for the courts to act, for we have been waiting for hundreds of years. We will not wait for the President, the Justice Department, nor Congress, but we will take matters into our own hands and create a source of power, outside any national structure that could and would assure us a victory." To those who have said, "Be Patient and Wait," we must say that, "Patience is a dirty and nasty word." We cannot be patient, we do not want to be free gradually, we want our freedom, and we want it now. We cannot depend on any political party, for both the Democrats and the Republicans have betrayed the basic principles of the Declaration of Independence.

We all recognize the fact that if any radical social, political and economic changes are to take place in our society, the people, the masses, must bring them about. In the struggle we must seek more than civil rights; we must work for the community of love, peace and true brotherhood. Our minds, souls, and hearts cannot rest until freedom and justice exist for *all the people*.

The revolution is a serious one. Mr. Kennedy is trying to take the revolution out of the street and put it in the courts. Listen, Mr. Kennedy, Listen Mr. Congressman, listen fellow citizens, the black masses are on the march for jobs and freedom, and we must say to the politicians that there won't be a "cooling-off" period.

* * * *

We won't stop now. All of the forces of Eastland, Barnett, Wallace, and Thurmond won't stop this revolution. The time will come when we will not confine our marching to Washington. We will march through the South, through the Heart of Dixie, the way Sherman did. We shall pursue our own "scorched earth" policy and burn Jim Crow to the ground—nonviolently. We shall fragment the South into a thousand pieces and put them back together in the image of democracy. We will make the action of the past few months look petty. And I say to you, WAKE UP AMERICA! ■

QUESTIONS FOR REVIEW

1.   How and why did SNCC play a crucial role in stimulating new levels of civil rights activism in many southern locales?

2.   What prompted the emergence of Albany, Georgia as America's leading site of civil rights activism in 1961–1962?

3.   Upon what motivations, strengths, and resources could local level civil rights activists such as the Albany Movement draw?

4.   How did white Albany, both its public officials and its business leaders, respond to blacks' demands for desegregation of local facilities?

5.   How did the news media and the Kennedy administration each respond to the Albany demonstrations?

6.   What attractions and advantages did Birmingham, Alabama offer to Martin Luther King, Jr. and the SCLC as the next major site for civil rights protests in the wake of the Albany campaign?

7.   Why was national media attention so crucial a factor in King's hopes for how the Birmingham protests would develop?

8.   What conclusions can be drawn from the federal government's response to the Albany and Birmingham campaigns?

9.   How did the 1963 March on Washington develop to the point where SNCC chairman John Lewis' proposed speech was significantly altered by pressure from his leadership colleagues?

10.   How did the Kennedys respond to civil rights activities in Albany and Birmingham?

ADDITIONAL RECOMMENDED READINGS

Forman, James. *The Making of Black Revolutionaries*. New York: Macmillan, 1972. An impassioned and extremely insightful account of Forman's own involvement in the movement when he was SNCC's executive secretary from 1961–1966.

Garrow, David J. *Bearing the Cross: Martin Luther King, Jr., and the Southern Christian Leadership Conference*. New York: William Morrow & Co., 1986. The most comprehensive study of Dr. King's role in the civil rights movement, including the Albany and Birmingham campaigns.

Navasky, Victor S. *Kennedy Justice*. New York: Atheneum, 1971. An influential early critique of the Kennedy administration's stance towards the civil rights movement.

Watter, Pat. *Down to Now: Reflections on the Southern Civil Rights Movement*. New York: Pantheon, 1971. An emotionally evocative account of the Albany Movement and the movement's spiritual evolution.

CHAPTER 6   MISSISSIPPI: IS THIS AMERICA? (1962–1964)

by CLAYBORNE CARSON

RELATED MEDIA:
EYES ON THE PRIZE
Television Program 5
"Mississippi: Is This
America?"

—Concentrates on the voting rights campaign in Mississippi

—Analyzes factors that led to an increased black and white activism in the deep south during this period and discusses the factors involved in ordinary citizens taking extraordinary personal risks and responsibility for social change

—Discusses the process of enfranchisement for black citizens in the south and describes the nature of white resistance to the sharing of political power in Mississippi

—Identifies Medgar Evers, Robert Moses, and Fannie Lou Hamer and describes their roles in the voting rights campaign

—Describes the involvement of the National Association for the Advancement of Colored People (NAACP), the Southern Christian Leadership Conference (SCLC), the Student Nonviolent Coordinating Committee (SNCC), and the Council of Federated Organizations (COFO) with respect to the voting rights campaign in Mississippi

—Dissects the various positions and involvement of the Kennedy and Johnson administrations in Mississippi during this period

OVERVIEW

Many student activists saw Mississippi as the stronghold of segregation and thus the ultimate testing ground for their idealism and commitment. The freedom riders who spent much of the summer of 1961 in Mississippi jails were the first wave of activists who entered the Mississippi movement, but the most determined assault came from Student Nonviolent Coordinating Committee (SNCC) "field secretaries" who first arrived late in the summer to establish a beachhead in McComb. The director of SNCC's project in McComb was Robert Moses, a school teacher from Harlem who had attended graduate school at Harvard. Influenced by Ella Baker's belief in group leadership, Moses established a model for community organization that would be followed in other communities. Stressing the need to work with local black leaders, Moses played down his own leadership role and sought to build the confidence of black residents who would carry on the struggle after SNCC had left. Moses later guided the voting rights campaign of the statewide Council of Federated Organizations (COFO), but he continued to emphasize the need for Mississippi residents to lead the suffrage effort and to see his role as a catalyst for the development of indigenous leadership.

Moses encouraged the emergence of a confident, resilient group of black leaders in Mississippi, but white resistance remained strong, and few blacks were added to the voter rolls. Indeed, antiblack violence, such as the killing of Herbert Lee in 1961, received little attention outside the state, and civil rights workers' calls for federal protection were largely ignored during the early 1960s. In 1963, the continuing violence and intimidation, as well as the assassination in Jackson of National Association for the Advancement of Colored People (NAACP) field secretary Medgar Evers, led Moses to rethink his initial opposition to the use of white student volunteers from outside the state. Recognizing that northern public opinion was not much affected by violence against Mississippi blacks, he surmised that the presence of white students might provide a protective shield against the more blatant acts of racial intimidation.

Moses followed the suggestion of white lawyer and activist Allard Lowenstein and, in the fall of 1963, planned a mock election similar to a black protest vote which Lowenstein had observed in South Africa. Lowenstein recruited white students, mostly from Stanford and Yale, to assist the effort, which would demonstrate the desire of blacks to vote. The mock election was considered a success, because over 80,000 blacks participated and attacks against civil rights workers decreased. Local blacks gained confidence, and Moses immediately began considering the idea of bringing a larger number of whites to the state during the following summer. He and other SNCC workers felt that the large-scale involvement of whites from prominent northern colleges and families would restrain white violence or perhaps, if violence occurred, provide a confrontation between federal and state authorities. Many black organizers on the COFO staff resisted the plan to use large numbers of whites, however, believing that it would hamper their long-term effort to build self-confident local black leadership. Despite this opposition, COFO voted to support a major project that would bring as many as a thousand volunteers to the state during the summer of 1964.

The 1964 Summer Project succeeded in greatly increasing national awareness of the extent of racial oppression in Mississippi, but it also exposed serious internal tensions in the movement to achieve civil rights reforms. Even as volunteers were arriving in the state in June, they learned that three civil rights workers—two whites, Andrew Goodman and Michael Schwerner, and a black, James Chaney—were missing after being released from the Philadelphia, Mississippi jail. They had gone to nearby Meridian to investigate a church bombing. The killings led to a massive investigation by the FBI, which had responded unenthusiastically to previous SNCC requests to investigate attacks on black Mississippians. Following a massive search involving military personnel, the bodies of the three men were found buried in an earthen dam. Months later, a group of whites that included police officials were implicated in the murders. They were eventually convicted of interfering with the civil rights of the victims.

The Summer Project, which continued despite the disappearance of the three workers, brought accomplishments and disappointments. Volunteers and COFO workers gained extensive experience in community organizing and in developing black-controlled institutions. Among the most successful aspects of the project were the "freedom schools," which used innovative teaching techniques to improve the academic and political skills of black children—and some adults—and to enhance their knowledge of Afro-American history. Both teachers and students alike were positively influenced by this unique educational experience, which inspired the subsequent free schools movement in the urban north.

Another important aspect of the Summer Project was the development of the Mississippi Freedom Democratic Party (MFDP), a political organization intended to challenge the legitimacy of the regular, all-white Mississippi delegation to the Democratic convention in Atlantic City, held in August 1964. The MFDP hoped to unseat the regulars by affirming its loyalty to the expressed principles of the national party and proclaiming its support of the reelection of President Lyndon B. Johnson. Despite MFDP's adherence to state regulations and its considerable support among northern delegates at the convention, the challenge did not succeed. The MFDP delegation voted to reject a compromise offered by Democratic leaders, who proposed that the challengers accept two at-large seats rather than the full recognition they sought.

The rejection of the compromise was a major turning point in the history of the southern black movement. It strengthened the belief of some activists that the Summer Project had been an unsuccessful experiment. Bitterness over the outcome of that convention challenge exacerbated

many of the racial tensions that had festered during the summer's unprecedented interactions between black activists and white volunteers in Mississippi. Many black organizers in SNCC became increasingly dubious about
the merits of interracialism as a strategy of black advancement and more
determined to seek fundamental social change rather than merely civil
rights legislation. The fall of 1964 was a period of reassessment for SNCC
and other civil rights organizations, and the ideological ferment that occurred during the period provided hints of the ideological debates that
dominated the late 1960s.

The struggle in Mississippi had brought black residents closer to the
goal of voting rights, but, like other social movements, new objectives and
concerns had emerged in the process of pursuing initial goals. After the
summer, organizers confronted the vexing question of whether it was
possible to alter the basic living conditions of poor blacks through traditional political processes or whether it was necessary to build new black-
controlled institutions. They also critically examined their tactics, political
assumptions, and organizing techniques to insure that they were consistent
with their desire to build new bases of black power rather than be forever
dependent upon the goodwill of white liberals. As white volunteers returned from a summer in Mississippi with greater militancy and distrust of
white-controlled institutions, many black organizers began to move in a
separatist direction, building black-controlled institutions, such as the
Lowndes County Freedom Organization (LCFO) in Alabama—better
known as the Black Panther Party. The struggle to achieve the vote for black
Mississippi provided a stimulus for subsequent movements to achieve a
fundamental transformation of American society.

READINGS

1. The struggle to gain the vote for black Mississippians began long before the arrival of
outside student activists. During the 1950s, NAACP members in the state
had faced fierce opposition to their efforts to encourage black voter registration, and in 1955, Rev. George Lee had been ambushed and killed after
protesting against black disenfranchisement. Among these early pioneers
was Amzie Moore, a World War II veteran who, after the war, organized
blacks to resist a series of racist killings designed to insure that returning
black soldiers did not disrupt the "southern way of life." In 1960, Moore

invited Robert Moses to bring students to the state in order to launch a voting rights campaign, and in 1961 Moses returned to work in McComb, Mississippi, where he worked with another local NAACP leader, C.C. Bryant. In the following selection, Moses describes the difficult process of launching a black movement in the most politically repressive of the southern states.

From: "Mississippi: 1961–1962" by Robert Moses, *Liberation*, 14 (January 1970). Used by permission of Robert Moses.

. . . I first came South July, 1960 on a field trip for SNCC, went through Alabama, Mississippi and Louisiana gathering people to go to the October conference. That was the first time that I met Amzie Moore. At that time we sat down and planned the voter registration drive for Mississippi. I returned in the summer of 1961 to start that drive. We were to start in Cleveland, Mississippi in the delta. However, we couldn't; we didn't have any equipment; we didn't even have a place at that time to meet. So we went down to McComb at the invitation of C.C. Bryant who was the local head of the NAACP. And we began setting up a voter registration drive in McComb, Mississippi.

What did we do? Well, for two weeks I did nothing but drive around the town talking to the business leaders, the ministers, the people in the town, asking them if they would support ten students who had come in to work on a voter registration drive. We got a commitment from them to support students for the month of August and to pay for their room and board and some of their transportation while they were there. . . . This means that we went around house-to-house, door-to-door in the hot sun everyday because the most important thing was to convince the local townspeople that . . . we were people who were responsible. What do you tell somebody when you go to their door? Well, first you tell them who you are, what you're trying to do, that you're working on voter registration. You have a form that you try to get them to fill out. . . .

Now we did this for about two weeks and finally began to get results. That is, people began to go down to Magnolia, Mississippi which is the county seat of Pike County and attempt to register. In the meantime, quite naturally, people from Amite and Walthall County, which are the two adjacent counties to Pike County, came over asking us if we wouldn't accompany them in schools in their counties so they could go down and try to register also. And this point should be made quite clear, because many people have been critical of going into such tough counties so early in the game. . . . The problem is that you can't be in the position of turning down the tough areas because the people then, I think, would simply lose confidence in you; so, we accepted this. . . .

* * * *

. . . we planned to make another registration attempt on the 19th of August. . . . This was the day then that Curtis Dawson and Preacher Knox and I were to go down and try to register. This was the day that Curtis Dawson drove to Steptoe's, picked me up and drove down to Liberty and we were to meet Knox at the courthouse lawn, and instead we were to walk through the town and on the way back were accosted by Billy Jack Caston and some other boys. I was severely beaten. I remember very sharply that I didn't want to go immediately back into McComb beause my shirt was very bloody and I figured that if we went back in we would probably be fighting everybody. So, instead, we went back out to Steptoe's where we washed down before we came back into McComb.

Well, that very same day, they had had the first sit-in in McComb, so when we got back everybody was excited and a mass meeting was planned for that very night. And Hoplis and Curtis had sat down in the Woolworth lunch counter in McComb and the town was in a big uproar. We had a mass meeting that night and made plans for two things: one, the kids made plans to continue their sit-in activity, and two, we made plans to go back down to Liberty to try to register some more. We felt it was extremely important that we try and go back to town immediately so the people in that county wouldn't feel that we had been frightened off by the beating and before they could get a chance there to rally their forces.

Accordingly, on Thursday, August 31, there was more activity in Liberty and McComb. In McComb, there were more sit-ins, in Liberty, another registration attempt coupled with an attempt by us to find the person who had done the beating and have his trial. Well, it turned out that we did find him, that they did have his trial, that they had a six-man Justice of the Peace jury, that in a twinkling of an eye the courthouse was packed. That is, the trial was scheduled that day and in two hours it began and in those two hours farmers came in from all parts of the county bearing their guns, sitting in the courthouse. We were advised not to sit in the courthouse except while we testified, otherwise we were in the back room. After we testified, the sheriff came back and told us that he didn't think it was safe for us to remain there while the jury gave its decision. Accordingly, he escorted us to the county line. We read in the papers the next day that Billy Jack Caston had been acquitted.

* * * *

To top it all off, the next week John Hardy was arrested and put in jail in Walthall County. He had been working there for two weeks and they had been taking people down, and finally one day he had taken some people down to the registrar's office, had walked in, they had been refused the right to register, and he had asked the registrar why. The registrar recognized him, took the gun out of his drawer and smacked John on the side of his head with a pistol. John staggered out onto the street and was walking down the street when he was accosted by the sheriff who arrested him and charged him with disturbing the peace. . . .

. . . A couple of days before John Hardy was arrested, we had gone back into Amite County to Liberty. This time I was not beaten, but Travis Britt was. I think that was on the 5th of September, and I stood by and watched Travis get pummeled by an old man, tall, reedy and thin, very, very, very mean with a lot of hatred in him. . . . At that particular occasion, Travis and I had been sitting out front of the courthouse and then decided to move around back because the people began to gather out front. Finally, everybody, about 15 people, gathered around back and began questioning Travis and myself. . . . They were asking him where he was from and how come a nigger from New York City could think that he could come down and teach people down here how to register to vote and have all those problems up there in New York City, problems of white girls going with nigger boys and all such like that. . . . Well, the Travis Britt incident followed by the John Hardy incident in Walthall County just about cleaned us out. The farmers in both those counties were no longer willing to go down; people in Pike County and McComb were in an uproar over the sit-in demonstrations and the fact that Brenda Travis, a sixteen-year-old girl, was in jail, and for the rest of the month of September we just had a tough time. Wasn't much we could do. The kids were in jail; people were in jail on the sit-in charges, had a $5,000 bail over their heads, and the problem was to raise that money and get them out of jail, and then sit down and see if we couldn't collect the pieces together.

Well, we got through September aided in great measure by some of the lawyers from the Justice Department who finally began to come in investigating the voting complaints. They stayed in for about a two-week period and while they were there they gave a lot of support and confidence to the people of the Negro community and allowed us to go back into Walthall and Amite Counties and to interview all the people who had been involved in the voter registration campaign and raise some hope that perhaps something would be done.

And then, finally, the boom lowered, on September 31: Herbert Lee was killed in Amite County. . . . The Sunday before Lee was killed, I was down at Steptoe's with John Doar from the Justice Department and he asked Steptoe was there any danger in that area, who was causing the trouble and who were the people in danger. Steptoe had told him that E.H. Hearst who lived across from him had been threatening people and that specifically he, Steptoe, Herbert Lee and George Reese were in danger of losing their lives. We went out, but didn't see Lee that afternoon. At night John Doar and the other lawyers from the Justice Department left. The following morning about 12 noon, Doc Anderson came by the Voter Registration office and said a man had been shot in Amite County. . . . I went down to take a look at the body and it was Herbert Lee; there was a bullet hole in the left side of his head just above the ear. . . .

Our first job was to try to track down those people . . . who had been at the shooting, who had seen the whole incident. . . . Essentially, the story was this: they were standing at the cotton gin early in the morning and they saw Herbert Lee drive up in his truck with a load of cotton, E.H. Hearst following behind him in an empty truck. Hearst got out of his truck and came to the cab on the driver's side of Lee's truck and began arguing with Lee. He began gesticulating towards Lee and pulled out a gun which he had under his shirt and began threatening Lee with it. One of the people that was close by said that Hearst was telling Lee, "I'm not fooling around this time, I really mean business," and that Lee told him, "Put the gun down. I won't talk to you unless you put the gun down." Hearst put the gun back under his coat and then Lee slid out on the other side, on the offside of the cab. As he got out, Hearst ran around the front of the cab, took his gun out again, pointed it at Lee and shot him. . . . Hearst was acquitted. He never spent a moment in jail. In fact, the sheriff had whisked him away very shortly after the crime was committed. I remember reading very bitterly in the papers the next morning, a little short article on the front page of the *McComb Enterprise Journal*, said that the Negro had been shot in self-defense as he was trying to attack E.H. Hearst. That was it. You might have thought he had been a bum.

There was not mention that Lee was a farmer, that he had a family, that he had nine kids, beautiful kids, that he had been a farmer all his life in Amite County and that he had been a very substantial citizen. It was as if he had been drunk or something and had gotten into [a] fight and gotten shot. . . . Now we knew in our hearts and minds that Hearst was attacking Lee because of the voter registration drive, and I suppose that we all felt guilty and felt responsible, because it's one thing to get beat up and it's another thing to be responsible, or to participate in some way in a killing. . . .

* * * *

Shortly after Lee was killed, the kids were released from jail who had been in jail for a month on the sit-in cases, including Brenda. Brenda was not allowed to go back in the school and in early October she and 115 students marched out and marched downtown. It's no doubt in my mind that part of the reason for the march, part of the reason for the willingness of so many students to do it, was the whole series of beatings culminating in the killing that had taken place in that area. Well, needless to say, the white community was completely on edge by this time. 115 students stopped in front of the city hall to begin praying one by one, Brenda first, then Curtis, then Hollis, then Bobby Talbort and then finally all of us herded up the steps and into the city courthouse, and Bob Zellner, who was the only white participant, was attacked on the steps as he went up and then the mob outside, waiting, milling around, threatening, and inside, the police brought the people down, the white people, the so-called good citizens of the town, to come down and take a look at this Moses guy, and they would come down and stand at the front of the jail and say, "Where's Moses?". . .

We were finally taken up one by one into a kind of kangaroo court which they held upstairs which was crowded with citizens from the town: the sheriff, the local county attorney, the local judges. . . . Well, they let all the kids who were under 18 off, and took those who were over 18 down to the county jail and we stayed in jail for several days. . . .

We were let out a few days later on a bail bond, and swept back into the problems in McComb where the balance of the hundred students who had marched out were now being required to fill out a slip saying that they would not participate in any more demonstrations in order to get back in the school. Most of them were refusing to do so, and the community was again in an uproar. . . . We finally decided to set up make-shift classes for them. We opened up Nonviolent High in McComb. That was pretty funny. We had about fifty to seventy-five kids in a large room trying to break them down with the elements of algebra and geometry, a little English, and even a little French, a little history, I think Deon taught physics and chemistry, and [Charles] McDew took charge of history, and I did something with math. . . . And we carried on our classes for a week or two weeks, until finally we got word from Campbell College in Jackson that they would accept them all and that they would make provisions for them immediately. . . .

* * * *

Well, we spent most of the month of November and on into December in jail; we . . . then regrouped to decide what could be done and what projects we needed to carry out next, how we could pick up the pieces. We had, to put it mildly, got our feet wet. We now knew something of what it took to run a voter registration campaign in Mississippi; we knew some of the obstacles we would have to face; we had some general idea of what had to be done to get such a campaign started. First there were very few agencies available in the Negro community that could act as a vehicle for any sort of campaign. The Negro churches could not in general be counted on; the Negro business leaders could also not in general be counted on except for under-the-cover help; and, in general, anybody who had a specific economic tie-in with the white community could not be counted on when the pressure got hot. Therefore, our feeling was that the only way to run this campaign was to begin to build a group of young people who would not be responsible economically to any sector of the white community and who would be able to act as free agents. And we began to set about doing this. . . . ∎

2. **T**he goal of the civil rights activists who went to Mississippi was to mobilize black residents who had spent all their lives in the state. Many of these residents had been poorly educated in the state's segregated and poorly funded public education system and were intimidated by the almost unlimited power that white people had over their lives. In the state where Emmett Till had been lynched, enormous courage was required to attempt to register to vote. Successful organizers in SNCC, the Congress of Racial Equality (CORE), and other groups worked diligently and patiently to gain the confidence of black residents and then to instill in those residents the necessary confidence to lead their own struggle for equal rights and political power. In the following selection, Mrs. Fannie Lou Hamer describes the experiences that suddenly and unexpectedly brought her into the Mississippi movement and subsequently transformed her into a confident and effective leader.

From: To Praise Our Bridges: An Autobiography of Mrs. Fanny Lou Hamer (Jackson: KIPCO, 1967), pages 5–17. Used by permission of Arybie Rose, Fannie Lou Hamer Living Memorial Charitable Trust Fund, and the Hamer family.

I was born October sixth, nineteen and seventeen in Montgomery County, Mississippi. My parents moved to Sunflower County when I was two years old, to a plantation about four and a half miles from here, Mr. E.W. Brandon's plantation.

. . . My parents were sharecroppers and they had a big family. Twenty children. Fourteen boys and six girls. I'm the twentieth child. All of us worked in the fields, of course, but we never did get anything out of sharecropping. . . .

* * * *

My life has been almost like my mother's was, because I married a man who sharecropped. We didn't have it easy and the only way we could ever make it through the winter was because Pap had a little juke joint and we made liquor. That was the only way we made it. I married in 1944 and stayed on the plantation until 1962 when I went down to the courthouse in Indianola to register to vote. That happened because I went to a mass meeting one night.

Until then I'd never heard of no mass meeting and I didn't know that a Negro could register and vote. Bob Moses, Reggie Robinson, Jim Bevel and James Forman were some of the SNCC workers who ran that meeting. When they asked for those to raise their hands who'd go down to the courthouse the next day, I raised mine. Had it up as high as I could get it. I guess if I'd had any sense I'd a-been a little scared, but what was the point of being scared. The only thing they could do to me was kill me and it seemed like they'd been trying to do that a little bit at a time ever since I could remember.

* * * *

Well, there was eighteen of us who went down to the courthouse that day and all of us were arrested. Police said the bus was painted the wrong color—said it was too yellow. After I got bailed out I went back to the plantation where Pap and I had lived for eighteen years. My oldest girl met me and told me that Mr. Marlow, the plantation owner, was mad and raising sand. He had heard that I had tried to register. That night he called on us and said, "We're not going to have this in Mississippi and you will have to withdraw. I am looking for your answer, yea or nay?" I just looked. He said "I will give you until tomorrow morning. And if you don't withdraw you will have to leave. If you do go withdraw, it's only how I feel, you might still have to leave." So I left that same night. Pap had to stay on till work on the plantation was through. Ten days later they fired into Mrs. Tucker's house where I was staying. They also shot two girls at Mr. Sissel's.

That was a rough winter. I hadn't a chance to do any canning before I got kicked off, so didn't have hardly anything. I always can more than my family can use 'cause there's always people who don't have enough. That winter was bad, though. Pap couldn't get a job nowhere 'cause everybody knew he was my husband. We made it on through, though, and since then I just been trying to work and get our people organized.

I reckon the most horrible experience I've had was in June of 1963. I was arrested along with several others in Winona, Mississippi. That's in Montgomery County, the county where I was born. I was carried to a cell and locked up with Euvester Simpson. I began to hear the sound of licks, and I could hear people screaming. . . .

After then, the State Highway patrolmen came and carried me out of the cell into another cell where there were two Negro prisoners. The patrolman gave the first Negro a long blackjack that was heavy. It was loaded with something and they had me lay down on the bunk with my face down, and I was beat. I was beat by the first Negro till he gave out. Then the patrolman ordered the other man to take the blackjack and he began to beat. . . .

. . . After I got out of jail, half dead, I found out that Medgar Evers had been shot down in his own yard.

* * * *

I've worked on voter registration here ever since I went to that first mass meeting. In 1964 we registered 63,000 black people from Mississippi into the Freedom Democratic Party. We formed our own party because the whites wouldn't even let us register. We decided to challenge the white Mississippi Democratic Party at the National Convention. We followed all the laws that the white people themselves made. We tried to attend the precinct meetings and they locked the doors on us or moved the meetings and that's against the laws they made for their ownselves. So we were the ones that held the real precinct meetings. At all these meetings across the state we elected our representatives to go to the National Democratic Convention in Atlantic City. But we learned the hard way that even though we had all the law and all the righteousness on our side—that white man is not going to give up his power to us.

We have to build our own power. We have to win every single political office we can, where we have a majority of black people. . . .

* * * *

The question for black people is not, when is the white man going to give us our rights, or when is he going to give us good education for our children, or when is he going to give us jobs—if the white man gives you anything—just remember when he gets ready he will take it right back. We have to take for ourselves. ∎

3. **T**he kinds of harassment suffered by Mrs. **Hamer received little national attention, and voting rights workers became increasingly angry about the failure of the federal government to protect them or the local blacks who assisted the movement. The 1963 report of the United States Commission on Civil Rights was important in the process of publicizing the extent of racial repression in Mississippi. The Commission called upon President Lyndon B. Johnson to study the possibility of legislation that would deny federal funds to any state, such as Mississippi, that failed to comply with the Constitution and federal laws regarding civil rights.**

From: Interim Report of the United States Commission on Civil Rights, April 16, 1963, pages 1–3.

Since October 1962, the open and flagrant violation of constitutional guarantees in Mississippi has precipitated serious conflict which, on several occasions, has reached the point of crisis. The United States Commission on Civil Rights has become increasingly alarmed at the defiance of the Constitution. Each week brings fresh evidence of the danger of a complete breakdown of law and order.

Citizens of the United States have been shot, set upon by vicious dogs, beaten and otherwise terrorized because they sought to vote. Since October, students have been fired upon, ministers have been assaulted and the home of the Vice Chairman of the State Advisory Committee of this Commission has been bombed. Another member and his wife were jailed on trumped up charges after their home had been defiled. Even children, at the brink of starvation, have been deprived of assistance by the callous and discriminatory acts of Mississippi officials administering Federal funds.

All this affronts the conscience of the Nation.

* * * *

The Commission notes the action taken by the President of the United States in employing the force necessary to assure compliance with the court decrees in the University of Mississippi case. It is mindful of the unequivocal public statements of the President expressing his belief that discriminatory practices are morally wrong. The Commission, nevertheless, believes that the President should, consistent with his Constitutional and statutory authority, employ to the fullest the legal and moral powers of his office to the end that American citizenship will not continue to be degraded in Mississippi. ■

4. The Summer Project of 1964 was a major test of interracialism in the southern struggle, for it led to an unprecedented degree of involvement by white activists in Mississippi black communities. From the time when the summer volunteers first arrived in the state, they encountered a variety of responses from black movement veterans and local residents, ranging from gratitude to suspicion to open resentment. Sally Belfrage's account of the initial orientation sessions in Oxford, Ohio reveal the racial tensions that would become increasingly evident during the course of the summer. Her subsequent experiences in Greenwood, Mississippi suggest some of the difficulties faced by white activists who sought to understand as well as assist an increasingly complex black movement.

From: *Freedom Summer* by Sally Belfrage (New York: Viking/Penguin, 1965), pages 80–81, 170–177. Copyright 1965 by Sally Belfrage. Used by permission of Viking/Penguin, Inc.

In describing the then Chairman of SNCC, with whom he was sharing a Mississippi jail cell, Bob Moses wrote in 1961 that "McDew . . . has taken on the deep hates and deep loves which America, and the world, reserve for those who dare to stand in a strong sun and cast a sharp shadow." This could as well describe many SNCC Negroes, whose deep hates and loves were often translated into simple whites and blacks. They were automatically suspicious of us, the white volunteers; throughout the summer they put us to the test, and few, if any, could pass. Implicit in all the songs, tears, speeches, work, laughter, was the knowledge secure in both them and us that ultimately we could return to a white refuge.

* * * *

. . . But we didn't *have* to come, did we? We could have stayed at home and gone to the beach, or earned the money we so badly needed for next semester at old Northern White. And here we are: We Came. Among all the millions who could have realized their responsibility to this revolution, we alone came. Few Northern Negroes even came. We came. Don't we earn some recognition, if not praise? *I want to be your friend, you black idiot*, was the contradiction evident everywhere.

SNCC is not populated with Toms who would wish to be white . . . who fill closets with bleaches and straighteners, who lead compromise existences between reality and illusion. They accept their color and are engaged in working out its destiny. To bend to us was to corrupt the purity of their goal. . . .

* * * *

It was the policy of the Summer Project to limit its activities this side of the Civil Rights Act, and not to engage in testing the law or desegregating public facilities. . . . There were people in Greenwood, however, particularly young admirers of Silas McGhee, who were quite unmoved by the idea of registering voters. The bill had been passed, and they wanted to see it work. Without COFO help or supervision, teenagers began to make forays over the tracks on their own. As the weeks passed, their frustration fed on itself, white outrage increased, and violence rose nearer to the surface daily.

Meanwhile, Silas and Jake [McGhee] kept going to the movies. On July 25 their house was shot into; on July 26 they went to the Leflore Theater. They had been joined near the end of the month by their elder half-brother Clarence Robinson, a six-foot-six paratrooper (again on furlough and still out on bail). Clarence had a thirty-six-inch reach and a 136 I.Q., and his Army hat was reinforced with a silver dollar sewn under the emblem: picked on in a bar once, he had swung the hat and downed two men. He walked down the street in his uniform like Wild Bill Hickok on the way to a duel, cool, tough, infinitely menacing.

He spoke at a mass meeting one night, using his voice as he used his body, with precision and power. "When I went in the Army in April of 1952, I raised my right hand and they told me that I was fighting for my country and my brothers, my sisters, my mother, and my fellow man. And after approximately four months of basic training to teach me how to fight, they sent me to Korea. Now when I come back here and try to go to the Leflore Theater, me and my two brothers, when I got ready to leave, there was a whole *mob* out there. . . ."

* * * *

". . . We walked to this car. I opened the rear door, let my two brothers in, and I stood outside for approximately thirty seconds looking around. Nobody threw a brick at me. They could have, they could have knocked my brains out. I'm the same as anybody else, I can be killed, very easy. But they didn't do it. Why? Because I showed that I didn't mind being hit. That if I could get the man that wants to hit me within my thirty-six-inch *reach* [he demonstrated], I'll prove to him that I'm a better man than he is. We left from the theater, because there were incidents. When you go to the theater you've got to expect incidents. Why? Because the white man is scared of you!"

The "incidents" had been reported to the national SNCC office as they occurred, and most of the mass meeting audience already knew what had happened. The brothers had seen the movie in peace that night—largely because those who objected to their presence inside were on the picket line outside. But when the movie finished there were nearly two hundred whites waiting for them in the street. The McGhees tried to call for a taxi but none would come. The manager ordered them to leave: the theater was closing. They couldn't risk walking. There was one alternative, to call the SNCC office. Two of our cars volunteered to go down to get them while the office phoned the FBI, relating the facts to local agent Schaum. Schaum, responding that the FBI would not give protection, was told that the purpose of the call was to request FBI witnesses on the scene. Schaum refused to commit himself. . . .

When the cars arrived at the Leflore from the office, the McGhees, inside in the lobby, asked two policemen on duty to escort them through the mob. The policemen took them outside; then one of them had a look at the crowd and said, "You got yourself into this, you can get yourself out." The brothers were abandoned between point one and point two.

They made their way toward the car. As they reached it, the whites began to scream at them. They managed to get inside, but the mob, cheated, closed in on them. A bottle was thrown at the rear window with such force that it broke through and sprayed the brothers with glass. Jake was hit by particles in the eye. Instead of returning to the office, they drove to the hospital, where Jake was admitted to the emergency ward.

In the office calls came in on every phone, and the staff, like synchronized parts of a machine, answered them and phoned out again. One of the two cars returned, its occupants reporting that they had been followed by a car of whites and that those at the hospital were in danger. The office sent another car to the hospital. When it arrived, Judy Richardson called in to say that they had been shot at from a roadhouse on the way, a white teen-agers' hangout. . . . At the hospital they found a throng of whites milling around, of whom at least five were seen (by Clarence, who knew such things) to be armed with .22 rifles and .38 pistols. After Jake was treated and discharged, a group trying to drive away was threatened with bricks and sticks and blocked at the exit by a car full of white men. They returned to the hospital.

* * * *

Something had to be done to avert a shooting war. The people in COFO were anxious for peace in which to conduct their work, but events were no longer in their control. The teen-agers were mesmerized by the brothers McGhee, and felt more and more uninterested in the tameness of the Freedom School, the Freedom Party: they wanted direct action. The Freedom School teachers, sensing this, invited Clarence Robinson to come to the Friendship Church to debate with Bob Zellner. The audience had defined the confrontation as "Nonviolence against Violence"; but Bob began by mentioning that he and Clarence would "just have a little discussion on the different approaches to social change." . . .

"It has been proven time and time again," Clarence said, "that when a man fights back, he is not attacked. Now, I've never been the one to start a fight. But if someone is pushing me, I have to defend myself. You got to learn to stay flexible, to fight when you have to, but *only* when you have to."

Bob's respect for Clarence was immediately apparent; he clearly didn't want to argue with him publicly. He began by quoting Gandhi: "If you can't be non-violent, be violent rather than a coward." Then: "Because we're organized we have to be nonviolent. We don't have the strength, even if we wanted to, to carry guns and fight back. We're facing organizations with more resources, more money, and with unlimited access to weapons."

Clarence: "I'm not talking about carrying guns. If everybody did that, pretty soon you'd have a revolution on your hands. And I'm not saying we should go out there and *start* a lot of violence. I'm saying that you only resort to violence after you have done everything possible to avoid it." Speaking to the children, and pointing to Bob: "This man can't go to the Leflore Theater and integrate it for you, because he's white." . . .

Bob: "There's more guts per person in the McGhees than in any other family you'll ever meet. They're trying to desegregate the Leflore and they're doing a great job. But we feel that our concentration has to be on voter registration now. Integrating all the movies in the South won't achieve anything basic."

Clarence: "You got to act in areas that people understand, not just a nebulous political argument beyond them all. This house-to-house activity is fine, but people are afraid of what they can't grasp. They never *have* voted, they don't know what it's all about. But they know they can't go to that movie. . . ."

The children broke in then. A solemn, composed girl of about sixteen raised her hand and spoke. "You say," she addressed Bob, "that we have to wait until we get the vote. But you know, by the time that happens the younger people are going to be too old to enjoy the bowling alley and the swimming pool. And the Civil Rights Act was passed this month." A little girl added, "Yeah, and do you mean we jus' s'pose to let The Man beat on our head?"

Bob: "Look, I try to be a disciplined man. That means I try to do what I say I'm goin' to do. When I joined with SNCC I said I'd behave nonviolently. I didn't say how I'd think, how I'd feel. But the reason I know I can do this, that I *can* behave nonviolently, is that I've done it. I was in McComb, Mississippi, in sixty-one. McComb is not a Freedom School or a playpen. I had eighteen men beatin' me, stompin' on me while the cops held my arms. They tried to pull my eyes out by the roots. And I was nonviolent, not only because I said I'd be, but because there were about five hundred people watching, and what am I goin' to do with five hundred people?"

Clarence: "If anyone has the guts to raise their right hand and say they'll be nonviolent, I respect that. I haven't got the guts to do that. If he's able to do this and maintain it, that's a fine thing." . . .

* * * *

. . . Clarence said that actual weapons were not the issue: "they bring trouble with the law, violations of the Sullivan Act. The point is you *got* a weapon—you got two hands and two feet, and I don't mean using them to run on. Only four people can get on a man at one time. If you bring certain death to the first *two*, then you won't have much trouble with the others. I'm just talking about if you're attacked, and you can do some damage, the next time they'll be a little more *cautious*. . . .

"Then there's this argument they're always having in the movement, you know, about what you are supposed to do if you're nonviolent and you're in a house where the man has a gun, and 'letting him do the dirty work' if you're attacked, and should he have that gun at all if you're involved. Well, all I'm saying is that in a case like that, I'm not doing your dirty work for you; I'm defending *my* right to have whom *I* want in *my* house."

Bob: "I agree. I don't see where you get off tellin' somebody else to be non-violent because you are." And he wanted to clear a few things up. "The way I am, I'd flatten anybody who came at me on the street. But when you're pledged to the discipline of a mass movement, you got to behave as you promised."

The children sat digesting it all for a while, then the same girl who had spoken before raised her hand and Bob recognized her. "How is it," she asked, "that SNCC has moved from a militant position to a rather subdued one?"

There was a little coughing. Bob said, "It depends on your definition of the word 'militant.' This is a policy worked out by the most militant people in the South today. As far as we're concerned, we're doing one of the most militant things anybody could be doing: building a new political structure." ■

5. The culmination of Mississippi Freedom Summer came in August when the Freedom Democratic Party tried to gain recognition as Mississippi's official delegation to the 1964 Democratic National Convention in Atlantic City. The MFDP effort to challenge the seating of the all-white "regular" delegation pitted the COFO-SNCC activists and the MFDP delegates against powerful Democratic politicians who wanted to avoid controversies that would undermine Lyndon Johnson's southern support in the coming campaign against Republican Barry Goldwater. Johnson supporters sought a compromise that would avoid a disruptive battle at the convention, but the southern struggle had made many black activists reject the notion that compromises could be arranged by leaders working behind closed doors. SNCC leader Charles Sherrod's description of his experiences at the convention reflects the radicalization process that affected many pro-MFDP activists and reveals a widening of the split between "establishment" liberals and "radical" activists.

From: "Mississippi at Atlantic City" by Charles M. Sherrod in *Grains of Salt*, Union Theological Seminary, Vol. 18, No. 3 (October 12, 1964). Used by permission of Charles Sherrod.

It was a cool day in August beside the ocean. Atlantic City, New Jersey was waiting for the Democratic National Convention to begin. In that Republican fortress history was about to be made. High on a billboard smiling out at the breakers was a picture of Barry Goldwater and an inscription "In your heart you know he's right." Later someone had written underneath, "Yes, extreme right." Goldwater had had his "moment," two weeks before on the other ocean. This was to be L.B.J.'s "moment," and we were to find out that this was also his convention. . . .

* * * *

No one could say that we were a renegade group. We had tried to work within the structure of the state Party. In fact, we were not only trying to be included in the state Party, but we also sought to insure that the state Party would remain loyal to the candidates of the National Democratic Party in November. . . .

* * * *

. . . No one could say that we had not tried. We had no alternative but to form a State Party that would include everyone.

So sixty-eight [Freedom Democratic Party] delegates from Mississippi—black, white, maids, ministers, carpenters, farmers, painters, mechanics, schoolteachers, the young, the old—they were ordinary people but each had an extraordinary story to tell. And they could tell the story! The Saturday before the convention began, they presented their case to the Credentials Committee, and through television, to the nation and to the world. No human being confronted with the truth of our testimony could remain indifferent to it. Many tears fell. Our position was valid and our cause was just.

141

But the word had been given. The Freedom Party was to be seated without voting rights as honored guests of the Convention. The [MFD] Party caucused and rejected the proposed "compromise." The slow and now frantic machinery of the administration was grinding against itself. President Johnson had given Senator Humphrey the specific task of dealing with us. They were desperately seeking ways to seat the regular Mississippi delegation without any show of disunity. The administration needed time!

Sunday evening, there was a somewhat secret meeting held at the Deauville Hotel, for all Negro delegates. The MFDP was not invited but was there. In a small, crowded, dark room with a long table and a blackboard, some of the most prominent Negro politicians in the country gave the "word," one by one. Then an old man seated in a soft chair struggled slowly to his feet. It was the black dean of politics, Congressman Charles Dawson of Chicago.

Unsteady in his voice, he said exactly what the other "leaders" had said: (1) We must nominate and elect Lyndon B. Johnson for President in November; (2) we must register thousands of Negroes to vote; and (3) we must follow leadership—adding, "we must respect womanhood"—and sat down.

With that a little woman, dark and strong, Mrs. Annie Devine from Canton, Mississippi, standing near the front, asked to be heard. The Congressman did not deny her. She began to speak.

"We have been treated like beasts in Mississippi. They shot us down like animals." She began to rock back and forth and her voice quivered. "We risk our lives coming up here . . . politics must be corrupt if it don't care none about people down there . . . these politicians sit in positions and forget the people put them there." She went on, crying between each sentence, but right after her witness, the meeting was adjourned.

. . . Here we were in a life-death grip, wrestling with the best political strategists in the country. We needed only eleven votes for a minority report from the Credentials Committee. . . .

A compromise was suggested by [Congresswoman] Edith Green (D.-Ore.), a member of the Credentials Committee. It was acceptable to the Freedom Party and could have been the minority report: (1) Everyone would be subjected to a loyalty oath, both the Freedom Party and the Mississippi regular party; (2) Each delegate who took the oath would be seated and the votes would be divided proportionally. It was minimal; the Freedom Party would accept no less.

The administration countered with another compromise. It had five points. (1) The all-white Party would take the oath and be seated; (2) The Freedom Democratic Party would be welcomed as honored guests of the Convention; (3) Dr. Aaron Henry and Rev. Edwin King, Chairman and National Committeeman of the Freedom Democratic Party respectively, would be given delegate status in a special category of "delegates at large"; (4) The Democratic National Committee would obligate states by 1968 to select and certify delegates through a process without regard to race, creed, color or national origin; and (5) The Chairman of the National Democratic Committee would establish a special committee to aid the states in meeting standards set for the 1968 Convention. . . .

The "word" had come down for the last time. We had begun to lose support in the Credentials Committee. This came mainly as a result of a squeeze play by the administration.

It was Tuesday morning when the Freedom Democratic Party delegation was hustled to its meeting place, the Union Temple Baptist Church. You could cut through the tension; it was so apparent. People were touchy and on edge. It had been a long fight; being up day and night, running after delegations, following leads, speaking, answering politely, always aggressive, always moving. Now, one of the most important decisions of the convention had to be made.

. . . The hot day dragged on; there were speeches and speeches and talk and talk—Dr. Martin Luther King, Bayard Rustin, Senator Wayne Morse, Edith Green, Jack Pratt, James Farmer, James Forman, Ella Baker, Bob Moses. Some wanted to accept the compromise and others did not. A few remained neutral and all voiced total support whatever the ultimate decision. But time had made the decision. The day was fast spent when discussion was opened to the delegation.

The administration had succeeded in baiting us into extended discussion and this was the end. . . .

The [administration's] proposal was rejected by the Freedom Democratic Delegation; we had come through another crisis with our minds depressed and our hearts and hands unstained. Again we had not bowed to the "massa." We were asserting a moral declaration to this country that the political mind must be concerned with much more than the expedient; that there are real issues in this country's politics and "race" is one. . . .

* * * *

. . . We could have accepted the compromise, called it a victory and gone back to Mississippi, carried on the shoulders of millions of Negroes across the country as their champions. But we love the ideals of our country; they mean more than a moment of victory. We are what we are—hungry, beaten, unvictorious, jobless, homeless, but thankful to have the strength to fight. This is honesty, and we refuse to compromise here. It would have been a lie to accept that particular compromise. It would have said to blacks across the nation and the world that we share the power, and that is a lie! The "liberals" would have felt great relief for a job well done. The Democrats would have laughed again at the segregationist Republicans and smiled that their own "Negroes" were satisfied. That is a lie! We are a country of racists with a racist heritage, a racist economy, a racist language, a racist religion, a racist philosophy of living, and we need a naked confrontation with ourselves. ■

M

6. ajor ideological debates took place within SNCC and other civil rights organizations
after the summer of 1964 as movement activists attempted to assess their
accomplishments and to decide their future direction. Because SNCC workers had been the spearhead of the struggle in Mississippi, the group's
discussions were especially intense and far-reaching, at times threatening
to destroy the bonds of trust that had held SNCC together. SNCC workers
faced the enduring dilemma of social reformers who seek to improve the
lot of the less privileged without creating new sources of dependency. They
tried to identify and confront the subtle injustices and inequities that
existed within the movement as well as those imposed by white society.
During the fall of 1964, SNCC workers argued about basic issues, such as
whether whites should organize black communities, whether education
should be a criterion for holding leadership roles, and whether the elimination of sexism should be a goal of the southern struggle. Although many
of the ideas expressed in the debates after the summer were rooted in
organizing experiences, the following selections demonstrate that movement activists were increasingly open to external ideological influences. In
particular, Malcolm X's influence grew after he abandoned the apolitical
stance of Elijah Muhammad's Nation of Islam and sought alliances with the
grass-roots leadership of the southern black movement.

From: In Struggle: SNCC and the Black Awakening of the 1960s by Clayborne Carson (Cambridge: Harvard
University Press, 1981), pages 133–137. Copyright 1981 by the President and Fellows of Harvard College.
Used and abridged by permission.

During the months after the Mississippi Summer Project, SNCC's staff began to
confront the difficult task of critically examining their past work and formulat-
ing a future strategy. They had accomplished much since coming together in
McComb three years before. They had roused thousands of southern blacks to
political action and had launched new black-controlled institutions, most notably the MFDP and the freedom schools. They had created a strong base of
northern financial support, prodded the federal government to act with increasing firmness on behalf of black civil rights, and brought together a coalition of
liberal forces in support of the MFDP challenge. They had done this by developing distinctive and effective techniques of community organizing that relied on
local leadership and on the use of militancy as a catalyst for mass mobilization.

Yet many SNCC workers had begun to doubt the value of their work, and their
uneasiness grew after the summer of 1964. . . .

Retaining a common belief in sustained, militant mass struggle as the major
agent of social change, staff members nevertheless differed in their proposals for
increasing SNCC's effectiveness and broadening its range. The bonds that held
the staff together in confrontations with southern racists also began to weaken
as SNCC came into increasing conflict with former liberal supporters. Like the
rest of American society, SNCC was entering a period of divisive conflict, with

staff members becoming more aware of the varied and sometimes subtle dimensions of social oppression. . . .

Spurred by the defeat of the MFDP challenge, SNCC workers began to look beyond their own experiences for ideological insights. An unexpected turn in this search for new ideas came in the fall of 1964 when SNCC accepted the invitation of Harry Belafonte to send a delegation to Africa. Belafonte, a long-time SNCC supporter, arranged for the trip through his contacts with the government of Guinea. Although Jim Forman later concluded that it was "a serious mistake" to approve the trip before resolving questions about SNCC's direction at home, the chance to tour Africa was irresistible. SNCC workers welcomed the opportunity for a break from the pressures of their work. Moreover, they had been inspired by the example of young black leaders of newly independent African nations. On many occasions they had rhetorically linked their struggle with the African nationalist movements and had appealed to Africans for support of civil rights efforts. In December 1963 a group of staff members had met with Oginga Odinga, the Kenyan leader, on his brief stop in Atlanta.

The African tour, which began on September 11, 1964, had a profound impact on the SNCC delegation. . . . As guests of the government of Guinea, a former French colony that had determined to remain politically independent of the West, they were able to see American society from a new perspective. Guinean President Sékou Touré, a proponent of African socialism and of nonalignment in the Cold War, encouraged them to take a broad view of the goals of their struggle, stating that there was a close relationship between what SNCC did in the United States and what happened in Africa. The delegates were impressed not only by their warm reception from government officials but also by their observations of daily life in a nation dominated by blacks. "I saw black men flying the airplanes, driving buses, sitting behind big desks in the bank and just doing everything that I was used to seeing white people do," [Fannie Lou] Hamer recalled.

The SNCC representatives, in becoming aware of how their own struggle was perceived by Africans, discovered that the United States government had far more control than they over the image of the American civil rights movement in the minds of Africans. [Julian] Bond expressed dismay about the misleading information provided by American information offices in Africa. "There were all these pictures of Negroes doing things, Negro judges, Negro policemen, and if you didn't know anything about America, like Africans would not, you would think that these were really commonplace things. That's the worst kind of deceit."

After the rest of the delegation returned to the United States on October 4, [John] Lewis and [Donald] Harris continued on a month-long tour of Liberia, Ghana, Zambia, Kenya, Ethiopia, and Egypt. Their meetings with African student leaders and Afro-American expatriates convinced them that SNCC should establish permanent ties with Africans. While in Zambia for that nation's independence ceremonies, they talked with African revolutionaries who, according to their subsequent report, also "knew the insides of many jails and the loneliness of being separated from family and friends." The revolutionaries told delegates

145

that they wanted closer contacts with SNCC: "As one brother said, 'Let's join hands so we can all be free together.' "

Perhaps the most significant episode of their stay in Africa was an unexpected encounter in Nairobi with Malcolm X, the Afro-American leader who had recently broken with the narrowly religious focus of Elijah Muhammad's Nation of Islam. Even before the meeting, Lewis and Harris had learned of Malcolm's considerable influence on the African continent, for Africans occasionally greeted them with "skepticism and distrust" because, as one explained, "if you are to the right of Malcolm, you might as well start packing right now 'cause no one'll listen to you.' " Malcolm, however, had resolved to abet the radical tendencies in the civil rights movement, and was eager to meet with representatives of SNCC, his favorite civil rights organization. At the meeting he criticized American civil rights groups for neglecting African affairs, despite the fact that African leaders and citizenry themselves supported the Afro-American struggle. Although Malcolm felt that Africans would not endorse particular groups or factions, he hoped that his recently formed Organization of Afro-American Unity (OAU) would bring together American blacks who were interested in closer ties with Africa.

The Nairobi meeting was followed by a series of attempts by Malcolm to forge links with SNCC. Malcolm's Pan-African perspective and his awareness of the need for black self-defense and racial pride converged with ideas gaining acceptance in SNCC. He spoke at an MFDP rally in Harlem and invited Hamer and the SNCC Freedom Singers to appear at a meeting of the OAU. . . . In February 1965 during the voting rights campaign in Selma, Malcolm addressed black demonstrators at the invitation of SNCC activists. Then on February 21, the developing ties between SNCC and Malcolm were severed by the nationalist leader's assassination in New York. Afterward Lewis commented that Malcolm, "more than any other single personality," had been "able to articulate the aspirations, bitterness, and frustrations of the Negro people," forming "a living link between Africa and the civil rights movement in this country."

* * * *

Enthusiasm for African revolutionary ideas was soon tempered by a realization of the enormous difficulties to be faced at home. Not only were SNCC workers exhausted after the summer ordeal, but many were uncertain of their future roles in the changing southern struggle. In addition they were coming under attack from liberals who were beginning to doubt whether SNCC militants would continue to play useful roles as the shock troops of the civil rights movement or would instead become the spearhead of a new assault against conventional liberalism.

* * * *

SNCC's deteriorating relations with more moderate civil rights organizations became evident at a meeting of the different groups in New York on September 18 to discuss future strategy in Mississippi. . . . SNCC was criticized for failing to cooperate with the other national civil rights groups in supporting a compromise at the Democratic convention and for controlling the MFDP. Program Director Courtland Cox, representing SNCC while the other officers were in

Africa, defended the group by insisting that the MFDP delegates, not the COFO staff, had rejected the seating compromise. He suggested that differences among the civil rights organizations should be resolved through a "low-level meeting" involving local black leaders from Mississippi. Although Andrew Young of SCLC supported this suggestion, others argued that policy issues should be resolved by leaders at the national level. Allard Lowenstein argued for "structured democracy" rather than SNCC's "amorphous democracy." [Gloster] Current [of the NAACP], who had "been listening to people from Mississippi cry for seventeen years," felt that a high-level meeting was needed "so we can cut away the underbrush." The gathering ended without a resolution of the differences and with increased suspicion among the SNCC representatives and civil rights moderates regarding each other's motives. ■

From: "To Mississippi Youth" by Malcolm X in *Malcolm X Speaks* (New York: Grove Press, 1965), pages 143–145. Copyright by Merit Publishers. Used by permission of Pathfinder Press.

In my opinion, the greatest accomplishment that was made in the struggle of the black man in America in 1964 toward some kind of real progress was the successful linking together of our problem with the African problem, or making our problem a world problem. Because now, whenever anything happens to you in Mississippi, it's not just a case of somebody in Alabama getting indignant, or somebody in New York getting indignant. The same repercussions that you see all over the world when an imperialist or foreign power interferes in some section of Africa . . . nowadays, when something happens to black people in Mississippi, you'll see the same repercussions all over the world. I wanted to point this out to you because it is important for you to know that when you're in Mississippi, you're not alone. . . . we here in the Organization of Afro-American Unity are with the struggle in Mississippi one thousand per cent. We're with the efforts to register our people in Mississippi to vote one thousand per cent. But we do not go along with anybody telling us to help nonviolently. . . . You get freedom by letting your enemy know that you'll do anything to get your freedom; then you'll get it. It's the only way you'll get it. ■

7. **A**fter the Mississippi Summer Project, veteran civil rights leader Bayard Rustin was one of the many civil rights leaders who became concerned about the increasingly radical direction of black activism. Rustin himself had been considered a radical in his early years and had been a leading organizer of the 1963 March on Washington. He had become convinced that in order for blacks to continue advancing, they must build alliances with liberal and labor forces in the Democratic party. Recognizing the increasingly angry mood of blacks, Rustin acknowledged that future reforms would have to extend beyond the traditional objectives of interracial reform. In the following essay, however, he supported the notion that it was time to move beyond the protest politics of the southern black struggle toward more conventional political approaches involving electoral alliances with other groups.

From: "From Protest to Politics: The Future of the Civil Rights Movement" by Bayard Rustin in *Commentary* (February 1964). Copyright 1964 by Bayard Rustin. Used by permission.

. . . in Mississippi, thanks largely to the leadership of Bob Moses, a turn toward political action has been taken. More than voter registration is involved here. A conscious bid for *political power* is being made, and in the course of that effort a tactical shift is being effected: direct-action techniques are being subordinated to a strategy calling for the building of community institutions or power bases. Clearly, the implications of this shift reach far beyond Mississippi. What began as a protest movement is being challenged to translate itself into a political movement. . . .

* * * *

. . . It is now concerned not merely with removing the barriers to full *opportunity* but with achieving the fact of *equality*. From sit-ins and freedom rides we have gone into rent strikes, boycotts, community organization, and political action. As a consequence of this natural evolution, the Negro today finds himself stymied by obstacles of far greater magnitude than the legal barriers he was attacking before: automation, urban decay, *de facto* school segregation. These are problems which, while conditioned by Jim Crow, do not vanish upon its demise. They are more deeply rooted in our socio-economic order; they are the result of the total society's failure to meet not only the Negro's needs, but human needs generally.

* * * *

I believe that the Negro's struggle for equality in America is essentially revolutionary. While most Negroes—in their hearts—unquestionably seek only to enjoy the fruits of American society as it now exists, their quest cannot *objectively* be satisfied within the framework of existing political and economic relations. The young Negro who would demonstrate his way into the labor market may be motivated by a thoroughly bourgeois ambition and thoroughly "capitalist" considerations, but he will end up having to favor a great expansion of the public sector of the economy. At any rate, that is the position the movement will be forced to take as it looks at the number of jobs being generated by the private economy, and if it is to remain true to the masses of Negroes.

* * * *

. . . How are these radical objectives to be achieved? The answer is simple, deceptively so: *through political power*.

* * * *

Neither . . . [the civil rights protest] movement nor the country's twenty million black people can win political power alone. We need allies. The future of the Negro struggle depends on whether the contradictions of this society can be resolved by a coalition of progressive forces which becomes the *effective* political majority in the United States. . . .

* * * *

Here is where the cutting edge of the civil rights movement can be applied. We must see to it that the reorganization of the "consensus [Democratic] party" proceeds along the lines which will make it an effective vehicle for social reconstruction, a role it cannot play so long as it furnishes Southern racism with its national political power. (One of Barry Goldwater's few attractive ideas was that the Dixiecrats belong with him in the same party.) And nowhere has the civil rights movement's political cutting edge been more magnificently demonstrated than at Atlantic City, where the Mississippi Freedom Democratic Party not only secured recognition as a bona fide component of the national party, but in the process routed the representatives of the most rabid racists—the white Mississippi and Alabama delegations. While I still believe that the FDP made a tactical error in spurning the compromise, there is no question that they launched a political revolution whose logic is the displacement of Dixiecrat power. They launched that revolution within a major political institution and as part of a coalitional effort. ■

QUESTIONS FOR REVIEW

1.   What practices had whites, particularly in the south, created to deny equality to blacks and ensure power and privilege to whites? How did blacks begin to confront these and what were some of the reasons for their increased activism?

2.   Why were whites so reluctant to allow blacks to register to vote in the south? Why did many blacks see this as one of the most significant barriers of discrimination?

3.   Why was Mississippi seen as one of the most important states in the south in which to mount challenges against segregation and white supremacy?

4.   What responses did SNCC workers receive as they began to move into the communities of the south and assist blacks with voter registration? In what way was SNCC's philosophy of development and support of local organizations and movements successful?

5.   What were the hopes of Robert Moses and the COFO staff as they began the drive to recruit large numbers of white students for SNCC's voter registration campaigns in the south? What risks were they taking?

6.   What did SNCC activists expect from the FBI in relationship to the activities of the Ku Klux Klan and segregationists? How did the activists attempt to make the FBI more responsive on civil rights enforcement?

7.   How important were SNCC's organizing tactics? How did SNCC develop and change as it gained experience in voting and civil rights campaigns in the south? How did SNCC adjust to the many violent reactions of whites, such as Robert Moses describes in his account of the killing of Herbert Lee?

8.   How were the voter registration and organizing efforts of SNCC conducive to the emergence of local leaders, such as Fannie Lou Hamer?

9.   How did the Kennedys respond to the new phase of civil rights activities in Mississippi and to the legal violations and violence it provoked?

10.   What were the major goals of the Mississippi Freedom Summer Project?

11.   How did the freedom schools fit into SNCC's long-range goals for community development? How does Sally Belfrage describe the intense interactions between northern whites and black SNCC members, as well as rural blacks?

12.   What was the purpose of the MFDP, and how did it represent black hopes and aspirations for substantive change?

13.   What was the significance of the MFDP challenge to the regular Mississippi delegation at the Democratic National Convention in 1964? How does Charles Sherrod describe the outlook of the party representatives and their treatment of the convention?

14.   Why did the MFDP refuse to accept the administration's compromise, despite intense pressure from established black leaders and white allies?

15.   Following the MFDP challenge and Freedom Summer, in what ways did movement leaders begin to shift their strategies?

16.   Why did SNCC begin to look more critically at white involvement within its own organization? To what extent did this represent an abandonment of the belief in "interracialism" that had been strong in SNCC up to this time?

17.   Why did Bayard Rustin feel that the civil rights movement had to move beyond protest to a political agenda?

ADDITIONAL RECOMMENDED READINGS

Holt, Len. *The Summer that Didn't End.* London: Heinemann, 1966. A participant account of the freedom summer, which also includes some of the significant documents associated with this period.

Loewen, James W., and Charles Sallis. *Mississippi: Conflict & Change.* New York: Pantheon Books (revised edition), 1982. Looks closely at the development of race relations over many years, the realities of segregation, and the development of black resistance in Mississippi.

Raines, Howell. *My Soul Is Rested: Movement Days in the Deep South Remembered.* New York: Putnam, 1977. A valuable collection of oral history interviews with some of the leaders, participants, and opponents of the southern black freedom movement.

Sellers, Cleveland, with Robert Terrell. *The River of No Return: The Autobiography of a Black Militant and the Life and Death of SNCC.* New York: William Morrow & Company, 1973. A rare and important book written by former SNCC activists that discusses the formation and development of SNCC, the issues and questions that its members struggled to solve, and factors that led to its decline.

by DAVID J. GARROW

RELATED MEDIA:
EYES ON THE PRIZE
Television Program 6
"Bridge to Freedom"

—Concentrates on 1965, Selma, Alabama, and the passage of the 1965 Voting Rights Act

—Analyzes the importance of voting as a measure of full citizenship

—Describes the protest strategies employed by Martin Luther King, Jr. and the Southern Christian Leadership Conference (SCLC) to make voting rights a major national issue

—Identifies the strategic and ideological differences that led to growing disagreements between King's SCLC and the younger activists of the Student Nonviolent Coordinating Committee (SNCC)

—Explains the position of white liberals in the south and discusses ways in which segregationist resistance to civil rights demonstrations aided the movement's cause

—Describes President Lyndon B. Johnson's commitment to the movement's legislative goals

—Analyzes the impact of national media and public opinion on the civil rights movement at this time

OVERVIEW

Following the 1964 passage of the landmark Civil Rights Act, Martin Luther King, Jr. and his colleagues on the Southern Christian Leadership Conference (SCLC) rightfully concluded that the next federal legislative goal of the black freedom struggle in the south should be congressional passage of a strong voting rights statute that would provide for direct federal action and intervention guaranteeing southern blacks widespread access to registration and the ballot. Despite the passage of previous laws—particularly the Civil Rights Acts of 1957 and 1960—aimed at protecting southern blacks' right to vote, in many heavily-black southern counties few, if any, black citizens were registered to vote due to discriminatory practices employed by white voter registrars.

One Alabama county with a record of consistent opposition to black voting was Dallas, whose county seat was Selma, a small city of 27,000 people 50 miles west of Montgomery, Alabama's capital. Despite its strongly segregationist politics, Dallas County had several hundred registered black voters as of 1964, thanks very largely to the long-term efforts of the Dallas County Voters' League (DCVL), the local black civic organization, and its two long-time leaders, Amelia and Samuel Boynton, the latter of who died in 1963. Mrs. Boynton, a courageous and dedicated woman, also had been instrumental in convincing the Student Nonviolent Coordinating Committee (SNCC) to make Selma, like McComb and Albany before it, one of those southern locales where a small number of full-time SNCC workers was deployed.

The succession of SNCC workers that began in 1963 met a violently hostile reception from white officials, particularly short-tempered Dallas County Sheriff James G. Clark, Jr. and a sometimes mixed welcome from Selma's black community. Clark's deputies and white volunteer "possemen" almost literally surrounded the first black community mass rally when it took place in May 1963. Likewise, an October 1963 Freedom Day voter registration effort, that brought hundreds of prospective black registrants to the downtown county courthouse on one of the few dates of the month when Alabama laws required voter registrars to open their offices, met with stiff resistance from Clark's lawmen.

By late 1964, in the aftermath of the disheartening experience at Atlantic City's Democratic National Convention, SNCC's commitment of people and resources to an active project in Selma seemed, to local black leaders like Mrs. Boynton and DCVL President Rev. F. D. Reese, to be weakening. Committed to keeping up some initiatives, Mrs. Boynton proposed to the SCLC's staff, who long had known of her invaluable work in Selma, that King and his organization make Selma their next national focal point. King, convinced that any campaign for a strong federal voting rights statute would need such a focus, quickly accepted Mrs. Boynton and the DCVL's invitation to come to Selma and take on trigger-tempered Sheriff Clark.

Throughout January and February 1965, the SCLC's staff, in conjunction with several SNCC workers who also had continued organizing efforts in Selma, mounted an ongoing series of demonstrations targeted at the Dallas County courthouse, which contained the offices of both the registrar and the combative Sheriff Clark. When initial police restraint made for low-key national news coverage of the Selma drive, King chose to be arrested and jailed to draw more attention to the protests. As demonstrations continued into mid-February, Sheriff Clark engaged in picturesque tactics that drew some news coverage to the campaign on several occasions, but SCLC decided to expand some of its efforts to the nearby small town of Marion, seat of Perry County. There, on Wednesday evening, February 17, a small civil rights march was attacked by lawmen and one participant, Jimmie Lee Jackson, was shot by an Alabama state trooper. Several days later Jackson died, and Marion activists, in conjunction with the SCLC staff, decided that a fitting movement response to his death would be a mass pilgrimage from Selma to the Alabama state capitol in Montgomery.

The march was scheduled for Sunday, March 7. The SCLC leaders, King and Ralph Abernathy, were in Atlanta preaching at their respective churches, and the 600-person column was led by the SCLC's Hosea Williams and SNCC chairman John Lewis. After crossing the Edmund Pettus Bridge over the Alabama River on the eastern edge of downtown Selma, the marchers' path was blocked by scores of Alabama state troopers and Clark's local lawmen. The troopers' commander instructed the marchers to turn around and walk back into Selma; when the column did not move, the gas-masked lawmen walked forward, pushing marchers to the ground and striking others with billy clubs as tear gas cannisters were fired at the peaceful parade. Within seconds the scene was a bloody rout with mounted possemen chasing the marchers back across the bridge into Selma. Over 50 participants were treated at local hospitals.

Television footage of the eerie and gruesome attack produced immediate national outrage. King issued a public call for civil rights supporters across the nation to come to Selma to show their support and join a second attempted march; congressmen of both parties called upon President Lyndon B. Johnson to intervene in Alabama and to speedily put voting rights legislation before Congress. Johnson's Justice Department aides already had been hard at work preparing a comprehensive voting rights bill, but the "bloody Sunday" attack and the national reaction to it spurred the White House to press for a faster completion of the drafting process.

At the same time, Attorney General Nicholas deB. Katzenbach and other administration officials strongly lobbied King to postpone the second march attempt until a federal court hearing and decision on the protesters' plea for government protection against any further brutalities could take place. King found himself painfully torn between the federal requests, from men who had committed themselves to spur passage of the voting rights legislation—his top goal—and the desire of hundreds of movement supporters who had poured into Selma for an immediate second march. Faced with those competing pressures, King in the end led the second march out to the place where the first column had been attacked, and then, when faced with another wall of lawmen, King called the group to kneel and pray and then turned the procession around and marched back into Selma. None of the marchers or King's civil rights colleagues had been informed of his intention to turn around. His less-than-forthright behavior and his sometimes contradictory characterizations of his actions brought down on his head an angry deluge of private criticism, especially from SNCC workers. The "Tuesday turnaround," as the event came to be called, pushed the underlying strategic and organizational tensions between SCLC and SNCC to a higher level than had ever been reached before.

On Monday evening, March 15, as King and his colleagues waited in Selma for the expected federal court approval of a fully-protected march to Montgomery, President Johnson addressed a joint session of Congress on national television to announce that his voting rights legislation was ready and that his administration was committed. He said that "we shall overcome . . . a crippling legacy of bigotry and injustice." Congressional leaders promised that the administration's bill would receive speedy consideration and endorsement from representatives who, with only a modest number of exceptions, were more than ready to support a legislative remedy for voting discrimination that Selma's televised brutalities had so effectively highlighted.

Following federal court approval and the deployment of substantial numbers of Federal Bureau of Investigation (FBI) agents and federalized National Guardsmen, the third attempt at a march from Selma to Montgomery got underway on Sunday, March 21, under heavy government protection and even heavier international news coverage. Walking an average of some ten miles a day, sometimes in heavy rain, and camping at night in open fields under simple tents, the marchers arrived in Montgomery on Tuesday, March 25, and held a large rally on the steps of the Alabama state capitol. Hours later, one participating white volunteer, Viola Liuzzo, a Michigan housewife, was shot and killed by Klansmen as she drove between Selma and Montgomery.

Little more than four months later, on August 6, 1965, the Voting Rights Act of 1965 was signed into law. In ensuing years, the black voter registration gains it made possible and the discriminatory election techniques it voided allowed black southerners in many small towns and rural counties to enjoy meaningful participation and representation in the American electoral process for the first time in their lives.

READINGS

1. **M**rs. Amelia Boynton, wife of long-time DCVL leader Samuel William "Bill" Boynton, **was a crucial local-level black activist in Selma who played major roles in involving SNCC and, later, the SCLC in that small Alabama city. In this excerpt from her autobiographical recollections of early civil rights activism in Selma, Mrs. Boynton—now Mrs. Amelia Robinson—describes some of the earliest efforts.**

From: Bridge Across Jordan—The Story of the Struggle for Civil Rights in Selma, Alabama by Amelia Platts Boynton (New York: Carlton Press, Inc., 1979), pages 81–82. Copyright 1979 by Amelia Platts Boynton Robinson. Used by permission.

For many years Negro leaders had tried to arouse the blacks and get them to realize that they were taxpayers and citizens who had the right to vote. For many years we urged black citizens to call on the local governments of Selma and Dallas County and ask for these rights. But it was like striking the pendulum offbeat. We got no results until 1965.

During the late 1920's a group of Selma and Dallas County black citizens formed the first city-county organization that unified them for one common cause—becoming registered voters. But the Dallas County Voters' League (DCVL) went to sleep for lack of enough interest. In 1936, just before election time, the DCVL members were called together by my husband Bill, and another attempt was made to serve the black community. C.J. Adams, a railroad clerk, was elected president again. He was truly the most dynamic person Selma had had, but most Negroes were afraid to follow him. They knew he was right, but the point was to please the "white folks," or they knew their lives would be in danger.

Mr. Adams was finally forced to leave Selma because of the economic pressure imposed by the whites, and afterward Bill became head of the League. He continued as president until his death in 1963. The harder the DCVL worked to get Negroes registered the harder the county, city and state worked to throw up barriers so high as to make registration impossible. In 1963 there were only 180 registered Negroes in the county, though clinics and schools had been held for several years. We found that other methods had to be used to break the complacency of the adults. If we succeeded, other parts of the South might do likewise. As Negroes gained political strength, they would certainly be able to gain more of their constitutional rights.

All the candidates running for local and state office were segregationists who preached their segregation when necessary to gain votes in the white community. It was usually unnecessary to mention it because it was the standard pattern, and seemingly no one was concerned with breaking it. That is, until 1954, when the Supreme Court ruled that schools should be desegregated with all deliberate speed. But Negroes were only fighting for the privilege to vote. We held regular meetings, and just before an election we would arrange to vote as a bloc for our candidates. Then our votes would count; if they did not listen to us we would not support them. Selecting the lesser of the evils to vote for was in most cases a toss-up. ■

2. **B**ernard Lafayette and his wife Colia Liddell Lafayette were among the first young SNCC workers to go into Selma. In this mid-1960s remembrance of their first experiences in Selma, Bernard Lafayette recalls how the black community responded to their encouragement.

From: "Selma, Alabama" by Bernard Lafayette in the songbook *Freedom Is a Constant Struggle* edited by Guy and Candie Carawan (New York: Oak Publications, 1968), pages 146–147. Used by permission of Guy and Candie Carawan.

"Colia and I first went to Selma in February, 1963. It was sort of our honeymoon; we'd been married about six weeks. The first SNCC worker there came back and said that we might as well scratch Selma off the list because the people there just weren't ready for a movement. We didn't get any different impression when we were there. We had trouble finding a place to live; most people were afraid to put us up. But we worked on this assumption: no matter how bad a place is, some people got courage. Those people are gonna be warm and friendly to you.

"It was Mrs. Amelia Boynton who befriended us. We used her office and began to work. The first thing we did was to just try to get people to loosen up, to talk about registration and to realize they needed to vote. We set up classes teaching people how to fill out the registration forms. We knew that the forms are irrelevant in terms of voting and have nothing to do with whether a person is qualified to vote or not. But it's a psychological thing to build people's confidence. They have to feel themselves that they can fill out the form before they feel they can go down and try to register.

"We tried to get people around the city to come, but it was slow. So we went out in the rural. The people out there are close to the earth, they're very religious and warm and friendly. And mostly they're unafraid. They own most of their own property and their little stores. They work hard and they want to see a future for their children. So we got these people to go and try to register to vote first.

"Then we used this as a leverage to try to embarrass many of the people in the city. City folks are sometimes critical and skeptical about country people. So we pointed out that these people were really getting ahead. When these city people began to go down it was really sort of a birth of a movement.

"Between February and September we got about 2,000 people to go down and try to register and about 600 of them actually did get registered.

"By this time we had the people teaching each other. When one person learned to fill out the form, he was qualified to help somebody else. We had recruited some local workers too. We didn't really have to be there anymore.

"We went back to school that Fall. Worth Long and James Love were the SNCC workers who took over in Selma. The situation continued to develop and I would get little bits of news from there.

"In the Fall of 1964 James Bevel and SCLC moved into Alabama and began to build on making Selma a national issue of Voter Registration.

"I went back in 1965 to help with some of the planning and strategy. I saw some great changes. Many, many people had gone to jail—people you never would have expected to stand up. Some of the kids I had worked with—whose parents, grandparents and teachers had all argued with them, threatened them and disciplined them—would run up to me:

"'Guess what happened! Man, my grandmother went to jail! Man, I can't believe it . . . my grandma's in jail!'

"The principal of one high school who had told the kids he would lower their grades if they participated in the Movement, actually led a march of teachers asking for the right to vote. Many of the informers—Negroes who used to carry messages downtown to the white people—were still message-carriers, but they were now bringing messages to us. So I saw a whole city change. Large numbers of adults were participating, both from Selma and from surrounding areas."

■

3. A major part of King's and the SCLC's political strategy for the Selma protest campaign involved drawing national news media attention to the political plight of Selma's largely-disenfranchised black citizens. On February 1, 1965, King himself was purposefully arrested and jailed as part of the SCLC's strategy for drawing national attention to the Selma situation. Even before he was incarcerated, the SCLC had prepared a fund solicitation advertisement that would appear in *The New York Times* that was designed to remind readers of King's already famous 1963 "Letter from Birmingham Jail."

Source: "A Letter from Martin Luther King from a Selma, Alabama Jail" run as an advertisement in *The New York Times* (February 1, 1965).

February 1, 1965.

Dear Friends:

When the King of Norway participated in awarding the Nobel Peace Prize to me he surely did not think that in less than sixty days I would be in jail. He, and almost all world opinion will be shocked because they are little aware of the unfinished business in the South.

By jailing hundreds of Negroes, the city of Selma, Alabama, has revealed the persisting ugliness of segregation to the nation and the world. When the Civil

Rights Act of 1964 was passed many decent Americans were lulled into complacency because they thought the day of difficult struggle was over.

Why are we in jail? Have you ever been required to answer 100 questions on government, some abstruse even to a political scientist specialist, merely to vote? Have you ever stood in line with over a hundred others and after waiting an entire day seen less than ten given the qualifying test?

THIS IS SELMA, ALABAMA. THERE ARE MORE NEGROES IN JAIL WITH ME THAN THERE ARE ON THE VOTING ROLLS.

But apart from voting rights, merely to be a person in Selma is not easy. When reporters asked Sheriff Clark if a woman defendant was married, he replied, "She's a nigger woman and she hasn't got a Miss or a Mrs. in front of her name."

This is the U.S.A. in 1965. We are in jail simply because we cannot tolerate these conditions for ourselves or our nation.

We need the help of all decent Americans. Our organization, SCLC, is not only working in Selma, Ala., but in dozens of other Southern communities. Our self-help projects operate in South Carolina, Georgia, Louisiana, Mississippi and other states. Our people are eager to work, to sacrifice, to be jailed—but their income, normally meager, is cut off in these crises. Your help can make the difference. Your help can be a message of unity which the thickest jail walls cannot muffle. With warmest good wishes from all of us.

Sincerely,
MARTIN LUTHER KING, JR.

■

4. Thousands of Americans were shocked and outraged when they first saw the television news film depicting Alabama lawmen's violent attack on the first Selma-to-Montgomery march on "bloody Sunday," March 7, 1965. In this excerpt from a longer account, journalist George B. Leonard recounts his own reactions and response to the graphic footage.

From: "Journey of Conscience—Midnight Plane to Alabama" by George B. Leonard in *The Nation* (May 10, 1965). Used by permission of Nation Associates, Inc. Copyright 1965.

. . . The chief function of the current Negro movement has been to awaken a nation's conscience. . . .

Such an awakening is painful. It may take years to peel away the layers of self-deception that shut out reality. But there are moments during this process when the senses of an entire nation become suddenly sharper, when pain pours in and the resulting outrage turns to action. One of these moments came, not on Sunday, March 7, when a group of Negroes at Selma were gassed, clubbed and trampled by horses, but on the following day when films of the event appeared on national television.

The pictures were not particularly good. With the cameras rather far removed from the action and the skies partly overcast everything that happened took on the quality of an old newsreel. Yet this very quality, vague and half silhouetted, gave the scene the vehemence and immediacy of a dream. The TV screen showed a column of Negroes standing along a highway. A force of Alabama state troopers blocked their way. As the Negroes drew to a halt, a toneless voice drawled an order from a loudspeaker: In the interests of "public safety," the marchers were being told to turn back. A few moments passed, measured out in silence, as some of the troopers covered their faces with gas masks. There was a lurching movement on the left side of the screen; a heavy phalanx of troopers charged straight into the column, bowling the marchers over.

A shrill cry of terror, unlike any sound that had passed through a TV set, rose up as the troopers lumbered forward, stumbling sometimes on fallen bodies. The scene cut to charging horses, their hoofs flashing over the fallen. Another quick cut: a cloud of tear gas billowed over the highway. Periodically the top of a helmeted head emerged from the cloud, followed by a club on the upswing. The club and the head would disappear into the cloud of gas and another club would bob up and down.

Unhuman. No other word can describe the motions. The picture shifted quickly to a Negro church. The bleeding, broken and unconscious passed across the screen, some of them limping alone, others supported on either side, still others carried in arms or on stretchers. It was at this point that my wife, sobbing, turned and walked away, saying, "I can't look any more."

We were in our living room in San Francisco watching the 6 P.M. news. I was not aware that at the same moment people all up and down the West Coast were feeling what my wife and I felt, that at various times all over the country that day and up past 11 P.M. Pacific Time that night hundreds of these people would drop whatever they were doing, that some of them would leave home without changing clothes, borrow money, overdraw their checking accounts; board planes, buses, trains, cars; travel thousands of miles with no luggage; get speeding tickets, hitchhike, hire horse drawn wagons; that these people, mostly unknown to one another, would move for a single purpose: to place themselves alongside the Negroes they had watched on television.

Within the next several hours I was to meet many of these travelers and we were to pass the time telling one another how and why we had decided to come. My own decision was simple. I am a Southerner living away from the South. Many of my friends and relatives have remained there to carry on the grinding day-after-day struggle to rouse the drugged conscience of a stubborn and deluded people. They are the heroes. A trip to Alabama is a small thing.

I had, of course, any number of excellent reasons for *not* going to Selma, not the least of which was a powerful disinclination to be struck on the head and gassed. But as I raised that point and every other negative argument, a matter-of-fact voice answered: "You better get down there."

At midnight, the San Francisco airport was nearly deserted. Three men stood at the Delta Air Lines counter, a Negro and a white man in business suits, and a tall, fair Episcopalian priest. I sensed something dramatic about the tall man. . . . I introduced myself and learned that the priest was going to Selma, that he had decided to go only that night, that he had no idea how he was going to get from Birmingham, where the flight ended, to Selma, ninety miles south. I told him I had wired to both Avis *and* Hertz for cars at Birmingham, somehow I would get him to Selma.

* * * *

Flight 808 to Dixie rose into the cloudless California night. As in countless other flights across America, I pressed my head to the window and wondered at the wilderness below. This nation, the most automated, urbanized civilization in the world, consists mostly of open space. Yet this is appropriate, for America is still unfinished; it is still a huge, untidy experiment, a series of hopeful statements ending with question marks. . . .

* * * *

Dawn came in Dallas as we waited between planes. The night had brought other flights in from the West; each had its cargo of pilgrims. All of us trooped aboard a rakish, shining Convair 880 for Birmingham—a score of clergymen both Negro and white, a lawyer from Palo Alto, a psychiatrist from Los Angeles, a Bay Area matron who had had a bit too much to drink, a young couple from Berkeley.

Inside the plane, a plump Negro minister from Los Angeles named Bohler kept leaping to his feet to introduce himself and everyone within earshot to each new passenger, most of whom were bound for Selma. Twice he told us that the previous night he had been wanting to go "more than anything," and that the phone had rung at about 10:30 with news that he had been given a ticket—at which he had murmured, "Oh, He's answered my prayers so quickly!" One of Bohler's companions admitted that "when I told my wife, all she said was buy as much insurance as possible."

* * * *

In Birmingham . . . the airport was in turmoil. People from all over the nation were streaming in. Many others, we learned, were landing in Atlanta, still more in Montgomery. I picked up my car and loaded my passengers and started out on a tricky, uneasy 90 miles through hostile territory.

* * * *

. . . in the back was an older couple who had sat in front of me on the plane from Dallas. . . .

* * * *

"We watched the news," Ruth Morris said, "and then we went in and sat down and were eating dinner. Our home is right on the ocean. It's a very pleasant place to live, rather gay in color. Our dining room is warm and gay and we were sitting

161

down to a very good dinner. We felt sort of guilty about being there enjoying ourselves after what we had just seen on TV.

"We both said it at the same time, it just seemed to come out of the blue: Why are we sitting here? Then I said, 'I'll pack,' and Bull said, 'I'll call for reservations.' "

* * * *

. . . we entered Selma . . . and we stayed on dirt roads all the way to the Negro church district that was our destination. As we pulled to a stop, three slim young Negro women walked past our car. One of them leaned over to us and said with absolute simplicity: "Thank you for coming." . . .

The scene inside the church burst upon me. Every seat, every aisle was packed. They were shoulder to shoulder—the Princeton professor and the sharecropper's child, the Senator's wife and the elderly Negro mammy. . . .

* * * *

. . . a doctor from New York was speaking: he was giving us, with scientific enthusiasm, our medical briefing. "Tear gas will *not* keep you from breathing. You may *feel* like you can't breathe for a while. Tear gas will not make you *permanently* blind. It may blind you *temporarily*. Do *not* rub your eyes." I looked around at the amused but somber smiles. The doctor's enthusiasm was carrying him away. "If you become unconscious, be sure somebody stays with you." A delighted, outraged laugh rose throughout the church. The doctor laughed, too. "I mean, if you see someone become unconscious, be sure to stay with him." He got the day's greatest ovation.

* * * *

Outside, in hazy sunlight, the marchers formed. . . . They moved in voiceless exaltation. I exchanged smiles with Jim Forman who walked arm in arm with Dr. King in the front rank. And behind them were all those with whom I had traveled. . . .

America's conscience has been sleeping, but it is waking up. . . . A trip to Alabama is a small thing, but out of many such acts, let us hope, may come a new America. I smiled at my friends and stepped into the ranks. ■

5. SNCC executive secretary James Forman was one of those movement activists who was most greatly troubled by the differences in political strategy that distinguished the SCLC from SNCC and by King's handling of the extremely difficult situation the movement found itself faced with on Monday night, March 8

and Tuesday, March 9, when federal officials pleaded with King to postpone any second march attempt while hundreds of movement supporters, newly arrived in Selma, eagerly but ominously looked forward to a renewed effort to march to Montgomery. In this excerpt from his first book, Forman gives his frank account of that tense period.

From: *Sammy Younge, Jr.* by James Forman (New York: Grove Press, Inc., 1968), pages 75–79. Copyright 1986 by James Forman. Republished by Open Hand Publishing, Inc. Used by permission of James Forman.

. . . SCLC decided to devote almost all of its organizational energy to a massive right-to-vote campaign, with headquarters in Selma. SNCC, already based in Selma, agreed to cooperate in this new venture. . . . But disagreement on such key issues as concepts of leadership, working methods, and organizing voters for independent political action versus Democratic Party politics, bred conflict between SNCC and SCLC staffs in Alabama.

As the vote campaign intensified, accompanied by innumerable arrests and beatings, the proposal emerged for a march on the Alabama Capitol to demand the vote, as well as new state elections. Basically SNCC was opposed to a Selma-Montgomery march because of the likelihood of police brutality, the drain on resources, and the frustrations experienced in working with SCLC. At a lengthy meeting of its executive committee on March 5 and 6, SNCC voted not to participate organizationally in the march scheduled for Sunday, March 7. However, it encouraged SNCC staffers to do so on a non-organizational basis if they so desired. SNCC was also to make available radios, telephone lines, and certain other facilities already committed by our Alabama staff.

Then we heard that Dr. King would not appear at the march he himself had called. Without his newsworthy presence, it seemed likely that the lives of many black people would be even more endangered. We therefore mobilized three carloads of staff workers from Mississippi, two-way radios, and other protective equipment. At our national office in Atlanta, a group of SNCC people—including Alabama project director Silas Norman and Stokely Carmichael, whose subsequent election as SNCC chairman was largely the result of his work in Alabama—chartered a plane rather than make the five-hour drive to Selma. Since we had heard of King's absence only after the marchers had begun to assemble, none of SNCC's people were able to arrive for the march itself. But it seemed important to have maximum support in the event that violence developed that evening. While our various forces headed for Selma, we tried repeatedly, but unsuccessfully, to contact Dr. King, to find out his reasons for not appearing and to discuss the situation.

Our fears proved all too well-founded: hundreds, including SNCC chairman John Lewis, were beaten, whipped, and tear-gassed by Jim Clark's deputies and Alabama state troopers at the bridge that Sunday.

A new attempt to march was scheduled for the following Tuesday; SCLC also filed a suit seeking to enjoin the Alabama Highway Patrol and Sheriff Jim Clark from interfering with the march. I arrived in Montgomery early Monday evening and found James Farmer, then director of CORE [Congress of Racial Equality], also at the airport. A.D. King, Martin's brother, told us that we were

163

wanted at a meeting. Gathered there were Martin Luther King, Ralph Abernathy, Andrew Young, Hosea Williams, and Bernard Lee of SCLC, together with Fred Gray and Solomon Seay, Jr., Montgomery attorneys.

Farmer and I were informed that Judge Frank Johnson of the Federal Court of the Middle District had promised the SCLC lawyers that if Tuesday's march from Selma to Montgomery was canceled, he would hold a hearing Thursday on the injunction suit which SCLC had filed. Judge Johnson's other conditions were that there be no demonstrations in Montgomery and that the march not proceed in any way before or during the hearing. He expected an answer by 9:00 P.M., said Fred Gray.

The group assembled wanted to know what James Farmer and I had to say. It was clear that the consensus was to accept Judge Johnson's offer; Hosea Williams was the only SCLC leader pushing for the march. Farmer stated that, while he had come down to march and emotionally understood the position of Hosea, rationally he had to agree with waiting until Thursday. I stated that, first, I had not come to march and, second, I had not yet talked with our Alabama staff, so none of my remarks could be binding. With these reservations, I offered my analysis of the situation: that the Judge's offer was legal blackmail. There was no guarantee of getting the injunction and no deadline for the completion of hearings on it. "So many times in the past," I added, "we have seen movements killed by placing the question in the courts, waiting for weeks or months to get an injunction—or just a hearing on one."

Martin Luther King decided to accept the Judge's condition. The march would be postponed.

The entire group left immediately for Brown's Chapel in Selma. There, to my amazement, King pledged before a mass meeting that the march would begin the next morning at eight o'clock!

Not having had a chance to talk with the SNCC staff, I decided not to raise any questions about King's announcement publicly. When asked to speak, I talked about the need for organizing politically when the vote was won. Immediately afterward, I met with the SNCC staff who were disturbed to hear of the way people had been misled.

Later, SCLC held a meeting to reconsider the decision against marching; the SNCC staff attended. After three hours, Dr. King was convinced that he should reverse his position. He telephoned Attorney General Nicholas Katzenbach at 4:30 A.M. to tell him that the march would proceed. According to King, they talked over forty-five minutes and Katzenbach was angry. "I really had to preach to him," said King. I then decided to participate in the march, as King urged, hoping that events might continue to move him away from the U.S. government. Developments in the years which followed, and in particular Dr. King's stand on the Vietnam war, indicate that this did take place to a considerable degree.

As we had anticipated, Judge Johnson issued a court order a few hours later against the march or any type of demonstration. Katzenbach had not sat idly by. But we knew it was impossible to enjoin a whole town and we also felt that, at this point, people had to move. We therefore urged that anyone who had not actually been served papers under the court order should participate. . . .

Hundreds stood ready to march, including many Northern supporters. But once again we were fooled. After crossing the bridge, going a few yards beyond the spot where people had been beaten on the previous Sunday, and then kneeling in prayer, Dr. King turned the march around and led it back to Selma. This was done, according to my own information and the press coverage of the time, in compliance with a "compromise" agreement made between the Administration and Dr. King through the intermediacy of LeRoy Collins, director of the Federal Community Relations Service. King did not inform the marchers of that agreement. Needless to say, people were dismayed, baffled, and angry.

Back in Selma, Dr. King stated that all marches in Selma or Montgomery would be postponed pending the outcome of the injunction suit. This was on Tuesday, March 9. Relations between SNCC and SCLC were at a very low point. We began holding meetings of the SNCC staff, as well as meetings between SNCC and SCLC, to resolve our difficulties. . . . ■

6. **I**n Selma, as in Montgomery, Albany, and Birmingham in previous years, the white population was not monolithically segregationist. In each city there existed a few—albeit not many—white natives or long-time residents who knew that segregation and racial discrimination was wrong and sought to find ways in which they could successfully help speed its elimination. In Selma the two best known white moderates or liberals were auto dealer Art Lewis and his wife Muriel. In this excerpt from a mid-March letter that the Lewises circulated to several dozens of their closest friends and relatives across the country, Muriel Lewis explained their feelings about the Selma crisis.

Source: Personal letter from Muriel and Art Lewis to her mother, from Selma, Alabama, March 19, 1965. Used by permission of Muriel Lewis.

Dear Mother,

This letter is being written to all our friends, relatives and a few acquaintances to try and explain our personal position in "the Selma situation." There are some few of you who understand the situation completely and our role in it, but for the most part we think you believe that we are either disinterested, not involved, partial segregationists, rednecks, fools, courageous or possibly even moderate or liberal in our thinking. We feel that we must set the record straight, as no story in recent years has so completely stirred the nation, or had such complete coverage.

This is almost the end of the ninth week of racial demonstrations in this locale, and for most of that time we have been walking on eggshells, balancing on a very thin tightrope while trying to do what we believe is right and just. But we must act differently, and think differently because Selma is our home, we love it and its people and we want to continue to live here.

We have long been aware of the white racist group in Selma (and it is very large), and we have worked in a small way to change this through overthrowing the political machine that has ruled this city and county for many many years. There has been some success along these lines; our new young Mayor, Joe Smitherman; the head of the City Council, Carl Morgan; and three other councilmen were elected partly through our efforts and support. Art is one of the few nonpolitical figures who can still talk with the Mayor, but sadly these past weeks none of his advice has been accepted. Prior to these past few months, there was a good line of communication between the Mayor and the local negro leaders. For the first time there had been biracial talks, and we can only hope that in time these will resume. The history of Selma is too long to go into now; let me get down to the Lewises.

. . . until the riot on the bridge on our terrible black Sunday we kept our views quiet. We could be called moderates but not liberals, for we believe in the rights of the negroes, their right to free speech and their right to demonstrate in *moderation*. We know that Selma has been used for the sole purpose of bringing national attention to the rights of the negroes, and we were well aware that there was a perfect setup here with "the villain" Jim Clark, and when Martin Luther King arrived there was the hero. Among the press, the negroes and some whites are known as "the devil and deLawd."

Anyhow, the past few weeks we have become more vocal. I started by talking with my friends. There are a pitiful few who feel as we do, and when the tensions become almost unbearable we have only each other with whom to talk. One of the great problems in the city is the lack of strong, nonpolitical, white, moderate leaders. We have known that there was formed a nucleus of old-family (important) business and professional men who are moderates, but they have [been] and are still meeting in secret. We too need a leader and we know to be successful he must have certain qualifications. Art does not quite fit these, because of the fact that we have only lived here 23 years (and so are still outsiders), we are Jewish and there is a health problem to consider. I personally have taken to writing letters to editors to try and show that Selma has human beings here who do not condone violence. So far the only one printed (that I know of) was in our Selma paper and that in re. the rights of local citizens to work with the CRS [Community Relations Service] to help our city attain what is right and to ensure peace. This one letter has had surprising results. I have been contacted by a group of local people who are too liberal and too new in town to have any long lasting effect, and as expected there has been a little hate mail. . . .

. . . we realize that we can no longer be afraid to speak out, but that does not mean that we are no longer a bit fearful, and we do not—nor should you, condemn our moderate friends for their silence. We know that this area is full of potential violence, not only from the radical whites, but from the many militant negroes. We go anywhere and everywhere in Selma, except Sylvan St., [and] we go about the necessary day to day activities, but for weeks we have thought of nothing else, have talked of nothing else. The tension has been ever present, and it will be here for a long long time. The name Selma will soon drop from the headlines, but we are working for a long range program of understanding between the races and for lasting peace.

* * * *

From our friends and relatives we have heard very little, and we have needed all the love and support possible. Some few of you have been concerned and kind and to you we have tried to make our ordeal seem much less than it has been. A very few of you have seen fit to question our motives and thoughts during this time. We hope that you will continue to acknowledge us, or we shall be truly lost, and you should not feel shame at writing SELMA on an envelope. There are decent people everywhere, and this town is no exception.

* * * *

We are confused, more than ever tonight. We must live with ourselves, but we also want to live here. It would be so easy to be quiet, but it would not let us sleep any easier than we do now. All we ask from you is partial understanding, and compassion. We hope that you will never be faced with a crisis in your lives that even remotely resembles this, and we hope that you will understand the purpose of this letter. We ask that you do not show it to your friends or even talk about it; this information is for the people who mean something important to us.

With fondest regards,
Muriel and Art Lewis
■

7. **O**ne county where a dramatic upsurge in southern black political activism took place directly after the 1965 Selma-to-Montgomery march—beginning even before the August passage of the Voting Rights Act—was Lowndes County, Alabama, the hard-core segregationist stronghold lying between Selma and Montgomery and through which the marchers had passed—with no small sense of foreboding—on their way to the Alabama state capitol. In the immediate aftermath of the march, several SNCC workers, including future SNCC chairman Stokely Carmichael (now Kwame Toure), who had already

earned his organizing spurs in the Mississippi Delta in 1963 and 1964, focused their efforts on Lowndes County. In this excerpt from *Black Power*, which Carmichael coauthored with black political scientist Charles V. Hamilton, the initial 1965–1966 SNCC effort in Lowndes is described. This effort produced the Lowndes County Freedom Organization (LCFO), which soon came to be called the Black Panther Party, after its visual symbol. Today one of the LCFO's first major activists, John Hulett, serves as Lowndes County sheriff, and one of Carmichael's SNCC colleagues, Robert Mants, serves as a Lowndes County commissioner.

From: Black Power—The Politics of Liberation in America by Stokely Carmichael and Charles V. Hamilton (New York: Vintage Books, 1967), pages 98–120. Copyright 1967 by Stokely Carmichael and Charles V. Hamilton. Used by permission of Random House, Inc.

. . . In March, 1965, not one black person was even registered to vote; over the next twenty months, close to 3,900 black people had not only registered but also formed a political organization, held a nominating convention and slated seven of their members to run for county public office. . . . If ever the political scientists wanted to study the phenomenon of political development or political modernization in this country, here was the place: in the heart of the "black belt," that range of Southern areas characterized by the predominance of black people and rich black soil.

Most local black people readily admit that the catalyst for change was the appearance in the county in March and April, 1965, of a handful of workers from SNCC. They had gone there almost immediately after the murder of Mrs. Viola Liuzzo, on the final night of the Selma to Montgomery March. Mrs. Liuzzo, a white housewife from Detroit, had been driving marchers home when she was shot down by Klansmen on that same Highway 80 in Lowndes County. For the black people of Lowndes, her murder came as no great surprise: Lowndes had one of the nation's worst records for individual and institutional racism, a reputation for brutality that made white as well as black Alabama shiver. In this county, eighty-one percent black, the whites had ruled the entire area and subjugated black people to that rule unmercifully. Lowndes was a prime area for SNCC to apply certain assumptions learned over the years of work in rural, backwoods counties of the South.

SNCC had long understood that one of the major obstacles to helping black people organize structures which could effectively fight institutional racism was *fear*. The history of the county shows that black people could come together to do only three things: sing, pray, dance. Any time they came together to do anything else, they were threatened or intimidated. For decades, black people had been taught to believe that voting, politics, is "white folks' business." And the white folks had indeed monopolized that business, by methods which ran the gamut from economic intimidation to murder.

The situation in Lowndes was particularly notable inasmuch as civil rights battles had been waged on an extensive scale in two adjoining counties for years: in Dallas County (Selma) and in Montgomery County. The city of Montgomery had seen a powerful movement, led by Dr. Martin Luther King, Jr., beginning in 1955 with the bus boycott. But Lowndes County did not appear affected by this activity. This is even more striking when one considers that at least seventeen percent of the black people in Lowndes work in Montgomery and at least sixty percent of the black people do their major shopping there. Lowndes was a truly totalitarian society—the epitome of the tight, insulated police state. SNCC people felt that if they could help crack Lowndes, other areas—with less brutal reputations—would be easier to organize. This might be considered a kind of SNCC Domino Theory.

There were several black organizations in Lowndes County, all centered around the church. . . . Some of the most politically-oriented people who subsequently formed the Lowndes County Freedom Organization were those experienced in the internal politics of the church. The ability and power of these local leaders, however, rested inside the black community and was geared toward religious and social affairs only. Many people who were very political *inside* those organizations were unwilling to enter the *public* political arena. They were afraid.

The black people most respected by the whites in Lowndes County were the school teachers and the two high school principals. But, as in many southern communities, they were at the mercy of the white power structure. They held their positions at the sufferance of the whites; the power they had was delegated to them by the white community. And what the master giveth, the master can take away. The power of the black principals and teachers did not come from the black community, because that community was not organized around public political power. In this sense, they were typical "Negro Establishment" figures.

The question of leadership in the county was crucial. If there was to be a sustained political assault on racism, the black people would have to develop a viable leadership group. The white-established Negro leaders—the teachers, principals—were looked up to by the black community because they could get certain things done. They could intercede with the white man, and they had certain overt credentials of success: a big car, a nice house, good clothes. The black ministers constituted another source of leadership. They have traditionally been the leaders in the black community, but their power lay inside the black community, not with the white power structure. In some cases, they could ask white people to do certain things for black people, but they did not have the relative power possessed by the white-made leaders. The ministers, likewise, could invoke the authority of God; they were, after all, "called to preach the gospel," and, therefore, their word had almost a kind of divine authority in the black community.

* * * *

There was another set of leaders in the black community of Lowndes County. This was a group of middle-aged ladies, who knew the community well and were well known. They were to play a very important role in the political organization of the blacks. They had considerable influence in the black community—being staunch church members, for example—but they possessed no power at all with the white community.

Economically, Lowndes County is not noted for its equitable distribution of goods and income. The average income of blacks, most of them sharecroppers and tenant farmers, is about $985 per year. Eighty-six white families own ninety percent of the land. Inside the black community, there were in 1965 few people who had running water in their houses; only about twenty families had steam heat, and the rest got by with stove burners and wood fireplaces to keep warm. The economic insecurity of the latter is obvious, yet as we have seen, even the "Negro Establishment" faced disaster if they started meddling in "white folks business."

Against these odds, there had somehow been in Lowndes County a long history of black men who started to fight—but were always cut down. Mr. Emory Ross, who later became an active participant in the Lowndes County Freedom Organization, had a father who was a fighter. He was shot at several times; his house riddled with bullets; his home burned down at one time. But he continued to struggle, and he was able to impart his determination to his son.

There were a few more like him. Spurred by the demonstrations and Dr. King's presence in Selma in early 1965, some seventeen brave people rallied around Mr. John Hulett, a lifelong resident of the County, to form the Lowndes County Christian Movement for Human Rights in March of that year. SNCC workers began moving around the county shortly afterward, talking a strange language: "Political power is the first step to independence and freedom." "You can control this county politically." It was exceptionally difficult at first to get black people to go to the courthouse to register—the first step. The fight at that point was waged simply in terms of being able to establish within the black community a sense of the *right* to fight racial oppression and exploitation. This was a battle of no small proportion, because black people in this county—many of them—did not even feel that they had the *right* to fight. In addition, they felt that their fight would be meaningless. They remembered those who had been cut down.

From March to August, 1965, about fifty to sixty black citizens made their way to the courthouse to register and successfully passed the registration "test." Then, in August, the 1965 Voting Rights Act was passed and federal "examiners" or registrars came into the county. No longer did a black man face literacy tests or absurdly difficult questions about the Constitution or such tactics as rejection because one "t" was not properly crossed or an "i" inadequately dotted. The voting rolls swelled by the hundreds. . . .

The *act* of registering to vote does several things. It marks the beginning of political modernization by broadening the base of participation. It also does something the existentialists talk about: it gives one a sense of being. The black man who goes to register is saying to the white man, "No." He is saying: "You have said that I cannot vote. You have said that this is my place. This is where I should remain. You have contained me and I am saying 'No' to your containment. I am stepping out of the bounds. I am saying 'No' to you and thereby I am creating a better life for myself. I am resisting someone who has contained me." That is what the first act does. The black person begins to live. He begins to create his *own* existence when he says "No" to someone who contains him.

But obviously this is not enough. Once the black man has knocked back centuries of fear, once he is willing to resist, he then must decide how best to use that vote. To listen to those whites who conspired for so many years to deny him the ballot would be a return to that previous subordinated condition. He must move independently. The development of this awareness is a job as tedious and laborious as inspiring people to register in the first place. In fact, many people who would aspire to the role of an organizer drop off simply because they do not have the energy, the stamina, to knock on doors day after day. That is why one finds many such people sitting in coffee shops talking and theorizing instead of organizing.

* * * *

The SNCC research staff discovered an unusual Alabama law which permits a group to organize a potential political party on a county-wide basis. . . . The black people of Lowndes County and SNCC then began the hard work of building a legitimate, independent political party with no help from anyone else. Virtually the entire country condemned this decision; it was "separatism"; it was traditionally doomed "third-party politics" and the only way to succeed was through one of the two established parties. Some even said that the black voters of Lowndes County should support the Democratic party out of gratitude for being given the vote. But the Democratic party did not give black people the right to vote; it simply stopped denying black people the right to vote.

In March, 1966, the Lowndes County Freedom Organization was born with the immediate goals of running candidates and becoming a recognized party. In building the LCFO, it was obviously wise to attempt first to recruit those black people who owned land and were therefore somewhat more secure economically than those without property. But there were few of them. Those without property, merely sharecropping on white-owned plantations, were subject to being kicked off the land for their political activity. This is exactly what had happened at the end of December, 1965; some twenty families were evicted and spent the rest of the winter living in tents, with temperatures often below freezing. Their fate, and it was shared by others later, intensified the fear, but it also served to instill a sense of the tremendous need to establish an independent base of group power within the community. That base could lend support, security. Thus, despite the ever-present threat of loss of home and job and even possibly life, the black people of Lowndes County continued to build. Mass meetings were held weekly, each time in a different part of the county. Unity and strength, already developing over the winter, grew.

In May, 1966, the time arrived to put up black candidates in the primary election. . . .

The black people of Lowndes County were ready and made themselves even readier. Workshops were held, with SNCC's assistance, on the duties of the sheriff, the coroner, the tax assessor, tax collector and members of the Board of Education—the offices up for election. Booklets, frequently in the form of picture books, were prepared by SNCC and distributed over the county. People began to see and understand that no college education or special training was needed to perform these functions. They called primarily for determination and

171

common sense, and black people in Lowndes had long since shown that they possessed these qualities.

* * * *

The campaign which followed was hardly a typical American political campaign. There were no debates (or offers to debate) between the candidates; black candidates certainly did not canvass white voters and no white candidates made open appeals for black votes.

[Despite tremendous LCFO efforts, on election day, Nov. 8, 1966, all of the black candidates lost to their white competitors by margins of roughly 600 votes— 2,200 to 1,600. Nonetheless, the LCFO drew clear lessons from the experience.]

* * * *

The new Lowndes County Freedom Party is also aware that somehow it must counteract the economic dependence which so seriously impedes organizing. It must begin thinking of ways to build a "patronage" system—some sort of mechanism for offering day-to-day, bread-and-butter help to black people immediately in need. A prime example occurred on election day at 1 P.M., when a black family's home was completely destroyed by fire; fourteen children, ranging in age from four to eighteen, and two adults were left homeless and penniless. Immediate assistance in the form of clothes, food, and dollars coming from the Party would have been politically invaluable. It is true that the Party does not have the local resources to help every family burned out of their homes or kicked off the land or in need of a job, but it must begin to move in that direction. Such "patronage" should always be identified as coming from the Party. If necessary (and it undoubtedly will be necessary), drives in selected northern communities could be launched to help until the Party can show more substantial victories. Only so many black people will rush to the banner of "freedom" and "blackness" without seeing some way to make ends meet, to care for their children.

One way or another, the fact is that the John Huletts of the South will participate in political decision-making in their time and in their land. November 8, 1966, made one thing clear: some day black people will control the government of Lowndes County. For Lowndes is not merely a section of land and a group of people, but an idea whose time has come. ■

QUESTIONS FOR REVIEW

1. What goal did Dr. King and the SCLC have uppermost in their minds for their 1965 protest campaign in Selma?

2. What advantages and attractions did Selma offer to King and the SCLC as a focal point for their 1965 voting rights campaign?

3. What was the history of civil rights activism in Selma prior to the arrival of King and the SCLC?

4. What role did King and the SCLC envision publicity and the news media playing in their Selma protest strategy?

5. Why was the national reaction to the March 7, 1965 attack by lawmen on voting rights marchers so important and pronounced?

6. What differences separated SNCC's approach to civil rights activism from that of King and the SCLC?

7. How would you analyze the choices King faced with regard to the second march on March 9, and the criticisms SNCC made of how King handled his predicament? What do you think would have happened if King had led the group of marchers to cross the Pettus Bridge that Tuesday? Consider George Leonard's article as you reply.

8. What tensions and divisions seem to have been most important in white Selma's response to the demonstrations?

9. How do you account for the changes in people mentioned by Bernard Lafayette? How had they become more prepared to take great risks?

10. In his letter from the Selma jail, King made it clear that voting rights was not the only issue of the struggle there. What else was at stake? What does Stokely Carmichael say about this?

11. George Leonard responded to an inner voice telling him to go to Selma. Are any such calls possible in our country today? If so, where? If not, why?

12. Forman expresses his hope "that events might continue to move [King] away from the U.S. government." What did he mean? Why would he have such a hope?

13. What different aspects of the importance of voting rights can you identify?

ADDITIONAL RECOMMENDED READINGS

Fager, Charles E. *Selma 1965: The March that Changed the South*. New York: Charles Scribner's Sons, 1974. A fast-paced narrative account of the Selma campaign written by a former SCLC staff worker.

Garrow, David J. *The FBI and Martin Luther King, Jr.: From "Solo" to Memphis*. New York: W.W. Norton, 1981. A detailed investigation of the FBI's animus towards King, based heavily upon Bureau documents released under Freedom of Information Act (FOIA) requests, which also analyzes the mixed and complicated behavior of Presidents Kennedy and Johnson toward King.

Garrow, David J. *Protest at Selma: Martin Luther King, Jr., and the Voting Rights Act of 1965*. New Haven: Yale University Press, 1978. The standard academic study of the Selma campaign and the passage of the Voting Rights Act.

Norrell, Robert J. *Reaping the Whirlwind: The Civil Rights Movement in Tuskegee*. New York: Knopf, 1985. A sensitive and insightful study of local-level civil rights activism in the Alabama town that served as SNCC's principal base in the state.

PART III

THE STRUGGLE CONTINUES

CHAPTER 8

WE THE PEOPLE: THE STRUGGLE CONTINUES

by VINCENT HARDING

—Reviews the significance of Supreme Court decisions, presidents, Congresses, and political parties in the struggle for social justice in America during the period 1954–1965

—Identifies the major differences among the National Association for the Advancement of Colored People (NAACP), the Southern Christian Leadership Conference (SCLC), the Student Non-violent Coordinating Committee (SNCC), and the Congress of Racial Equality (CORE) during the decade

—Characterizes the differing experiences and needs of southern rural black Americans and northern urban black Americans at the end of the decade

—Analyzes some of the reasons leadership of the civil rights movement became more diffuse after the assassination of Martin Luther King, Jr.

—Describes the roles of religion, black religious organizations, and grass-roots community organizations in the movement

—Reviews the contributions of A. Philip Randolph, Ralph Bunche, Roy Wilkins, Bayard Rustin, John Lewis, Stokely Carmichael, Malcolm X, Amelia Boynton, Rev. Fred Reese, Viola Liuzzo, Rosa Parks, Martin Luther King, Jr., Coretta Scott King, Ralph Abernathy, and Juanita Abernathy to the struggle for social justice during the period 1954–1965

—Identifies the issues and individuals that become significant in the movement during the period 1966–1986

On March 25, 1965, as thousands of marchers poured into the concourse of Montgomery's Dexter Avenue, moving like a dark and light river toward the capitol at the far end of the thoroughfare, they carried among themselves a symbolic power too forceful to overlook. Many layers of history and meaning were caught up in this convergence of people, time, and place, this climax of another stage in the long, black-led journey toward a more perfect union.

After four days of marching through rain, mud, sunshine, and sudden chills, carrying their American flags, accompanied by federalized guard units and army personnel, still always aware of the presence of danger, but always singing their songs ("Oh, Wallace! Segregation's got to fall . . . you never can jail us all"), they had finally come to Montgomery.

This city represented many realities, each spiralling into the other. It had been the first capital of the Confederacy, stark symbol of the south's blood-red, Civil War resistance to the demands for black freedom. But now, marching toward the capitol were also many of the human sources of the city's transformation. Here, among the thousands of persons spreading all over the streets were hundreds of women and men who represented the historic black determination to "swamp the foundations" of injustice, to possess the land, and to re-create the meaning of Montgomery. As they marched down Dexter Avenue, such persons were living signs of a continuing struggle to define and live out freedom, a struggle that had been going on, in its most recent manifestation, for a century.

A. Philip Randolph was there, perhaps the oldest of the long-time freedom-moving contingent, continuing a tradition he had carried on ever since World War I. Ralph Bunche, first black American Nobel Peace Prize winner, a direct link to the powerful days of Howard University in the 1930s, had joined the line on that day. So had Roy Wilkins, bearing witness to the persistent presence of the National Association for the Advancement of Colored People (NAACP) for more than half a century in the struggle to re-create the Union. Bayard Rustin, veteran of the national and international nonviolent movements for peace and justice, returned to the city where he had first helped Martin Luther King, Jr. In the line, too, was John Lewis, SNCC chairman, his head still bandaged from the Pettus Bridge beating, representing the new generation of black students who had given a powerful, decisive impetus to the movement. He marched along with Stokely Carmichael, the tall indefatigable young organizer from Harlem and Trinidad who already dreamed of what *black power* might be like. (Perhaps, in his own way, Malcolm—now beyond even El-Hajj Malik El-Shabazz—was also there, marching, testifying.) And, of course, courageous local leaders like Mrs. Amelia Boynton and Reverend Fred Reese of Selma, reminded the world that it was their commitment and the persistent determination of grass-roots leaders like them everywhere, which usually formed the base of every attempt to reshape the nation in the direction of democracy, justice, and freedom.

But who could have marched on Dexter Avenue that day bearing more dreams and memories than Rosa Parks and Martin and Coretta King and Ralph and Juanita Abernathy and the thousands of black Montgomerians who just 10 years ago had brought a new moment to the historic struggle? Following their lead, in less than a decade, an aroused southern black community, eventually joined by white allies from everywhere, had confounded all the conventional wisdom about who they were and what power they did or did not possess. In the process they had surprised and shaken their nation and encouraged millions of people around the world.

Disciplined by a profound sense of place, deep reservoirs of religious faith, a commitment to nonviolence and an American optimism, this black-shaped force had lifted up the richest implications of the 1954 Supreme Court decision and joined its faith in God to a faith in democracy and, finally, in themselves. Thus armed, they had taken on in direct confrontation the harsh and often murderous system of legalized and quasi-legal segregation in the south and had broken its essential power. In the process they had made it impossible for the United States ever to return to its explicit, pre-World War II commitment to black submissiveness, white domination, and a schizophrenic democracy. Rising from the bottom, they had pressed the nation forward.

By 1965 they had smashed almost all of the humiliating "colored" and "white" signs, and though the unsigned realities still persisted, though the supporters of the old order swore never to give up, the audacious power of a religiously inspired human freedom movement was against them. Now churches, schools, courthouses, registration lists, restrooms, motels, U.S. military units, some political offices, parks, pools, beaches—every public facility and rest-room—were all feeling the rising force of the flooding black movement.

In the course of their struggle, these black marchers had also been freeing white people all over the south and north, opening the locked doors for both the prisoners and the wardens. Indeed, an observer needed only to look at the parading, celebrating, marching lines as they made their way toward the capitol that day in order to see one of the most powerful and pervasive effects of the post-1954 black freedom struggle. Clearly, it had opened the way for the white religious communities of the nation to respond more fully to their God of truth, justice, and love. Priests and rabbis, Catholic sisters and Orthodox bishops, monks and lay people of every persuasion were in the lines, joining their lives in the search for a just community, a more perfect union, assuming that the quest for such human community was an act of divine communion. Thus the singing, preaching, believing black movement had once more brought into the streets its long tradition of liberation spirituality, theology, and action, and thousands of white sisters and brothers were set free to begin anew, set free by the descendants of America's slaves.

It was the same for young white people. The Montgomery bus boycott had begun at a time when all the keepers of the societal wisdom were identifying white young folks (the only ones they saw) as "the silent generation." College students of the period were put down as a set of fearful, self-centered youth, cowed by the domestic, anticommunist crusades of the "cold war," refusing to take risks or to live with political ideologies. Into the midst of these analyses walked the black children and teenagers who took the words of *Brown v. the Board of Education of Topeka* and transmuted them into costly deeds, testifying to the presence of far more than the wise men had seen. Then, while commissions and academic conferences were continuing to explain why college students were obsessed by panty-raids and telephone-booth-stuffing contests, a creative black youth storm blew into the face of official public segregation, becoming sit-ins and freedoms rides and dangerous voter registration organizing and campaigning.

Black youth were on fire in the cause of justice, living on subsistence salaries (when the checks arrived), standing in solidarity with the people under threat, drawing much of it to themselves. Quickly, the power of their commitment, the audacity of their movement, and the justice of their cause began to draw thousands of white young people out of their hiding places into the light of the surging movement toward a new society. The white youth were never the same again, as many went on to challenge their universities, their government, and eventually their own souls. (Again, in spite of the conventional wisdom of our own time, it is likely that the last has not been heard from some of the men and women whose young lives were transformed in the crucible of the black-led freedom movement.) In Selma they were present, looking for the America that had not yet come into being in their lives. Indeed, white Americans of every age were responding to the power of the challenging black surge. They understood that it was also a movement for their liberation from a distortion of democracy. That was why Viola Liuzzo came from Detroit, to serve, to risk, and finally, to die.

Of course, the powerful dynamic of the movement had moved not only white youth, religious peoples, and other citizens who were believers in justice, but it had insistently, amazingly, challenged the major institutions of our national government as well. So not only had the highest courts been forced to face the meaning of the Constitution and its Preamble, but now presidents, Congresses, and political parties were pressed to decide how they would stand, what they would say, what they would do in response to the black challenge to re-create America, to redefine "we the people." Now, all over the world, wherever women and men honored the hope of social justice, the southern black freedom movement was a source of inspiration, and its songs—especially "We Shall Overcome"—began to be heard everywhere.

At the same moment, as one might expect, the black community was re-creating, repossessing, and challenging itself, discovering the possibilities of a power that had long been denied, from within and without. One fascinating aspect of this self-renewal was evidenced in the fact that the black people of the north had gained new respect for the courage and creativity of their supposedly backward relatives in the churning precincts of the south. Indeed, faithful to a long tradition among many freedom-obsessed peoples, a stunning dialectic had been set in motion: A people determined to change the world around them had begun again, as well, to change the world within them, to take into themselves the words of their song, words as old as humankind: "The truth shall make us free." For now the marchers could hopefully envision the freedom of their children and their grandchildren, could see the new beauty about to be born as a result of their costly, risky struggles, and could repeat the words of the black woman of the bus boycott: "My feets is tired, but my soul is rested." Indeed, all through the south, a fascinating testimony was constantly repeated: wherever the freedom movement heightened its activities in a black community, at the same time, the crime rate in that community plummeted to its lowest levels.

So the history and the hope the marchers brought into Montgomery that day were long and deep, at once centuries-old and yet less than a decade into their newest motion. Of course, a decade is a short time in the development of human struggles for justice, especially when their highest goal has been defined as "redeeming the soul of America," especially when they intend "to [inject] new meaning into the veins of history and of civilization," especially when their only weapons are courage, hope, commitment, and intelligent, powerful love.

Martin Luther King, Jr., whose greatest gift may well have been his capacity to imbibe, transform, and return to the people their best hopes and dreams, understood how short a time a decade was. He knew this was especially the case for people whose unarmed struggle pits them against fierce opponents in persons and structures, sets them against systems of inertia and fear. So, that Thursday afternoon, when he finally stood on the steps of the capitol in Montgomery, rounding off a century, closing out a decade, facing the exultant crowd, he clearly understood the great pride of the people in what they had already accomplished to "establish justice, insure domestic tranquility, provide for the common defense, and promote the general welfare," as well as to "secure the blessings of liberty" to themselves and their posterity. At the same moment, he realized that civil rights acts, voter registration laws, and the smashing of outward signs were only the end of the beginning of the long journey toward a new America.

Working from that consciousness and from his own deep sense of compassion and courage, the black leader urged the responsive crowd of some 25,000 persons—as well as the onlooking nation and world—to keep moving on the long journey. In a portion of his speech that is rarely quoted, King obviously recognized the necessarily limited nature of the important, costly victories which had been won in the south. But he then pointed the way toward the next stages of the struggle—pointed the way to the poor, toward the cities, toward the north, saying,

> We are on the move now. The burning of our churches will not deter us. We are on the move now. The bombing of our homes will not dissuade us. We are on the move now. The beating and killing of our clergymen and young people will not divert us. We are on the move now. The arrest and release of known murderers will not discourage us. We are on the move now.
>
> Like an idea whose time has come, not even the marching of mighty armies can halt us. We are moving to the land of freedom.
>
> Let us therefore continue our triumph and march to the realization of the American dream. Let us march on segregated housing, until every ghetto of social and economic depression dissolves and Negroes and whites live side by side in decent, safe, and sanitary housing.
>
> Let us march on segregated schools until every vestige of segregated and inferior education becomes a thing of the past and Negroes and whites study side by side in the socially healing context of the classroom.
>
> Let us march on poverty until no American parents have to skip a meal so that their children [may eat. Let us] march on poverty until no starved man walks the streets of our cities and towns in search of jobs that do not exist.
>
> Let us march on ballot boxes, march on ballot boxes until race baiters disappear from the political arena. Let us march on ballot boxes until the Wallaces of our nation tremble away in silence.

He knew, of course, that "The road ahead is not altogether a smooth one." He said, "There are no broad highways to lead us easily and inevitably to quick solutions." But he pressed on, challenging the crowd, the nation: "We must keep going."

Within the context of such a statement, we can understand that what is usually called "the civil rights movement" was only one element—albeit a crucial, necessary element—of what many persons considered a larger, deeper, historically-grounded movement: the struggle—often led by black people—to transform America, its values, institutions, and people toward a more perfect union. (Thus the grass-roots level leaders and participants rarely spoke of fighting for "civil rights." More often they saw themselves as true freedom fighters, and the songs which ran deep into the soul of the movement were not called "civil rights songs" but "freedom songs," and all through the nights the chant, "Everybody wants free-e-e-DOM!" went out.)

As a result, there could be a real sense of pride and joy when in the summer of 1965 Congress finally passed the Voting Rights bill and it was signed into law. Everybody knew how fully this governmental action had been spurred by the confrontations on Pettus Bridge, by the march to Montgomery, by the deaths on the way. But there was also a sense of sobriety when in that same summer the fires of Watts broke loose. There had been intimations of such volatility in Birmingham in 1963 and in Harlem and other scattered cities in 1964, but Watts was the great explosion which some people (like Malcolm X) had been sensing for years. Indeed, anyone who looked at the conditions of the black urban communities, anyone who recognized the all-too-American commitment to violent solutions then being acted out in Vietnam, anyone who felt the increasing white resistance to deep probes into the structural problems of the nation—anyone with such insights knew that something like Watts was coming.

In a sense, the rounding off of the classic southern phase of the movement in Selma that spring and the summertime explosion in black Los Angeles (as well as in places like Chicago and Philadelphia) proved to mark a turning point. From there on, the growing attention, energies, and action of the black freedom movement were geared toward the north, toward the cities, toward the problems of political powerlessness, economic exploitation, social disruption (from within and without), and explosive, sometimes cathartic rage. All of this was set in the context of what most movement leaders considered a cruel, unjust, and wasteful war being waged by the United States against the Vietnamese people. Finally, the entire domestic setting was shaped and fundamentally influenced by the powerful black nationalist fervor which was emerging with sometimes volcanic force in the black communities everywhere, especially after the February 1965 assassination of Malcolm X.

By the middle of 1966, all of these transitional elements were drawn together in Mississippi in what was called the March Against Fear. Late in the spring of that year, James Meredith, the somewhat reluctant hero of the hard struggle to integrate the University of Mississippi, had decided to set off on this solitary march down through the heart of his native state. After he fell victim to a shotgun blast at the beginning of his march, other movement leaders attempted to continue, but the strains among them concerning the future of the freedom struggle, concerning the role of white allies, concerning outspoken criticism of the federal government, were too great for all of them to go into Mississippi together. So the march developed as a fascinating encounter among the Student

Nonviolent Coordinating Committee (SNCC), the Southern Christian Leadership Conference (SCLC), and the Congress of Racial Equality (CORE), against the background of white Mississippi's continuing, sometimes brutal resistance to the movement of history. The most powerful result of the march was likely the emergence of SNCC's call for *black power*, identified primarily with its radical, charismatic, and often provocative, new chairperson, Stokely Carmichael, veteran of Alabama's hard organizing campaigns and many other battlegrounds in the south.

In that same explosive period of transition, SNCC and other movement forces were also attracted to another kind of charisma. This was identified with the young, California-based Black Panther Party and their dramatic projection of the necessity of "picking up the gun" in the defense of the black communities of the north against the familiar force of police arrogance and brutality. King, meanwhile—against much powerful advice—followed his compassion and had gone into Chicago to try to find some way to use his movement experience and contacts to challenge the harsh world of poverty, political powerlessness, and despair that he found in the northern urban black communities. Of course, these were often communities where women and men had no deeply projected sense of place, no history of sustained, disciplined, and often victorious struggles for change. Coming out of such a setting in the south, King thought he could use his southern movement resources and transform them in such a way as to organize a real challenge to the powerful, paternalistic political machine of Mayor Richard Daley, thereby suggesting a ray of hope to Afro-Americans locked in similar situations across the north. Great resistance to this new vision emerged in the white communities of the north, and many black northerners were ambivalent as well.

Meanwhile, the summer explosions in the black communities of America continued. By 1967, when thousands of U.S. troops had to be called out to control the two major uprisings of that summer, in Newark, New Jersey, and Detroit, Michigan, many persons were talking of the possibility of seeing widespread racial warfare erupt in America. But for the black participants in the rebellions they never quite took on that character, for these men and women were striking out more against the enveloping hopelessness of their situation than against white persons as individuals. The deaths in the riots were overwhelmingly black, usually at the hands of police or other enforcers of law and order. From the perspective of many black persons, if a war existed, it was between the forces of unjust law and crippling order that were so often set against the northern, urban black need to break out into fresh air, into a new sense of what it means to be taken seriously as "we the people," as shapers of their own destiny and that of the nation.

In a parallel movement, King, SNCC, and CORE had decisively and often harshly identified the war in Vietnam (and the American president who was obsessed with winning it) as a major obstacle to any real national attempt to deal with the problems of structural racism, poverty, militarism, and political powerlessness. Indeed, the black freedom workers made it clear that they considered all of these aspects of the nation's way of life to be part of the bloody, entangling web in Vietnam, part of the obstruction to the necessary, continuing internal movement toward a more perfect union.

In a sense, King was a repository of much of the symbolic and actual

181

energies that had now flowed from the southern black freedom movement into the larger, less definable task of "redeeming the soul of America." In the last year of his life, King was calling more and more for what he loosely identified as "a revolution of values" in the United States. But he was going further as well. For by that time it was clear to him, he said, that

> the black revolution is much more than a struggle for the rights of Negroes. It is forcing America to face all its interrelated flaws—racism, poverty, militarism and materialism. It is exposing the evils that are rooted deeply in the whole structure of our society. It reveals systematic rather than superficial flaws and suggests that radical reconstruction of society itself is the real issue to be faced. [1]

By the time of his assassination, King was consumed with the compassionate, ambiguous search for the way to "radical reconstruction" of this country he loved so deeply. Constantly facing the threat of death and the reality of harsh criticism from many former allies, he groped for a way which would challenge the best energies and indignation of the black community—especially its young people—and move them into a higher level of nonviolence than had yet been discovered in the freedom struggle. He was no longer dependent on the goodwill of the federal government's leaders toward him and his cause. For by 1967–68 there was almost none. Instead, King sought to recruit the poor and their allies of every community—Appalachian whites, native Americans, Hispanics, as well as northern and southern black people, rural and urban together. These were the persons who had gained very little in concrete benefits from the victories of the southern movement.

But in those years, the shadow of assassination seemed to fall everywhere. On April 4, 1968, its movement cut short King's attempt to organize a Poor People's Campaign. At its best this was meant to be an audacious, multiracial movement of America's poor people and their friends to challenge the unfriendly, Vietnam-obsessed federal government with massive civil disobedience in the search for economic justice, for a more perfect union, for a nonviolent revolution. King had seen the faces of the poor. Like the grass-roots SNCC organizers of an earlier time, like Malcolm X, he had felt more and more deeply the needs of the locked-out. Thus, he had gone beyond civil rights to try to take on the structural problems of racism, poverty, militarism, materialism, and paranoid anticommunism in American life. But he could not go beyond the edges of his own life, and, therefore, left much undone, much to be done.

At the same time, other persons who had been deeply involved in the freedom struggle were losing energy, focus, vision, and direction. Some, facing a time of assassinations, murderous police riots, and extensive government subversion, were losing courage and hope. Others had drifted into self-destructive ways of life, deeply wounded veterans of a long and costly struggle. SNCC was in organizational disarray. CORE was fighting a series of harsh internal battles. It was simply not clear how persons and organizations, rising out of the traditions of the black-led freedom struggle, might confront and respond to the need for "radical reconstruction" of the nation's life systems. In other words, it was hard to know how to keep going, how to keep eyes on the prize. It was especially difficult for many persons to find the internal resources necessary for venturing onto new, uncertain, and dangerous ground.

As part of the black search for the way ahead, the period surrounding King's assassination saw an electric outpouring of black energy, creativity, and activism. Conferences and conventions flourished in a spirit reminiscent of the early days of the post-Civil War Reconstruction, bringing together politics, religion, economics, and culture. Black caucuses erupted in almost every predominantly white organization, often accompanied by hard, confrontative stands over issues of power, control, financing, and direction. (Some of the most vigorous of these caucuses sprang up in the churches, both Protestant and Roman Catholic. They were the sources of much of the black theology movement which broke through the traditions of a white, Euro-American theology which had previously made many self-assured, but unfounded, claims to universalism.) Black power conventions in Newark—while the odor of burning was still in the air—and then in Philadelphia were transmuted in 1970 into the first Congress of African Peoples in Atlanta, a testimony to the powerful revival of black nationalism and Africa-consciousness. Of course it was also a testimony to the transformation that was at work in Atlanta itself: A Congress of African People in Joe Louis Auditorium at Morris Brown College in Atlanta! Surely the times were changing.

During this period, many conferences were called by teachers, parents, students, and others which convened scholars, activists, political leaders, and many professionals to engage in vibrant, sometimes marvelously unscholarly discussions and debates on the need for black history and black studies in American life. White academic institutions in the north, feeling a postassassination pressure unlike any they had known before, were pushed to find black faculty, to recruit black students, to discover black-focused curriculum, and campuses rocked with confrontational actions.

Small, often creative, independent black institutions, especially those intent on the education of children, on the repossession of young minds, sprang up in hundreds of locations across the nation. Regularly they claimed the names, words, and traditions of DuBois, Garvey, Robeson, Ida B. Wells, and other historical figures as they searched for a past on which to build their vision of the future. It was a time of powerful, sometimes abrasive cultural renaissance—matched in power and scope only by the highest days of the Universal Negro Improvement Association—as poets, playwrights, graphic artists, dancers, and musicians seemed to be flourishing everywhere in the early 1970s. If nothing more, their presence seemed to suggest that the coming "radical reconstruction" of America would have to include systems of culture and belief, systems of education and identity, especially as these were revisioned and re-created by black people.

Much of the thrust and energy of this period was caught up in the first National Black Political Convention held in March 1972, in Gary, Indiana, a new beachhead city for the rising force of another black electoral power. Symbolically enough, the convention was called by the gifted, charismatic black artist and nationalist, Amiri Baraka (LeRoi Jones); by one of the representatives of traditional black congressional power, U.S. Representative Charles Diggs of Detroit (who had courageously attended the Mississippi trial of Emmett Till's murderers in 1955); and by the newly elected mayor of Gary, Richard Hatcher, host of the exciting, historic gathering.

Most persons among those hundreds who attended from across the country had some sense of agreement with the preamble to the convention's declaration: "We stand on the edge of history. We cannot turn back." Although interpretations of that announcement were varied, it was easy to forget the differences in the midst of the high energy of the convention. Indeed, some persons thought they might be witnessing the beginning of a new age in the black freedom struggle, or at least a new stage, when toward the end of the convention they were treated to this sight: On the stage, Jesse Jackson, Coretta Scott King, Shirley Chisholm (the first black woman elected to the U.S. House of Representatives), Baraka, Diggs, Hatcher, and others stood with clasped hands raised high, suggesting the prospects of a new union of forces for the transformation of black and white America.

Unfortunately, the millennium was not at hand. Much traditional politics and many personal agendas stood in the way. So it was necessary to deal with King's 1965 warning again: "There are no broad highways to lead us easily and inevitably to quick solutions." So, many persons left Gary and continued to move into the ambiguous years of the 1970s, sometimes guided only by the conviction that "We must keep going." Perhaps that was all that was possible for anyone to know with any certainty while moving on the edge of history.

As black men and women pressed on beyond Gary, trying to find ways to respond to the internal and external challenges of past, present, and future, they chose a number of alternatives, many bearing familiar elements of earlier times in the freedom movement. Some went the way of traditional American political participation, believing that the rising black numbers would somehow make a difference in a system still dominated by unprincipled compromise, the overwhelming desire for reelection, and a blindness to the needs for "radical restructuring." Others moved toward independent black institutions, finding their way to traditional black settings, or creating new ones. Many persons became deeply involved in organizations and movements focused on African liberation, participating in the continuing drama of the search for independence and for unity in the homeland. Sometimes they also seemed to be signaling a belief that the possession of this land had proved impossible—or at least incompatible with their sense of black integrity. Meanwhile a relative few developed scenarios for armed rebellion in the United States and some of them tried at times to live that out, often with disastrous results.

For a time, a significant movement of black people continued into the Nation of Islam. Then, after the death of the Honorable Elijah Muhammad, the organization went through a series of radical changes, leading finally to the creation of a break-away, revivalist movement headed by Minister Louis Farrakhan. These transformations and internal divisions made it difficult for many seekers, and some turned toward the path of more traditional Islam. (Indeed, a significant number of movement activists from the 1960s are now seriously engaged in religious communities.)

In the course of the 1970s, powerful debates were carried on in some circles of the black community over the relative merits of black nationalism and black Marxism as adequate ways to the future. Some of this proved enlightening and it opened up important issues concerning the "radical reconstruction" of the nation that King called for; however, other aspects of the debate were far more focused on personalities than on issues, always a dangerous trend. Indeed, by the end of the 1970s it was especially clear that black people needed to be wary of all cults of personality, for they watched in horror as the story unfolded concerning one such cult, led by James Jones, a renegade white Christian minister, and learned how hundreds of largely poor, religiously committed Afro-Americans had been driven to a terrible mass suicide in Guyana. But the death of Jonestown also carried the continuing, insistent message that men and women of every kind wanted and needed to be called to transformation, to work for the re-creation of themselves and their society, wanted to develop that work on some spiritually nourishing base in community with others. In other words, all over America, among many peoples, a deep hunger existed to participate actively in the search for a more perfect union.

As a result, much of the debate over affirmative action, self-help, government aid, entitlements, and other important recent issues somehow seemed to miss the depth and power of the call that was coming from many persons for a way to engage in the re-creation of their personal lives and the life of their nation. Perhaps the continuing hope for such an alternative was part of what drew so many men and women to Jesse Jackson's political candidacy in 1984, as the great grandson of slaves boldly entered the arena of presidential politics and offered to lead a nation badly in need of some direction. For Jackson and those who search with him to find a way to challenge, and perhaps transform America, many of the issues raised by a black scholar-activist at the beginning of the 1980s are still relevant. Referring to the 1970s as "a long, hard winter to endure," he asked,

If we are actually in the midst of so elemental a time of turning, if indeed we stand at the edge of history, then the central question for us all, but especially for those of us who are young, is, how shall we live responsibly in this momentous period of humankind's evolution? In the light of what we have seen and been and done over the last twenty years, what is our best response to this hour, to our forebears, to our children—to our own deepest hopes and human longings? Considering the lessons of the 1970s, how do we move forward?

Do we turn aside into divisionary and essentially private pursuits, refusing to face our need for solidarity and community, resisting the struggle-honed development of our own most humane and creative selves? Or do we move forward, emerging renewed and enlarged out of the spiritual pilgrimages of this decade, ready to advance in the company of our brothers and sisters into the uncharted arena of the new time?

At the edge of history, how shall we move? Do we continue to trail behind the most revolutionary insights that our struggle has already achieved? Do we turn away from the radical directions that Malcolm, Martin, and Fannie Lou had already approached in the 1960s? Or do we stand with them, move with them, move beyond them, move on for them and for ourselves and our children to remake this nation?

Absorbing the meaning of the 1970s, do we ignore the call of Gary? Or do we take its best insights and press on to create our own courageous summons to the newest stages of our struggle? How do we take all that we have learned and move it into the deeper internal spaces of our beings which this decade of winter has allowed us to explore? How, from so spacious and solid a center do we then move forward, beyond our best actions, beyond our best dreams, to participate fully in the creation of a fundamentally new reality, in ourselves, in our people, in this nation, and in this world?

185

These are no longer wild and visionary questions. The winter of our constrictions is finally passing. Are we ready for all the necessary birth pangs, all the searching floodlights, all the unexpected new pathways of spring?

Because the questions remain alive among us (when we allow ourselves to be alive with them), it may be helpful to close this section with the words of the poem "Creation-Spell" by Ed Bullins.

> Into your palm I place the ashes
> Into your palm are the ashes of your brothers
> burnt in the Alabama night
> Into your palm that holds your babies
> into your palm that feeds your children
> into your palm that holds the work tools
> I place the ashes of your father
> here are the ashes of your husbands
> Take the ashes of your nation
> and create the cement to build again
> Create the spirits to move again
> Take this soul dust and begin again.

Is it possible that beginning again, building again on the foundation of the long historic struggle for freedom—in every generation—is the only way to "possess this land," to possess ourselves, to create, and to re-create a more just, compassionate, and perfect union for ourselves and our posterity? Is that possibly what it means to keep your eyes on the prize?

Note

1. James Melvin Washington, ed., *A Testament of Hope* (San Francisco: Harper & Row, 1986), page 315.

QUESTIONS FOR REVIEW

1. Why do you think singing was so important to the post-World War II southern black freedom movement? In what ways do you think it is the same for justice movements in other parts of the world?

2. Why did white allies, often at the risk of their lives, join the black freedom struggle?

3. By 1965, what were some of the major external and internal accomplishments of the southern freedom movement?

4. If you were a college student (white or black) in the early 1960s, would you have participated in the movement? If so, why? If not, why not? If you did get involved, how and where might you have done so?

5. What opportunities exist in this generation for young people to participate in movements for social justice in attempts to create "a more perfect union?"

6. What were some of the ways in which people and the institutions of the U.S.A. responded to the challenge of the southern freedom movement?

7. Why might someone who is participating in the freedom movement say "my soul is rested?"

8. The author reports that "wherever the freedom movement heightened its activities in a black community, at the same time, the crime rate in such a community plummeted to its lowest levels." What are some of the implications of that statement for our crime-ridden communities?

9. What is the difference between a struggle for civil rights and a struggle for freedom and justice? What is the difference between working for black rights and working to create a more perfect union? Can you have one without the other?

10. In 1965 what did King sense to be the future direction of the black-led movement for freedom and justice?

11. What were the differences and similarities between the experiences and goals of Martin Luther King, Jr. and Malcolm X?

12. By the end of his life, King was describing the freedom struggle as "the black revolution" and saying that "radical reconstruction of society itself is the real issue to be faced." What do you think of the statement from which those quotations are taken? What might "radical reconstruction" of American society have meant to King?

13. In what ways were the *black power* conferences and the Black Political Convention of 1972 significant?

RECOMMENDED READINGS

Blumberg, Rhoda. *Civil Rights*. Boston: Twayne Publishers, 1984. One of the more recent attempts to synthesize the story of the movement of the 1950s and 1960s. Written for a popular audience.

Carawan, Guy and Candie. *We Shall Overcome* and *Freedom Is a Constant Struggle*. New York: Oak Publishers, 1963 and 1968. Two books comprising the most complete collection of the songs of the freedom movement. Along with the SNCC Freedom Singers, the authors were central in the role of sharing those songs throughout the movement.

Good, Paul. *The Trouble I've Seen*. Washington, D.C.: Howard University Press, 1974. A provocative account by a white journalist of some of his experiences reporting on the freedom movement of the early 1960s, particularly the events of 1964.

Jones, LeRoi and Larry Neal, eds. *Black Fire*. New York: William Morrow & Co., 1968. A sometimes overpowering collection of some of the writing that was pouring out of the black cultural renaissance of the 1960s.

King, Martin Luther, Jr. *Where Do We Go From Here: Chaos or Community?* New York: Harper & Row, 1967. This is King's attempt to set forward his sense of a direction that the freedom movement needed to take in the post-1965 period.

PART IV

THE LATER YEARS
1966–1986

CHAPTER 9

A NEW BLACK CONSCIOUSNESS (1966–1968)

by DARLENE CLARK HINE

—Compares the meaning of *black power* with the meanings of previous slogans of the black freedom struggle and discusses the significance attributed to this new slogan by the news media

—Explores the effect on the civil rights movement of American's increasing involvement in Vietnam

—Identifies a continuing shift in civil rights activities from a southern-based movement to one focused on urban ghettos in the north, explores reasons for the shift, and differentiates between traditional civil rights movement activities and those that were initiated during this period

—Analyzes why liberal northern whites who were previously supportive of civil rights goals were less involved with black concerns during this period

—Gives examples of the new style of black consciousness in literature, politics, and higher education

OVERVIEW

The two years between James Meredith's March Against Fear through Mississippi and the assassination of Martin Luther King, Jr. marked a turning point in the history of the civil rights movement in America. Although a significant body of legislation had been enacted to guarantee the basic rights of freedom to black Americans, rights that were already enjoyed by their fellow white citizens, gross inequities still existed. Southern blacks lacked political power, school desegregation remained a distant dream, poverty and economic disparities underscored their subordinate position, and a shroud of fear left few free to test their newly acquired rights. To be sure, massive change was evident throughout the south. Gone, for the most part, were many of the signs of overt segregation and discrimination, yet progress was negligible when measured in terms of real political and economic empowerment, and many blacks began to grow impatient with the slow gradualistic pace of desegregation.

In the summer of 1966 James Meredith resolved to demonstrate to fellow black Mississippians that they could indeed overcome fear and use the ballot to bring about effective social change. Many black leaders cautioned Meredith against undertaking a march from Memphis, Tennessee to Jackson, Mississippi. He was adamant, and on June 5th he set out on his trek. A very short distance from where he began Meredith was felled by an attempted assassination. Civil rights leaders of prominent rights organizations rushed to the wounded Meredith's hospital room and decided then that they would continue the march, beginning at the point he had been attacked.

Before long it became apparent that this march would be different from previous marches of the civil rights movement. The young members of the Student Nonviolent Coordinating Committee (SNCC) had already begun to seriously question the efficacy of nonviolence. Under the leadership of Stokely Carmichael, the newly elected chairman of SNCC, a new course was charted and the movement for black rights took a radical turn; thus, when Carmichael assumed the platform one evening during the march and declared that what black people really wanted was *black power,* the die was cast. Almost immediately massive media attention was directed towards Carmichael and the other adherents of *black power.* Millions of whites grew alarmed, unsure as to what the phrase meant and where they, particularly the more sympathetic ones, would fit into this new movement.

Initially few people knew what *black power* meant. Some suspected and speculated that it was a call for blacks to achieve their rights by any means necessary, including violence. Such impressions were reinforced by the organization of the Black Panther Party (BPP). Suddenly black people, especially those in the ghetto areas of northern cities, were acting defiantly different. No longer did they call themselves Negro; the new terminology was *black.* A host of new voices now demanded to be heard, espousing philosophies of cultural and revolutionary nationalism. Among their heroes were the recently slain Malcolm X, the 1920s black nationalist leader Marcus Garvey, and Frantz Fanon, the author of *The Wretched of the Earth*. Young blacks let their hair grow long, adopted African names, identified with the liberation struggles of the Third World, and challenged every fundamentally American value.

There could be no question that a social revolution of profound consequence was in the process of being born. But even more disturbing manifestations of the change were occurring within black America. Martin Luther King, Jr.'s sudden attack against the Vietnamese War and his call for an immediate cease-fire shocked both black and white veteran supporters of the civil rights movement. Many sought to distance themselves from him and even questioned whether his newly announced position would do serious damage to the civil rights movement as it had been known.

Meanwhile *black power* was slowly acquiring definition and strategy. *Black power* called for black people to organize themselves, to build group solidarity and pride, and with some white support to seek control of the institutions which governed their lives. The election of Richard Hatcher of Gary, Indiana and of Carl B. Stokes of Cleveland, Ohio as mayors of their respective cities announced that *black power* could work. But on college campuses other manifestations of the effects of *black power* on the development of a new consciousness were apparent. Black students, many of whom were the first generation of blacks to be admitted into predominantly white colleges, began to demand that these institutions create black studies departments and courses, hire black faculty, and recruit more black students. Their demands would shake the foundations of the American higher education establishment.

READINGS

1. On June 5, 1966 James Meredith began his march from Memphis, Tennessee to Jackson, Mississippi to serve as an example of individual courage so that other blacks in the state would overcome their fear and actively seek to exercise their right to vote. A shotgun blast abruptly ended Meredith's march, but only provoked in members of SNCC, the Southern Christian Leadership Conference (SCLC), and the Congress of Racial Equality (CORE) a fierce determi-

nation to resume the trek from where Meredith had been ambushed. The march, however, possessed an even greater significance for it was during this march that the slogan *black power*, symbolizing a radical new departure in the civil rights movement, was first proclaimed and embraced by young blacks grown weary of the slow pace of legislative and legalistic progress. Continued school and residential segregation and the entrenched poverty of rural and ghetto blacks shook the faith of young blacks for black liberation. Cleveland Sellers was program secretary of SNCC during the period of the Meredith march. In his autobiography Sellers describes the events and issues underlying the transformation of the march against fear into one for *black power.*

From: *The River of No Return—The Autobiography of a Black Militant and the Life and Death of SNCC* by Cleveland Sellers with Robert Terrell (New York: William Morrow & Company, Inc., 1973), pages 156–168. Copyright 1973 by Cleveland Sellers and Robert Terrell. Used by permission.

. . . What is Black Consciousness? More than anything else, it is an attitude, a way of seeing the world. Those of us who possessed it were involved in a perpetual search for racial meanings . . . the construction of a new, black value system. A value system geared to the unique cultural and political experience of blacks in this country.

Black Consciousness signaled the end of the use of the word *Negro*. . . . Black Consciousness permitted us to relate our struggle to the one being waged by Third World revolutionaries in Africa, Asia and Latin America. It helped us understand the imperialistic aspects of domestic racism. It helped us understand that the problems of this nation's oppressed minorities will not be solved without revolution.

* * * *

. . . We were in Little Rock, Arkansas, talking with Project Director Ben Greenich and some of his staff when a lawyer came up and told us that James Meredith had been killed.

* * * *

. . . Even though I'd always believed that Meredith's intention to march across Mississippi in order to prove that blacks didn't have to fear white violence any longer was absurd, I was enraged.

We didn't find out until two hours later that Meredith had not actually been murdered. The pellets from the shotgun, which had been fired from about fifty feet, had only knocked him unconscious. . . .

When we arrived at the hospital the next afternoon, Dr. [Martin Luther] King and CORE's new national director, Floyd McKissick, were visiting Meredith. Stanley [Wise], Stokely [Carmichael] and I joined them. . . . Meredith had agreed that the march should be continued without him. . . .

* * * *

Later that afternoon, a group, which included Stokely, Stanley Wise, Dr. King, McKissick and me, drove out on the highway to the spot where Meredith had been ambushed, and we walked for about three hours. We wanted to advertise that the march would be continued. . . .

* * * *

Late that night, a planning meeting was held at the Centenary Methodist Church, whose pastor was an ex-SNCC member, the Reverand James Lawson. The meeting was attended by representatives from all those groups interested in participating in the march, including Roy Wilkins and Whitney Young, who had flown in earlier in the day.

Participants in the meeting were almost immediately divided by the position taken by Stokely. He argued that the march should deemphasize white participation, that it should be used to highlight the need for independent, black political units, and that the Deacons for Defense, a black group from Louisiana whose members carried guns, be permitted to join the march.

Roy Wilkins and Whitney Young were adamantly opposed to Stokely. They wanted to send out a nationwide call to whites; they insisted that the Deacons be excluded and they demanded that we issue a statement proclaiming our allegiance to nonviolence.

* * * *

. . . Despite considerable pressure, Dr. King refused to repudiate Stokely. Wilkins and Young were furious. Realizing that they could not change Stokely's mind, they packed their briefcases and announced that they didn't intend to have anything to do with the march. . . .

The march began in a small way. We had few people, maybe a hundred and fifty. That was okay. We were headed for SNCC territory and we were calling the shots. . . .

* * * *

The Deacons for Defense served as our bodyguards. Their job was to keep our people alive. . . .

We had our first major trouble with the police on June 17, in Greenwood. It began when a contingent of state troopers arbitrarily decided that we could not put up our sleeping tent on the grounds of a black high school. When Stokely attempted to put the tent up anyway, he was arrested. Within minutes, word of his arrest had spread all over town. The rally that night, which was held in a city park, attracted almost three thousand people—five times the usual number.

Stokely, who'd been released from jail just minutes before the rally began, was the last speaker. He was preceded by McKissick, Dr. King and Willie Ricks. Like the rest of us, they were angry about Stokely's unnecessary arrest. Their speeches were particularly militant. When Stokely moved forward to speak, the crowd greeted him with a huge roar. He acknowledged his reception with a raised arm and clenched fist.

Realizing that he was in his element, with his people, Stokely let it all hang out. "This is the twenty-seventh time I have been arrested—and I ain't going to jail no more!" The crowd exploded into cheers and clapping.

"The only way we gonna stop them white men from whuppin' us is to take over. We been saying freedom for six years and we ain't got nothin'. What we gonna start saying now is Black Power!"

The crowd was right with him. They picked up his thoughts immediately.

"BLACK POWER!" they roared in unison.

Willie Ricks, who is as good at orchestrating the emotions of a crowd as anyone I have ever seen, sprang into action. Jumping to the platform with Stokely, he yelled to the crowd, "What do you want?"

"BLACK POWER!"

"What do you want?"

"BLACK POWER!!"

"What do you want?"

"BLACK POWER!! BLACK POWER!!! BLACK POWER!!!!"

Everything that happened afterward was a response to that moment. More than anything, it assured that the Meredith March Against Fear would go down in history as one of the major turning points in the black liberation struggle. . . .

* * * *

From SNCC's point of view, the march was a huge success. Despite the bitter controversy precipitated by Stokely's introduction of Black Power, we enjoyed several important accomplishments: thousands of voters were registered along the route; Stokely emerged as a national leader; the Mississippi movement acquired new inspiration, and major interest was generated in independent, black political organizations. ■

2. In this 1966 essay, Stokely Carmichael, as the recently elected chairman of SNCC, attempts to give meaning to the concept of the empowerment of black people, yet this essay is quite clearly directed towards an audience of white liberals and radical intellectuals who wanted to know what role whites would be allowed to play in the black power movement. Both the Carmichael essay and

the Ruth Turner Perot article which follows it define *black power* in terms of black people organizing themselves and their communities in order to gain political rights and advantage. The slogan quickly attracted many adherents from among the younger, more radical black youths grown increasingly disillusioned with Martin Luther King's philosophy of non-violence. Perot was Special Assistant to the National Director of CORE at the time.

From: "What We Want" by Stokely Carmichael in *New York Review of Books* (September 22, 1966). Copyright 1966 by New York Review of Books-New York Review, Inc. Used by permission.

One of the tragedies of the struggle against racism is that up to now there has been no national organization which could speak to the growing militancy of young black people in the urban ghetto. There has been only a civil rights movement, whose tone of voice was adapted to an audience of liberal whites. It served as a sort of buffer zone between them and angry young blacks. None of its so-called leaders could go into a rioting community and be listened to. In a sense, I blame ourselves—together with the mass media—for what has happened in Watts, Harlem, Chicago, Cleveland, Omaha. Each time the people in those cities saw Martin Luther King get slapped, they became angry; when they saw four little black girls bombed to death, they were angrier; and when nothing happened, they were steaming. We had nothing to offer that they could see, except to go out and be beaten again. We helped to build their frustration.

* * * *

An organization which claims to be working for the needs of a community—as SNCC does—must work to provide that community with a position of strength from which to make its voice heard. This is the significance of black power beyond the slogan.

Black power can be clearly defined for those who do not attach the fears of white America to their questions about it. We should begin with the basic fact that black Americans have two problems: they are poor and they are black. All other problems arise from this two-sided reality: lack of education, the so-called apathy of black men. Any program to end racism must address itself to that double reality.

* * * *

. . . the concept of "black power" is not a recent or isolated phenomenon: It has grown out of the ferment of agitation and activity by different people and organizations in many black communities over the years. Our last year of work in Alabama added a new concrete possibility. In Lowndes County, for example, black power will mean that if a Negro is elected sheriff, he can end police brutality. If a black man is elected tax assessor, he can collect and channel funds for the building of better roads and schools serving black people—thus advancing the move from political power into the economic arena. In such areas as Lowndes, where black men have a majority, they will attempt to use it to exercise control. This is what they seek: control. Where Negroes lack a majority, black power means proper representation and sharing of control. It means the creation of power bases from which black people can work to change statewide or nationwide patterns of oppression through pressure from strength—instead of weakness. Politically, black power means what it has always meant to SNCC: the coming-together of black people to elect representatives and *to force those representatives to speak to their needs*. It does not mean merely putting black faces into office. A man or woman who is black and from the slums cannot be automatically expected to speak to the needs of black people. Most of the black politicians we see around the country today are not what SNCC means by black power. The power must be that of a community, and emanate from there.

* * * *

Ultimately, the economic foundations of this country must be shaken if black people are to control their lives. The colonies of the United States—and this includes the black ghettoes within its borders, north and south—must be liberated. For a century, this nation has been like an octopus of exploitation, its tentacles stretching from Mississippi and Harlem to South America, the Middle East, southern Africa, and Vietnam; the form of exploitation varies from area to area but the essential result has been the same—a powerful few have been maintained and enriched at the expense of the poor and voiceless colored masses. This pattern must be broken. As its grip loosens here and there around the world, the hopes of black Americans become more realistic. For racism to die, a totally different America must be born.

* * * *

White America will not face the problem of color, the reality of it. The well-intended say: "We're all human, everybody is really decent, we must forget color." But color cannot be "forgotten" until its weight is recognized and dealt with. White America will not acknowledge that the ways in which this country sees itself are contradicted by being black—and always have been. Whereas most of the people who settled this country came here for freedom or for economic opportunity, blacks were brought here to be slaves. When the Lowndes County Freedom Organization chose the black panther as its symbol, it was christened by the press "the Black Panther Party"—but the Alabama Democratic Party, whose symbol is a rooster, has never been called the White Cock Party. No one ever talked about "white power" because power in this country *is* white. All this adds up to more than merely identifying a group phenomenon by some catchy name or adjective. The furor over that black panther reveals the problems that white America has with color and sex; the furor over "black power" reveals how deep racism runs and the great fear which is attached to it.

* * * *

I have said that most liberal whites react to "black power" with the question, What about me?, rather than saying: Tell me what you want me to do and I'll see if I can do it. There are answers to the right question. One of the most disturbing things about almost all white supporters of the movement has been that they are afraid to go into their own communities—which is where the racism exists—and work to get rid of it. They want to run from Berkeley to tell us what to do in Mississippi; let them look instead at Berkeley. They admonish blacks to be nonviolent; let them preach nonviolence in the white community. They come to teach me Negro history; let them go to the suburbs and open up freedom schools for whites. Let them work to stop America's racist foreign policy; let them press this government to cease supporting the economy of South Africa.

There is a vital job to be done among poor whites. We hope to see, eventually, a coalition between poor blacks and poor whites. That is the only coalition which seems acceptable to us, and we see such a coalition as the major internal instrument of change in American society. SNCC has tried several times to organize poor whites; we are trying again now, with an initial training program in Tennessee. It is purely academic today to talk about bringing poor blacks and whites together, but the job of creating a poor-white power bloc must be attempted. The main responsibility for it falls upon whites. . . .

* * * *

But our vision is not merely of a society in which all black men have enough to buy the good things of life. When we urge that black money go into black pockets, we mean the communal pocket. We want to see money go back into the community and used to benefit it. We want to see the cooperative concept applied in business and banking. We want to see black ghetto residents demand that an exploiting store keeper sell them, at minimal cost, a building or a shop that they will own and improve cooperatively; they can back their demand with a rent strike, or a boycott, and a community so unified behind them that no one else will move into the building or buy at the store. The society we seek to build among black people, then, is not a capitalist one. It is a society in which the spirit of community and humanistic love prevail. . . . ∎

From: "Black Power: A Voice Within" by Ruth Turner Perot in *Oberlin Alumni Magazine*, LXIII (May 1967). Used by permission of *Oberlin Alumni Magazine*.

. . . Black power to CORE means the organization of the black community into a tight and disciplined group, for six purposes:

1. Growth of political power.
2. Building economic power.
3. Improvement of self-image.
4. Development of Negro leadership.
5. Demanding federal law enforcement.
6. Mobilization of Negro consumer power.

Let me give some examples of how CORE programs the concept:

• In Baltimore, MFU, an independent union organized by CORE, raised wages of nearly 100 members, workers regular labor unions did not want to organize, from 35¢ to $1.50.

• Baltimore, CORE's 1966 Target City, also demonstrated black power in the November elections. As a result of intensive mobilizing and organizing by CORE and other groups, Negroes switched 35 to 1 to vote for Republican [Spiro] Agnew over "Home is your castle" [George P.] Mahoney. Mahoney was defeated. We were so effective, in fact, that the Ku Klux Klan has chosen Baltimore as [its] Target City.

• CORE ran eight Negro candidates for school board elections in Democratic primaries in Louisiana. All won, first time since Reconstruction.

• Also—Louisiana (Opelousas)—Sweet potato cooperative. 375 farmers, 15 white, growing and marketing their sweet potato crops. This is economic black power.

• Watts, Operation Bootstraps, "Learn, Baby, Learn." 12 teenagers, graduates of [a] computer course, have set up their own business, offering up-to-date skills for pay.

• Freedom School in Baltimore and plans for Black Arts and Afro-American Institute. A place where black people learn of history and contributions to world culture and civilization. Power of self-knowledge. Also in Baltimore, a leadership training [program] for neighborhood people.

• As a result of CORE insistence, federal examiners sent to South Carolina and Mississippi counties. Result: registration climbed.

We believe that these building blocks will become a bulwark that will protect the next Adam Clayton Powell, multiplied many times over. There is no other choice. If power for the powerless is not achieved so that changes within its structure can be made, this nation will not survive. ■

3. **A**s the traditional integrationist goals appeared increasingly illusory, younger, radical black leaders concluded that the strategy of nonviolence and legislative intervention was largely a failure. Recruits into the new black power movement searched for new heroes to give voice and vision to their struggle for black self-determination and identity. It was in this context that Malcolm X became canonized, Marcus Garvey was resurrected, and Frantz Fanon's *The Wretched of the Earth* became required reading and the most often quoted text. Young urban blacks adopted new ways of dressing, greeting, and communicating with each other. A black arts movement soon flourished as poets, playwrights, painters, and novelists created a revolution in the cultural consciousness of black Americans. Black was beautiful. It was all right for black people to love themselves and each other, and, moreover, it was

imperative that they construct a new value system and aesthetic to resist what was perceived to have been the corrupt materialism of white America. The three readings that follow—from Fanon, Sonia Sanchez, and Yusef Iman—are major examples of this black aesthetic.

From: *The Wretched of the Earth* by Frantz Fanon (New York: Grove Press, Inc., 1963), pages 222–223. Copyright 1963 by Présence Africaine. Used by permission of Grove Press, Inc.

If we wanted to trace in the works of native writers the different phases which characterize this evolution we would find spread out before us a panorama on three levels. In the first phase, the native intellectual gives proof that he has assimilated the culture of the occupying power. His writings correspond point by point with those of his opposite numbers in the mother country. His inspiration is European and we can easily link up these works with definite trends in the literature of the mother country. This is the period of unqualified assimilation. We find in this literature coming from the colonies the Parnassians, the Symbolists, and the Surrealists.

In the second phase we find the native is disturbed; he decides to remember what he is. This period of creative work approximately corresponds to that immersion which we have just described. But since the native is not a part of his people, since he only has exterior relations with his people, he is content to recall their life only. Past happenings of the bygone days of his childhood will be brought up out of the depths of his memory; old legends will be reinterpreted in the light of a borrowed estheticism and of a conception of the world which was discovered under other skies.

Sometimes this literature of just-before-the-battle is dominated by humor and by allegory; but often too it is symptomatic of a period of distress and difficulty, where death is experienced, and disgust too. We spew ourselves up; but already underneath laughter can be heard.

Finally in the third phase, which is called the fighting phase, the native, after having tried to lose himself in the people and with the people, will on the contrary shake the people. Instead of according the people's lethargy an honored place in his esteem, he turns himself into an awakener of the people; hence comes a fighting literature, a revolutionary literature, and a national literature. During this phase a great many men and women who up till then would never have thought of producing a literary work, now that they find themselves in exceptional circumstances—in prison, with the Marquis, or on the eve of their execution—feel the need to speak to their nation, to compose the sentence which expresses the heart of the people, and to become the mouthpiece of a new reality in action. ■

From: "Malcolm" by Sonia Sanchez in *Homecoming* (Detroit: Broadside Press, 1969), page 32. Used by permission of Sonia Sanchez.

Do not speak to me of martyrdom
of men who die to be remembered
on some parish day.
I don't believe in dying
though I too shall die
and violets like castanets
will echo me.

Yet this man
this dreamer,
thick-lipped with words
will never speak again
and in each winter
when the cold air cracks
with frost, I'll breathe
his breath and mourn
my gun-filled nights.

He was the sun that tagged
the western sky and
melted tiger-scholars

while they searched for stripes.
He said, "Fuck you white
man. we have been
curled too long. nothing
is sacred now. not your
white face nor any
land that separates
until some voices
squat with spasms."

Do not speak to me of living.
life is obscene with crowds
of white on black.
death is my pulse.
what might have been
is not for him/or me
but what could have been
floods the womb until I drown.

■

"Love Your Enemy" by Yusef Iman in *Black Fire: An Anthology of Afro-American Writing*, edited by LeRoi Jones and Larry Neal (New York: William Morrow & Co., 1968), page 387–388. Used by permission of Yusef Iman.

Brought here in slave ships and
    pitched over board.
Love your enemy.
Language taken away, culture taken away.
Love your enemy.
Work from sun up to sun down.
Love your enemy.
Work for no pay.
Love your enemy.
Last hired, first fired.
Love your enemy.
Rape your mother.
Love your enemy.
Lynch your father.
Love your enemy.
Bomb your churches.
Love your enemy.
Kill your children.
Love your enemy.
Forced to fight his wars.
Love your enemy.
Pay the highest rent.

Love your enemy.
Sell you rotten foods.
Love your enemy.
Sell dope to your children.
Love your enemy.
Forced to live in the slums.
Love your enemy.
Dilapidated schools.
Love your enemy.
Puts you in jail.
Love your enemy.
Bitten by dogs.
Love your enemy.
Water hose you down.
Love your enemy.
    Love.
    Love.
    Love.
    Love.
    Love.
    Love, for everybody else.
But when will we love ourselves?

■

4. **M**artin Luther King, Jr. opposed the war in Vietnam for many years, but when he delivered this speech at the Riverside Church in New York, few would have predicted the extent of criticism that was targeted at him. He addressed the adverse consequences of continued American involvement in the war: moral isolation, the strengthening of the military-industrial complex, and the growing threat of nuclear confrontation. King's stance on Vietnam clashed with the Johnson administration and brought upon King the wrath of J. Edgar Hoover of the FBI. In response to questions of whether it was wise, politic, or expedient for the civil rights movement to become embroiled in the battle over Vietnam, King replied, "Ultimately a genuine leader is not a searcher for consensus but a molder of consensus. On such positions, cowardice asks the question, 'Is it safe?' Vanity asks the question, 'Is it popular?' But conscience asks the question, 'Is it right?' There comes a time when one must take a position that is neither safe nor politic nor popular but must take it because conscience tells him that it must be right." ("The Future of Integration" in *The Humanist*, March/April 1968)

From: "Beyond Vietnam" a speech by Martin Luther King, Jr. given at Riverside Church Meeting, sponsored by Clergy and Laymen Concerned about Vietnam, New York, April 4, 1967. Copyright 1967 by Martin Luther King, Jr. Used by permission of Joan Daves.

. . . I come to this platform tonight to make a passionate plea to my beloved nation. This speech is not addressed to Hanoi or to the National Liberation Front. It is not addressed to China or to Russia.

* * * *

Since I am a preacher by trade, I suppose it is not surprising that I have several reasons for bringing Vietnam into the field of my moral vision. There is at the outset a very obvious and almost facile connection between the war in Vietnam and the struggle I, and others, have been waging in America. A few years ago there was a shining moment in that struggle. It seemed as if there was a real promise of hope for the poor—both black and white—through the Poverty Program. There were experiments, hopes, new beginnings. Then came the build-up in Vietnam and I watched the program broken and eviscerated as if it were some idle political plaything of a society gone mad on war, and I knew that America would never invest the necessary funds or energies in rehabilitation of its poor so long as adventures like Vietnam continued to draw men and skills and money like some demoniacal destructive suction tube. So I was increasingly compelled to see the war as an enemy of the poor and to attack it as such.

Perhaps the more tragic recognition of reality took place when it became clear to me that the war was doing far more than devastating the hopes of the poor at home. It was sending their sons and their brothers and their husbands to fight and to die in extraordinarily high proportions relative to the rest of the population. We were taking the black young men who had been crippled by our society and sending them 8,000 miles away to guarantee liberties in Southeast Asia which they had not found in Southwest Georgia and East Harlem. So we have been repeatedly faced with the cruel irony of watching Negro and white boys on TV screens as they kill and die together for a nation that has been unable to seat them together in the same schools. . . .

My third reason moves to an even deeper level of awareness, for it grows out of my experience in the ghettoes of the North over the last three years—especially the last three summers. As I have walked among the desperate, rejected and angry young men I have told them that Molotov cocktails and rifles would not solve their problems. I have tried to offer them my deepest compassion while maintaining my convictions that social change comes most meaningfully through non-violent action. But they asked—and rightly so—what about Vietnam? They asked if our own nation wasn't using massive doses of violence to solve its problems, to bring about the changes it wanted. Their questions hit home, and I knew that I could never again raise my voice against the violence of the oppressed in the ghettos without having first spoken clearly to the greatest purveyor of violence in the world today—my own government. . . .

For those who ask the question, "Aren't you a Civil Rights leader?" and thereby mean to exclude me from the movement for peace, I have this further answer. In 1957 when a group of us formed the Southern Christian Leadership Conference, we chose as our motto: "To save the soul of America." We were convinced that we could not limit our vision to certain rights for black people, but instead affirmed the conviction that America would never be free or saved from itself unless the descendants of its slaves were loosed completely from the shackles they still wear. . . .

* * * *

And as I ponder the madness of Vietnam and search within myself for ways to understand and respond in compassion my mind goes constantly to the people of that peninsula. I speak now not of the soldiers of each side, not of the junta in Saigon, but simply of the people who have been living under the curse of war for almost three continuous decades now. I think of them too because it is clear to me that there will be no meaningful solution there until some attempt is made to know them and hear their broken cries.

* * * *

They watch as we poison their water, as we kill a million acres of their crops. They must weep as the bulldozers roar through their areas preparing to destroy the precious trees. They wander into the hospitals, with at least 20 casualties from American firepower for one Vietcong-inflicted injury. They wander into the towns and see thousands of the children, homeless, without clothes, running in packs on the streets like animals. They see the children degraded by our soldiers as they beg for food. They see the children selling their sisters to our soldiers, soliciting for their mothers. . . .

Perhaps the more difficult but no less necessary task is to speak for those who have been designated as our enemies. What of the National Liberation Front— that strangely anonymous group we call VC or Communists? What must they think of us in America when they realize that we permitted the repression and cruelty of Diem which helped to bring them into being as a resistance group in the South? What do they think of our condoning the violence which led to their own taking up of arms? How can they believe in our integrity when now we speak of "aggression from the North" as if there were nothing more essential to the war? How can they trust us when now we charge them with violence after the murderous reign of Diem, and charge them with violence while we pour every new weapon of death into their land? Surely we must understand their feelings even if we do not condone their actions. Surely we must see that the men we supported pressed them to their violence. Surely we must see that our own computerized plans of destruction simply dwarf their greatest acts.

How do they judge us when our officials know that their membership is less than 25 per cent Communist and yet insist on giving them the blanket name? What must they be thinking when they know that we are aware of their control of major sections of Vietnam and yet we appear ready to allow national elections in which this highly organized political parallel government will have no part? They ask how we can speak of free elections when the Saigon press is censored and controlled by the military junta. And they are surely right to wonder what kind of new government we plan to help form without them—the only party in real touch with the peasants. They question our political goals and they deny the reality of a peace settlement from which they will be excluded. Their questions are frighteningly relevant. Is our nation planning to build on political myth again and then shore it up with the power of new violence?

Here is the true meaning of value and compassion and non-violence when it helps us to see the enemy's point of view, to hear his questions, to know his assessment of ourselves. For from his view we may indeed see the basic weaknesses of our own condition, and if we are mature, we may learn and grow and profit from the wisdom of the brothers who are called the opposition.

So, too, with Hanoi. In the North, where our bombs now pummel the land, and our mines endanger the waterways, we are met by a deep but understandable mistrust. To speak for them is to explain this lack of confidence in western words, and especially their distrust of American intentions now. In Hanoi are the men who led the nation to independence against the Japanese and the French, the men who sought membership in the French commonwealth and were betrayed by the weakness of Paris and the willfulness of the colonial armies. It was they who led a second struggle against French domination at tremendous costs, and then were persuaded to give up the land they controlled between the 13th and 17th parallel as a temporary measure at Geneva. After 1954 they watched us conspire with Diem to prevent elections which would have surely brought Ho Chi Minh to power over a united Vietnam, and they realized they had been betrayed again. . . .

At this point I should make it clear that while I have tried in these last few minutes to give a voice to the voiceless on Vietnam and to understand the arguments of those who are called enemy, I am as deeply concerned about our own troops there as anything else. For it occurs to me that what we are submitting them to in Vietnam is not simply the brutalizing process that goes on in any war where armies face each other and seek to destroy. We are adding cynicism to the process of death, for they must know after a short period there that none of the things we claim to be fighting for are really involved. Before long they must know that their government has sent them into a struggle among Vietnamese, and the more sophisticated surely realize that we are on the side of the wealthy and the secure while we create a hell for the poor.

* * * *

If we continue there will be no doubt in my mind and in the mind of the world that we have no honorable intentions in Vietnam. It will become clear that our minimal expectation is to occupy it as an American colony and men will not refrain from thinking that our maximum hope is to goad China into a war so that we may bomb her nuclear installations. If we do not stop our war against the people in Vietnam immediately, the world will be left with no other alternative than to see this as some horribly clumsy and deadly game we have decided to play.

* * * *

In order to atone for our sins and errors in Vietnam, we should take the initiative in bringing a halt to this tragic war. I would like to suggest five concrete things that our Government should do immediately to begin the long and difficult process of extricating ourselves from this nightmarish conflict:

1. End all bombing in North and South Vietnam.

2. Declare a unilateral cease-fire in the hope that such action will create the atmosphere for negotiation.

3. Take immediate steps to prevent other battlegrounds in Southeast Asia by curtailing our military build-up in Thailand and our interference in Laos.

4. Realistically accept the fact that the National Liberation Front has substantial support in South Vietnam and must thereby play a role in any meaningful negotiations and in any future Vietnam government.

5. Set a date that we will remove all foreign troops from Vietnam in accordance with the 1954 Geneva Agreement.

Part of our ongoing commitment might well express itself in an offer to grant asylum to any Vietnamese who fears for his life under a new regime which included the Liberation Front. Then we must make what reparations we can for the damage we have done. We must provide the medical aid that is badly needed, making it available in this country if necessary.

Meanwhile we in the churches and synagogues have a continuing task while we urge our Government to disengage itself from a disgraceful commitment. We must continue to raise our voices if our nation persists in its perverse ways in Vietnam. We must be prepared to match actions with words by seeking out every creative means of protest possible. ■

5. **I**n politics, *black power* meant running black candidates for office and mobilizing and organizing black votes to elect them. The most notable successes of this strategy were the elections of Richard Hatcher as mayor of Gary, Indiana, and of Carl Stokes as mayor of Cleveland, Ohio. The unified black ghetto vote combined with some white support would eventually witness the election of scores of blacks to mayoral positions in many of the larger cities in the country. The following reading discusses the strategy used and the larger significance of the election of a black mayor in 1967.

From: "The Making of the Negro Mayors 1967" by Jeffrey K. Hadden, Louis H. Masotti, and Victor Thiessen in *Trans-Action*, Vol. 5, No. 3. Copyright 1968 by Transaction, Inc. Used by permission.

Throughout most of 1967, black power and Vietnam kept this nation in an almost continual state of crisis. The summer months were the longest and hottest in modern U.S. history—many political analysts even felt that the nation was entering its most serious domestic conflict since the Civil War. Over a hundred cities were rocked with violence.

As the summer gave way to autumn, the interest of the nation shifted a little from the summer's riots to the elections on the first Tuesday of November. An unprecedented number of Negroes were running for office, . . . In Cleveland, Carl B. Stokes, a lawyer who in 1962 had become the first Democratic Negro legislator in Ohio, was now seeking to become the first Negro mayor of a large American city. . . .

Normally, the nation couldn't care less about who would become the next mayors of Cleveland [and] Gary. . . . But the tenseness of the summer months gave these elections enormous significance.

* * * *

Cleveland

By early 1967, the city Cleveland had seemingly hit rock bottom. A long procession of reporters began arriving to write about its many problems. The racial unrest of the past several years had, during the summer of 1966, culminated in the worst rioting in Cleveland's history. This unrest was continuing to grow as several militant groups were organizing. Urban renewal was a dismal failure; in January, the Department of Housing and Urban Development even cut off the city's urban-renewal funds, the first such action by the Federal Government. The exodus of whites, along with business, shoved the city to the brink of financial disaster. In February, the Moody Bond Survey reduced the city's credit rating. In May, the Federal Government cut off several million dollars of construction funds—because the construction industry had failed to assure equal job opportunities for minority groups. In short, the city was . . . in deep trouble. And while most ethnic groups probably continued to believe that Cleveland was the "Best Location in the Nation," the Negro community—and a growing number of whites—were beginning to feel that Cleveland was the "Mistake on the Lake," and that it was time for a change.

Carl Stokes's campaign for mayor was his second try. In 1965, while serving in the state House of Representatives, he came within 2100 votes of defeating Mayor Ralph S. Locher. Stokes had taken advantage of a city charter provision that let a candidate file as an independent and bypass the partisan primaries. Ralph McAllister had earned the enmity of the Negro community. The Republican candidate was Ralph Perk, the first Republican elected to a county-wide position (auditor) in many years. A second-generation Czech-Bohemian, Perk hoped to win by combining his ethnic appeals with his program for the city (Perk's Plan). He had no opposition for his party's nomination. The fourth candidate was Mayor Locher, who had defeated Mark McElroy, county recorder and perennial candidate for something in the Democratic primary.

It was in the 1965 Democratic primary that the first signs of a "black bloc" vote emerged. The Negroes, who had previously supported incumbent Democratic mayoral candidates, if not enthusiastically at least consistently, made a concerted effort to dump Locher in favor of McElroy. There were two reasons.

• Locher had supported his police chief after the latter had made some tactless remarks about Negroes. Incensed Negro leaders demanded an audience with the mayor, and when he refused, his office was the scene of demonstrations, sit-ins, and arrests. At that point, as one of the local reporters put it, "Ralph Locher became a dirty name in the ghetto."

• Stokes, as an independent, and his supporters hoped that the Democratic primary would eliminate the *stronger* candidate, Locher. For then a black bloc would have a good chance of deciding the general election because of an even split in the white vote.

• Despite the Negro community's efforts, Locher won the primary and went on to narrowly defeat Stokes. Locher received 37 percent of the vote, Stokes 36 percent, Perk 17 percent, and McAllister 9 percent. Some observers reported that a last-minute whispering campaign in Republican precincts—to the effect that "A vote for Perk is a vote for Stokes"—may have given Locher enough Republican votes to win. The evidence: The popular Perk received only a 17 percent vote in a city where a Republican could be expected to receive something closer to 25 percent. Had Perk gotten anything close to 25 percent, Stokes would have probably been elected two years earlier.

Although he made a strong showing in defeat, Carl Stokes's political future looked bleak. No one expected the Democratic leaders to give Stokes another opportunity to win by means of a split vote. Nor were there other desirable elected offices Stokes could seek. Cleveland has no Negro Congressman largely because the heavy Negro concentration in the city has been "conveniently" gerrymandered. The only district where Stokes might have had a chance has been represented by Charles Vanik, a popular and liberal white, and as long as Vanik remained in Congress Stokes was locked out. Stokes's state Senate district was predominantly white; and a county or state office seemed politically unrealistic because of his race. So, in 1966, Stokes sought re-election to the State House unopposed.

Between 1965 and 1967, Cleveland went from bad to worse, physically, socially, and financially. With no other immediate possibilities, Stokes began to think about running for mayor again. . . .

* * * *

The first part of his strategy was a massive voter-registration drive in the Negro wards—to reinstate the potential Stokes voters dropped from the rolls for failing to vote since the 1964 Presidential election. The Stokes organization—aided by Martin Luther King Jr. and the Southern Christian Leadership Conference, as well as by a grant (in part earmarked for voter registration) from the Ford Foundation to the Cleveland chapter of CORE—did succeed in registering many Negroes. But there was a similar drive mounted by the Democratic Party on behalf of Locher. . . .

The second part of the Stokes strategy took him across the polluted Cuyahoga River into the white wards that had given him a mere 3 percent of the vote in 1965. He spoke wherever he would be received—to small groups in private homes, in churches, and in public and private halls. While he was not always received enthusiastically, he did not confront many hostile crowds. He faced the race issue squarely and encouraged his audience to judge him on his ability.

Stokes's campaign received a big boost when the *Plain Dealer*, the largest daily in Ohio, endorsed him. Next, the *Cleveland Press* called for a change in City Hall. . . .

More people voted in this primary than in any other in Cleveland's history. When the ballots were counted, Stokes had 52.5 percent of the votes—he had defeated Locher by a plurality of 18,000 votes . . .

What produced Stokes's clear victory?. . . . The decisive factor was the size of the Negro turnout. While Negroes constituted only about 40 percent of the voters, 73.4 percent of them turned out, compared with only 58.4 percent of the whites. . . .

Stokes emerged from the primary as the odds-on favorite to win—five weeks later—in the general election. And in the first few days of the campaign, it seemed that Stokes had everything going for him.

• Stokes was bright, handsome, and articulate. His opponent, Seth Taft, while bright, had never won an election, and his family name, associated with the Taft-Hartley Act, could hardly be an advantage among union members. In addition, he was shy and seemingly uncomfortable in a crowd.

• Both the *Plain Dealer* and the *Cleveland Press* endorsed Stokes in the general election.

• The wounds of the primary were quickly (if perhaps superficially) healed, and the Democratic candidate was endorsed by both the Democratic Party and Mayor Locher.

• Labor—both the A.F.L.–C.I.O. and the Teamsters—also endorsed Stokes.

• He had a partisan advantage. Of the 326,003 registered voters, only 34,000 (10 percent) were Republican. . . .

• Stokes had 90,000 or more Negro votes virtually assured, with little possibility that Taft would make more than slight inroads.

The Gary Race

The race for mayor in Gary, Ind., was not overtly racist. Still, the racial issue was much less stable than it was in Cleveland. When Democratic chairman John G. Krupa refused to support Richard D. Hatcher, the Democratic candidate, it was clear that the reason was race. When the Gary newspaper failed to give similar coverage to both candidates and sometimes failed to print news releases from Hatcher headquarters (ostensibly because press deadlines had not been met), it was clear that race was a factor.

Even though race was rarely mentioned openly, the city polarized. While Stokes had the support of the white-owned newspapers and many white campaign workers, many of Hatcher's white supporters preferred to remain in the background—in part, at least, because they feared reprisals from white racists. Hatcher didn't use the black-power slogan, but to the community the election was a contest between black and white. And when the Justice Department supported Hatcher's claim that the election board had illegally removed some 5000 Negro voters from the registration lists and added nonexistent whites, the tension in the city became so great that the Governor, feeling that there was "imminent danger" of violence on election night, called up 4000 National Guardsmen.

Negroes constitute an estimated 55 percent of Gary's 180,000 residents, but white voter registration outnumbers Negroes by 2000 or 3000. Like Stokes, Hatcher—in order to win—had to pull some white votes or have significantly higher Negro turnout.

The voter turnout and voting patterns in Cleveland and Gary were very similar. In both cities, almost 80 percent of the registered voters turned out at the polls. In the Glen Park and Miller areas, predominantly white neighborhoods, Joseph B. Radigan—Hatcher's opponent—received more than 90 percent of the votes. In the predominantly Negro areas, Hatcher received an estimated 93 percent of the votes. In all, Hatcher received about 4000 white votes, while losing probably 1000 Negro votes, at most, to Radigan. This relatively small white vote was enough to give him victory. . . . ■

6. **O**ne of the most controversial manifestations of the new black consciousness was acted out on predominantly white college campuses, including the University of Wisconsin, Cornell, Harvard, Yale, and Northwestern Universities. Confronting institutional racism head on, this first generation of black students on white campuses demanded what were perceived to be drastic reforms in curriculum; moreover, they insisted that university officials not only pay attention to their socio-cultural and educational needs but also to those racial and economic ills oppressing the larger black community. Many, both white and black, criticized the black studies movement vehemently. Some black leaders and educators argued that black studies would encourage and support racial segregation and were nothing more than exercises in "ethnocentric manipulation." White scholars warned that a "cowardly surrender" to all black student demands would be destructive to the university as an institution of higher learning and to Afro-American society in general. Few seemed to appreciate the particular pain, isolation, and alienation black students experienced on predominantly white campuses that were devoid of black faculty and had no curriculum programs that reflected their historical and cultural lives. The following document, prepared by the black students of Northwestern University, is one example of black student demands that swept across the country in the late 1960s.

From: "Revised Demands of the Black Students" in "Black and White at Northwestern University: Documents," *Integrated Education*, Vol. VI (May–June 1968). Used by permission of *Equity & Excellence*, formerly *Integrated Education*.

Having rejected the basic principles on which our demands were based, the administration has forced us to speak for the last time on those matters discussed at the meeting of Wednesday, April 24, 1968. We demand that such action be taken to meet this, our final list of demands. The University must show itself flexible enough to take in the "peculiarities" of our culture and background. . . .

Policy Statement

Northwestern cannot begin to deal effectively with racism on this campus until it first realizes and openly acknowledges the extent of racism in American society. For this reason we reject the statement given to us in response and demand that a "new" policy statement be issued and made public from President J. Roscoe Miller asserting that the racism of American society which has penetrated all American institutions has also penetrated Northwestern University, and has thus affected the social and academic life here.

This statement is to include a declaration that the University is attempting to provide a multi-racial and cultural society within the university walls and that any racist attack and/or abuses shall be considered in direct opposition to the University's goals and a danger to the peaceful existence of such a society. The extent of this danger is such that the perpetrator shall be immediately excluded from this institution.

In order to alter the racist structure of this University, a change has to take place in the judiciary structures, attitudes, and practices. As of now, the University Disciplinary Committee [U.D.C.] is ineffective in dealing with racism on campus. . . . We demand that this judiciary be changed and implemented to bring about swifter and fairer decisions, or that a special judiciary be created to deal with these special cases.

On acknowledging the racist structure of this country and this institution, Northwestern is committed to understand the negative effects of racism on Black people and other oppressed people. The entire concept of justice has to be re-evaluated for this reason. Justice for Black people at this time does not mean equal treatment before a law or rule which is insensitive to our oppressive position in this country. We contend that justice for Black people means that extra consideration and efforts are to be made in order to balance the effects of racism. This means in effect that the U.D.C. decision to place 3 white students and 2 Black students on disciplinary warning is not justice and is thus unacceptable in our eyes.

Our experience in America has not been characterized by justice in any way. No white institution can right our hundreds of years of history and experience by suddenly treating us the same as white people (only at those times when it is strategic to do so) and call it justice and equality. No matter how one looks at it, idealistically or realistically, Black people know that we are still getting the short end of the deal. A new basis for administering justice must be developed and put into effect and it is with this that U.D.C., or any new judiciary which intends to deal with racism, has to concern itself.

The only concrete response from the administration was the establishment of a special University Committee on Human Relations. However, we are not satisfied with that response and demand the right of the Black student community to approve all appointments to this committee and to determine at least 50% of these appointments.

* * * *

Curriculum
Dean Strotz received a copy of our demands on April 21, 1968 as did the rest of the administration. It is our understanding that Dean Strotz heads the Committee for Curriculum Revisions. We have received no reply either from him or through the administration on the creation of a Black Studies Course. Therefore, we assume that he has either denied our request or he is thoroughly disinterested in the condition of the Black student at Northwestern.

Through University funds, the Administration has the influence to promote the hiring of Black faculty members. We demand that this influence be immediately put into effect and used to its fullest extent.

One concrete step in meeting our demand would be the creation of a visiting chair in Black Studies. However, we demand that the Black community have the ultimate decision as to which professor would occupy this chair from year to year.

* * * *

Open occupancy

... We realize that the factors leading to our presently being students at Northwestern were basically politically motivated and had little or nothing to do with a social interest in the plight of Black people in America. Being brought here essentially for purposes of exploitation, Northwestern has subsequently shown little interest in our needs except for those which were compatible with theirs. Therefore, the main responsibility for reconciling the tension between us lies with the Administration and not with us. All we can say is that if our demands are impossible, then peace between us is impossible, too.

In summary, we demand positive responses from the Administration to the following:

* * * *

That each forthcoming freshman class consist of 10%-12% Black students, half of which are from the inner city school systems.

That the Administration will institute a committee selected by the Black community to aid the Admissions Office, especially in recruitment, and which will have shared power with the Office of Admissions and Financial Aid in making decisions relevant to us.

That the members constituting this committee be in a salaried position.

* * * *

That the process of evaluating financial need and administering financial aid be restructured in conjunction with our Admissions and Financial Aid Committee.

That our scholarships be increased to cover what is now included in our "required" jobs and that funds be allocated for those who want or need to attend summer session.

That the University provide us with a Black living unit or commit themselves to immediately getting rid of the present fraternity and sorority housing arrangements.

That any hiring of personnel in the position of counseling the Black community of NU be approved by that Black community.

That a committee of Black students selected by us work with the Administration in meeting our needs for a Black Student Union.

That we have access to the committee studying open occupancy and discrimination with review rights to the matters which they are discussing. ■

Questions for Review

1.   What did James Meredith hope to accomplish through his March Against Fear?

2.   What were some of the causes of the widening schism among black leaders of the four major civil rights organizations—NAACP, SCLC, SNCC, and CORE?

3.   Define *black power*.

4.   What was so new about the new black consciousness?

5.   What were some of the forces operating in the larger American society which created a need for changing strategies and objectives among black rights activists?

6.   In what ways were the problems confronting rural southern blacks similar to or different from those plaguing the lives of blacks in northern urban centers?

7.   Why weren't proponents of nonviolent direct action more successful in persuading young urban blacks to adopt the philosophy of nonviolence?

8.   What did Stokely Carmichael see as the best way to bring about social change in a racist society?

9.   How did the assassination of Malcolm X affect or alter the evolution of the quest for black rights in white America?

10.   Define *cultural nationalism*.

11.   What important writers and historical figures foreshadowed and influenced the rise of the new black consciousness?

12.   Why did many civil rights leaders initially criticize Martin Luther King, Jr. for his stance against American involvement in Vietnam? Why did King criticize the administration's efforts in the Vietnamese War?

13.   What is the significance of the mayoral elections of Richard Hatcher of Gary, Indiana and of Carl Stokes of Cleveland, Ohio?

14.   In what ways did the black studies movement challenge American institutions of higher learning?

15.   Define *institutional racism*.

ADDITIONAL RECOMMENDED READINGS

Barbour, Floyd. *A New Black Consciousness*. Boston: Porter-Sargent, 1968. An indispensable collection of documents. The author sheds light on the meaning of *black power* and provides insight into the new emerging nationalism of that period.

Carmichael, Stokely and Charles V. Hamilton. *Black Power: The Politics of Liberation in America*. New York: Random House, 1967. One of the earliest detailed statements defining the slogan and the significance undergirding the cry for *black power*.

Malcolm X and Alex Haley. *The Autobiography of Malcolm X*. New York: Grove Press, 1966. One of the most read autobiographies of the time. This classic book traces the evolution of Malcolm's life and thought. It details his emergence as one of the most articulate spokesmen for the Nation of Islam and his potent criticisms of the nonviolent direct-action oriented civil rights movement.

Sitkoff, Harvard. *The Struggle for Black Equality, 1954–1980*. New York: Hill and Wang, 1981. This good and succinct narrative is an historical synthesis of the civil rights era from *Brown* down to the recent past. It contains a useful bibliographical essay.

CHAPTER 10

REVOLT AND REPRESSION (1967–1970)

by CLAYBORNE CARSON

RELATED MEDIA:
EYES ON THE PRIZE
Audio Programs 2A and 2B
"Revolt and Repression"

—Identifies and discusses the roots of black urban violence of the period

—Identifies the forms and analyzes the causes of white resistance to black nationalism at both individual and federal levels

—Examines the involvement of blacks in the Vietnamese War

—Differentiates between the goals, tactics, and sources of support of the Student Nonviolent Coordinating Committee (SNCC) and the Black Panther party

—Compares the politics of nonviolence with the politics of violence

—Contrasts black student activism of the early 1960s with black student activism of the late 1960s with respect to goals, strategies, and sources of support

—Identifies ideological differences among blacks with respect to black nationalism

OVERVIEW

During the late 1960s, American society became increasingly divided along racial lines. Civil rights legislation had heightened black expectations while bringing few tangible gains for the black masses. Black Americans, encouraged by previous civil rights gains and influenced by the innovative ideas of the southern black struggle, pressed vigorously for more far-reaching economic and political changes. The national black advancement organizations sought to continue their work, but found that the tactics and strategies that had been used successfully in pursuit of civil rights in the south were not as effective in dealing with the problems of poverty and powerlessness that were major concerns during the last half of the 1960s. Although the Congress of Racial Equality (CORE) and the Student Nonviolent Coordinating Committee (SNCC) adopted the rhetoric of *black power,* they and other established organizations were challenged by more radical groups, such as the Black Panther party, which were more in tune with the angry mood of urban blacks; moreover, white support for civil rights reform declined as a result of both a general backlash against racial militancy and a growing belief among northern whites that black gains would come at their expense. The festering anger and frustration of blacks was expressed through the increasing popularity of the *black power* slogan and through many varied kinds of militancy. White resistance to further racial reforms stimulated even more extreme forms of black rebelliousness, which in turn generated greater white resistance that often took the form of brutal police repression.

The most visible form of black militancy during 1967 and 1968 was the black urban uprising or riot, which spread to many major cities during the summer of 1967. The most serious outbreaks were in Newark, New Jersey, where 26 persons—24 blacks and 2 whites—died, and in Detroit, Michigan, where at least 40 people were killed. Dozens of other cities experienced serious racial disorders during the first nine months of 1967. In April 1968, the final major wave of urban uprisings occurred, prompted by the assassination of Martin Luther King, Jr. Some government officials claimed that the militant speeches of black leaders were responsible for the violence. Maryland Governor Spiro T. Agnew, for example, gained national prominence when he blamed SNCC leader H. Rap Brown for racial violence in Cambridge, Maryland during July 1967. Although little evidence existed that any black leader was capable of initiating—much less controlling—widespread insurgencies, opponents of racial reform exploited news accounts of the inflamatory rhetoric of Brown, Stokely Carmichael, and other firebrands in order to garner white support. Politicians used the congressional debate over proposed civil rights legislation, which eventually became the Civil Rights Act of 1968, as an opportunity to request antiriot amendments, thereby publicly displaying their opposition to black agitators.

Nonviolent black activism remained evident during 1967 and 1968,   215 but it became increasingly difficult for proponents of nonviolent strategies to attract media attention and to achieve gains that would demonstrate their effectiveness. King attempted to reinvigorate the nonviolent movement in 1967 by launching his Poor People's Campaign, an effort designed to mobilize the poor of all races. Even before King's assassination, however, the campaign was widely seen as a failure and another indication that moderate black leaders were losing ground to more militant ones. Resurrection City, U.S.A., a shantytown constructed in Washington, DC after King's death was plagued by logistical problems and leadership conflicts and did not have its intended effect of spurring Congressional action. New black spokesmen, who saw King as overly cautious and too committed to integrationist goals, insisted that revolutionary changes would soon occur as blacks of all classes became more militant.

During the late 1960s, a resurgence of black student activism appeared. Southern black college campuses, which had generally been dormant politically since the early 1960s, were once again settings for protest. Without northern support, however, the southern student protests received little attention in the press. Thus in February 1968, when police officers killed three protesting black students at South Carolina State College and wounded 27 others, the Orangeburg Massacre, as it was called by blacks, received only distorted and superficial coverage. Similarly, when two black students were killed in May 1970 at Jackson State University in Mississippi, the incident received only a fraction of the press coverage given the killing the same month of white students at Kent State. Black students at predominantly white universities demonstrated in support of black student unions, increased black admissions, and black studies courses. Black college athletes joined the student revolt by protesting against demeaning treatment, and a few star athletes participated in a boycott of the 1968 Olympics, which featured a clenched-fist *black power* salute by two black sprinters.

Urban black communities became centers of political and cultural activity as black residents displayed a new racial consciousness through a wide range of activities. In many cities, blacks successfully used peaceful means to increase black political power. A major electoral trend had begun in 1967 when black mayors were elected in Cleveland, Ohio and Gary, Indiana, an achievement soon replicated in other cities. The dramatic increase in the number of black elected officials during subsequent years was accompanied, initially at least, by a growing level of militant grass-roots political activity. The Black Panther party was the most highly publicized black radical group to emerge in the urban north during the last half of the 1960s, but many other black institutions arose that reflected the increasing desire of blacks to challenge the *status quo.* Until pressures from besieged municipal officials stymied this promising experiment, the federal "war on poverty" hired community organizers— including some veterans of civil rights activism—to encourage blacks to build self-help institutions and to protect their rights. In many cities, black united fronts or black congresses were formed to encourage cooperation among the varied groups. Resisting the trend toward separatist racial strategies, the National Welfare Rights Organization also had some success in organizing the poorest classes of blacks.

The transformation of consciousness was also evident in the military, which included an increasing proportion of black soldiers. While the war in Vietnam contributed to the climate of radicalism in the United States, blacks fighting in the war were influenced by the antiwar stances of black leaders. Although King did not take a public stand against the war until 1967, more than a year after SNCC's initial statement, he was uniquely able to articulate the belief of many blacks that they should not be asked to use violence to free the Vietnamese while being asked to remain nonviolent in struggling for human rights at home. Rebelliousness among black soldiers became increasingly evident during the late 1960s and early 1970s as the military began to draft young blacks who had participated in the urban rebellions and had absorbed the spirit of racial militancy.

Black prisoners were similarly affected by the racial activism of the 1960s. Imprisonment had often been a radicalizing experience for blacks, and some black leaders, including Malcolm X, Huey Newton, and Eldridge Cleaver, had been prisoners themselves before joining the black struggle. The rebellious spirit of black prisoners during the late 1960s was captured in the eloquent letters of George Jackson, whose campaign to avoid conviction on charges of murdering a prison guard attracted widespread support, including that of black philosopher Angela Davis. Jackson was killed in 1971 during a bloody escape attempt at a courthouse in California. During the same year, 43 prisoners and guard-hostages died during the Attica State Correctional Facility rebellion, which lasted several weeks until it was suppressed by New York State police. Although New York authorities reported that the hostages' throats had been slashed by inmates, subsequent investigation indicated that the hostages were killed by overzealous police, who had also shot many inmates in the back.

In summary, the black militancy of the late 1960s and early 1970s produced some lasting gains, but it also encountered brutal repression. The black urban rebellions were crushed, and the ranks of groups such as the Panthers were decimated as a result of deadly confrontations with police. The widespread recruitment of police informers heightened feelings of distrust in black militant groups and made them increasingly concerned with ideological conformity. In addition to the "iron fist" of police repression, black militancy also confronted the "velvet glove" of co-optation—the use of poverty program jobs and other incentives to buy off potential rebels. On one occasion, for example, antipoverty officials scheduled hiring interviews designed to attract young blacks to coincide with planned protests at the trial of boxer Muhammad Ali, who 217 had refused induction into military service.

The external forces seeking to undermine black militancy exploited and exacerbated the internal division that existed in the black militant community. To some extent these divisions were based on ideological differences. Although black power proponents expected that militant racial consciousness would be a unifying force in black communities, ideological differences among blacks actually became more pronounced—and even a source of violent intrablack conflict—during the late 1960s. Advocates of *black power* conceived of it in many different ways, ranging from an advocacy of revolution to support for black capitalism. Even among the proponents of black nationalism, major ideological divisions were apparent, often described as between the revolutionary nationalism of groups such as the Panthers and the cultural nationalism of Maulena Karenga's United Slaves (US) organization or Amiri Baraka's (formerly LeRoi Jones) black arts movement. Rhetoric that stressed ideological purity and utilized "blacker than thou" assumptions to attack other blacks led to the rise of small isolated racial cults that justified their lack of popular support by insisting that most blacks lacked sufficiently high levels of consciousness. Unlike the southern black organizers of the early 1960s, who had developed their ideas through active involvement in a mass struggle, the militant black ideologues of the late 1960s were more likely to see their role as providing ideological direction for mass insurgences that lacked leadership.

Thus, ironically, the 1968 plan of the Federal Bureau of Investigation (FBI) to crush black militancy by preventing the rise of a "messiah" who could "unify and electrify" the black movement unwittingly reflected the views of black orators seeking to bring blacks under their ideological banner. Although many black activists tried to maintain the illusion of racial unity by staging black power conferences and, during the 1970s, national black political conventions, the period was characterized by increasing fragmentation in black leadership. Overall, the late 1960s were years of tremendous activity and intellectual excitement, but they were also a period of ruthless repression and political infighting. Although many of the civil rights gains of the early 1960s were consolidated, particularly in the realm of electoral politics, the momentum of the black struggle had waned by the beginning of the 1970s.

READINGS

1. T he black urban rebellions of the mid-1960s were aspects of a shift in the focus of black politics from the south, where blacks were seeking basic political rights, to the urban north, where many blacks remained poor and powerless despite having civil rights. The Oakland-based Black Panther party was one of many northern black groups that reflected the militant mood of northern ghetto residents. In some respects the Panthers were the northern counterpart of SNCC, displaying a similar brash, youthful style of activism and a similar willingness to confront white authority. Indeed, Black Panther founders Huey Newton and Bobby Seale were greatly influenced by Stokely Carmichael's calls for *black power* and took the name of their party from SNCC's successful effort to build a Panther party in Lowndes County, Alabama. The following selection by Newton indicates, however, that the Black Panther party's political orientation was shaped by experiences that differed in important ways from those of the black students who initiated the sit-ins of the early 1960s. Although Newton and Seale initially sought to establish an alliance with the more experienced leaders of SNCC, the party's militaristic form of organization and ghetto base contrasted sharply with SNCC's initial consensus mode of decision-making and college student constituency.

From: *Revolutionary Suicide* by Huey P. Newton with the assistance of J. Herman Blake (New York: Harcourt Brace Jovanovich, 1973), pages 110–127. Copyright 1973 by Stronghold Consolidated Productions, Inc. Used by permission of Harcourt Brace Jovanovich, Inc.

We had seen Watts rise up the previous year. We had seen how the police attacked the Watts community after causing the trouble in the first place. We had seen Martin Luther King come to Watts in an effort to calm the people, and we had seen his philosophy of nonviolence rejected. Black people had been taught nonviolence; it was deep in us. What good, however, was nonviolence when the police were determined to rule by force? . . . We had seen all this, and we recognized that the rising consciousness of Black people was almost at the point of explosion. . . .

Out of this need sprang the Black Panther Party. Bobby [Seale] and I finally had no choice but to form an organization that would involve the lower-class brothers.

* * * *

All that summer we circulated in the Black communities of Richmond, Berkeley, Oakland, and San Francisco. Wherever brothers gathered, we talked with them about their right to arm. In general, they were interested but skeptical about the weapons idea. . . . The way we finally won the brothers over was by patrolling the police with arms.

Before we began the patrols, however, Bobby and I set down in writing a practical course of action. . . .

I started rapping off the essential points for the survival of Black and oppressed people in the United States. Bobby wrote them down, and then we separated those ideas into two sections, "What We Want" and "What We Believe. . . ."

. . . This is the program we wrote down:

OCTOBER 1966
BLACK PANTHER PARTY
PLATFORM AND PROGRAM
WHAT WE WANT
WHAT WE BELIEVE

1.   *We want freedom. We want power to determine the destiny of our Black Community.*

* * * *

2.   *We want full employment for our people.*

* * * *

3.   *We want an end to the robbery by the capitalists of our Black Community.*

* * * *

4.   *We want decent housing, fit for shelter of human beings.*

* * * *

5.   *We want education for our people that exposes the true nature of this decadent American society. We want education that teaches us our true history and our role in present-day society.*

* * * *

6.   *We want all Black men to be exempt from military service.*

* * * *

7.   *We want an immediate end to POLICE BRUTALITY and MURDER of Black people.*

* * * *

8.   *We want freedom for all Black men held in federal, state, county and city prisons and jails.*

* * * *

9.   *We want all Black people when brought to trial to be tried in court by a jury of their peer group or people from their Black communities, as defined by the Constitution of the United States.*

* * * *

10.   *We want land, bread, housing, education, clothing, justice, and peace. And as our major political objective, a United Nations-supervised plebiscite to be held throughout the Black colony in which only Black colonial subjects will be allowed to participate, for the purpose of determining the will of Black people as to their national destiny.*

We started now to implement our ten-point program. Interested primarily in educating and revolutionizing the community, we needed to get their attention and give them something to identify with. This is why the seventh point—police action—was the first program we emphasized. . . . This is a major issue in every Black community. The police have never been our protectors. Instead, they act as the military arm of our oppressors and continually brutalize us. Many communities have tried and failed to get civilian review boards to supervise the behavior of the police. . . . We recognized that it was ridiculous to report the police to the police, but we hoped that by raising encounters to a higher level, by patrolling the police with arms, we would see a change in their behavior. Further, the community would notice this and become interested in the Party. Thus our armed patrols were also a means of recruiting.

At first, the patrols were a total success. Frightened and confused, the police did not know how to respond, because they had never encountered patrols like this before. They were familiar with the community-alert patrols in other cities, but never before had guns been an integral part of any patrol program. With weapons in our hands, we were no longer their subjects but their equals.

Out on patrol, we stopped whenever we saw the police questioning a brother or a sister. We would walk over with our weapons and observe them from a "safe" distance so that the police could not say we were interfering with the performance of their duty. . . .

* * * *

The Black Panthers were and are always required to keep their activities within legal bounds. . . . So, we studied the law about weapons and kept within our rights. . . .

. . . The police, invariably shocked to meet a cadre of disciplined and armed Black men coming to the support of the community, reacted in strange and unpredictable ways. In their fright, some of them became children, cursing and insulting us. We responded in kind, calling them swine and pigs, but never cursing—this would be cause for arrest—and we took care not to be arrested with our weapons. . . .

* * * *

In addition to our patrols and confrontations with the police, I did a lot of recruiting in pool halls and bars, sometimes working twelve to sixteen hours a day. I passed out leaflets with our ten-point program, explaining each point to all who would listen. . . .

* * * *

This recruiting had an interesting ramification in that I tried to transform many of the so-called criminal activities going on in the street into something political, although this had to be done gradually. Instead of trying to eliminate these activities—numbers, hot goods, drugs—I attempted to channel them into significant community actions. . . . Many of the brothers who were burglarizing and participating in similar pursuits began to contribute weapons and material to community defense. In order to survive they still had to sell their hot goods, but at the same time they would pass some of the cash on to us. That way, ripping off became more than just an individual thing.

Gradually the Black Panthers came to be accepted in the Bay Area community. We had provided a needed example of strength and dignity by showing people how to defend themselves. More important, we lived among them. They could see every day that with us the people came first. ■

2. **As indicated by Newton in the previous selection, the Black Panthers attracted considerable support from blacks who admired their bravado. Among the many new recruits who joined the party during 1967 was Eldridge Cleaver, who had become a follower of Malcolm X while serving a prison term. After his release on parole, Cleaver's writing talent enabled him to join the staff of the new left journal _Ramparts_, a job that brought him into contact with white leftists as well as leading black militants. By the time of Cleaver's initial contact with the Black Panthers, he had become impatient with the apolitical stance of black cultural nationalists. His decision to join the Panthers came soon after witnessing an incident involving Betty Shabazz, the widow of Malcolm X. The confrontation described below demonstrated the distinctly brash—and sometimes reckless—tactics that attracted support and notoriety to the Panthers. Ironically, Cleaver was later ousted from the Panther party when Newton and Seale refused to go along with his calls for revolutionary violence spearheaded by the downtrodden black "lumpen proletariat."**

From: _Eldridge Cleaver: Post-Prison Writings and Speeches_ edited by Robert Scheer (New York: Random House, 1969), pages 32–36. Used by permission of Eldridge Cleaver.

On the day that Sister Betty and Hakim Jamal were to arrive in San Francisco, I was sitting in my office tinkering with some notes for an article. One of the secretaries burst through the door. Her face was white with fear and she was shouting, "We're being invaded! We're being invaded!"

I couldn't tell just who her invaders were. Were the Chinese coming? Had the CIA finally decided to do _Ramparts_ in? Then she said, "There are about twenty men outside with guns!"

I knew that Hakim Jamal and Sister Betty had arrived with their escort of armed Black Panthers.

* * * *

I waded through *Ramparts* staff jammed into the narrow hallways, fending off the frightened inquiries by repeating, "It's all right, it's all right." The lobby resembled certain photographs coming out of Cuba the day Castro took Havana. There were guns everywhere, pointed toward the ceiling like metallic blades of grass growing up out of the sea of black faces beneath the black berets of the Panthers. I found Hakim Jamal and Sister Betty surrounded by a knot of Panthers, who looked calm and self-possessed in sharp contrast to the chaotic reactions their appearance had set off. Outside . . . a massive traffic jam was developing and sirens could be heard in the distance as cops sped our way.

* * * *

When it was agreed that it was time to leave, Huey Newton took control. Mincing no words, he sent five of his men out first to clear a path through the throng of spectators clustered outside the door, most of whom were cops. He dispatched a phalanx of ten Panthers fast on their heels, with Hakim Jamal and Sister Betty concealed in their midst. Newton himself, along with Bobby Seale and three other Panthers, brought up the rear.

I went outside and stood on the steps of *Ramparts* to observe the departure. When Huey left the building, [a] TV cameraman who had been tossed out was grinding away his camera. Huey took an envelope from his pocket and held it up in front of the camera, blocking the lens.

"Get out of the way!" the TV man shouted. When Huey continued to hold the envelope in front of the lens, the TV man started cursing, and reached out and knocked Huey's hand away with his fist. Huey coolly turned to one of the score of cops watching and said:

"Officer, I want you to arrest this man for assault."

An incredulous look came into the cop's face, then he blurted out: "If I arrest anybody, it'll be you!"

Huey turned on the cameraman, again placing the envelope in front of the lens. Again the cameraman reached out and knocked Huey's hand away. Huey reached out, snatched the cameraman's collar and slammed him up against the wall, sending him spinning and staggering down the sidewalk, trying to catch his breath and balance the camera on his shoulder at the same time.

Bobby Seale tugged at Huey's shirt sleeve. "C'mon, Huey, let's get out of here."

Huey and Bobby started up the sidewalk toward their car. The cops stood there on the point, poised as though ready to start shooting at a given signal.

"Don't turn your backs on these back-shooting dogs!" Huey called out to Bobby and the other three Panthers. By this time the other Panthers with Sister Betty and Jamal had gotten into cars and melted into the traffic jam. Only these five were still at the scene.

At that moment a big, beefy cop stepped forward. He undid the little strap holding his pistol in his holster and started shouting at Huey, "Don't point that gun at me! Stop pointing that gun at me!" He kept making gestures as though he was going for his gun.

This was the most tense of moments. Huey stopped in his tracks and stared at the cop.

"Let's split, Huey! Let's split!" Bobby Seale was saying.

Ignoring him, Huey walked to within a few feet of the cop and said, "What's the matter, you got an itchy finger?"

The cop made no reply.

"You want to draw your gun?" Huey asked him.

The other cops were calling out for this cop to cool it, to take it easy, but he didn't seem to be able to hear them. He was staring into Huey's eyes, measuring him.

"O.K.," Huey said. "You big fat racist pig, draw your gun!"

The cop made no move.

"Draw it, you cowardly dog!" Huey pumped a round into the chamber of the shotgun. "I'm waiting," he said and stood there waiting for the cop to draw.

All the other cops moved back out of the line of fire. I moved back, too, onto the top step of *Ramparts*. I was thinking, staring at Huey surrounded by all those cops and daring one of them to draw, "Goddam, that nigger is c-r-a-z-y!"

Then the cop facing Huey gave it up. He heaved a heavy sigh and lowered his head. Huey literally laughed in his face and then went off up the street at a jaunty pace, disappearing in a blaze of dazzling sunlight.

"Work out, soul brother!" I was shouting to myself. "You're the baddest mother-fucker I've ever seen!" I went back into *Ramparts* and we all stood around chattering excitedly, discussing what we had witnessed with disbelief. ∎

3. The militancy of such groups as the Black Panthers prompted increased police and governmental repression, which in turn led black militants to become even more hostile toward the dominant political system and more committed to armed self-defense. Although black political activists had endured considerable police violence in the south, the repression of the late 1960s became increasingly effective because it was carried out by powerful urban police forces and the federal government and was backed by many northern

politicians who feared a "white backlash" against black militancy. The antiblack activities of the FBI were particularly destructive because the bureau was able to exploit growing internal divisions among black militants. Although the FBI asserted that its counterintelligence activities—called COINTELPRO—were directed against "black nationalist hate groups" engaged in violence, the targets of COINTELPRO included King and sometimes contributed to the climate of racial violence. A Senate investigation of the abuses of power that led to the Watergate scandal produced the following account of the FBI's campaign to promote violence between the Panthers and members of the US organization, led by Maulana Karenga.

From: Final Report of the Senate Select Committee to Study Governmental Operations with Respect to Intelligence Activities, Supplementary Detailed Staff Reports on Intelligence Activities and the Rights of Americans, Book III (1976), pages 187–193.

In August 1967, the FBI initiated a covert action program—COINTELPRO—to disrupt and "neutralize" organizations which the Bureau characterized as "Black Nationalist Hate Groups." The FBI memorandum expanding the program described its goals as:

1.   Prevent a coalition of militant black nationalist groups. . . .
2.   Prevent the rise of a messiah who could unify and electrify the militant nationalist movement . . . Martin Luther King, Stokely Carmichael and Elijah Muhammad all aspire to this position. . . .
3.   Prevent violence on the part of black nationalist groups. . . .
4.   Prevent militant black nationalist groups and leaders from gaining respectability by discrediting them. . . .
5.   . . . prevent the long-range growth of militant black nationalist organizations, especially among youth.

The targets of this nationwide program to disrupt "militant black nationalist organizations" included groups such as the Southern Christian Leadership Conference (SCLC), the Student Nonviolent Coordinating Committee (SNCC), the Revolutionary Action Movement (RAM), and the Nation of Islam (NOI). It was expressly directed against such leaders as Martin Luther King, Jr., Stokely Carmichael, H. Rap Brown, Maxwell Stanford, and Elijah Muhammad.

The Black Panther Party (BPP) was not among the original "Black Nationalist" targets. In September 1968, however, FBI Director J. Edgar Hoover described the Panthers as:

"the greatest threat to the internal security of the country.
"Schooled in the Marxist-Leninist ideology and the teaching of Chinese Communist leader Mao Tse-tung, its members have perpetrated numerous assaults on police officers and have engaged in violent confrontations with police throughout the country. Leaders and representatives of the Black Panther Party travel extensively all over the United States preaching their gospel of hate and violence not only to ghetto residents but to students in colleges, universities and high schools as well."

By July 1969, the Black Panthers had become the primary focus of the program, and was ultimately the target of 233 of the total 295 authorized "Black Nationalist" COINTELPRO actions.

Although the claimed purpose of the Bureau's COINTELPRO tactics was to prevent violence, some of the FBI's tactics against the BPP were clearly intended to foster violence, and many others could reasonably have been expected to cause violence. For example, the FBI's efforts to "intensify the degree of animosity" between BPP and the Blackstone Rangers, a Chicago street gang, included sending an anonymous letter to the gang's leader falsely informing him that the Chicago Panthers had "a hit out" on him. The stated intent of the letter was to induce the Ranger leader to "take reprisals against" the Panther leadership.

* * * *

James Adams, Deputy Associate Director of the FBI's Intelligence Division, told the Committee:

> None of our programs have contemplated violence, and the instructions prohibit it, and the record of turndowns of recommended actions in some instances specifically say that we do not approve this action because if we take it it could result in harm to the individual.

But the Committee's record suggests otherwise. For example, in May 1970, after US organization members had already killed four BPP members, the Special Agent in Charge of the Los Angeles FBI office wrote to FBI headquarters:

> Information received from local sources indicate that, in general, membership of the Los Angeles BPP is physically afraid of US members and take premeditated precautions to avoid confrontations.
> In view of their anxieties, it is not presently felt that the Los Angeles BPP can be prompted into what could result in an internecine struggle between the two organizations. . . .
> The Los Angeles Division is aware of the mutually hostile feelings harbored between the organizations and the first opportunity to capitalize on the situation will be maximized. It is intended that US Inc. will be appropriately and discreetly advised of the time and location of BPP activities *in order that the two organizations might be brought together and thus grant nature the opportunity to take her due course.* [Emphasis added in Report.]

* * * *

In November 1968, the FBI took initial steps in its program to disrupt the Black Panther Party in San Diego, California by aggravating the existing hostility between the Panthers and US. A memorandum from FBI Director Hoover to 14 field offices noted a state of "gang warfare" existed, with "attendant threats of murder and reprisals," between the BPP and US in southern California and added:

> In order to fully capitalize upon BPP and US differences as well as to exploit all avenues of creating further dissention in the ranks of the BPP, recipient offices are instructed to submit imaginative and hard-hitting counterintelligence measures aimed at crippling the BPP.

As the tempo of violence quickened, the FBI's field office in San Diego developed tactics calculated to heighten tension between the hostile factions. . . . the San Diego field office requested permission from headquarters to mail derogatory cartoons to local BPP offices and to the homes of prominent BPP leaders around the country. . . .

* * * *

In mid-March 1969, the FBI learned that a BPP member had been critically wounded by US members at a rally in Los Angeles. The field office concluded that shots subsequently fired into the home of a US member were the results of a retaliatory raid by the BPP. Tensions between the BPP and US in San Diego, however, appeared to lessen, and the FBI concluded that those chapters were trying "to talk out their differences." . . .

* * * *

On March 27, 1969—the day that the San Diego field office learned that the local BPP leader had promised that his followers "would not hold a grudge" against local US members for the killings in Los Angeles—the San Diego office requested headquarters' approval for three more cartoons ridiculing the BPP and falsely attributed to US. One week later, shortly after the San Diego office learned that US and BPP members were again meeting and discussing their differences, the San Diego field office mailed the cartoons with headquarters' approval.

On April 4, 1969 there was a confrontation between US and BPP members in Southcrest Park in San Diego at which, according to an FBI memorandum, the BPP members "ran the US members off." On the same date, US members broke into a BPP political education meeting and roughed up a female BPP member. The FBI's Special Agent in Charge in San Diego boasted that the cartoons had caused these incidents. . . .

The fragile truce had ended. On May 23, 1969, John Savage, a member of the BPP in Southern California, was shot and killed by US member Jerry Horne, aka Tambuzi. . . .

* * * *

Despite this atmosphere of violence, FBI headquarters authorized the San Diego field office to compose an inflammatory letter over the forged signature of a San Diego BPP member and to send it to BPP headquarters in Oakland, California. The letter complained of the killing of Panthers in San Diego by US members, and the fact that a local BPP leader had a white girlfriend.

According to a BPP bulletin, two Panthers were wounded by US gunman on August 14, 1969, and the next day another BPP member, Sylvester Bell, was killed in San Diego by US members. On August 30, 1969, the San Diego office of US was bombed. The FBI believed the BPP was responsible for the bombing.

The San Diego office of the FBI viewed this carnage as a positive development and informed headquarters: "Efforts are being made to determine how this situation can be capitalized upon for the benefit of the Counterintelligence Program. . . . " The field office further noted:

> In view of the recent killing of BPP member Sylvester Bell, a new cartoon is being considered in the hopes that it will assist in the continuance of the rift between BPP and US.

The San Diego FBI office pointed with pride to the continued violence between black groups:

> Shootings, beatings, and a high degree of unrest continues to prevail in the ghetto area of southeast San Diego. Although no specific counterintelligence action can be credited with contributing to this overall situation, *it is felt that a substantial amount of the unrest is directly attributable to this program.* [Emphasis added in Report.] ■

4. The racial violence of the period from 1965 through 1968 prompted calls for greater use of police forces and the enactment of new antiriot legislation, but the violence also prompted serious efforts to determine the basic causes of the worsening racial climate. In the aftermath of the 1967 riots in Detroit and Newark, President Lyndon B. Johnson appointed an 11-member National Advisory Commission on Civil Disorders, which undertook a major investigation of the racial violence. Their efforts produced an account of both the distinctive factors that precipitated outbreaks in particular cities and the general causes of black discontent. In its 1968 report, the Kerner Commission, as it was called, warned that America was "moving toward two societies, one black, one white—separate and unequal." It charged that "white racism" was chiefly responsible for the "explosive mixture" of discrimination, poverty, and frustration that existed in black urban communities. White society, the Commission asserted, "is deeply implicated in the ghetto. White institutions created it, white institutions maintain it, and white society condones it." The report was a forceful statement about American race relations, but its recommendations to bridge the deepening racial divisions did not receive much support from white Americans and few were implemented.

From: "Detroit" in *Report of the National Advisory Commission on Civil Disorders* (New York: E.P. Dutton & Co, 1968), pages 84–108.

On Saturday evening, July 22, the Detroit Police Department raided five "blind pigs." The blind pigs had their origin in prohibition days, and survived as private social clubs. . . .

* * * *

Police expected to find two dozen patrons in the [fifth] blind pig. That night, however, it was the scene of a party for several servicemen, two of whom were back from Vietnam. Instead of two dozen patrons, police found 82. Some voiced resentment at the police intrusion.

An hour went by before all 82 could be transported from the scene. The weather was humid and warm . . . and despite the late hour, many people were still on the street. In short order, a crowd of about 200 gathered.

* * * *

On 12th Street, with its high incidence of vice and crime, the issue of police brutality was a recurrent theme. A month earlier the killing of a prostitute had been determined by police investigators to be the work of a pimp. According to rumors in the community the crime had been committed by a Vice Squad officer.

At about the same time, the killing of Danny Thomas, a 27-year old Negro Army veteran, by a gang of white youths, had inflamed the community. . . .

* * * *

. . . A few minutes after 5:00 A.M., just after the last of those arrested had been hauled away, an empty bottle smashed into the rear window of a police car. A litter basket was thrown through the window of a store. Rumors circulated of excess police force used by the police during the raid. A youth, whom police nicknamed "Mr. Greensleeves" because of the color of his shirt, was shouting: "We're going to have a riot!" and exhorting the crowd to vandalism.

At 5:20 A.M. Commissioner [Ray] Girardin was notified. He immediately called Mayor Jerome Cavanagh. Seventeen officers from other areas were ordered into the 10th Precinct. By 6:00 A.M. police strength had grown to 369 men. Of these, however, only 43 were committed to the immediate riot area. By that time the number of persons on 12th Street was growing into the thousands and widespread window-smashing and looting had begun.

* * * *

By 7:50 A.M., when a 17-man police commando unit attempted to make the first sweep, an estimated 3,000 persons were on 12th Street. They offered no resistance. As the sweep moved down the street, they gave way to one side, and then flowed back behind it.

A shoe store manager said he waited vainly for police for two hours as the store was being looted. At 8:25 A.M. someone in the crowd yelled "The cops are coming!" The first flames of the riot billowed from the store. Firemen who responded were not harassed. The flames were extinguished.

229

By mid-morning, 1,122 men . . . had reported for duty. Of these, 540 were in or near the six-block riot area. One hundred and eight officers were attempting to establish a cordon. There was, however, no interference with looters. . . .

* * * *

Numerous eyewitnesses interviewed by Commission investigators tell of the carefree mood with which people ran in and out of stores, looting and laughing, and joking with the police officers. Stores with "Soul Brothers" signs appeared no more immune than others. . . .

* * * *

A police officer in the riot area told Commission investigators that neither he nor his fellow officers were instructed as to what they were supposed to be doing. Witnesses tell of officers standing behind saw-horses as an area was being looted—and still standing there much later, when the mob moved elsewhere. A squad from the commando unit, wearing helmets with face-covering visors and carrying bayonet-tipped carbines, blockaded a street several blocks from the scene of the riot. Their appearance drew residents into the street. Some began to harangue them and to question why they were in an area where there was no trouble. . . .

By that time a rumor was threading through the crowd that a man had been bayoneted by the police. Influenced by such stories, the crowd became belligerent. . . . Numerous officers reported injuries from rocks, bottles, and other objects thrown at them. Smoke billowed upward from four fires, the first since the one at the shoe store early in the morning. When firemen answered the alarms, they became the target for rocks and bottles.

At 2:00 P.M. Mayor Cavanagh met with community and political leaders at police headquarters. Until then there had been hope that, as the people blew off steam, the riot would dissipate. Now the opinion was nearly unanimous that additional forces would be needed.

A request was made for state police aid. By 3:00 P.M. 360 officers were assembling at the armory. At that moment looting was spreading from the 12th Street area to other main thoroughfares.

* * * *

Some evidence that criminal elements were organizing spontaneously to take advantage of the riot began to manifest itself. . . .

A spirit of carefree nihilism was taking hold. To riot and to destroy appeared more and more to become ends in themselves. Late Sunday afternoon it appeared to one observer that the young people were "dancing amidst the flames."

* * * *

In the midst of the chaos there were some unexpected individual responses.

Twenty-four-year-old E.G., a Negro born in Savannah, Georgia, had come to Detroit in 1965 to attend Wayne State University. Rebellion had been building in him for a long time . . .

When a friend called to tell him about the riot on 12th Street, E.G. went there expecting "a true revolt," but was disappointed as soon as he saw the looting begin: "I wanted to see the people really rise up in revolt. When I saw the first person coming out of the store with things in his arms, I really got sick to my stomach and wanted to go home. Rebellion against the white suppressors is one thing, but one measly pair of shoes or some food completely ruins the whole concept."

* * * *

At 4:20 P.M. Mayor Cavanagh requested that the National Guard be brought into Detroit. . . . The first troops were on the streets by 7:00 P.M.

At 7:45 P.M. the mayor issued a proclamation instituting a 9:00 P.M. to 5:00 A.M. curfew. At 9:07 P.M. the first sniper fire was reported. Following his aerial survey of the city, Governor [George] Romney, at or shortly before midnight, proclaimed that "a state of public emergency exists" in the cities of Detroit, Highland Park, and Hamtramck.

* * * *

By 2:00 A.M. Monday, Detroit police had been augmented by 800 State Police officers and 1,200 National Guardsmen. An additional 8,000 Guardsmen were on the way. Nevertheless, Governor Romney and Mayor Cavanagh decided to ask for federal assistance. . . .

* * * *

Shortly before noon the President of the United States authorized the sending of a task force of paratroopers to Selfridge Air Force Base, near the city. . . .

* * * *

As the riot alternately waxed and waned, one area of the ghetto remained insulated. On the northeast side the residents of some 150 square blocks inhabited by 21,000 persons had, in 1966, banded together in the Positive Neighborhood Action Committee (PNAC). With professional help from the Institute for Urban Dynamics, they had organized block clubs and made plans for the improvement of the neighborhood. In order to meet the need for recreational facilities, which the city was not providing, they had raised $3,000 to purchase empty lots for playgrounds. Although opposed to urban renewal, they had agreed to co-sponsor with the Archdiocese of Detroit a housing project to be controlled jointly by the archdiocese and PNAC.

When the riot broke out, the residents, through the block clubs, were able to organize quickly. Youngsters, agreeing to stay in the neighborhood, participated in detouring traffic. While many persons reportedly sympathized with the idea of a rebellion against the "system," only two small fires were set—one in an empty building.

During the daylight hours Monday, nine more persons were killed by gunshots elsewhere in the city, and many others were seriously or critically injured. Twenty-three-year old Nathaniel Edmonds, a Negro, was sitting in his back yard when a young white man stopped his car, got out, and began an argument with him. A few minutes later, declaring he was "going to paint his picture on him with a shotgun," the white man allegedly shotgunned Edmonds to death.

Mrs. Nannie Pack and Mrs. Mattie Thomas were sitting on the porch of Mrs. Pack's house when police began chasing looters from a nearby market. During the chase officers fired three shots from their shotguns. The discharge from one of these accidentally struck the two women. Both were still in the hospital weeks later.

* * * *

. . . At 11:20 P.M. the President signed a proclamation federalizing the Michigan National Guard and authorizing the use of the paratroopers.

* * * *

Within hours after the arrival of the paratroopers the area occupied by them was the quietest in the city, bearing out General [John L.] Throckmorton's view that the key to quelling a disorder is to saturate an area with "calm, determined, and hardened professional soldiers." Loaded weapons, he believes, are unnecessary. Troopers had strict orders not to fire unless they could see the specific person at whom they were firing. Mass fire was forbidden.

During five days in the city, 2,700 Army troops expended only 201 rounds of ammunition, almost all during the first few hours, after which even stricter fire discipline was enforced. (In contrast, New Jersey National Guardsmen and State police expended 13,326 rounds of ammunition in three days in Newark.) . . .

General Throckmorton ordered the weapons of all military personnel unloaded, but either the order failed to reach many National Guardsmen, or else it was disobeyed.

* * * *

With persons of every description arming themselves, and guns being fired accidentally or on the vaguest pretext all over the city, it became more and more impossible to tell who was shooting at whom. Some firemen began carrying guns. One accidentally shot and wounded a fellow fireman. Another injured himself.

* * * *

On a number of occasions officers fired at fleeing looters, then made little attempt to determine whether their shots had hit anyone. . . .

* * * *

Prosecution is proceeding in the case of three youths in whose shotgun deaths law enforcement personnel were implicated following a report that snipers were firing from the Algiers Motel. In fact, there is little evidence that anyone fired from inside the building. Two witnesses say that they had seen a man, standing outside of the motel, fire two shots from a rifle. The interrogation of other persons revealed that law enforcement personnel then shot out one or more street lights. Police patrols responded to the shots. An attack was launched on the motel.

* * * *

Although by late Tuesday looting and fire-bombing had virtually ceased, between 7:00 and 11:00 P.M. that night there were 444 reports of incidents. Most were reports of sniper fire.

* * * *

In all, more than 7,200 persons were arrested. Almost 3,000 of these were picked up on the second day of the riot, and by midnight Monday 4,000 were incarcerated in makeshift jails. . . .

* * * *

Of the 43 persons who were killed during the riot, 33 were Negro and 10 were white. Seventeen were looters, of whom two were white. Fifteen citizens (of whom four were white), one white National Guardsmen, one white fireman, and one Negro private guard died as a result of gunshot wounds. Most of these deaths appear to have been accidental, but criminal homicide is suspected in some.

Two persons, including one fireman, died as a result of fallen power lines. Two were burned to death. One was a drunken gunman; one an arson suspect. One white man was killed by a rioter. One police officer was felled by a shotgun blast when his gun, in the hands of another officer, accidentally discharged during a scuffle with a looter.

Action by police officers accounted for 20 and, very likely, 21 of the deaths. Action by the National Guard for seven, and, very likely, nine. Action by the Army for one. Two deaths were the result of action by store owners. Four persons died accidentally. Rioters were responsible for two, and perhaps three of the deaths; a private guard for one. A white man is suspected of murdering a Negro youth. The perpetrator of one of the killings in the Algiers Motel remains unknown.

Damage estimates, originally set as high as $500 million, were quickly scaled down. The city assessor's office placed the loss—excluding business stock, private furnishings, and the buildings of churches and charitable institutions—at approximately $22 million. Insurance payments, according to the State Insurance Bureau, will come to about $32 million, representing an estimated 65 to 75 percent of the total loss.

By Thursday, July 27, most riot activity had ended. The paratroopers were removed from the city on Saturday. On Tuesday, August 1, the curfew was lifted and the National Guard moved out. ■

5. **T**hroughout his career as a protest leader, Martin Luther King, Jr. had insisted that nonviolence did not involve passive acceptance of injustice but was a militant force for broad social change. In a 1964 magazine article, for example, he had stated, "When the white power structure calls upon the Negro to reject violence but does not impose upon itself the task of creating necessary social change, it is in fact asking for submission to injustice. Nothing in the theory of nonviolence counsels this suicide course." Far from becoming contented with the gains of the early 1960s, King grew increasingly determined to use nonviolent tactics to bring about a radical transformation of the American social and economic structure. The following posthumously published essay reveals his steadfast belief that nonviolent struggle offered the best means of reversing the trend of escalating racial violence and hostility that characterized American society during the last few years of his life.

From: "A Testament of Hope" by Martin Luther King, Jr. in *Playboy* (January 1969), pages 175–194. Copyright 1968 by the Estate of Martin Luther King, Jr. Used by permission of Joan Daves.

I am not sad that black Americans are in rebellion; this was not only inevitable but eminently desirable. Without this magnificent ferment among Negroes, the old evasions and procrastinations would have continued indefinitely. Black men have slammed the door shut on a past of deadening passivity. Except for the Reconstruction years, they have never in this long history on American soil struggled with such creativity and courage for their freedom. These are our bright years of emergence; though they are painful ones, they cannot be avoided. . . .

Justice for black people will not flow into society merely from court decisions nor from fountains of political oratory. Nor will a few token changes quell all the tempestuous yearnings of millions of disadvantaged black people. White Americans must recognize that justice for black people cannot be achieved without radical changes in the structure of our society. The comfortable, the entrenched, the privileged cannot continue to tremble at the prospect of change in the *status quo*.

Stephen Vincent Benet had a message for both white and black Americans in the title of a story, *Freedom Is A Hard Bought Thing*. When millions of people have been cheated for centuries, restitution is a costly process. Inferior education, poor housing, unemployment, inadequate health care—each is a bitter component of the oppression that has been our heritage. Each will require billions of dollars to correct. Justice so long deferred has accumulated interest and its cost for this society will be substantial in financial as well as human terms. This fact has not been fully grasped, because most of the gains of the past decade were obtained at bargain prices. The desegregation of public facilities cost nothing; neither did the election and appointment of a few black public officials. . . .

Millions of Americans are coming to see that we are fighting an immoral war that costs nearly 30 billion dollars a year, that we are perpetuating racism, that we are tolerating almost 40 million poor during an overflowing material abundance. Yet they remain helpless to end the war, to feed the hungry, to make brotherhood a reality; this has to shake our faith in ourselves. If we look honestly at the realities of our national life, it is clear that we are not marching forward; we are growing and stumbling; we are divided and confused. Our moral values and our spiritual confidence sink, even as our material wealth ascends. In these trying circumstances, the black revolution is much more than a struggle for the rights of Negroes. It is forcing America to face all its interrelated flaws—racism, poverty, militarism and materialism. It is exposing evils that are rooted deeply in the whole structure of our society. It reveals systemic rather than superficial flaws and suggests that radical reconstruction of society itself is the real issue to be faced. ■

6. **United States involvement in the war in Vietnam affected the black struggle in numerous ways. First of all, the military draft made it more difficult for young blacks to participate in the struggle. In addition, the war and the controversies surrounding it absorbed the attention of the public and national leaders and made it more difficult for black protest activity to attract attention and white participants. The war also diverted government funds that might have been used to deal with black economic problems. Finally, the war affected the attitudes of many black activists, creating a wide chasm between those who criticized national policy and those who did not. Most of the activists who had been deeply involved in the southern struggle had become distrustful of the motives of the federal government and identified themselves with nonwhite people elsewhere who were fighting against white domination. As demonstrated in the following selections, such attitudes were also evident in muted form among the black soldiers who served in Vietnam, particularly those who had been drafted in the late 1960s.**

From: *Bloods: An Oral History of the Vietnam War by Black Veterans* by Wallace Terry (New York: Random House, 1984), pages 167, 83, 10–11. Copyright 1984 by Wallace Terry. Used by permission of Random House, Inc.

Staff Sergeant Don F. Browne:
When I heard that Martin Luther King was assassinated, my first inclination was to run out and punch the first white guy I saw. I was very hurt. All I wanted to do

was to go home. I even wrote Lyndon Johnson a letter. I said that I didn't understand how I could be trying to protect foreigners in their country with the possibility of losing my life wherein in my own country people who are my heroes, like Martin Luther King, can't even walk the streets in a safe manner. I didn't get an answer from the President, but I got an answer from the White House. It was a wonderful letter, wonderful in terms of the way it looked. It wanted to assure me that the President was doing everything in his power to bring about racial equality, especially in the armed forces. A typical bureaucratic answer.

* * * *

Specialist 5 Emmanuel J. Holloman:
Black people seemed to get along better with the Vietnamese, even though they fought the Communists harder than the white GIs. Two or three of the NVAs [North Vietnamese Army] I interrogated told me they knew when black soldiers were in action, because they would throw everything they could get their hands on—grenades, tear gas, anything. They feared the black soldier more than the white soldier, because the black soldier fought more fiercely, with more abandonment.

But I think blacks got along better with the Vietnamese people, because they knew the hardships the Vietnamese went through. The majority of the people who came over there looked down on the Vietnamese. They considered them ragged, poor, stupid. They just didn't respect them. I could understand poverty. I had five brothers and three sisters. My mother worked, still works, in an old folks' home. An attendant, changing beds and stuff. My father works in a garage in New York. They are separated, and I had to leave school after the eighth grade to work in North Carolina.

Anything blacks got from the Vietnamese, they would pay for. You hardly didn't find a black cursing a Vietnamese. And a black would try to learn some of the words. And try to learn a few of their customs so they wouldn't hurt them. . . .

* * * *

Private First Class Reginald Edwards:
When I went home, they put me in supply, probably the lowest job you can have in the Marines. But they saw me drawing one day and they said, "Edwards can draw." They sent me over to the training-aids library, and I became an illustrator. I reenlisted and made sergeant.

When I went to Quantico, my being black, they gave me the black squad, the squad with most of the blacks, especially the militant blacks. And they started hippin' me. I mean I was against racism. I didn't even call it racism. I called it prejudice. They hipped me to terms like "exploitation" and "oppression." And by becoming an illustrator, it gave you more time to think. And I was around people who thought. People who read books. I would read black history where the white guys were going off on novels or playing rock music. So then one day, I just told them I was black. I didn't call them *blanco*, they didn't have to call me Negro. That's what started to get me in trouble. I became a target. Somebody to watch.

Well, there was this riot on base, and I got busted. It started over some white guys using a bunch of profanity in front of some sisters. I was found guilty of attack on an unidentified Marine. Five months in jail, five months without pay. And a suspended BCD [Bad Conduct Discharge]. In jail they didn't want us to read our books, draw any pictures, or do anything intellectually stimulating or what they thought is black. They would come in my cell and harass me. So one day I was just tired of them, and I hit the duty warden. I ended up with a BCD in 1970. After six years, eight months, and eight days, I was kicked out of the Corps. I don't feel it was fair. If I had been white, I would never have gone to jail for fighting. That would have been impossible.

With a BCD, nothing was happenin'. I took to dressin' like the Black Panthers, so even blacks wouldn't hire me. So I went to the Panther office in D.C. and joined. I felt the party was the only organization that was fighting the system.

I liked their independence. The fact that they had no fear of the police. Talking about self-determination. Trying to make Malcolm's message reality. This was the first time black people had stood up to the state since Nat Turner. I mean armed. It was obvious they wasn't gonna give us anything unless we stood up and were willing to die. . . . ∎

7. The killing of black student protesters at Jackson State College marked the culmination of a period of black student activism. The numbers of black college students had expanded greatly during the late 1960s, particularly at predominantly white colleges, and the new wave of black students brought with them an unwillingness to accept the college environment as it was. San Francisco State, Cornell, Northwestern, and Howard were among the many universities that experienced major insurgencies involving black students. A few students lost their lives, while others felt compelled to devote much of their time to protest activity rather than studies. The positive results of their sacrifices included a broadening of the realm of student political activity, a major transformation of college curricula to include black-related courses, and a dramatic increase in the numbers of black students and faculty members.

From: "Jackson State" in *The Report of the President's Commission on Campus Unrest* (Washington: U.S. Government Printing Office, 1970), pages 411–459.

Two nights of campus demonstrations at Jackson State College in May 1970 ended in violent confrontation and tragedy. After 28 seconds of gunfire by

Mississippi Highway Safety Patrolmen and Jackson city policemen, two black youths lay dying and 12 others were wounded.

* * * *

The Commission has not attempted to assess guilt or innocence but has sought to learn what happened and why. . . .

* * * *

Causes of Student Conduct
Jackson State College is a black school situated in a white-dominated state. This is the starting point for analyzing the causes of the student disorders of May 13 and 14, 1970.

The stark fact underlying all other causes of student unrest at Jackson State is the historic pattern of racism that substantially affects daily life in Mississippi.

The National Advisory Commission on Civil Disorders emphasized that racism is a fact in American society. No state or community is totally exempt. What happened in Jackson could have happened on any number of campuses where black students are protesting—on white campuses as well as black ones.

* * * *

It is important to emphasize that in any normal sense of the term, "student unrest" does not exist on the Jackson State campus. There is virtually no student movement as such and no deep or serious grievance expressed by students with respect to the administration of the school. This is not because Jackson State students are insensitive to the issues that concern students on other campuses in this country. On the contrary, roughly 500 students attended the student-organized rally on May 7 protesting the move into Cambodia by American troops and expressing their sympathy for the four students slain at Kent State.

* * * *

Interviews with black students reveal that in general they take for granted that the United States should withdraw from Indochina, and that the social conditions which breed poverty and crime in this country should be eliminated. But Jackson State students do not agitate or protest or propagandize for these policies in any organized fashion.

There are three basic reasons why almost all Jackson State students are disinclined to participate in protest activities. . . .

* * * *

The students perceive that years of protest—by turns vigorous and muted—have not brought white Mississippians to respect the full human dignity of black people. It is a fact, for example, that Jackson State College remains a separate, black state school. . . .

Second, Jackson State students do not readily engage in protest activities because they cannot afford to, especially given their belief that the utility of such action is marginal at best. In their daily life in Mississippi, Jackson State students are too busy fighting for their physical, economic, social, and psychological lives to engage in protests. . . .

There is a third reason why Jackson State students do not readily protest: Southern black people as a group still believe that the American system will respond to their legitimate demands without the necessity of bringing to bear the pressure of protest activities. . . .

* * * *

Causes of Police Conduct

We have said it is impossible to understand the actions of the students who participated in the events of May 13 and 14 without recognizing the central role of racial antagonisms. That is equally true of the reaction of those peace officers who fired their weapons at Alexander Hall.

Many white Mississippi law enforcement officers—and all officers who fired were white—are afraid of what black men may do to them in hostile surround-ings. Whether that fear is justified is of little consequence; the fear exists. That fear is intensified enormously in a violent confrontation—one in which foul language is made more threatening by thrown bricks and bottles and by the knowledge that there are Blacks with guns in the immediate area.

Moreover, many white police officers are influenced by their disdain or hatred of Blacks. One officer characterized the rock-throwing on Wednesday night as follows: "It's just a bunch of damn niggers." . . .

* * * *

The Commission concludes that racial animosity on the part of white police officers was a substantial contributing factor in the deaths of two black youths and the gunshot injuries of twelve more.

One of the most tragic aspects of the Jackson State College deaths, however, is that—despite the obvious existence of racial antagonisms—the confrontation itself could have been avoided.

The Commission concludes that the 28-second fusillade from police officers was an unreasonable, unjustified overreaction. Even if we were to assume that two shots were fired from a window in the west wing of Alexander Hall, the 28-second fusillade in response was clearly unwarranted. . . .

* * * *

Law enforcement officers stated that they did not fire to disperse the crowd in front of Alexander Hall, but rather were responding to what they believed was a sniper located in the west wing. Every officer who admits firing stated that he fired either into the west wing or into the air. The physical evidence and the positions of the victims, however, indicate that the officers were firing indis-criminately into the crowd, at ground level, on both sides of Lynch Street.

Even though the officers did fire into the crowd, it appears that no one would have been killed if birdshot had been used rather than buckshot. . . .

This change in policy lends some support to the view, widespread among Jackson State students, that police, particularly highway patrolmen, have be-come more hostile in recent years to Blacks and more inclined to deal harshly with black protestors. Some students say that national, state, and local officials have created a favorable climate for such police attitudes.

Finally, the Commission concludes that a significant cause of the deaths and injuries at Jackson State College is the confidence of white officers that if they fire weapons during a black campus disturbance they will face neither stern departmental discipline nor criminal prosecution or conviction.

This view received confirmation by the Mississippi Highway Safety Patrol investigation and by the report of the Hinds County grand jury. . . .

* * * *

. . . Its underlying philosophy is summarized in the following passage from the report: "When people . . . engage in civil disorders and riots, they must expect to be injured or killed when law enforcement officers are required to re-establish order."

That position, which the grand jury drew almost verbatim from grand jury charges by Federal District Judge Harold Cox and State Circuit Judge Russell Moore, may reflect the views of many Americans today. It is a view which this Commission urges Americans to reject.

The Commission categorically rejects rhetorical statements that students must "expect" injury or death during civil disorders. Such statements make no distinction between legitimate dissent and violent protest. It is the duty of public officials to protect human life and to safeguard peaceful, orderly, and lawful protest. When disorderly protest exists, it is their duty to deal with it firmly, justly, and with the minimum force necessary; lethal force should be used only to protect the lives of officers or citizens and only when the danger to innocent persons is not increased by the use of such force. ■

QUESTIONS FOR REVIEW

1. How did the focus of the civil rights movement change following the growth of black cultural awareness in the late 1960s? How well did the established civil rights organizations and leaders adjust to these new trends?

2. What methods were used by the FBI and other law enforcement agencies in response to civil rights and militant organizations? How did federal authorities manipulate and encourage differences that existed among militants in regard to the strategies and rhetoric of black liberation?

3. How were the responses of black youth to civil rights issues in the late 1960s different from those of the early 1960s? What does this indicate about the nature of the black freedom struggle during the decade?

4. How did the black struggle at home affect black soldiers in the Vietnamese War and black veterans at home?

5. How did police behavior affect attitudes in black urban communities and to what extent did it contribute to urban unrest?

6. In what ways did the mid-1960s struggle for civil rights become a broader drive for human rights and against poverty and injustice?

7. Compare the politics of violence with the politics of nonviolence. Why did it become increasingly difficult to mobilize around tactics of nonviolence?

8. What were the findings of the Kerner Commission about the causes of and solutions to black urban unrest? In what ways did black militants make themselves more vulnerable to police repression?

9. Define *black consciousness*. How did this express itself in the actions, dress, mannerisms, and art of black Americans in the late 1960s?

10. How did the assassination of Martin Luther King, Jr. affect the struggle for black equality in America? What was the federal response to the outburst of rage in black ghettos?

11. Where did the Black Panther Party for Self-defense have its origins?

12. In what ways was the increasingly militant black struggle in America influenced by events in other parts of the world?

13. To what extent did black militancy alienate white liberals who had previously supported civil rights reform? What was the significance of this loss?

14. Compare the views of Huey Newton and Stokely Carmichael with regard to methods of bringing about social change.

ADDITIONAL RECOMMENDED READINGS

Cleaver, Eldridge, *Soul on Ice*. New York: Random House, 1968. A best seller, detailing the rhetoric of the American *black power* movement. Cleaver takes the reader on a journey through black consciousness, discussing his own experiences as a youth and in prison. He also discusses the influence that such leaders as Malcolm X had on young black men of that time and how the international call for justice in Africa and Asia affected black Americans.

Foner, Philip S., ed. *The Black Panthers Speak*. Philadelphia/New York: J.B. Lippincott Company, 1970. A collection of documents which provide a detailed look at the development of the Black Panther party and the personalities and issues that were the focus of its program.

Gilbert, Ben W. and staff of *The Washington Post. Ten Blocks From The White House*. New York: Frederick A. Praeger, Publishers, 1968. A well-written book that looks at the development of the riot in Washington, DC that followed Martin Luther King, Jr.'s murder.

Goff, Stanley and Robert, Sanders. *Brothers: Black Soldiers in the 'Nam*. San Francisco: Presidio Press, 1982. The first book to deal in any depth with the issue of black involvement in the Vietnamese War. Based on the accounts of two black soldiers, it provides a strong complement to the Terry book.

Lewis, David L. *King, A Biography*. Urbana/Chicago: University of Illinois Press, 1978. A well-written biography on the renowned civil rights and religious leader. It provides a full and critical account of the life of Martin Luther King, Jr. placed in the context of the many leaders and issues of the movement. Also includes a bibliography and index of King's works.

Oates, Stephen. *Let the Trumpet Sound: The Life of Martin Luther King, Jr.* New York: Harper & Row Publishing, 1982. A quite readable biography, based on a more extensive study of primary sources than Lewis had available.

CHAPTER 11

DEFINING EQUALITY: THE NEW LEGAL BATTLES OVER RACE AND CIVIL RIGHTS (1970–1986)

BY DAVID J. GARROW

RELATED MEDIA:
EYES ON THE PRIZE
Audio Programs
3A and 3B
"Defining Equality:
The New Legal Battles
Over Race and
Civil Rights"

. . . Concentrates on the legal and legislative aspects of the freedom struggle during the late 1960s and the 1970s

. . . Identifies the significant provisions of the 1964 Civil Rights Act and the 1965 Voting Rights Act and describes their impact on American life

. . . Analyzes the position of the Supreme Court on civil rights issues during the 1967–1971 period

. . . Discusses the significance of the busing issue to American race relations and racial attitudes in the early 1970s

. . . Describes the development of American affirmative action policies during the 1960s and 1970s and identifies the major interpretations of this phrase

. . . Analyzes the significance of neoconservative arguments for adopting totally "color blind" policies throughout American life

OVERVIEW

The Civil Rights Act of 1964 and the Voting Rights Act of 1965 did much to transform many aspects of southern society and American life. Formal and overt racial segregation and discrimination was outlawed from virtually all facets of American public life, and black southerners for the first time in the 20th century were able to begin registering, voting, and electing members of their race to public offices in substantial numbers. Along with the provisions of the Civil Rights Act of 1968, which outlawed racial discrimination in most portions of the American housing market, those two statutes had a profound impact upon American society and politics.

Even in the deep south, however, federal statutes by themselves did not fundamentally transform the lives of most black citizens. As some civil rights activists such as Ella Baker and Bayard Rustin had been stressing since the early 1960s, simply having the legal right to walk into a restaurant to order a hamburger did not mean that people who suffered from inferior education, limited job opportunities, and poverty-level income would actually have the means to do so.

The period immediately after Selma and the passage of the Voting Rights Act was one in which movement activists became even more aware of the fundamental economic limitations on the impact and meaningfulness of federal antidiscrimination statutes. The events and experiences of those years also brought home to movement veterans another painful and previously underappreciated lesson: that simply the issuing of court decisions and the enactment of federal statutes did not mean that those legal commands would quickly or completely take effect. Indeed, one of the major lessons of the 1960s was that implementation of such measures rarely took place with any speed and never took place to as great an extent as proponents initially had presumed.

In the deep south, the impact of the 1964 and 1965 acts was substantial, although not as thorough-going as some observers had hoped. Almost immediately, thanks to the provisions of the voting rights measure, the substantial increase in the number of black citizens who were able to register to vote brought about drastic changes in the rhetoric and demeanor of many once rabidly-segregationist white politicians. Even such figures as Selma's Sheriff James Clark and former Alabama Public Safety Director Al Lingo, who ran for sheriff in Birmingham's Jefferson County, courted black voters during their unsuccessful 1966 races.

Nonetheless, changes in the behavior of white candidates, who oftentimes now were willing to support public works improvements in black neighborhoods that they previously had ignored, did not mean that blacks themselves suddenly were able to win elective office in numbers anywhere near approaching their percentage of the southern population; even in some towns and counties with black population majorities, white influence—especially white control over the jobs and other economic opportunities of local blacks—kept blacks out of all local elective offices, even 20 years after the Voting Rights Act had become law.

In addition to the fact that the effects of the 1964 and 1965 acts on the south were more complicated, incomplete, and subtle than often assumed, the impact and implementation of the Supreme Court's 1954 and 1955 school desegregation decisions in *Brown I* and *Brown II* was much slower and more modest in taking effect. Not until 1968 and 1969 did the Supreme Court take meaningful steps to see that more than token-level desegregation was taking place in more than a handful of southern school districts. Only in 1971, in the landmark case of *Swann* v. *Charlotte-Mecklenburg*, did the Supreme Court move forcefully to implement significant levels of integration by approving the use of busing as one tool among many for hastening the dismantling of the south's dual school systems; nonetheless, throughout the late 1960s and early 1970s, as actual school desegregation came to many southern communities for the first time, many white families withdrew their children from the public schools and enrolled them in privately-supported "segregation academies," leaving the public schools of many towns and counties nearly all black.

Although the Supreme Court's firm endorsement of school busing in *Swann* gave clear judicial support to a desegregation technique that many northern urban whites vociferously opposed when it was applied to their own *de facto* segregated schools systems, the major 1970s legal controversy involving race became the question of affirmative action, or reverse discrimination, rather than busing. While the issue of remedial measures designed to recompense black citizens for the ongoing effects of years and years of past discrimination had first emerged—and created little controversy—in the mid-1960s, in the 1970s, when more and more elite colleges and professional schools began implementing special admissions programs for minority students, affirmative action became a major national controversy.

The first definitive Supreme Court ruling on affirmative action came in 1978 in *Regents of the University of California* v. *Allan Bakke*, where the Supreme Court struck down a rigid radical quota in the Medical School admissions program. It also, with equal emphasis, declared that educational institutions *could* take an applicant's race into account, as one of many measures of student diversity, in making admissions decisions. Over the ensuing eight years, the Supreme Court continued to uphold a wide variety of affirmative action programs, especially in the area of employment, always stressing that racially-conscious affirmative action measures were remedies for previous violations of black American's constitutionally-protected rights to be free of discriminatory treatment.

By the late 1970s, criticism of racially-conscious remedy measures was growing steadily, and the 1980 election of Ronald Reagan brought into the Justice Department for the first time a group of policy-makers who strongly supported the elimination of any affirmative action efforts except where individual, identifiable victims of past discrimination could make legally-provable claims against distinct firms or institutions. The most principled exponents of such a "race-blind" approach to legal issues argued that if America was ever to get beyond and above the pernicious uses of race that had dominated the country's first 350 years since European settlement, it had better begin immediately by eliminating *all* uses of race from the law, rather than trying to distinguish affirmative from negative ones.

The first half of the 1980s witnessed a slowly emerging realization among proponents of real racial equality that constitutional claims and court litigation would likely play a continuously decreasing role in ongoing efforts to improve the lives of black Americans. Although the years from 1954 through 1965 had witnessed a series of landmark events that fundamentally erased the legal obstacles to formal black equality, the 1980s signalled that future activism would increasingly focus on questions of government policy and politics, and not on the law.

READINGS

1. Although Selma may seem a relative success story in terms of how substantial the changes have been in its politics and racial practices over the past two decades, many places in the rural deep south still remain where such changes have *not* occurred. The following 1985 *New York Times* story offers an important and at times poignant analysis of how the old ways of the segregation era still survive in many southern locales.

From: "Across the Rural South, Segregation as Usual," by E.R. Shipp in *The New York Times* (April 27, 1985). Copyright 1985 by The New York Times Company. Used by permisson.

DAWSON, Ga.—When a well-dressed black visitor to the Terrell County Courthouse here recently asked a white secretary in the probate judge's office for directions to the ladies' room, she was told, "Just go downstairs."

On her way down rickety wooden stairs to the basement, the visitor asked further directions from a white-haired black man, the courthouse janitor. He told her to go back upstairs to the sheriff's office, across the lobby from the probate judge's office, for the key to the ladies' room that is located on the main floor.

The first-floor restroom, it turns out, is generally used by white women, whose exclusive preserve it was in the days of Jim Crow laws, while black women generally continue to use the basement restroom. The two are not far apart, but the steps between them are steps into a time warp, steps that many blacks in this rural southwest Georgia town take every business day.

For here in Dawson, a predominantly black town of 5,700, as in countless other rural towns across the states that made up the Confederacy, an unwritten code perpetuates what was once enshrined in law and announced by "Colored Entrance" or "Whites Only" signs. These are the towns and rural areas that the civil rights movement and the Civil Rights Act of 1964 largely bypassed as black-white relations in the region as a whole were indelibly changed.

The civil rights laws of the 1960's barred overt segregation, but some changes are slow to develop. They are governed by a combination of adherence to tradition, fear by blacks, racism by whites and the facets of economics.

In many of the towns, there are bars where blacks know they cannot buy drinks, restaurants in which they cannot eat, motels in which they cannot get a room and golf courses at which they cannot tee off.

This situation exists, said Steve Suitts, executive director of the Atlanta-based Southern Regional Council, a private research organization, "because the Federal Government's arm isn't that long and business doesn't require a different practice."

"No one would do that, as a rule, in Atlanta," he said, "not because Atlanta doesn't believe in it, but simply because it would be bad for business."

Determining who is responsible for the perpetuation of segregation is difficult. Many whites say people want to stick with their own kind; blacks say they are discriminated against. Whites also feel that race relations are good and that there are no racial problems; blacks say the opposite is true.

* * * *

One 23-year-old woman, who identified herself only as Helen, explained why she was among those blacks who enter Dr. G. Fain Martin's dental office through the side door, sit in the "east" waiting room at the Terrell County Medical Clinic and use the basement restrooms at the courthouse. "That's where we always went," she said, "so that's where we go."

Huelett Phillips, a black 48-year-old Atlantan who is incarcerated at the Terrell County Prison Camp for possession of marijuana, said blacks "know their place" in the rural South. The prisoners, two-thirds of whom are black, maintain county roads and buildings and collect garbage. Mr. Phillips is the courthouse janitor.

"It's changed in the big cities," he added, "but it hasn't changed in small towns like this."

* * * *

For blacks who live in these areas, said Charles H. King Jr., a race relations consultant based in Atlanta, "the name of the game is survival."

"Their whole livelihood depends on the white people, the white system," said Mr. King, who is black. "Civil rights, drinking water from a public fountain, eating in restaurants, going to bathrooms—all that is secondary to survival."

White resistance comes as no shock to Charles Sherrod, a black who is a member of the Albany, Ga., City Council, who came to southwest Georgia in 1961 with the Student Nonviolent Coordinating Committee.

"Those people who shot at us and blew up churches and all that 20 years ago, they haven't gone anywhere," said Mr. Sherrod. "The attitudes are still there. Their behavior has changed because we have got a little power. They won't do anything they can't get away with."

* * * *

Economics also plays a role, according to many experts. So long as blacks must depend on whites for jobs, credit and small favors, they will not rock the boat.

* * * *

It is where an independent class of blacks has emerged, as doctors, lawyers or undertakers, that they have challenged the old system, said David Garrow, an associate professor of political science at City College, in New York. . . .

* * * *

. . . As in other areas of the South, whites speak to a visitor of racial harmony while blacks quietly complain of racism.

* * * *

Several whites, including John Thacker, president of the local Chamber of Commerce, insisted that Dawson had never had any "racial problems." But that overlooks the history of what civil rights activists and older blacks still refer to as "Terrible Terrell."

They recall the two churches that were burned in 1962, churches that were being used for voter registration drives. Dr. [Martin Luther] King and Jackie Robinson, the baseball player, came to Dawson to lend their encouragement.

And they remember that a third church was torched by three drunken men, one of whom told the local newspaper, *The Dawson News*, that they had been angry.

Blacks also recall how in 1964 D.U. Pullum, then in his 70's and president of the local N.A.A.C.P., was brutally beaten by unidentified white men.

They remember the people who lost their jobs when they registered to vote or when it was discovered that they belonged to the N.A.A.C.P. And they remember the Dawson Five case, which in 1977 brought international attention to a bastion of Old South that existed in the shadows of President Carter's New South.

Five illiterate or semiliterate black youths who had been charged with murdering a white man spent 18 months in jail awaiting trial. The only evidence was two confessions that proved to have been coerced. After a hearing, the confessions were thrown out and the charges dismissed. According to testimony at a pretrial hearing, one youth was told that the polygraph machine to which he was fastened was an electric chair.

The town felt itself on trial, and neither blacks nor whites liked what they saw, for conflicting reasons. Whites still say the town was falsely portrayed. But many blacks, including Mr. [Robert L.] Albritten, the City Council member, trace the "reawakening" of blacks to the Dawson Five case.

Within two years, following a lawsuit that challenged the at-large voting system, blacks were elected to the City Council and the County Commission for the first time. Two blacks were named to the school board. And blacks began holding jobs they had never held before, as bank tellers, as City Hall secretaries, as factory supervisors or as personnel directors.

But most white children still attend the Terrell Academy, which was established in 1970, shortly after the school board agreed to let blacks attend white schools on a "freedom-of-choice" basis. The city owned a swimming pool near the courthouse, but sold it to the hastily formed Terrell County Youth Foundation in the 1960's, thus avoiding integration.

Today, blacks swim in a city-owned pool in a black neighborhood. Whites use the facilities at the Terrell Country Club, which has no black members.

* * * *

As for socializing, Mr. [J.R.] Melton [a barber] said blacks have their bars and whites theirs. Adults might get together at the softball games sponsored by the County Recreation Department. "But just straight socializing, a white couple and black couple getting together? No."

Asked why, he said, "It's just the way we were brought up, the way we were raised."

Blacks, when asked, say they do not care to socialize with whites, anyway. And so the pattern, established by law in years past, continues now by force of habit.

There are two activities that may help draw the children of Dawson closer than their parents are: basketball and the 4–H Club.

Whites from the academy will come to watch basketball games at the Terrell County High School, which is 95 percent black. In 1984 the boys won the state championship; this year the girls did. A recent victory parade through downtown Dawson drew blacks and whites.

About 450 students from fifth grade up work together on 4–H projects, go to camps together and compete with each other.

But whether any of this is a sign that the next generation will create a more integrated society in the Dawsons of the South remains to be seen.

Mr. Gamble, the County Commission chairman said, "I think it's going to be a while."

Mr. Garrow, the political science professor, put it this way: "I think the distance in time between small, rural towns and an Atlanta or a Birmingham is a difference of decades." ■

2. T**he Supreme Court's unanimous 1971 opinion in** *James E. Swann* **v.** *Charlotte-Mecklenburg Board of Education* **was the most important ruling on race since the** *Brown* **decisions of 1954 and 1955. In** *Swann,* **the high court upheld a wide-ranging desegregation decree issued by the local federal district court, a decree that included the use of student busing to eliminate one-race schools, for at the time that the** *Swann* **case had begun, nearly 60 percent of black students in the Charlotte-Mecklenburg district attended schools that were 99 percent or more black, even though the system as a whole was over 70 percent white.**

From: James E. Swann et al. v. *Charlotte-Mecklenburg Board of Education* et al. Decided April 20, 1971.

Mr. Chief Justice Burger delivered the opinion of the Court.

* * * *

This case and those argued with it arose in States having a long history of maintaining two sets of schools in a single school system deliberately operated to carry out a governmental policy to separate pupils in schools solely on the basis of race. That was what *Brown* v. *Board of Education* was all about. These cases present us with the problem of defining in more precise terms than heretofore the scope of the duty of school authorities and district courts in implementing *Brown I* and the mandate to eliminate dual systems and establish unitary systems at once. . . .

* * * *

Nearly 17 years ago this Court held, in explicit terms, that state-imposed segregation by race in public schools denies equal protection of the laws. At no time has the Court deviated in the slightest degree from that holding or its constitutional underpinnings. . . .

* * * *

Over the 16 years since *Brown II*, many difficulties were encountered in implementation of the basic constitutional requirement that the State not discriminate between public school children on the basis of their race. Nothing in our national experience prior to 1955 prepared anyone for dealing with changes and adjustments of the magnitude and complexity encountered since then. Deliberate resistance of some to the Court's mandates has impeded the good-faith efforts of others to bring school systems into compliance. The detail and nature of these dilatory tactics have been noted frequently by this Court and other courts.

* * * *

The central issue in this case is that of student assignment, and there are essentially four problem areas:

    (1)   to what extent racial balance or racial quotas may be used as an implement in a remedial order to correct a previously segregated system;

(2) whether every all-Negro and all-white school must be eliminated as an indispensable part of a remedial process of desegregation;

(3) what the limits are, if any, on the rearrangement of school districts and attendance zones, as a remedial measure; and

(4) what the limits are, if any, on the use of transportation facilities to correct state-enforced racial school segregation.

* * * *

We see therefore that the use made of mathematical ratios was no more than a starting point in the process of shaping a remedy, rather than an inflexible requirement. From that starting point the District Court proceeded to frame a decree that was within its discretionary powers, as an equitable remedy for the particular circumstances. . . . A school authority's remedial plan or a district court's remedial decree is to be judged by its effectiveness. Awareness of the racial composition of the whole school system is likely to be a useful starting point in shaping a remedy to correct past constitutional violations. In sum, the very limited use made of mathematical ratios was within the equitable remedial discretion of the District Court.

* * * *

The importance of bus transportation as a normal and accepted tool of educational policy is readily discernible. . . . The District Court's conclusion that assignment of children to the school nearest their home serving their grade would not produce an effective dismantling of the dual system is supported by the record.

Thus the remedial techniques used in the District Court's order were within that court's power to provide equitable relief; implementation of the decree is well within the capacity of the school authority.

The decree provided that the buses used to implement the plan would operate on direct routes. Students would be picked up at schools near their homes and transported to the schools they were to attend. The trips for elementary school pupils average about seven miles and the District Court found that they would take "not over 35 minutes at the most." . . . In these circumstances, we find no basis for holding that the local school authorities may not be required to employ bus transportation as one tool of school desegregation. Desegregation plans cannot be limited to the walk-in school.

An objection to transportation of students may have validity when the time or distance of travel is so great as to either risk the health of the children or significantly impinge on the educational process. . . . It hardly needs stating that the limits on time of travel will vary with many factors, but probably with none more than the age of the students. The reconciliation of competing values in a desegregation case is, of course, a difficult task with many sensitive facets but fundamentally no more so than remedial measures courts of equity have traditionally employed.

. . . On the facts of this case, we are unable to conclude that the order of the District Court is not reasonable, feasible and workable. . . .

At some point, these school authorities and others like them should have achieved full compliance with this Court's decision in *Brown I*. . . .

It does not follow that the communities served by such systems will remain demographically stable, for in a growing, mobile society, few will do so. Neither school authorities nor district courts are constitutionally required to make year-by-year adjustments of the racial composition of student bodies once the affirmative duty to desegregate has been accomplished and racial discrimination through official action is eliminated from the system. This does not mean that federal courts are without power to deal with future problems; but in the absence of a showing that either the school authorities or some other agency of the State has deliberately attempted to fix or alter demographic patterns to affect the racial composition of the schools, further intervention by a district court should not be necessary. ■

3. The Supreme Court's 1978 opinion in *Regents of the University of California* v. *Bakke* remains the Supreme Court's most influential decision with regard to affirmative action. When an unsuccessful applicant to the Medical School at University of California at Davis, Allan P. Bakke, challenged his rejection on the grounds that a special minority admissions program had unconstitutionally allowed for the admission of minority students with lower qualifications than his own, the Supreme Court ruled not only on Bakke's individual claim for admission but also on the far broader question of whether an applicant's race could be considered as part of an educational institution's admissions decisions.

From: Regents of the University of California v. *Allan Bakke.* Decided June 28, 1978.

Mr. Justice Powell announced the judgment of the Court.

This case presents a challenge to the special admissions program of the petitioner, the Medical School of the University of California at Davis. . . .

For the reasons stated in the following opinion, I believe that so much of the judgment of the California court holds petitioner's special admissions program unlawful and directs that respondent be admitted to the Medical School must be affirmed. . . .

I also conclude . . . the portion of the court's judgment enjoining petitioner from according any consideration to race in its admissions process must be reversed. . . .

Affirmed in part and reversed in part.

The Medical School of the University of California at Davis opened in 1968 with an entering class of 50 students. In 1971, the size of the entering class was increased to 100 students, a level at which it remains. . . . Over the next two years, the faculty devised a special admissions program. . . .

* * * *

The special admissions program operated with a separate committee, a majority of whom were members of minority groups. On the 1973 application form, candidates were asked to indicate whether they wished to be considered as "economically and/or educationally disadvantaged" applicants; on the 1974 form the question was whether they wished to be considered as members of a "minority group," which the Medical School apparently viewed as "Blacks," "Chicanos," "Asians," and "American Indians." . . . No formal definition of "disadvantaged" was ever produced, but the chairman of the special committee screened each application to see whether it reflected economic or educational deprivation. Having passed this initial hurdle, the applications then were rated by the special committee. . . . About one-fifth of the total number of special applicants were invited for interviews in 1973 and 1974. . . . The special committee then presented its top choices to the general admissions committee. The latter did not rate or compare the special candidates against the general applicants, but could reject recommended special candidates for failure to meet course requirements or other specific deficiencies. The special committee continued to recommend special applicants until a number prescribed by faculty vote were admitted. . . . [I]n 1973 and 1974 . . . the prescribed number of special admissions [was] 16.

From . . . 1971 through 1974, the special program resulted in the admission of 21 black students, 30 Mexican-Americans, and 12 Asians, for a total of 63 minority students. Over the same period, the regular admissions program produced one black, six Mexican-Americans, and 37 Asians, for a total of 44 minority students. Although disadvantaged whites applied to the special program in large numbers, none received an offer of admission through that process. Indeed, in 1974, at least, the special committee explicitly considered only "disadvantaged" special applicants who were members of one of the designated minority groups.

Allan Bakke is a white male who applied to the Davis Medical School in both 1973 and 1974. . . . His 1973 interview[er] . . . considered Bakke "a very desirable applicant to [the] medical school." Despite a strong benchmark score of 468 out of 500, Bakke was rejected. [In 1974, his] faculty interviewer . . . found Bakke "rather limited in his approach" to the problems of the medical profession and found disturbing Bakke's "very definite opinions which were based more on his personal viewpoints than upon a study of the total problem." . . . Again, Bakke's application was rejected. . . . In both years, applicants were admitted under the special program with grade point averages, MCAT scores, and benchmark scores significantly lower than Bakke's. . . .

* * * *

. . . Petitioner prefers to view [the special admissions program] as establishing a "goal" of minority representation in the Medical School. Respondent, echoing the courts below, labels it a racial quota.

This semantic distinction is beside the point: The special admissions program is undeniably a classification based on race and ethnic background. To the extent that there existed a pool of at least minimally qualified minority applicants to fill the 16 special admissions seats, white applicants could compete for only 84 seats in the entering class, rather than the 100 open to minority applicants. Whether this limitation is described as a quota or a goal, it is a line drawn on the basis of race and ethnic status.

* * * *

Although many of the Framers of the Fourteenth Amendment conceived of its primary function as bridging the vast distance between members of the Negro race and white "majority," the Amendment itself was framed in universal terms, without reference to color, ethnic origin, or condition of prior servitude. . . .

Over the past 30 years this Court has embarked upon the crucial mission of interpreting the Equal Protection Clause with the view of assuring to all persons "the protection of equal laws" in a Nation confronting a legacy of slavery and racial discrimination. . . .

Petitioner urges us to adopt for the first time a more restrictive view of the Equal Protection Clause and hold that discrimination against members of the white "majority" cannot be suspect if its purpose can be characterized as "benign." The clock of our liberties, however, cannot be turned back to 1868. It is far too late to argue that the guarantee of equal protection to *all* persons permits the recognition of special wards entitled to a degree of protection greater than that accorded others. . . .

* * * *

. . . there are serious problems of justice connected with the idea of preference itself. First, it may not always be clear that a so-called preference is in fact benign. Courts may be asked to validate burdens imposed upon individual members of a particular group in order to advance the group's general interest. Nothing in the Constitution supports the notion that individuals may be asked to suffer otherwise impermissible burdens in order to enhance the societal standing of their ethnic groups. Second, preferential programs may only reinforce common stereotypes holding that certain groups are unable to achieve success without special protection based on a factor of having no relationship to individual worth. Third, there is a measure of inequity in forcing innocent persons in respondent's position to bear the burdens of redressing grievances not of their making.

* * * *

If it is the individual who is entitled to judicial protection against classifications based upon his racial or ethnic background because such distinctions impinge upon personal rights, rather than the individual only because of his membership in a particular group, then constitutional standards may be applied consistently. Political judgments regarding the necessity for the particular classification may be weighed in the constitutional balance . . . but the standard of justification will remain constant. This is as it should be, since those political judgments are the product of rough compromise struck by contending groups within the democratic process. When they touch upon an individual's race or ethnic background, he is entitled to a judicial determination that the burden he is asked to bear on that basis is precisely tailored to serve a compelling governmental [interest].

* * * *

In this case . . . there has been no determination by the legislature or a responsible administrative agency that the University engaged in a discriminatory practice requiring remedial efforts. Moreover, the operation of petitioner's special admissions program . . . prefers the designated minority groups at the expense of other individuals who are totally foreclosed from competition for the 16 special admissions seats in every Medical School class. Because of that foreclosure, some individuals are excluded from enjoyment of a state-provided benefit—admission to the Medical School—they otherwise would receive. When a classification denies an individual opportunities or benefits enjoyed by others solely because of his race or ethnic background, it must be regarded as suspect.

. . . The special admissions program purports to serve the purposes of: (i) "reducing the historic deficit of traditionally disfavored minorities in medical schools and in the medical profession;" (ii) countering the effects of societal discrimination; (iii) increasing the number of physicians who will practice in communities currently underserved; and (iv) obtaining the educational benefits that flow from an ethnically diverse student body. It is necessary to decide which, if any, of these purposes is substantial enough to support the use of a suspect classification.

. . . If petitioner's purpose is to assure within its student body some specified percentage of a particular group merely because of its race or ethnic origin, such a preferential purpose must be rejected not as insubstantial but as facially invalid. Preferring members of any one group for no reason other than race or ethnic origin is discrimination for its own sake. This the Constitution forbids.

. . . The State certainly has a legitimate and substantial interest in ameliorating, or eliminating where feasible, the disabling effects of identified discrimination. . . . That goal was far more focused than the remedying of the effects of "societal discrimination," an amorphous concept of injury that may be ageless in its reach into the past.

We have never approved a classification that aids persons perceived as members of relatively victimized groups at the expense of other innocent individuals in the absence of judicial, legislative, or administrative findings of constitutional or statutory violations. After such findings have been made, the governmental interest in preferring members of the injured groups at the expense of others is substantial, since the legal rights of the victims must be vindicated. In such a case, the extent of the injury and the consequent remedy will have been judicially, legislatively, or administratively defined. Also, the remedial action usually remains subject to continuing oversight to assure that it will work the least harm possible to other innocent persons competing for the benefit. Without such findings of constitutional or statutory violations, it cannot be said that the government has any greater interest in helping one individual than in refraining from harming another. Thus, the government has no compelling justification for inflicting such harm.

* * * *

Hence, the purpose of helping certain groups . . . perceived as victims of "societal discrimination" does not justify a classification that imposes disadvantages upon persons like respondent, who bear no responsibility for whatever harm the beneficiaries of the special admissions program are thought to have suffered. To hold otherwise would be to convert a remedy heretofore reserved for violations of legal rights into a privilege that all institutions throughout the Nation could grant at their pleasure to whatever groups are perceived as victims of societal discrimination. That is a step we have never approved.

. . . Petitioner identifies . . . improving the delivery of health care services to communities currently underserved. It may be assumed that in some situations a State's interest in facilitating the health care of its citizens is sufficiently compelling to support the use of a suspect classification. But there is virtually no evidence in the record indicating that petitioner's special admissions program is either needed or geared to promote that goal. . . .

. . . The fourth goal asserted by petitioner is the attainment of a diverse student body. . . . Academic freedom, though not a specifically enumerated constitutional right, long has been viewed as a special concern of the First Amendment. The freedom of a university to make its own judgments as to education includes the selection of its student body. . . .

* * * *

Thus, in arguing that its universities must be accorded the right to select those students who will contribute the most to the "robust exchange of ideas," petitioner invokes a countervailing constitutional interest, that of the First Amendment. In this light, petitioner must be viewed as seeking to achieve a goal that is of paramount importance in the fulfillment of its mission.

. . . Physicians serve a heterogeneous population. An otherwise qualified medical student with a particular background—whether it be ethnic, geographic, culturally advantaged or disadvantaged—may bring to a professional school of medicine experiences, outlooks, and ideas that enrich the training of its student body and better equip its graduates to render with understanding their vital service to humanity.

Ethnic diversity, however, is only one element in a range of factors a university properly may consider in attaining the goal of a heterogeneous student body. Although a university must have wide discretion in making the sensitive judgments as to who should be admitted, constitutional limitations protecting individual rights may not be disregarded. . . .

. . . [P]etitioner's argument that this is the only effective means of serving the interest of diversity is seriously flawed. . . . Petitioner's special admissions program, focused *solely* on ethnic diversity, would hinder rather than further attainment of genuine diversity.

* * * *

The experience of other university admissions programs, which take race into account in achieving the educational diversity valued by the First Amendment, demonstrates that the assignment of a fixed number of places to a minority group is not a necessary means toward that end. An illuminating example is found in the Harvard College program:

> "In recent years Harvard College has expanded the concept of diversity to include students from disadvantaged economic, racial and ethnic groups. . . .
>
> ". . . When the Committee on Admissions reviews the large middle group of applicants who are 'admissible' and deemed capable of doing good work in their courses, the race of an applicant may tip the balance in his favor just as geographic origin or a life spent on a farm may tip the balance in other candidates' cases. . . ."

* * * *

In such an admissions program, race or ethnic background may be deemed a "plus" in a particular applicant's file, yet it does not insulate the individual from comparison with all other candidates for the available seats. The file of a particular black applicant may be examined for his potential contribution to diversity without the factor of race being decisive when compared, for example, with that of an applicant identified as an Italian-American if the latter is thought to exhibit qualities more likely to promote beneficial educational pluralism. Such qualities could include exceptional personal talents, unique work or service experience, leadership potential, maturity, demonstrated compassion, a history of overcoming disadvantage, ability to communicate with the poor, or other qualifications deemed important. In short, an admissions program operated in this way is flexible enough to consider all pertinent elements of diversity in light of the particular qualifications of each applicant, and to place them on the same footing for consideration, although not necessarily according them the same weight. Indeed, the weight attributed to a particular quality may vary from year to year depending upon the "mix" both of the student body and the applicants for the incoming class.

This kind of program treats each applicant as an individual in the admissions process. The applicant who loses out on the last available seat to another candidate receiving a "plus" on the basis of ethnic background will not have been foreclosed from all consideration for that seat simply because he was not the right color or had the wrong surname. . . .

It has been suggested that an admissions program which considers race only as one factor is simply a subtle and more sophisticated—but no less effective—means of according racial preference than the Davis program. A facial intent to discriminate, however, is evident in petitioner's preference program and not

257

denied in this case. No such facial infirmity exists in an admissions program where race or ethnic background is simply one element—to be weighed fairly against other elements—in the selection process. . . . And a Court would not assume that a university, professing to employ a facially nondiscriminatory admissions policy, would operate it as a cover for the functional equivalent of a quota system. In short, good faith would be presumed in the absence of a showing to the contrary in the manner permitted by our cases. . . .

. . . [W]hen a State's distribution of benefits or imposition of burdens hinges on ancestry or the color of a person's skin, that individual is entitled to a demonstration that the challenged classification is necessary to promote a substantial state interest. Petitioner has failed to carry this burden. For this reason, that portion of the California court's judgment holding petitioner's special admissions program invalid under the Fourteenth Amendment must be affirmed.

In enjoining petitioner from ever considering the race of any applicant, however, the courts below failed to recognize that the State has a substantial interest that legitimately may be served by a properly devised admissions program involving the competitive consideration of race and ethnic origin. For this reason, so much of the California court's judgment as enjoins petitioner from any consideration of the race of any applicant must be reversed.

With respect to respondent's entitlement to an injunction directing his admission to the Medical School, petitioner has conceded that it could not carry its burden of proving that, but for the existence of its unlawful special admissions program, respondent still would not have been admitted. Hence, respondent is entitled to the injunction, and that portion of the judgment must be affirmed.

■

4. **I**n this excerpt from an important 1979 law review article, well-known legal scholar William Van Alstyne argues that the Supreme Court must not forget the "race blind" approach to American law that Justice John Marshall Harlan, the only dissenter in the Supreme Court's infamous 1896 *Plessy* v. *Ferguson* decision endorsing racial segregation, had unsuccessfully argued for sixty years before *Brown* actually vanquished formal segregation from American law. This excerpt from Van Alstyne's argument begins with him discussing the meaning of the three crucial Constitutional Amendments, the 13th, 14th, and 15th, adopted in the late 1860s in the wake of the Civil War.

From: "Rites of Passage: Race, the Supreme Court, and the Constitution" by William Van Alstyne in *University of Chicago Law Review*, 46 (Spring 1979). Used by permission of *The University of Chicago Law Review* which retains the copyright to this article.

[The thirteenth Constitutional amendment] prohibits all forms of involuntary servitude and allows Congress an ample power to police that ban through federal law. The fourteenth amendment is far more lengthy than the thirteenth, but in its most essential parts it establishes a constitutional definition of citizenship and forbids the states to abridge the incidents of national citizenship. It also forbids the states to deny equal protection to any person or to deprive any person of life, liberty, or property "without due process of law," and it vests in Congress an ample power to enforce these protections. The last—the fifteenth amendment—is more limited: it more explicitly protects the right to vote from abridgment "on account of race, color, or previous condition of servitude," again concluding with a section vesting in Congress ample power to vindicate that protection. The extent to which these three amendments enacted a color-blind restriction on the recurring temptation of government to regulate or allocate by race, however, was a question plainly not settled between 1866 and 1870. It remains unsettled even now.

At one level, the sheer stamina of the question, despite the passage of a century's opportunity for its resolution, is not surprising. The texts of these amendments are sufficiently unspecific that, even in the aggregate, with their obvious connections with one another and with the Civil War, they compel no single answer. Similarly, the welter of accompanying legislative history is amenable to more than one reasonable perspective. That people should disagree, and that mutually earnest scholars do disagree, is, therefore, rather to be expected even at this very late date. . . .

What is less explicable, at least to nonlawyers, is that after a century of periodic judicial review there is still no formal resolution of the question. . . . Laws regulating on the basis of race were in existence before the Civil War amendments were adopted; many were judicially examined in litigation prompted by the passage of these amendments. Other laws regulating on the basis of race were enacted after ratification of all three amendments, and still others are tenaciously put forward today; many of these have similarly been tested in the Supreme Court. One would surely suppose that, for judicial purposes at least, so old and so obvious an issue would long ago have been settled to provide us with some steady impression of the extent to which government may regulate or allocate by race. But it is not so.

* * * *

The first [rite of] passage for the Court came with the immediate adjudication of race-related cases on the heels of the Civil War amendments. With the exception of a few notable cases striking down the most egregious race regulations, the Supreme Court adopted a wholly tolerant and deferential rendering of all three amendments, imputing to them only the most modest consequences. Federal statutes flatly forbidding racial discrimination by commercial enterprises were held to be excessive, as acts of an unwarranted color-blind zeal. . . .

* * * *

The Court's view—that the laws would be sustained if "reasonable"—gen-uflected to the wisdom of legislative bodies to sort out good from bad uses of race. . . . Regulation by race was not commendable or censurable as such; only unfair, one-sided, or unevenhanded race regulation or allocation was forbidden. If individuals could be equally protected, albeit racially regulated, then nothing in the command or ethos of the fourteenth amendment was deemed to deny the use of racial classification to the body of American politics.

This view of the matter steadily developed between 1873 and the twilight of the 19th century. It was cemented in 1896 in the "separate-but-equal" decision of *Plessy* v. *Ferguson*. The decision upheld a state law requiring separate passenger cars for white and for black riders: neither was worse off than the other in the quality of accommodations to be furnished to each; neither was more or less protected than the other (rather, each was equally protected) by the racial regulation a legislative body deemed reasonable in the public interest.

There was but one dissent that took a less measured view and would have imposed upon the fourteenth amendment a more categorical imperative. Less flexible than others on the Supreme Court at the time, Justice Harlan was prepared to read into the Civil War amendments what was, to be sure, neither explicitly provided by their terms nor compelled by their compromised legisla-tive history. Proceeding from a more basic premise than that either of these considerations necessarily controlled the matter, Harlan put his finger on the lessons of his own contemporary history. Prior to the Civil War amendments, race was the basis on which status had been determined, worth assigned, entitlements settled, and legal rights measured. It had been iniquitous from the very beginning, and it subsequently proved to be a disaster for the entire country. He believed the enactment of the Civil War amendments should therefore be construed by the Court as altogether disallowing it. Government could not determine worth, assign entitlements, or measure legal rights by race *at all*. . . . The point of emphasis [in *Plessy* v. *Ferguson*] is fundamental. It is not that when race is used, all persons identified to each race must be as well regarded as all persons identified to some other race. The thing condemned is not that members of each race must be "equally" protected under laws dis-tinguishing them by their race, nor that they are assigned entitlements un-equally on the basis of race. The thing condemned, rather, is the assignment of entitlements by race. It is the impropriety of the *basis* of assignment, not the modicum thus assigned, that constitutes the government's offense. . . .

* * * *

The Harlan opinion passed into history at the time, . . . discredited by the dominant view that the fourteenth amendment had not withdrawn from legisla-tive bodies a political license to regulate by race. . . .

In the swift consecutive series of . . . decisions issued by the Supreme Court during the two years following *Brown*, the Court. . . . appeared more com-pletely to enact Harlan's view that the Civil War amendments altogether "remov-ed the race line from our governmental systems."

Between 1955 and 1976, moreover, virtually every other race-related decision by the Supreme Court appeared to convey this same message. . . . In each instance, the fulcrum of judicial leverage was an *existing governmental* race line, which the particular judicial order sought to remove. The object was thus to disestablish particular, existing uses of race, not to establish new ones. Indeed, decrees that would subsequently presume to require race-conscious decisions for any other purpose, for example, to maintain "proportions" or "balances" by race designation, were swiftly reversed.

This second rite of passage was accompanied by consistent developments in the 1960s in the Supreme Court and then, encouragingly, in congress and the executive branch as well. For the Court's part, long dormant Reconstruction statutes were revived and given a reinvigorated and uniformly race-blind application. . . .

* * * *

In this twenty-year pattern of development, from 1954 to 1974, the Supreme Court's ambiguous "lesson" thus seemed to be that race was indeed constitutionally withdrawn from the incorrigible temptations of governmental use. . . .

Thus the lesson . . . is . . . not merely that regulation and allocation by race are wrong. Rather, the message is commendably even stronger. Laws that divide and index people to measure their civil rights by race are unconstitutional. Laws that encourage others to do so are similarly invalid. And laws attempting to advance either policy even in disguise will likewise be struck down whenever it is within the capacity of conscientious courts to see beneath their cellophane wrappers.

* * * *

. . . But under the more flexible "test"—which allows allocation by race when certain criteria are met—to strike down a statute it is not enough to show that the law itself explicitly treats the rights of one person differently from those of any other by making race itself a sufficient reason for that difference. Rather, one must also "decide," even in every case arising in each of the above categories, two additional matters:

> (1)   what kinds of public purposes are sufficiently compelling to justify explicitly treating some people less well than others on racial grounds; and
> (2)   who is to say (and on what basis) that a law, which on its face is nominally very well connected with a sufficient public purpose, making its purposive racial discrimination "justifiable" under (1), was indeed enacted solely to promote that objective *rather than to enact some baser interest with which it is equally well connected?*

This is not, I think, a constitutional standard at all. It is, rather, a sieve—a sieve that encourages renewed race-based laws, racial discrimination, racial competition, racial spoils systems, and mere judicial sport. It is *Plessy* v. *Ferguson* all over again, in new and modish dress. . . .

. . . An actual example was well provided last year in *Regents of the University of California* v. *Bakke*. The Regents' Supreme Court brief treated the case as though the use of race itself to establish separate and unequal admission standards at the Davis medical school were really not the issue. Rather, the issue was better to be seen as a revised, updated version of *Plessy* v. *Ferguson*: that it is not the use of race as a means of assigning students to different schools that is at issue, but the reason for making such assignments. . . .

* * * *

We have had three hundred years of national experience to notice that *whenever* race has been an admissible criterion of governmental action, its licitness left people in public office without shelter against the organized efforts of those who would demand that they have a duty to act on that licitness: that they carry the alleged "merits" of race into appropriate legislation. We are also not without example of the inevitable necessity, the instant such regulation or allocation by race has been understood to be acceptable to the Supreme Court, for the Court ultimately to have to decide several other things as well. Among the more obvious issues, as additional groups, people, agencies, and parties are inevitably drawn in, are these: *which* races, *how much* to each race, *by what test* is each of us to be assigned "our" race? When these things were proper—as they were before *Brown* v. *Board of Education*—it was enough to be the government-designated member of a given "race" by being one-eighth of that "race." That, as the Supreme Court itself will recall, was the manner of imputing "race" to Mr. Plessy for the *Plessy* v. *Ferguson* experiments in racial designation and racial allocation. The odiousness of these issues will be no less should the Court now reopen this governmental license than it was some years ago.

* * * *

Nearly all who have urged the Supreme Court to readmit the legitimacy of race as an explicit basis of governmental regulation or allocation have done so with some reserve, some measure of diffidence, hedged about that, in any event, it should only be for a time. . . .

* * * *

Ironically, the basic suggestion to relicense racial discrimination by government is put forward not despite its intrinsic tendency to set race against race, but as a good, benign, and thoughtful way to get beyond racism. But "getting beyond" racism in this fashion, we have reason to believe, is as little likely to succeed as the now discredited idea that in order to "get beyond" organized government, it is first indispensable to organize a virtual dictatorship that, once it extirpates the evils that made organized government necessary, will itself just naturally wither away. We have not seen governments wither by the paradox of assigning them even greater power. We shall not now see racism disappear by employing its own ways of classifying people and of measuring their rights.

Rather, one gets beyond racism by getting beyond it now: by a complete, resolute, and credible commitment *never* to tolerate in one's own life—or in the life or practices of one's government—the differential treatment of other human beings by race. Indeed, that is the great lesson for government itself to teach: in all we do in life, whatever we do in life, to treat any person less well than another or to favor any more than another for being black or white or brown or red, is wrong. Let that be our fundamental law and we shall have a Constitution universally worth expounding. ■

5. I n this excerpt from an insightful 1983 essay, Yale Law School professor Drew S. Days, III, a former staff member at the National Association for the Advancement of Colored People (NAACP) Legal Defense and Educational Fund, who also served as assistant attorney general for civil rights in the Carter Administration (1977–1981), reviews the recent history of race in American law and argues that civil rights proponents must realize that unlike the 1950s and 1960s, litigation is not likely to be a productive pathway for further civil rights advances.

From: "Seeking a New Civil Rights Consensus" by Drew S. Days, III in *Daedalus*, 112 (Fall 1983). Used by permission of *Daedalus*, Cambridge, Massachusetts, Journal of the American Academy of Arts and Sciences.

The Supreme Court decision of 1954 outlawing segregation in public schools, *Brown* v. *Board of Education*, ushered in an era of unparalleled advancement in racial justice and the protection of civil rights in America. Since *Brown*, all official barriers to the participation of blacks on an equal basis with whites in education, as well as in employment, voting, housing, and public accommodations, have been removed. Moreover, blacks have not been the only beneficiaries of this movement. Other racial minorities, women, and the disabled have successfully relied upon principles established by *Brown* to strike down discriminatory practices impeding their progress. Yet despite the achievement in the years since *Brown*, the nation cannot yet legitimately claim to have eradicated the present effects of past discrimination based upon race, color, sex, or disability. As proof of this, we need only look at the degree to which blacks and other racial minorities continue to occupy the lowest rungs on our socioeconomic ladder, to which women find meaningful educational and professional opportunities closed to them, and to which the disabled are arbitrarily excluded from the mainstream of daily life.

Many of our major public and private institutions continue to recognize that the job of achieving racial justice and effective protection of civil rights in America has not been completed, and the direction of the movement is still forward. But the *momentum* of civil rights advancement has slowed significantly in recent years, and public debate over the pace and direction of further civil rights efforts has become increasingly divisive. . . .

* * * *

. . . [By] the late 1960s and 1970s. . . . [it] became obvious that it would not be enough merely to strike down segregationist laws and to forbid more subtle forms of discrimination. Enjoining Southern school boards from assigning children by race often did not result in any significant change in segregated attendance patterns. Furthermore, even after the courts directed that persons be employed on a nondiscriminatory basis, blacks did not rush to apply for jobs with employers who had been guilty of racially biased hiring practices. It was apparent that more than simple nondiscrimination measures would be required to overcome the inertia created by generations of segregation and the fears of blacks, often well founded, that taking advantage of these new opportunities would almost surely invite white reprisals. Thus, school boards were given the principal responsibility for desegregating their systems, and employers were required to recruit and hire blacks actively—and, subsequently, other racial minorities and women—as part of the remedy for past acts of discrimination. In some instances, courts or administrative agencies imposed specific goals and timetables for hiring members of groups that had been discriminated against in order to have more than the employer's assertions of "good faith" by which to judge compliance. Moreover, the courts proclaimed that the victims of discrimination were entitled to awards of back pay for wages lost as a result of their mistreatment, and to placement in the seniority ranks according to the position they would have held had they been treated fairly. In voting, electoral systems were ordered restructured to ensure fair participation by blacks and Hispanics.

For some, these developments with respect to remediation violated assumptions underlying the original civil rights consensus in several ways. For one, race and sex criteria had to be employed to ensure their effectiveness: unless school boards, for example, took race into consideration, they could not be expected to avoid perpetuating one-race schools in the desegregation process. For another, these remedies sometimes upset settled expectations of males and whites. Taking the school desegregation example a bit further, not only were black children ensured of a right to attend formerly all-white schools, but white children were required to attend formerly all-black schools as part of the process. Members of racial minorities and women found to have been denied their "rightful place" in the ranks were given seniority superior to that of incumbent whites and males, rendering the latter employees more vulnerable to layoffs in the event of economic retrenchment. Finally, this type of remediation necessitated in some cases the expenditure of significant sums of money. Equality was no longer available "on the cheap."

* * * *

. . . [Since the 1960s] we have looked primarily to litigation to correct the effects of generations of exclusionary practices. This reliance has created its own problems for the civil rights movement.

Congress enacted the modern civil rights laws because it concluded that blacks, principally, and other minorities and women to a lesser degree, had been victims of "societal discrimination," that is, actions by various combinations of American institutions, both public and private. Rather than legislating directly to create both opportunities for members of these groups and new federal agencies to see to the enforcement of such requirements, it decided instead to impose upon the victims of discrimination the principal responsibility for vindicating, through the courts, their newly established rights. There were other alternatives. The Congress could have, for example, required America's institutions to provide immediate access to blacks, other minorities, and women. . . . Federal agencies could have been given the responsibility for determining which institutions were "out-of-compliance" with such requirements and for obtaining their obedience under penalty of certain sanctions.

Moreover, the Congress could have allocated major resources to assist those institutions found not to be guilty of overt, blatant discrimination against racial minorities or women—or those seeking to reform voluntarily—to "integrate" more than token numbers from those groups into their operations or afford them greater opportunities to enjoy services to which they were previously denied access. Special programs limited solely to racial minorities or women could have been established to provide them with education and training that was deemed necessary to take advantage of opportunities only recently opened up on a nondiscriminatory basis. In these ways, Congress might have ensured that the burden of rectifying the effects of "societal discrimination" was spread relatively evenly across the society in general. Since the country, collectively speaking, was guilty of the violations, it could have followed that it was also responsible for providing a remedy—collectively. . . .

But Congress did not do this. Instead, private parties were expected to go to court seeking relief against individuals or institutions for what they claimed were acts of illegal discrimination. If they proved their case, the individual defendants would be ordered by the courts to provide adequate relief. Certain federal agencies were given litigating authority, of course. But their activities were limited explicitly by statute, in some instances, and by practical considerations otherwise, to addressing only "patterns or practices" of discrimination. Moreover, the authority for even administrative enforcement envisioned that private parties would shoulder much of the responsibility for triggering agency action through the complaint process. In practice, private litigation efforts, pursuant to the "implied private right of action" doctrine, long ago supplanted in importance agency enforcement of statutes that Congress anticipated would be handled principally through the administrative process. Such agencies have lacked the will, often for political reasons, or the resources to carry out their enforcement functions responsibly and effectively.

This arrangement served tolerably well for many years after the modern acts were passed, largely because the wrongs were obvious and long-standing and the remedies relatively straightforward: employers who categorically refused to hire blacks and women were ordered to open their doors. There appeared to be nothing particularly inappropriate about placing upon defendants found guilty of such blatant, vicious racial or sex discrimination the burden of remedying the effects of their patently illegal actions. They merely "got what they had coming to them." Ambiguities were not to be found here.

The real problems have arisen only in recent years. On the plaintiffs' side, the layers of requirements that the federal courts have imposed upon them to prove violations of civil rights laws and the sheer complexity of antidiscrimination cases have combined to make it impossible for other than the most well-established organizations or private practitioners to bring major lawsuits. But of greater significance, this arrangement has become less and less defensible to some in cases where defendants have been found to have engaged in only "technical" violations of civil rights laws rather than in outright and purposeful discrimination.

Where, for example, an employer is held liable for a violation of employment discrimination because it used an aptitude test that disproportionately screened out blacks and was found not to be supported by "business necessity" (proven to test effectively qualifications for the job in question), such a defendant has argued that the discriminatory effect is not caused by its wrongdoing but rather by the cumulative impact of denials of equal opportunity to blacks—in education, for example—by other societal institutions. Moreover, even in those instances where some intentional discrimination can be established, legitimate questions can be raised over whether a school board that engaged in certain segregative conduct twenty years ago should be expected to remedy singlehandedly present-day segregative patterns, since common sense alone tells us that the current problem is not entirely of the present school board's making. Private choice, private discrimination, and segregative actions by a complex combination of public agencies, such as housing and transportation authorities, have had a significant impact in ways beyond the ability of a school board to control or remedy. In both instances, there is the understandable reaction of some that the "little guy" is bearing unfairly the responsibility for remedying transgressions for which he was only partially responsible, if at all.

All of this is not meant to suggest that corrective measures should not be taken to end practices that exclude blacks or other groups from job opportunities or that we should wink at the abysmal degree of present racial segregation in our public schools. This is no brief for barring the disabled from entering the "mainstream." Rather, it is designed to raise candidly the question of whether we can continue to look to the litigation model as the principal method for achieving civil rights progress, given its significant shortcomings and waning public acceptance.

Ironically, our reliance on the litigation model has affected negatively efforts by public and private institutions to address lingering problems of discrimination voluntarily. In none of the three major affirmative action (or "reverse discrimination") cases decided by the Supreme Court since 1977 has "remedying the effects of societal discrimination" been accepted by a clear majority as a legitimate justification for the racially explicit selection programs at issue. Consequently, the decisions have been interpreted by some commentators and lower courts to require that such programs be designed to remedy the effects of discrimination particular to the institution in which they originate, and that the institutions themselves be legally "competent" to determine the need for such corrective measures in the first place. In any event, the ambiguity and opaqueness of these decisions have probably done little to reduce the extent to which voluntary affirmative action programs are challenged in court. Indeed, they seem to have provided additional fuel to the already heated public debate over the propriety of such practices.

* * * *

. . . The origins and current manifestations of discrimination are far too complex for lawsuits to sort out to anyone's satisfaction. Litigation, a mechanism designed principally to resolve disputes between individuals, can no longer be relied upon to resolve the problems of *class* inequality caused by institutions, except in the most obvious cases of exclusion. To do so gives merely the impression of fairness and progress, leaving to succeeding generations of Americans the task of devising realistic solutions.

In sum, what has to be accepted is that solving the current problems of discrimination will be possible only through a sustained effort, properly funded by both public and private institutions, that focuses explicitly on the inferior status of blacks, other racial minorities, women, and the disabled. It will take time, and it will not occur without substantial impact upon the settled ways in which whites, males, and the "able-bodied" have been accustomed to functioning in this society.

However all of this sorts out, of one thing we can be certain. Problems of discrimination are not going to disappear on their own. Our experience since *Brown* has taught us that treating such problems "with all deliberate speed" merely postpones the inevitable and exacts a higher price in human and financial terms than would have been the case at an earlier time. So the new consensus on civil rights comes down to a simple proposition: we have to agree once and for all to pay now rather than later. ■

QUESTIONS FOR REVIEW

1. In what ways do the politics of a once hard-core southern town like Selma, Alabama seem to have changed since the passage of the Voting Rights Act of 1965?

2. What aspects of southern life and racial discrimination seem to have gone partially, if not largely, unaffected by federal antidiscrimination statutes such as the Voting Rights Act and the 1964 Civil Rights Act?

3. How do the concepts of right, violation, and remedy play the most central roles in the Supreme Court's analysis in *Swann* v. *Charlotte-Mecklenburg* of the constitutional necessity of achieving meaningful integration in once-segregated southern public schools?

4. How does the Supreme Court's analysis of the constitutionality of affirmative action in *Bakke* seem to follow from the right-violation-remedy framework that the Supreme Court employed in *Swann*?

5. What is the prescription for a constitutionally-correct approach to considering race in college or graduate school admissions decisions that Justice Powell offers in *Bakke*?

6. How persuasive do you find the "race blind" argument offered in Professor Van Alstyne's article? How would you defend it? How would you argue against it?

7. To what extent do you believe that Professor Day's conclusion that court cases and constitutional rulings are likely to play a smaller role in ongoing civil rights activism than was true in the 1950s and 1960s will probably prove correct? Why?

Additional Recommended Readings

Bullock, Charles S., III and Charles M. Lamb, eds. *Implementation of Civil Rights Policy*. Monterey: Brooks/Cole Publishing Co., 1984. A solid academic survey of civil rights changes in the fields of voting rights, education, employment, and open housing.

Burstein, Paul. *Discrimination, Jobs, and Politics: The Struggle for Equal Employment Opportunity in the United States Since the New Deal*. Chicago: University of Chicago Press, 1985. An insightful academic study of the long fight against racial discrimination in American employment.

Dreyfuss, Joel and Charles Lawrence, III. *The Bakke Case: The Politics of Inequality*. New York: Harcourt Brace Jovanovich, 1979. The best available journalistic survey of America's 1970s debates about questions of affirmative action.

Lawson, Steven F. *In Pursuit of Power: Southern Blacks and Electoral Politics, 1965–1982*. New York: Columbia University Press, 1985. A comprehensive academic survey of voting rights developments in the south since the passage of the Voting Rights Act.

Wilkinson, J. Harvie, III. *From Brown to Bakke: The Supreme Court and School Integration, 1954–1978*. New York: Oxford University Press, 1979. A recounting of the Supreme Court's handling of school desegregation by a conservative young jurist currently serving on the federal Fourth Circuit Court of Appeals.

Chapter 12

Black America – A Better Life? (1970–1986)

by Clayborne Carson

RELATED MEDIA:
EYES ON THE PRIZE
Audio Programs 4A and 4B
"Black America—A Better
Life?"

. . . Concentrates on the economic and social issues relevant to the freedom struggle during the late 1960s and 1970s

. . . Identifies economic changes experienced by black Americans between the 1950s and the 1980s

. . . Describes major federal economic and social welfare policies of this period and analyzes their effect on black Americans

. . . Identifies and analyzes the concerns that underlie the current public policy debate on the status of the black family in America

. . . Explores the question: Has black America divided into a middle- and upper-class that is economically successful and an underclass, and if so, how does this affect American society?

OVERVIEW

Are present-day black Americans better off because of the black struggles of the 1950s and 1960s? Few blacks would voluntarily return to an era when they were subjected to various forms of degrading and often legally sanctioned racial segregation; nevertheless, as the readings in this chapter indicate, not all blacks have benefited in tangible ways from the civil rights reforms of the 1960s. Although many significant social changes have taken place since the 1960s, many blacks remain poor and powerless despite the passage of anti-discrimination and voting rights legislation. Recognition of this fact has led some commentators to criticize federal racial policies and programs and to urge blacks to abandon the insurgent strategies of the past. Thus, current debate over the status of black Americans is closely linked to discussions about the future course of Afro-American politics.

Echoing the decline in white support for black civil rights efforts, conservatives and neo-liberals of the 1970s and 1980s have attacked the idea that government should or could rectify the remaining inequalities that separate blacks from whites. Although some of these criticisms have been directed against expanded concepts of the role of government, their main target has been affirmative action programs and other race-specific remedies that are said to benefit blacks at the expense of other groups. As sociologist Nathan Glazer complained, "Intending in 1964 to create a color-blind America, we discovered to our surprise in the 1970s that we were creating an increasingly color-conscious society" (Ethnic Dilemmas 1964–1982, Harvard University Press). In addition to attacking federal programs to help blacks on ideological grounds, some conservatives, notably Charles Murray, author of *Losing Ground* (New York: Basic Books, Inc. 1984), have argued that these programs were counterproductive and even immoral.

Such justifications of government inaction have received little support from blacks, but the fact that civil rights reforms did not eliminate black poverty have led some commentators to suggest that the strategies of mass protest and insurgency that promoted the reforms are no longer appropriate. Even as early as 1965, Bayard Rustin argued that the shift in black goals from "removing barriers to full *opportunity*" to "achieving the fact of *equality*" required forsaking mass militancy in favor of electoral coalitions. Martin Kilson, Adolph L. Reed, and other social scientists have argued that electoral politics provide more effective mechanisms for expressing black aspirations than do mass demonstrations. For different reasons, many black nationalists of the late 1960s also abandoned mass militancy while pursuing strategies that stressed cadre formation and cultural transformation rather than community mobilization. By 1972, when the nationalist upsurge culminated in the National Black Assembly at Gary, Indiana, black elected officials had clearly displaced insurgent leaders in shaping black political objectives at the national level.

It is clear that civil rights reforms did not address all black problems; however, suggestions that blacks should break with the past and embark upon a new political course usually betray a narrow conception of the black struggles of the 1950s and 1960s. Although these struggles were often identified as a civil rights movement, these mass insurgencies were concerned with more than the achievement of civil rights reforms. The Montgomery bus boycott, for example, did not initially involve a demand to end segregation on buses but did call for the hiring of more black bus drivers. The 1963 March on Washington called for jobs as well as freedom. The movement in Lowndes County, Alabama, demanded *"black power* for black people" in addition to the vote. In most southern black communities where sustained mass struggles occurred, blacks sought political and economic objectives as well as civil rights reforms and saw the achievement of the civil rights of the 1960s as only the first stage in a continuing effort to improve their lives.

Thus, many current critiques of government racial policies and programs merely restate criticisms that were expressed more profoundly by participants in the struggles of the 1960s. The civil rights legislation and government programs that were prompted by the black struggle indicated the limits of what the American political system was willing to concede rather than the limits of black aspirations. Many black activists recognized that simply eliminating racial barriers would not aid blacks who could not compete on an equal basis with whites because of the damaging effects of past discrimination. Their support for affirmative action was not based on the belief that this was the best means of redistributing wealth but on the realization that it was the most feasible way of insuring more than token compliance with antidiscrimination legislation. By the end of the 1960s, the National Association for the Advancement of Colored People (NAACP) and other major civil rights organizations resisted efforts to undermine previous civil rights reforms while also seeking to deal with worsening black poverty and unemployment.

While movement activists recognized how much the values that guided federal racial policies diverged from the emergent values of the black struggle, few argued that government should abandon its social welfare functions. Instead, they insisted that government programs be made more effective and responsive to the desires of those they were intended to help. Rather than racial dependency, local black movements consistently sought to acquire self-sufficiency through the development of local leadership and black-controlled institutions. These efforts were often subverted by the insufficient government responses to black demands. Notions of participatory democracy that had guided black organizers in their efforts to encourage the emergence of indigenous leadership and to mobilize community institutions were quickly discarded by the federal "war on poverty." Social welfare programs functioned to

271

control as well as help the poor. The racial pride engendered through years of struggle dissipated as mass militancy declined and militant organizations of the 1960s became victims of outside repression and internal conflicts.

The legacy of the struggles of the 1960s may still provide important insights as black Americans chart their political future in the often hostile political climate of the 1980s. As revealed in previous chapters, these struggles were not simply characterized as a set of protest tactics but also as a generalized way of achieving social change through the mobilization of black communities. The local black movements of the 1960s were unique settings that allowed many thousands of black people to assume more appealing social roles and to develop latent talents. New leaders, drawn from every social class, and new institutions emerged from the southern struggle, and these are still important resources for contemporary black advancement efforts. The black struggle stirred feelings of racial pride that have remained evident in contemporary black literature, music, and other forms of cultural expression. The radical ideals and organizing techniques of the struggles of the 1960s invigorated black political life and provided inspiration for numerous movements involving nonblacks. A crucial question for the future is whether black Americans will utilize this valuable legacy as they confront today's difficult problems.

READINGS

1. **D**id the civil rights reforms of the 1960s actually result in tangible improvements in the living standards of blacks? This question was at the center of many discussions of the 1970s and 1980s regarding national racial policies. The question is difficult to answer definitively, because blacks with different levels of education and living in different regions of the nation were affected in dissimilar ways by civil rights legislation; moreover, legislation to eliminate explicit racial barriers to equality of opportunity, even if firmly enforced by government, did not guarantee changes in entrenched wealth distribution patterns that would produce equality of results. Americans debated the issue of whether government should or *could* reverse the growing gulf between the wealth of blacks and whites or, more generally,

between rich and poor. Although this debate was fundamentally rooted in different notions of the role of the American state, it was also based on conflicting interpretations of statistics regarding the relative status of black Americans.

The median net worth of black Americans was less than one-tenth that of white Americans, according to the United States Census Bureau. The Bureau reported that the median net worth of white householders was $39,140, while the net worth of blacks was $3,400. The corresponding figures for married couples was $54,180 for whites and $13,060 for blacks. Nearly one-third of all black households in the survey reported no net assets or were in debt, compared to fewer than one in ten whites who had no assets at all.

The following selections summarize data gathered by various federal agencies on the changing condition on black Americans.

From: America's Black Population: 1970 to 1982—A Statistical View by William C. Matney and Dwight L. Johnson (Washington: U.S. Government Printing Office, 1983), pages 1–18.

INTRODUCTION

Statistics from the latest Bureau Current Population Surveys (CPS) and the 1980 census show improvement in income levels of Black married-couple families, educational attainment and school enrollment, and home ownership among Blacks during the 1970's. But the data also reveal setbacks influenced by high Black unemployment, sharply increased divorce and separation rates, and a rise in family households maintained by Black females.

A recessionary economy coupled with inflation eroded both Black and White family income during the 1970 decade and together, they were major factors contributing to an increase in poverty among Blacks, especially women.

The disproportionate impact on Blacks of the economic downturn beginning in 1974 and of the relatively sluggish economy continuing through 1982, effectively brought to a halt the momentum of overall social and economic improvement apparent at the beginning of the decade.

POPULATION GROWTH AND DISTRIBUTION

Between 1970 and 1980, the Black population increased by 17.3 percent, from 22.6 million to 26.5 million. In 1980, Blacks represented approximately 12 percent of the total population.

In 1980, Blacks constituted more than 20 percent of the population in seven States—Mississippi (35 percent), South Carolina (30 percent), Louisiana (29 percent), Georgia (27 percent), Alabama (26 percent), Maryland (23 percent), and North Carolina (22 percent). . . .

New York had the largest Black population of any city (1,784,337) in 1980, followed by Chicago (1,197,000), Detroit (758,939), Philadelphia (638,878), and Los Angeles (505,210).

Of the 100 cities with the largest Black population, the city with the highest percentage was East St. Louis, Ill. (96 percent). In Washington, D.C., about 70 percent of the population was Black in 1980, about the same as in 1970, although the total population in the city actually dropped during the decade.

The traditional large Black migration from the South to points North and West appeared to end in the 1970 decade. Between 1975 and 1980, about 415,000 Blacks moved to the South, whereas, only about 220,000 left, thereby reversing the longstanding Black exodus from the South. In 1980, the proportion of the total Black population residing in the South was 53 percent, the same as in 1970.

* * * *

SOME INCOME GAIN
While income for all Black families continued to lag behind that of the general population, Black married-couple families registered a 6.9 percent gain in real median income between 1971 and 1981, improving from $18,370 to $19,620 in constant dollars. The comparable figures for White married-couple families were $25,130 in 1971 and $25,470 in 1981.

While the income levels for Black married-couple families [were] climbing during the decade of the 1970's, this group experienced a decline in the proportion they constituted of all Black families, dropping from 64 percent in 1972 to 55 percent in 1982.

In real terms, the 1981 median income for all Black families ($13,270) dropped 8.3 percent from 1971 and dropped 5.2 percent between 1980 and 1981. Median income for White families in 1981 was $23,520, down only 2.7 percent from 1980 when adjusted for inflation.

In 1971, the median income for Black families was 60 percent of the median income of White families—$14,460 versus $23,970. By 1981, this ratio was 56 percent.

According to survey data, the decline in Black family median income reflects, in part, the increase in the proportion of families maintained by females with no husband present and the lack of income gains for these families. Among Blacks, such families totaled 2.6 million in 1982 or about 41 percent of all Black families, up from the 32 percent in 1972. The median income for families maintained by Black female householders with no husband present was $7,510 in 1981, about 38 percent of the median of Black married-couple families ($19,620).

POVERTY RATE INCREASES
Persistent inflation, a stagnant economy, and family dissolution were reflected in the rising number of persons classified as poor between 1979 and 1981. During this period, the total number of persons in poverty increased by 5.4 million.

In 1970, about 8 million Blacks (34 percent) and 17 million Whites (10 percent) had incomes below the poverty level. By 1981, the number increased to 9 million for Blacks (34 percent) and 22 million for Whites (11 percent). (The poverty level for 1981 was $9,287 for a family of four.)

During the 1970s an increasing concentration of the poor in families maintained by females was especially evident among Blacks. The number of poor Black families with a female householder rose from 834,000 in 1970 to 1.4

million in 1981. These families accounted for 70 percent of all poor black families in 1981, substantially up from 56 percent in 1970.

LABOR FORCE
About 11 million Black persons were in the civilian labor force in 1982, an increase of 2.7 million over 1972—a 31 percent increase. Also between 1972 and 1982, the number of employed Black persons grew by 1.4 million (19 percent), whereas, the number of unemployed Black persons increased by 1.3 million (140 percent) (900,000 in 1972 to 2.1 million in 1982).

In 1982, the labor force participation rate for Black men and women 16 years and over was 70 and 54 percent, respectively. Black men in the labor force slightly outnumbered Black women (5.8 million to 5.5 million).

The unemployment rate for Blacks in 1972 was twice that for Whites (10.3 percent versus 5.0 percent). By 1982, when the unemployment rate for both Blacks and Whites was the highest since anytime in post-World War II history, the Black unemployment rate was still double that of Whites—18.9 percent compared to 8.6 percent.

Among Black teenagers, the unemployment rate reached 48 percent in 1982, 28 percentage points higher than that of White teenagers (20.4 percent). The rate was higher for Black male teens (48.9 percent) than for females (47.1 percent).

* * * *

FEMALE FAMILY HOUSEHOLDERS
Families maintained by Black women increased during the decade. In 1970, about 28 percent of the 4.9 million Black families were maintained by women. By 1982, however, almost 41 percent of the 6.4 million Black families were maintained by a woman. The comparable percentages for Whites during this period increased from only 9 percent to 12 percent. In 1982, the majority of Black families were still maintained by married-couples. However, since 1970, the percentage of all Black families maintained by married couples has declined from 68 to 55 percent.

Among Black women in 1982 who maintained families, 32 percent had never married, compared to 11 percent for White families maintained by a woman.

LIVING ARRANGEMENTS OF CHILDREN
As a consequence of the above changes, the number of Black children living with both parents dropped sharply between 1970 and 1982 while the percentage of Black children living in one-parent situations increased from 32 to 49 percent. About 8 percent of the children lived with neither parent in 1982, but in most cases resided with another relative. White children living with one parent also increased, doubling from 9 percent in 1970 to 17 percent in 1982. Still, 81 percent of White children lived with both parents in 1982, compared with 42 percent of Black children.

Black children constituted just 15 percent of all children under 18 years of age in 1982, but represented 34 percent of all children living with only one parent.

LIFE EXPECTANCY AND MORTALITY

Blacks are now living longer, according to the most recent data from the National Center for Health Statistics. The life expectancy of Black males in 1981 averages 66 years and Black females 75 years, doubling their rates of the early 1900's. But Whites still are expected to live about 4 years longer than Blacks—males to 71 and females to 79.

Blacks and Whites generally fared better in health care during the 1970s. The death rate from heart disease dropped 10 percent for Blacks and 7 percent for Whites. In contrast to the overall pattern, the picture for cancer was worse for Blacks, whose death rate for this disease went up 16 percent, while the White rate decreased 13 percent.

The homicide rate for Blacks dropped slightly between 1974 and 1979, from 39.7 to 37.9 deaths per 100,000 persons, but remained significantly higher than Whites, which increased from 5.8 to 6.5 over the same period. Black males experienced the highest homicide death rate (64.6) followed by Black females (13.8), White males (10.1) and White females (3.0).

INCREASED DIVORCE RATIO

In 1982, the divorce ratio was highest for Blacks, particularly women. This ratio is defined as the number of persons who are currently divorced per 1,000 married persons living with their spouses. In 1982, the combined divorce ratio for Black men and women (220 per 1,000) was about double that for White men and women (107 per 1,000). At this same time, the divorce ratio for Black women was 265 per 1,000. This represents a dramatic rise from 1970, when the divorce ratio for Black women stood at only 104 per every 1,000 married couples. The divorce ratio among White women rose from 56 to 128 per 1,000 during this same period.

■

BLACK AMERICA IN NUMBERS – 1986

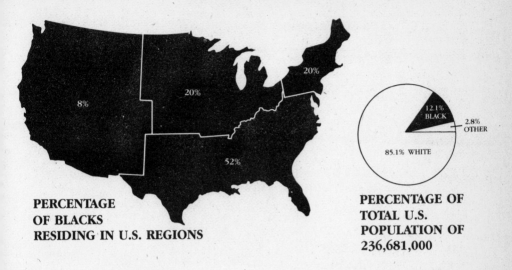

**PERCENTAGE
OF BLACKS
RESIDING IN U.S. REGIONS**

**PERCENTAGE OF
TOTAL U.S.
POPULATION OF
236,681,000**

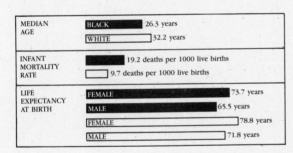

LIFE AND DEATH

MEDIAN AGE	BLACK	26.3 years
	WHITE	32.2 years
INFANT MORTALITY RATE		19.2 deaths per 1000 live births
		9.7 deaths per 1000 live births
LIFE EXPECTANCY AT BIRTH	FEMALE	73.7 years
	MALE	65.5 years
	FEMALE	78.8 years
	MALE	71.8 years

**MARITAL STATUS OF
PERSONS 15 YEARS
AND OVER**

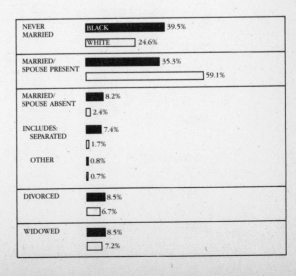

NEVER MARRIED	BLACK	39.5%
	WHITE	24.6%
MARRIED/ SPOUSE PRESENT		35.3%
		59.1%
MARRIED/ SPOUSE ABSENT		8.2%
		2.4%
INCLUDES: SEPARATED		7.4%
		1.7%
OTHER		0.8%
		0.7%
DIVORCED		8.5%
		6.7%
WIDOWED		8.5%
		7.2%

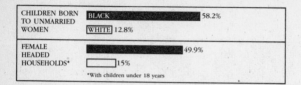

CHILDREN BORN TO UNMARRIED WOMEN

BLACK 58.2%
WHITE 12.8%

FEMALE HEADED HOUSEHOLDS* 49.9%
15%

*With children under 18 years

SINGLE MOTHERS

LIVING ARRANGEMENTS OF CHILDREN UNDER 18 YEARS

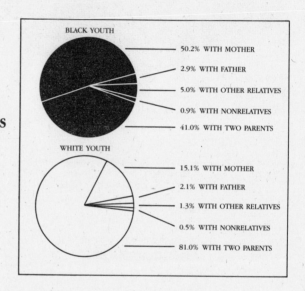

BLACK YOUTH
50.2% WITH MOTHER
2.9% WITH FATHER
5.0% WITH OTHER RELATIVES
0.9% WITH NONRELATIVES
41.0% WITH TWO PARENTS

WHITE YOUTH
15.1% WITH MOTHER
2.1% WITH FATHER
1.3% WITH OTHER RELATIVES
0.5% WITH NONRELATIVES
81.0% WITH TWO PARENTS

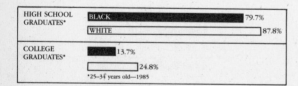

HIGH SCHOOL GRADUATES*
BLACK 79.7%
WHITE 87.8%

COLLEGE GRADUATES*
13.7%
24.8%

*25–34 years old—1985

EDUCATION

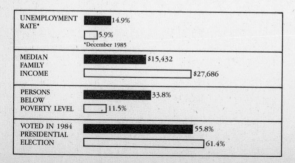

UNEMPLOYMENT RATE*
14.9%
5.9%
*December 1985

MEDIAN FAMILY INCOME
$15,432
$27,686

PERSONS BELOW POVERTY LEVEL
33.8%
11.5%

VOTED IN 1984 PRESIDENTIAL ELECTION
55.8%
61.4%

OTHER STATISTICS

2. **I**n the following selection, Reynolds Farley, a sociologist at the Population Studies Center of the University of Michigan, summarizes the consequences of the "civil rights revolution." Excerpted from a larger study of racial trends in the United States, Farley's generally optimistic view of black prospects contrasts sharply with the writings of other social scientists who link many black problems to the existence of a large, permanent black "underclass." Farley's "scorecard on black progress" is based not only on economic statistics but also on more subtle psychological factors that have affected black perceptions of racial gains and setbacks of the period since the 1960s.

From: *Blacks and Whites: Narrowing the Gap?* by Reynolds Farley (Cambridge: Harvard University Press, 1984), pages 193–206. Copyright 1984 by the President and Fellows of Harvard College. Used by permission.

What has the civil rights revolution accomplished? . . .

* * * *

Is it true that progress has been widespread and that discrimination is rapidly fading? Or has the observed racial progress been superficial, so that the status of blacks relative to whites has hardly changed? Or is the black population becoming economically polarized, so that some blacks are much better off than they were in the past while a larger group have gained little from the civil rights revolution of the 1960s?

Blacks in the United States are a diverse group, larger than the total population of Argentina, Australia, Canada, South Africa, or Yugoslavia. No simple generalization can adequately describe racial trends. Each of the views contains some truth, but each also fails to capture the complexity of the changes that have occurred.

There is good reason to be particularly critical of the view that black gains are superficial. In the important areas of education, occupations, and earnings, racial differences declined substantially. This is not tokenism. Throughout the entire economy and in all regions, racial differences on the most important indicators are smaller now than before. . . .

There is also good reason to doubt that the black community is becoming increasingly polarized into an elite and an underclass. Some aspects of this perspective are accurate: there has always been a prosperous segment of the black community and a large impoverished group. In recent decades the black elite has grown larger and more visible, and the black poor have moved to cities where they are also more visible. The welfare of the poor apparently has improved because of the expansion of government services. Nonetheless, the indicators of social and economic polarization are mixed. One type of economic polarization is certainly occurring, but it is quite different from the polarization by social class that is described most frequently. That is, the income gap separating husband-wife families from those families headed by women is growing.

The view that black gains are widespread and significant is the most accurate of the three, but its optimism needs to be tempered. As I have stressed again and again, many more decades of change similar to the 1960s and 1970s will be necessary if racial differences are to disappear.

* * * *

The trends I have described—the increased political power of blacks, the lasting impact of the civil rights movement, and changes in the attitudes of whites—will all cause racial differences to diminish in the future. The speed with which these differences decrease may depend upon the rate of economic growth and the future strength of the civil rights movement. The greatest threats to further black gains may be an economic depression and a federal administration that assigns a low priority to civil rights issues.

* * * *

It is probable that all future federal administrations will endorse the principles of civil rights, nondiscrimination, and equal opportunities. But the change in the actual status of blacks will depend upon whether an administration gives these issues high or low priority. This, in turn, may depend upon the strength and effectiveness of the civil rights movement.

* * * *

Throughout the nation's history there has been a tendency to underestimate the magnitude of racial differences, to overestimate the progress that has been made, and to oversimplify the solutions to remaining racial problems. Many people probably believe that during the 1960s and 1970s enough effort was devoted to the struggle for civil rights and the numerous laws and court rulings solved racial difficulties. The evidence I have presented makes it clear that much has been accomplished. People may focus upon these gains and assume that the time has indeed come for a strategy of benign neglect.

But in congratulating ourselves as a nation for the real and impressive progress we have made toward racial equality, we should not lose sight of the distance that remains to be traveled. Black men are still twice as likely as white men to be out of work. A high—and growing—proportion of black families have incomes below the poverty line. . . . And the public schools in New York, Chicago, Los Angeles, Philadelphia, and Washington were as racially segregated in 1980 as two decades earlier. Much remains to be done before we will be able to say unequivocally that the economic and social gap between the races has been closed. ■

3. **W**illiam Wilson's "The Declining Significance of Race" was one of the most important and controversial studies of black Americans to appear during the 1970s. A black sociologist at the University of Chicago, Wilson believed that the problems of poor blacks would not be addressed until black leaders recognized that racial discrimination was not the primary cause of black poverty. His book was primarily intended to challenge the views of middle-class blacks who, he contended, gained from programs designed to benefit all blacks rather than specific economic classes within the black populace. Wilson's discussion of his conclusions is followed by a selection written by black political theorist Manning Marable, who challenges the thesis that race is declining in significance.

From: "The Declining Significance of Race: Myth or Reality," by William Julius Wilson in *The Declining Significance of Race? A Dialogue among Black and White Social Scientists* edited by Joseph R. Washington, Jr. (University of Pennsylvania, Afro-American Studies Program, 1979), pages 4, 16–17. Used by permission of Joseph Washington, Jr. and the Afro-American Studies Program, University of Pennsylvania.

For poor blacks the problem is that even if all racial discrimination in labor-market practices were eliminated tomorrow, their economic conditions would not significantly improve because of structural barriers to decent jobs. Racial oppression in the past created the large black underclass as disadvantages were accumulated and passed on from generation to generation, and today the economic and technological revolution of an advanced capitalist society threatens to solidify that position. With the lack of job expansion in the manufacturing sector and the fact that the better paid jobs in the service industries require training and education, poor urban blacks face a situation in which the higher paying jobs that can be obtained without higher education and/or special skills are decreasing in central cities not only in relative terms but often in absolute numbers. Accordingly, poor blacks are increasingly confronting a situation in which the only jobs to which they have access are those that are dead-end, menial, frequently lacking in union protection, and that provide little or no opportunities for advancement.

In view of these developments, it would be difficult indeed to comprehend the plight of inner-city blacks by exclusively focusing on racial discrimination. For in a very real sense, the current problems of lower-class blacks are substantially related to fundamental structural changes in the economy. A history of discrimination and oppression created a huge black underclass, and the technological and economic revolutions have combined to insure it a permanent status. By the same token, it would be difficult to explain the rapid economic improvement of the more privileged blacks by arguing that the traditional forms of racial segregation and discrimination still characterize the labor market in American industries.

As the black middle class rides on the wave of political and social changes and benefits from the expansion of employment opportunities in the growing corporate and government sectors of the economy, the black underclass falls behind the larger society in every conceivable respect.

* * * *

. . . whereas the black poor would gain from a shift in emphasis from race to economic dislocation, more privileged blacks tend to emphasize, and if I may say, have, for the moment a vested interest in keeping race as the single most important issue in developing policies to promote black progress.

Thus, many black leaders and intellectuals have become either so accustomed or committed to the view that race is at the very center of all major problems plaguing blacks that they vigorously resist arguments dealing with color-blind structural barriers to meaningful employment. The black elites' definition of the current problems of black Americans are embodied in an ideology of culture and politics which obscures class differences among blacks—an ideology which therefore stresses a single or uniform black experience and which proposes solutions, such as affirmative action, that have, to repeat, effectively dealt with the concerns of privileged blacks but have not been designed to alleviate the problems of the black poor.

Unfortunately the groups that would have the most to gain by a shift in emphasis from race to economic dislocation, the black lower class, is not the group that is really defining the issues. Rather the issues are being defined by the articulate black intelligentsia—the very group that has benefited the most in recent years from antidiscrimination programs. Thus some of them vigorously resist a shift in emphasis, if only partially, and they continue to perpetuate the myth that blacks are a monolithic socio-economic group, that there are no class divisions to speak of in the black community, or no evidence of a growing gap between the haves and have-nots in the black community. This stance leads therefore to the sole concentration on policy programs that deal with racial bias thereby making it difficult for blacks to recognize how their fate is inextricably tied up with the structure of the modern American economy. ■

From: From the Grassroots: Social and Political Essays Toward Afro-American Liberation by Manning Marable (Boston: South End Press, 1980) pages 215–217. Used by permission.

When *The Declining Significance of Race* appeared . . . it presented nothing new—that is, its social analysis which minimized the role of racism within the composition of black economic and cultural life was not original. Others in the field of sociology had said as much in other ways, and will assuredly continue to do so. What was surprising to black academicians was, first, its lack of scholarly subtlety, the clear and unequivocal break from race that it proposed. Let us consider what would have occurred had Wilson selected the title, "The Increasing Significance of Class." The manuscript would have been published, but few people outside the field of sociology would have noticed. The fierce criticism from black researchers, social scientists, and activists would have been virtually nonexistent. Wilson set the entire tone for the debate by choosing "race" as the central focus for discussion. In doing so, he sold many more copies of the book. . . .

More important were the social implications of Wilson's study for public policies affecting blacks. White intellectuals were looking for a theoretical framework to justify their assault against affirmative action, and *The Declining Significance of Race* provided them with new academic ammunition. . . .

In its popular context, Wilson was understood as saying: 1) that racial prejudice and discrimination were no longer major problems within the capitalist economic system; 2) that affirmative action programs for blacks were no longer necessary, and were in fact destructive to the black group's own best interest; and 3) that economic development along liberal, welfare capitalist lines could alleviate any residual dilemmas with which blacks were afflicted. Race had "declined in significance" for public policy making. In the future, federal bureaucrats at the Department of Health, Education and Welfare could concentrate their corrective efforts toward "poorly trained and educationally limited blacks of the inner city," rather than toward blacks as a group. In effect, this approach minimizes the continuing burden of racism as the major feature in all black peoples' lives, regardless of their economic status, cultural achievement and educational mobility. . . .

. . . by any measure, *The Declining Significance of Race* prepares the way for a white reaction against black folks as a group and blackness in general. ■

4. T he modern women's liberation movement was greatly influenced by the southern black struggle, because the southern movement offered women greater opportunities than did the surrounding society. In 1964, two white staff members of SNCC, Casey Hayden and Mary King, wrote one of the first manifestos of the modern women's movement. They acknowledged that their consciousness of their own oppression as women had resulted from their exposure to the egalitarian ideals of the black struggle. Black women activists believed that racial concerns should take priority over feminist ones. The following selection reveals, however, that the prevailing conceptions of black militancy in the late 1960s were primarily shaped by black males, who assumed most of the major leadership roles while relegating women to supportive functions. By the end of the 1960s, black women became increasingly outspoken on issues of sexual equality. Some formed alliances with white feminists, while others created new feminist groups such as the Third World Women's Alliance.

During the first heady years of the Civil Rights Movement, Black men and women shared a unity of purpose and camaraderie—particularly in the student movement. As is historically true, in periods of racial assertion Black women's feminist reactions tend to be muted. Nevertheless, there was male chauvinism within the movement, and when the movement began to deteriorate after 1964, the intensity of that chauvinism increased. At the same time, with the movement in decline, Black women were less willing to tolerate such attitudes and became more openly critical of men, as they had done a century before. This was particularly true of women who had played prominent roles in organizations like SCLC and SNCC.

* * * *

By 1966, the movement had taken a decided turn—to the North. There, manhood was measured by wages, oppression had no face, and powerlessness no refuge. And in the North, the exhibitionism of manhood was not mitigated by the strength of Black institutions whose most vital resource was women. Both Black men and radical-chic White men—women, too—applauded the *machismo* of leather-jacketed young men, armed to the teeth, rising out of the urban ghetto. The theme of the late sixties was "Black Power" punctuated by a knotted fist. It sought a common ethos between northern and southern Blacks. Although it may not have been consciously conceived out of the need to affirm manhood, it became a metaphor for the male consciousness of the era. As Floyd McKissick, who replaced James Farmer as head of CORE, explained, "The year 1966 shall be remembered as the year we left our imposed status as Negroes and became Black men."

Two years later, the assassination of Martin Luther King, Jr., renewed the conviction that a violent struggle was inevitable, and Black men proclaimed their willingness to die for it. Black Panther Huey P. Newton wrote a book entitled *Revolutionary Suicide*; Stokely Carmichael announced that in the coming racial war Black people would "stand on our feet and die like men. If that's our only act of manhood," he said, echoing the lines of the Claude McKay poem written a half-century before: "then Goddamnit we're going to die." H. Rap Brown, who headed SNCC at one time and became associated with the phrase *burn, baby, burn,* believed that any lesser action was tantamount to impotence: "One loses a bit of manhood with every stale compromise," he warned.

* * * *

Black activist and writer Imamu Amiri Baraka infused into most of the activities he was associated with in the period the idea that "Nature had made women submissive, she must submit to man's creation order for it to exist.". . . Amina Baraka, an activist and wife of Amiri, reiterated the teachings of Ron Karenga which proclaimed: "What makes a woman appealing is femininity and she can't be feminine without being submissive." Another position paper disclosed: "We understand that it is and has been traditional that the man is the head of the house. He is the leader of the house/nation because his knowledge of the world is broader, his awareness is greater, his understanding is fuller and his application of this information is wiser."

It was but a short step from this sort of thinking to advocate that women remain politically barefoot and literally pregnant. Another Baraka orchestration, the Black Power Conference held in Newark in 1967, passed an anti-birth control resolution along with other serious-minded intentions. The idea had a surprisingly wide distribution. A May 1969 issue of *The Liberator* warned, "For us to speak in favor of birth control for Afro-Americans would be comparable to speaking in favor of genocide." A year earlier, an *Ebony* article had published the views of a physician who saw a revolutionary baby boom as a tactical advantage. He believed if Black women kept producing babies, Whites would have to either kill Blacks or grant them full citizenship.

There were protests, though usually belated, from Black women in the face of this anachronistic thinking. Linda La Rue remarked on the irony of "the rebirth of liberation struggles in the sixties with a whole platform of 'women's place' advocates who immediately relegated Black women to home and babies." It was a reflection of "Puritan-Americanism and/or the lack of simplest imagination," she concluded. Frances Beal called the demand to make Black women submissive "counterrevolutionary" and said, "Women who feel that the most important thing that they can contribute to the Black nation is children are doing themselves a great disservice." Beal also reminded the movement that the object of the "revolution was the freeing of all members of the society from oppression." The sexist emphasis of this period was also criticized by Sonia Pressman, writing in *The Crisis:* "When most people talk about civil rights, they mean the rights of Black people. And when they talk about the rights of Black people, they generally mean the rights of Black males."

Some Black intellectuals of the time were not content merely to relegate Black women to the political—or biological—back seat of the movement. Sociologists, psychiatrists, and the male literati accused Black women of castrating not only their men but their sons; of having low self-esteem; of faring badly when compared to the virtues of White women. Black women were unfeminine, they said; how could they expect the unflagging loyalty and protection of Black men?

■

QUESTIONS FOR REVIEW

1. How have blacks fared economically in comparison to the general population?

2. What problems confront inner-city blacks as they seek jobs and prosperity? How can these problems be solved?

3. In what ways does black family life often differ from the norm of white families? How do these differences contribute to or hinder black economic progress?

4. How does Reynolds Farley assess the economic and social status of black Americans?

5. Why does William Wilson reject the notion that the problems of the chronically poor, often called the "underclass," can be solved by focusing only on racial discrimination? What does he say about the role of middle-class blacks?

6. How does Wilson feel that class stratification in the black community has affected race relations, affirmative action, and the civil rights agenda?

7. How does Manning Marable respond to Wilson's thesis that class is more important today than racial distinctions? How does he indicate that this has been exploited by white Americans?

8. To what extent is racism still a major factor in the lives of American minority groups?

9. What unique problems for black women does Paula Giddings identify, both involving black men and in American society as a whole? What kind of impact, in her view, did the civil rights movement have for black women?

10. What results might you anticipate if the federal commitment to social services continues to decline while poverty and unemployment patterns show continued growth?

11. What factors are causing many blacks to reassess family roles and male-female relationships?

12. How have social scientists and historians analyzed the black family over the years? To what extent do problems faced by black families have their roots in society as a whole?

13. How will education improve the condition of the black community? How is this issue being addressed at the elementary, high school, and college levels?

14. How does the concept of black capitalism differ from the concept of black empowerment? Is black capitalism an effective means of improving the living standards of the black community as a whole?

ADDITIONAL RECOMMENDED READINGS

Blackwell, James E. *The Black Community: Diversity and Unity.* New York: Harper & Row Publishers, 1985. An overview of contemporary sociological issues relevant to the black community that contains recent data and recommends alternative solutions.

Cross, Theodore. *The Black Power Imperative: Racial Inequality and the Politics of Nonviolence.* New York: Faulkner Books, 1986. An important new work that looks extensively at the current economic and political status of black Americans, while examining the causes of black inequality. Cross also suggests strategies that could create greater opportunities for black empowerment.

Davis, George, and Glegg Watson. *Black Life in Corporate America: Swimming in the Mainstream.* New York: Doubleday and Co., 1982. A recent study that examines strategies that lead to success in the corporate world for blacks.

Glasgow, Douglas. *The Black Underclass.* New York: Vintage Books, 1981. Analyzes and recommends solutions for this neglected segment of the American population.

Marable, Manning. *How Capitalism Underdeveloped Black America.* Boston: South End Press, 1982. An analysis of the plight of black Americans in a capitalist economy, written from a socialist perspective.

Murray, Charles. *Losing Ground: American Social Policy, 1950–1980.* New York: Basic Books, 1984. A conservative analysis of the war on poverty which attacks the Great Society concept. Murray argues that relief programs actually worsen the plight of minorities and the poor.

Staples, Robert. *The Black Family: Essays and Studies.* Belmont, California: Wadsworth Publishing Company, 1978. A compilation of works by noted scholars on such topics as male-female relationships, child raising, family roles, and the heritage of the black family.

CHAPTER 13

WHERE DO WE GO FROM HERE? (1984–1986)

BY CLAYBORNE CARSON

RELATED MEDIA:
EYES ON THE PRIZE
Audio Programs 5A and 5B
"Where Do We Go From
Here?"

. . . Examines the impact of the growing black electorate during the period after the National Black Political Convention in 1972

. . . Identifies various alternative ideologies, including nationalism, socialism, and conservatism in recent black American politics

. . . Presents the views of black neoconservatives and discusses their significance

. . . Describes the impact of the increasing number of black elected officials after 1965

. . . Discusses the significance of Rev. Jesse Jackson's 1984 presidential campaign

. . . Explores the future political roles of black Americans

OVERVIEW

The television series title "Eyes on the Prize" pays homage to the integral role which music of the black church played in the civil rights movement. The song "Keep Your Eyes on the Prize" is based on a traditional gospel song and was often used to sustain movement participants.

The only chain that a man can stand,
Is the chain of hand in hand,
Keep your eyes on the prize,
Hold on, hold on.

We're gonna board that old Greyhound,
Carrying love from town to town,
Keep your eyes on the prize,
Hold on, hold on.

The only thing we did wrong,
Stayed in the wilderness a day too long,
Keep your eyes on the prize,
Hold on, hold on.

But the one thing we did right,
Was the day we started to fight,
Keep your eyes on the prize,
Hold on, hold on.

Even as black protesters sang this "freedom song" in the mid-1960s, they had increasingly varied conceptions of the illusive prize at the end of their struggle.

During subsequent years, those who had participated in the southern movement—and many who had not—engaged in intense discussions regarding alternative roads to future black advancement. The fact that mass activism among blacks declined during the period did not lessen the urgency of the intellectual debate. The decline confirmed the need for a reassessment of tactics, strategies, and goals.

As the following documents indicate, the debate has remained vigorous during the 1980s. Contemporary commentators not only disagree regarding the goals of black politics but even question whether racial politics are appropriate at all in what some call a "post-civil rights" era. Many, observing the continuing impact of antiblack sentiment in American politics and the escalating moral conflict in South Africa, reaffirm the statement of W. E. B. DuBois: "The problem of the twentieth century is the problem of the color-line." Others who insist that there is still a need for black political unity, disagree about whether blacks should attempt to revive mass activism or rely on conventional political activity. Debate over political goals is often rooted in basic differences regarding the causes of the current economic problems of black Americans. Are they the result of racial discrimination on the part of employers or do they result from other factors, such as inadequate occupational skills?

Although black businesses have always been in black communities, over the last twenty years, these establishments have lost their traditional customer base as it became more acceptable for blacks to shop in white establishments and as white-owned corporations have introduced products directed to black consumers. A recent *Washington Post* article asked, "Why have other minority groups recently found their way to the great middle class while blacks still find themselves at or near the bottom rung of the economic ladder?" (September 7, 1986) The article suggests that while other minorities have found their "path to success" in small, independent businesses, black mobility has been defined "in terms of education at universities and professional schools, employment in large corporations or government bureaucracies, or celebrity in sports and entertainment."

Among the questions being asked today are: Can or should the government seek to redress historical patterns of discrimination against Afro-Americans by giving special assistance to present-day blacks? Should blacks attempt to build political alliances with other groups? If so, which groups?

Certainly, the political power of blacks has increased markedly in the last twenty years. During the period from 1970 to 1986, the number of black Congresspeople doubled to 20, and almost 300 cities, including Detroit, Newark, Los Angeles, Chicago, Philadelphia, and New Orleans, elected black mayors; however, what is not as clear, is the impact on the lives of black people that black political power is having.

Black Americans will continue to disagree about such issues, for there is no such thing as a single black position. Among the by-products of the gains of the 1960s has been an increasing degree of diversity among blacks. Although differences in economic status are often reflected in differences over political issues, diversity has some positive benefits for black political life. If black Americans are no longer as united by common experiences as they once appeared to be, they now have far more political resources that can be mobilized to achieve their chosen objectives. It is hardly surprising that black people are no longer as likely to be engaged in mass activism as they were in the 1960s. What is remarkable is the degree to which they have remained more united about major political issues than any other large group. Black voters of all classes, for example, have consistently expressed their support for social welfare programs designed to help poor people of all races. As a group, black Americans remain a crucial source of support for social reform in the United States.

There is considerable evidence, therefore, that Afro-Americans as a group have not abandoned the ideals of the 1960s, but blacks are striving to find new ways of achieving their goals. Widespread black support for the movement to end American economic and political support for the white regime in South Africa is merely one indication of the continued volatility of black political life. Protest against South African apartheid also suggests that the future Afro-American struggle may be increasingly linked to international concerns and the black diaspora throughout the globe. Although many black leaders, most notably Martin Luther King, Jr. and Malcolm X, spoke out on international issues, contemporary black leaders, and the black populous as a whole, are likely to have greater concern for and knowledge of the outside world than was typical during the 1960s. Thus, for example, Jesse Jackson's long-standing contacts with Arab nations allowed him to play an important role in the January 3, 1984 release of a black American pilot who was detained after being shot down over Lebanon. Contemporary black leaders recognize the multinational scope of modern business and finance. This has led to increased emphasis on the connections between black concern over poverty and unemployment in the United States and the decisions of American corporations to relocate their manufacturing operations and capital abroad.

Although some aspects of past struggles are not likely to be replicated in the future, the many legacies of those struggles remain valuable resources for future black movements. It would be a mistake to assume that these legacies consist only of militant tactics, such as mass protest, for the essential quality of previous black struggles was that they demonstrated the ability of blacks to mobilize community resources to achieve common goals. The less visible economic boycotts and subtle political pressures were important supplements to the highly publicized sit-ins and marches. It would also be a mistake to assume that black Americans no longer possess the legacy of great leadership that was present in the 1950s and 1960s. Prominent leaders, such as Martin Luther King, Jr., did not initiate the black movements of that period; instead they exhibited their unique qualities in response to the demands of leading an historic movement. It would be fortunate indeed to have another great leader like King to guide future struggles, but it is not wise to depend on the appearance of such a leader. Perhaps the most valuable of all the legacies of previous black struggles is the knowledge that leadership qualities exist in great abundance among people at every level of the social order. The unexpected convergence of such leaders as Fannie Lou Hamer, Malcolm X, and thousands of other less-known grass-roots leaders should caution those who ask, where are our leaders?

As in the past those who search for leadership in their effort to improve the world should begin by looking in a mirror.

READINGS

1. Jesse Jackson's campaign for the presidency in 1984 was an important event in black political history. It not only mobilized black communities but also attracted a considerable amount of white support. Jackson's experiences in the southern struggle and in northern ghetto organizing, combined with his skills as an orator, gave him unique assets for his campaign. Although resented by many black leaders at the national level, Jackson was able to attract the support of many black voters. His efforts to bring nonblacks into his "rainbow coalition," which exceeded the predictions of most political experts, might have been even more successful, if he had not alienated Jewish voters by making a remark that was considered disparaging to Jews. Jackson's address to the Democratic National Convention provided an opportunity to try to heal these wounds as well as to summarize the themes of his campaign and set forth his vision of the future.

From: "Address by The Reverend Jesse Jackson" in *Proceedings of the Democratic National Convention,* July 17, 1984, pages 294–301. Copyright 1984 by The Reverend Jesse Jackson. Used by permission.

Our flag is red, white and blue, but our Nation is a rainbow—Red, Yellow, Brown, Black and White—we're all precious in God's sight.

America is not like a blanket—one piece of unbroken cloth, the same color, the same texture, the same size. America is more like a quilt—many patches, many pieces, many colors, many sizes, all woven and held together by a common thread. The White, the Hispanic, the Black, the Arab, the Jew, the woman, the Native American, the small farmer, the businessperson, the environmentalist, the peace activist, the young, the old, the lesbian, the gay and the disabled make up the American quilt.

Even in our fractured state, all of us count and fit somewhere. We have proven that we can survive without each other. But we have not proven that we can win and make progress without each other. We must come together.

From Fannie Lou Hamer in Atlantic City in 1964 to the Rainbow Coalition in San Francisco today; from the Atlantic to the Pacific, we have experienced pain but progress as we ended America's apartheid laws, we got public accommodations, we secured voting rights, we obtained open housing, as young people got the right to vote. We lost Malcolm, Martin, Medgar, Bobby and John and Viola. The team that got us here must be expanded, not abandoned.

Twenty years ago, tears welled up in our eyes as the bodies of Schwerner, Goodman, and Chaney were dredged from the depths of a river in Mississippi. Twenty years later, our communities, Black and Jewish, are in anguish, anger and in pain. Feelings have been hurt on both sides.

There is a crisis in communications. Confusion is in the air, but we cannot afford to lose our way. We may agree to agree or agree to disagree on issues; we must bring back civility to the tensions.

We are co-partners in a long and rich religious history—the Judeo-Christian traditions. Many Blacks and Jews have a shared passion for social justice at home and peace abroad. We must seek a revival of the spirit inspired by a new vision and new possibilities. We must return to higher ground.

We are bound by Moses and Jesus, but also connected with Islam and Mohammed. These three great religions—Judaism, Christianity, and Islam—were all born in the revered and Holy City of Jerusalem.

We are bound by Dr. Martin Luther King, Jr., and Rabbi Abraham Heschel, crying out from their graves for us to reach common ground. We are bound by shared blood and shared sacrifices. We are much too intelligent; much too bound by our Judeo-Christian heritage; much too victimized by racism, sexism, militarism, and anti-Semitism; much too threatened as historical scapegoats to go on divided one from another. We must turn from finger-pointing to clasped hands. We must share our burdens and our joys with each other once again. We must turn to each other and not on each other, and choose higher ground.

Twenty years later, we cannot be satisfied by just restoring the old coalition. Old wine skins must make room for new wine. We must heal and expand. The Rainbow Coalition is making room for Arab Americans. They, too, know the pain and hurt of racial and religious rejection. They must not continue to be made pariahs. The Rainbow Coalition is making room for Hispanic Americans who this very night are living under the threat of the Simpson-Mazzoli bill. And [for] farm workers from Ohio who are fighting the Campbell Soup Company with a boycott to achieve legitimate workers' rights.

The Rainbow is making room for the Native American, the most exploited people of all, a people with the greatest moral claim amongst us. We support them as they seek the restoration of land and water rights, as they seek to preserve their ancestral homelands and the beauty of a land that was once all theirs. They can never receive a fair share for all they have given us. They must finally have a fair chance to develop their great resources and to preserve their people and their culture.

The Rainbow Coalition includes Asian Americans, now being killed in our streets, scapegoats for the failures of corporate, industrial and economic policies.

The Rainbow is making room for young Americans. . . .

The Rainbow includes disabled veterans. The color scheme fits in the Rainbow. The disabled have their handicap revealed and their genius concealed; while the able-bodied have their genius revealed and their disability concealed. But ultimately, we must judge people by their values and their contribution. Don't leave anybody out. I would rather have Roosevelt in a wheelchair than Reagan on a horse.

The Rainbow is making room for small farmers. . . .

The Rainbow includes lesbians and gays. No American citizen ought to be denied equal protection under the law.

We must be unusually committed and caring as we expand our family to include new members. All of us must be tolerant and understanding as the fears and anxieties of the rejected . . . express themselves in many different ways. Too often, what we call hate, as if it were some deeply rooted philosophy or strategy, is simply ignorance, anxiety, paranoia, fear and insecurity.

* * * *

In 1984, my heart is made to feel glad, because I know there is a way out—justice. The requirement for rebuilding America is justice. The linchpin of progressive politics in our Nation will not come from the North. . . . [It] in fact will come from the South.

That is why I argue over and over again. We look from Virginia around to Texas. There is only one Black Congressperson out of 115. Nineteen years later, we are locked out of the Congress, the Senate, and the Governor's Mansion.

What does this large black vote mean? Why do I fight to win second primaries and fight gerrymandering and annexation and at-large elections? Why do we fight over that? Because I tell you, you cannot hold someone in the ditch unless you linger there with them. . . .

If you want a change in this Nation, you enforce that Voting Rights Act. We will get 12 to 20 Black, Hispanic, female and progressive congresspersons from the South. We can save the cotton, but we have got to fight the boll weevils. We have got to make a judgment. . . .

It is not enough to hope ERA will pass. How can we pass ERA? If Blacks vote in great numbers, progressive Whites win. It is the only way progressive Whites win. If Blacks vote in great numbers, Hispanics win. When Blacks, Hispanics, and progressive Whites vote, women win. When women win, children win. When women and children win, workers win. We must all come together. We must come up together.

* * * *

I have a message for our youth. I challenge them to put hope in their brains and not dope in their veins. I told them that like Jesus, I, too, was born in the slum, and just because you are born in the slum does not mean the slum is born in you, and you can rise above it if your mind is made up. I told them in every slum there are two sides. When I see a broken window, that is the slummy side. Train some youth to become a glazier; that is the sunny side. When I see a missing brick, that is the slummy side. Let that child in the union and become a brick mason and build; that is the sunny side. When I see a missing door, that is the slummy side. Train some youth to become a carpenter; that is the sunny side. And when I see the vulgar words and hieroglyphics of destitution on the walls, that's the slummy side. Train some youth to become a painter, an artist; that is the sunny side.

We leave this place looking for the sunny side because there is a brighter side somewhere. I am more convinced than ever that we can win. We will vault up the rough side of the mountain. We can win. I just want young America to do me one favor. . . .

Exercise the right to dream. You must face reality—that which is; but then dream of the reality that ought to be—that must be. Live beyond the pain of reality with the dream of a bright tomorrow. Use hope and imagination as weapons of survival and progress. Use love to motivate you and obligate you to serve the human family.

Young America, dream. Choose the human race over the nuclear race. Bury the weapons and don't burn the people. Dream—dream of a new value system.

Teachers who teach for life and not just for a living, teach because they can't help it. Dream of lawyers more concerned about justice than a judgeship. Dream of doctors more concerned about public health than personal wealth. Dream of preachers and priests who will prophesy and not just profiteer. Preach and dream! Our time has come. Our time has come.

Suffering breeds character, character breeds faith, and faith will not disappoint. Our time has come. Our faith, hopes and dreams will prevail. Our time has come. Weeping has endured for night, but now joy cometh in the morning.

Our time has come. No grave can hold our body down. Our time has come. No lie can live forever. Our time has come. We must leave the racial battleground and find the economic common ground and moral higher ground. America, our time has come.

We come from disgrace to Amazing Grace. Our time has come. Give me your tired, give me your poor, your huddled masses who yearn to breathe free, and come November there will be a change because our time has come.

Thank you and God bless you. ■

2. **B**lack activism has been less conspicuous during the 1980s than the 1960s, but the tradition of Afro-American radicalism and militancy remains alive, particularly in the writings of Manning Marable. A proponent of democratic socialism, Marable was a member of the executive commmittee of the National Black Political Assembly, a body that emerged from the National Black Political Convention in Gary in 1972. A professor of political sociology at Purdue, Marable is a prolific writer who has written numerous books and has published his articles in many black newspapers as well as in leading

academic and political journals. The following selection argues against the notion that race is becoming less important in America and suggests that, in the future, blacks should abandon "the politics of the black elite" in favor of strategies that are, in Marable's view, in the interest of the black majority.

From: From the Grassroots: Social and Political Essays Toward Afro-American Liberation by Manning Marable (Boston: South End Press, 1980), pages 224–227. Copyright 1980 by Manning Marable. Used by permission.

The black majority, located within the working class, view themselves and their political activities through the prism of race, primarily because their children still attend largely black schools, they still live in mostly black neighborhoods, they still attend all-black civic associations, fraternal societies and churches; and because they still perceive whites as a whole discriminating against them because of their race. The black elite, on the other hand, employs race as an ideological and cultural tool to maintain and extend its own influence, its hegemony, over the bulk of working class black society. The N.A.A.C.P., for instance, projects an image of a multi-class, largely black organization; but in practice it carries out pre-corporate, pro-integrationist policies which cut against the real interests of the black majority.

The politics of the black elite can be described in two words, "equal opportunity." The new leaders of black society do not wish to transform what they view as fundamentally "a good thing." They are not interested even in structural *reforming* of basic property relations. What it desires *above all else* is the *chance,* the *opportunity,* to compete for society's surplus value, the economic profits obtained from black and white workers, on a roughly equal basis with white elites. Equal opportunity within the existing status quo, to the N.A.A.C.P., means lending support to the promulgation of nuclear power plants, so long as blacks are hired as engineers and industrial workers equally. Equal opportunity in Exxon corporation means providing affirmative action gains within the corporate hierarchy for black executives and middle managers, without having an overview on the relationship between Exxon's monopoly of energy sources and the dependence of blacks on this energy.

The challenge in the 1980s for black activists and scholars, black community organizers and trade unionists, is twofold—first, we must break the hegemony of the black elite within our cultural institutions, media, economic centers and educational institutions; and secondly, we must make a case not for equal opportunity but for full equality, and for the prerequisites of equality, in every aspect of economic, social and political relations, involving not just blacks, but every U.S. citizen. This will not be an easy task.

Equality, as I am defining the term, must become the principle theoretical foundation for a new humanistic Movement within society, a movement which will stand on the shoulders of the Civil Rights Movement of the 1950s and 1960s and the Black Power Movement of the late 1960s. Equality within the mode of production means an equal share of decision making power from the shop floor of a factory to the upper echelons of the managerial elite. Equality, defined as the principle of human *fairness,* must take the place of equal opportunity, which is defined as an equal chance to become our own oppressors.

Equality must mean more than simply the attainment of full employment, the guarantee of a job for every individual. Equality must also involve the responsibility of work, of training black youth to view work as a means toward redefining themselves in relationship to their environment, and in contributing to a better kind of society for everyone. We have to teach our youth that the ultimate dehumanization is life without work; that work provides us with a way of confronting ourselves and others toward building a new world.

Equality should mean that the federal government should commit itself to the pursuit of the prerequisites of a fair and just life for all people, without turning people into dependents and non-productive individuals. Part of the solution toward real economic equality might mean that the federal government would provide several billions of dollars in interest-free loans and outright grants to minority businessmen and contractors and to black economic cooperatives, not as a dole, but to allow them to have the prerequisites to compete more equally with larger, white-owned corporations. Cultural equality would mean in part, massive federal fiscal support to all traditionally black colleges, without federal pressure to desegregate these institutions.

Equality must revive the ideal of poverty and self sacrifice. This is in direct conflict with the natural assumption of wealth which is part of the American Dream. We cannot all be wealthy. We should not all be wealthy. In an ideally democratic society, no one should have an income or an accumulation of wealth which he does not personally need, nor acquire economic power sufficient to destroy the aspirations and lives of others. As in everything, absolute power corrupts absolutely. "If civilization is to turn out millionaires," DuBois wrote, "it will also turn out beggars and prostitutes. A simple healthy life on limited income is the only reasonable ideal of civilized folk."

If we devote all our energies simply in the acquisition of individual wealth, we will neglect the ideals of philanthropy and service. It was not too many years ago that the majority of black middle class people devoted a regular portion of their incomes toward the construction of black colleges and trade schools, black churches and civic organizations. We must instill in our young adults the gift of giving toward others less fortunate within our communities. Equality must promote a certain depth of purpose, a belief in sharing and assistance.

Equality must connote, more than everything else, the construction of a sensible, democratic economic alternative for U.S. society, an alternative which socializes the accumulation of capital. We must stop thinking of ourselves as "minorities" and calling our interest "special interests," and begin to view our demands as the basis for a new beginning to the needs of the oppressed and exploited classes of the United States. As Martin Luther King wrote in 1966, "the long journey ahead requires that we emphasize the needs of all America's poor, for there is no way merely to find work, or adequate housing, or quality-integrated schools for Negroes alone. We shall eliminate unemployment for Negroes," Martin believed, "when we demand full and fair employment for *all.*"

The central problem of the twentieth century was in large measure, as DuBois accurately termed it, the problem of the color line—the relations of the darker to the lighter races in Africa, Asia, the United States, and throughout the world.

Many of the problems within societies are still racial or ethnic confrontations. But in our country, in our time, an even greater problem has emerged that underlies even the crisis of race—can we achieve real equality for all people, in every aspect of economic, social and political relations. As we destroy the economic illusions of U.S. society, the crisis of equality looms as the great unresolved riddle for democracy in the U.S. For the sake of our children, and for the future of the world, we must address the problem and master it, without uprooting the best of black cultural and social traditions which were created during the former period of segregation and inequality. We must resolve ourselves to struggle for the basic principles of fairness and equality for all people.

■

3. **B**lack political thought has always in-cluded conservative as well as radical themes. Black conservatism has usually emphasized the building and maintenance of community institutions, especially economic ones, rather than challenges to white-controlled institutions. Booker T. Washington made major contributions to black conservative thought through his advocacy of black vocational education and black business development. Like most black conservatives, Washington urged blacks to ally themselves with powerful white business leaders rather than pursue risky class-conflict strategies. Thomas Sowell, author of the following selection, is one of the foremost contemporary black conservatives. Sowell, an economist at the Hoover Institution at Stanford University, believes that market forces should be allowed to operate freely. Sowell has strongly criticized black leaders who call for government programs to assist blacks. He has argued that such programs are often harmful to blacks. His writings and those of other neoconservatives have been cited as justifications for the dismantling of some Great Society social welfare programs.

From: Civil Rights: Rhetoric or Reality? by Thomas Sowell (New York: William Morrow, 1984), pages 117–121. Copyright 1984 by Thomas Sowell. Used by permission of William Morrow & Company.

An attorney and former official of the NAACP Legal Defense Fund inadvertently revealed much of the evolution of that organization when he noted that by the mid-1960s "the long golden days of the civil rights movement had begun to wane," and the legal tools which it had developed "now threatened to collect dust." They needed new missions—and they found them, the crusade against the death penalty being just one. But they continued to call themselves "civil rights" organizations and the media have largely repeated that designation. In reality, the crusade for civil rights ended years ago. The scramble for special privilege, for turf, and for image is what continues on today under that banner and with that rhetoric.

The possibility that "too much" would be done to benefit minorities, women or others is the least likely of the consequences of the new conception of civil rights. There is much reason to fear the harm that it is currently doing to its supposed beneficiaries, and still more reason to fear the long-run consequences of polarizing the nation. Resentments do not accumulate indefinitely without consequences. Already there are signs of hate organizations growing in parts of the country and among more educated social classes than ever took them seriously before. As a distinguished writer has said in a different context: "It takes a match to start a fire but the match alone is not enough." Many racial policies continually add to the pile of combustible material, which only needs the right political arsonist to set it off.

Risks must be taken for genuine civil rights. But the kinds of internal struggles that have torn other multi-ethnic societies apart must be for something more than the continuing visibility of organizations or the continued employment of their lawyers.

The dangers of the present course are both insidious and acute. Among the insidious dangers are the undermining of minority and female self-confidence by incessant reiteration of the themes of pervasive discrimination, hypocritical standards, and shadowy but malign enemies relentlessly opposing their progress. However successful this vision may be in creating a sense of dependence on "civil rights" and "women's liberation" movements, it also obscures the urgency of acquiring economically meaningful skills or developing the attitudes to apply them with the best results. Pride of achievement is also undermined by the civil rights vision that assumes credit for minority and female advancement. This makes minority and female achievement suspect in their own eyes and in the eyes of the larger society.

The more acute dangers are longer run. The spread of hate organizations may be a symptom of much more unorganized resentment among people who are still not yet prepared to join fascistic or messianic movements. The dangers of continually adding to those resentments are all the greater the more heedlessly preferential doctrines are pushed in the courts, in the federal bureaucracy and by activists.

The resentments are not only against the particular policies but also against the manner in which the law, plain honesty, and democracy itself are sacrificed on the altar of missionary self-righteousness. The covert methods by which affirmative action has been foisted on a society that rejects it, the vengeful manner in which busing has been imposed without regard for the welfare of children, and the lofty contempt of a remote and insulated elite for the mass of citizens whose feelings and interest are treated as expendable, or dismissed as mere "racism," provide the classic ingredients of blindness and hubris that have produced so many human tragedies.

However much history may be invoked in support of these policies, *no* policy can apply to history but can only apply to the present or the future. The past may be many things, but it is clearly irrevocable. Its sins can no more be purged than its achievements can be expunged. Those who suffered in centuries past are as much beyond our help as those who sinned are beyond our retribution. To dress up present-day people in the costumes and labels of history and symbolically try to undo the past is to surpass Don Quixote and jeopardize reality in the name of visions. To do so in ways that harm the already disadvantaged is to skirt the boundaries of sanity and violate the very claims of compassion used to justify it.

"Realists" who claim that preferential policies are part of a "widespread" drive for equality, and therefore "here to stay" are the most out of touch of all. Polls show no such widespread preoccupation with imposing equal results, but instead a repeated rejection of such a goal, at low- as well as high-income levels, and among blacks and women, among other groups. The axiomatic and passionate nature of various beliefs among contemporary intellectuals does not make those intellectuals "everybody" or those beliefs valid or inevitable. That so many act as if it does is part of the problem. No idea is "here to stay" unless we choose to accept it. History is littered with predictions of inevitability and "waves of the future."

Sincerity of purpose is not the same as honesty of procedure. Too often they are opposites. Lies and deceptions "in a good cause" are all too common, and nowhere more so than in political and legal doctrines that falsely sail under the flag of "civil rights." The perversions of the law by federal judges appointed for life have been especially brazen. While they may be personally immune to the outrage they create, neither the law nor respect for the law is immune. Courts receive unprecedentedly low ratings in polls and contempt for the law is all too apparent in all too many ways. Demoralizing a people is not a small responsibility.

Civil rights is only one of the areas in which the vision of the morally self-anointed has overridden the upholding of law or the preservation of freedom. That it has been done sincerely is not to say that it has been done honestly—or that the dishonesty has gone undetected or unresented. When judges reduce the law to a question of who has the power and whose ox is gored, they can hardly disclaim responsibility, or be morally superior, when others respond in kind. We can only hope that the response will not someday undermine our whole concept of law and freedom. Fascism has historically arisen from the utter disillusionment of the people with democratic institutions.

We are not yet at that point, and our course need never take us there, though that is the direction in which we are currently drifting. Civil rights in the original and genuine sense are still solid. The very need of organizations like the NAACP and the ACLU to find ever more remote activities are evidence of that. If there is an optimistic aspect of preferential doctrines, it is that they may eventually make so many Americans so sick of hearing of group labels and percentages that the idea of judging each individual on his or her own performance may become more attractive than ever. ■

4. The American civil rights movement has been a long-term endeavor, with periods of intense activism and confrontation, followed by lulls and periods of serious introspection. Even as black Americans have benefited from the sacrifice and struggle of the 1960s activists, increased diversity within the black community and subtle changes in the ways many Americans view minorities and minority concerns have resulted in varied opinions as to what is yet to be accomplished.

As public concern about the civil rights agenda waned in the 1970s and 1980s, it became increasingly difficult to mobilize large numbers of people around civil rights issues. In the following essay, Dr. Benjamin L. Hooks, executive director of the National Association for the Advancement of Colored People (NAACP) since 1977, defines the future goals of his organization, the oldest civil rights group. The NAACP, considered moderate by some and radical by others, has been involved with the entire range of 20th century civil rights history, from W.E.B. DuBois in the 1920s through the great legal battles for desegregation that were waged and won in the 1950s and 1960s. Today, like most national organizations concerned with the struggle for social justice in America, the NAACP continues to reassess the gains and redefine the strategies that will produce a more equal and just America.

Source: "The Road Ahead" by Benjamin Hooks, executive director, National Association for the Advancement of Colored People. Used by permission.

James Weldon Johnson's mighty anthem, "Lift Ev'ry Voice," which we of the National Association for the Advancement of Colored People sing with great fervor, tells of the long struggle of black Americans to find their rightful place in this land. "Stony the road we trod," the song says.

The anthem reminds us of the bitter chastening rod, whose scourge we have endured. And it reminds us that we now stand "where the white gleam of our bright star is cast."

So it is with the contemporary civil rights movement. We have come over a long and weary way. We have gained many of our objectives.

But we dare not forget that our struggle is a continuing one. A long, long, road still stretches ahead. Our march along that road will require constant vigilance and unending struggle.

What is the nature of that struggle?

The goal of the struggle is what it has always been: We intend to eliminate every vestige of discrimination.

In today's struggle, we confront three basic problems:

• Implementation and enforcement of rights previously won;
• Maintenance of the gains already made, even as we continue to press forward;
• The elimination of a dual economic system—achieving economic parity.

At the beginning of our struggle, we fought for the right of blacks to sit at the front of the bus and the street car.

Today, we seek the right to have blacks as senior managers—and to own the bus company.

Yesterday, we fought—and some of us died—for the right to vote.

Today, we struggle to have our vote—our undiluted vote—counted.

Yesterday, we fought for the right to live in the neighborhood of our choice if we could afford the rent or the mortgage.

Today, we seek a fair share with the banks and mortgage companies.

Yesterday, we sought the right to check into the hotel.

Today, we are fighting to have enough money to check out of the hotel.

Yesterday, we sought the right to buy a hot dog at a lunch counter.

Today, we are fighting for the right to sell the ingredients that go into the hot dog.

Yesterday, we asked for charity.

Today, we seek economic parity.

Yesterday, we asked to be allowed to drink from any water fountain that was convenient.

Today, we want the right to produce and sell water fountains.

Yesterday, we sought to integrate segregated schools.

Today, we demand that schools be staffed by teachers who can and will motivate our children to learn in an integrated environment.

Yesterday, we sought the enactment of new laws to protect our rights.

Today, we seek to hold the line against a roll-back to our hard-won gains.

Yesterday, we fought to end discrimination in the work place.

Today, we fight subtle forms of prejudice in hiring and promotion.

Yesterday, we tried to get the news media to cover our protests.

Today, we struggle to get fair reporting for our efforts—and we fight to make certain that news-media employment reflects the rich diversity of the United States.

In this continuing struggle, we of the NAACP and civil rights community have had to make adjustments. We must fight today's battles with today's strategies and today's weapons. We understand that.

The first component of the new struggle in which we find ourselves is the battle to implement and enforce the laws, court decrees, regulatory rulings and other legal assertions of right that have been won at such great cost. To that end, we must be alert to see that laws forbidding discrimination in housing are enforced. We must be watchful to make certain that banks and insurance companies don't engage in red-lining our neighborhoods. We must be vigilant against schemes that are designed to dilute the power of the black vote. We must be sensitive to the unequal administration of justice in the criminal-justice system.

All this is the nitty-gritty day-by-day work of civil rights. It lacks glamor and sensationalism. But it must be done. Our task is to make certain that the laws that were written to protect the people we serve are living, vital forces, not dead words of legalese on parchment.

The second phase of the contemporary struggle is the effort to maintain past victories, while struggling and seeking to avail ourselves of new opportunities. That means standing watch upon the walls to see that the President and the Congress do not roll back progress. To that end, we and others labored to secure the extension of the Voting Rights Act. We have fought against the emasculation of Executive Order 11246, which requires employers who hold federal contracts to practice affirmative action in hiring. We have waged a successful battle to prevent the confirmation to high offices and judgeships of . . . men bent on thwarting our advancement.

The third element of our struggle is the fight for economic parity. As long as black Americans are confronted with an unemployment rate twice as high as that for whites, we must struggle. As long as black youth are unemployed at three times the rate of white youth, we must struggle. As long as the median family income of black Americans is 56 percent of the median family income of whites, we must struggle. As long as blacks have a mere one-tenth of the wealth of whites—and one-third of blacks have no wealth at all—we must struggle.

We fully intend to undo this nation's two-tier economic system. That system represents a kind of economic apartheid that has relegated blacks to economic "Bantustans." The system must be broken—and it will be, just as we eliminated the dual school system, tore down the "colored" drinking fountains, took down the signs from the "whites-only" restrooms, brought blacks to the front of the bus, and wrote the obituary for Jim Crow.

In pursuit of economic parity, the NAACP will continue to work for a full-employment economy. We recognize that unless the nation's economy as a whole is healthy the chronic economic paralysis of black America cannot be addressed. The NAACP stands behind the economic report it issued in 1981 and presented to the Administration.

That report called for policies to stimulate growth in inner cities, urged a series of programs—including job-training programs—to combat unemployment, and proposed tax relief for the working poor. But our document was clear in its assertion that "economic growth alone is not sufficient and provisions must be made for unemployment resulting from government policies, from recessions which are a part of the business cycle and, as a matter of right, for the care of those unable to find jobs even when the economy is at full employment."

We recognize that the mere creation of more jobs in the general economy will not automatically mean that blacks will receive a just share of the newly created jobs. Accordingly, we created our fair share program in 1981. Fair share seeks to ensure that blacks get their proportionate share of employment opportunities. We recognize minority ownership as an integral part of reaching that objective. In the past 20 years, 80 percent of all the new jobs created in the United States were created by small business. This fact is clear evidence of the importance of stimulating minority business.

These, then, are the milestones of the road ahead: the enforcement and implementation of rights; the maintenance of hard-won gains; the elimination of economic apartheid.

And other problems press upon us: the rise in teenage pregnancy; the growth of female-headed households; the staggering dropout rate among black, inner-city high school students.

These problems will be confronted, as they must be. That is our duty. ■

QUESTIONS FOR REVIEW

1.   What problems continue in black access to the ballot box despite passage of the 1965 Voting Rights Act?

2.   Explain the significance of the National Black Political Convention held in Gary, Indiana in 1972.

3.   To what extent was Jesse Jackson's presidential campaign successful? What did it accomplish?

4.   How has the increase in the number of black elected officials over the last twenty years affected the status and political influence of blacks as a whole? Locally? Nationally?

5.   What is coalition politics and what changes in American politics and society does it seek?

6.   How does Thomas Sowell distinguish between the struggle for civil rights and the struggle for position, privilege, and image? Is such a distinction appropriate today?

7.   How have blacks responded to the rise of conservatism in American political thought?

8.   Compare the views of neoconservatives such as Thomas Sowell regarding black economic advancement with those of Booker T. Washington, Malcolm X, Elijah Muhammed, and Martin Luther King, Jr.

9. What does Benjamin Hooks think should be the major objectives of the contemporary civil rights movement? How does this agenda compare to the one set forth by Manning Marable?

10. To what extent is the nationalistic tradition exemplified by *black power* in the late 1960s appropriate in the 1980s?

11. What advantages and disadvantages might result from a strategy to form a black independent political party?

12. What are some reasons some blacks have shifted from their traditional support of the Democratic party to support of the Republican party?

ADDITIONAL RECOMMENDED READINGS

Harding, Vincent and Rosemarie Freeney. *Martin Luther King, Jr. and the Company of the Faithful.* Washington, D.C.: Sojourners, 1986. A recent look at the enduring legacy of Martin Luther King, Jr. and the importance of his teachings for blacks in the world today.

Henderson, Lenneal J., Michael B. Preston, and Paul Puryear. *The New Black Politics: The Search for Political Power.* New York: Longman, Inc., 1982. A collection of essays that describe the development of modern black political institutions and examine the roles played by black organizations, politicians, and voters in the quest for greater freedom and political awareness.

Hine, Darlene Clark. *The State of Afro-American History: Past, Present, and Future.* Baton Rouge: Louisiana State University Press, 1986. A collection of essays that analyze the status of Afro-American Studies issues and research.

Karenga, Maulana. *Introduction to Black Studies.* Los Angeles: Kawaida Publications, 1982. An introductory text for black studies courses that includes an extensive bibliography and study questions.

Marable, Manning. *Black American Politics: From the Washington Marches to Jesse Jackson.* London: Verso, 1985. This book combines socialist theoretical analysis and several recent case studies on the results of black political activity with historical background on black America's political legacy.

Reed, Adolph L. *The Jesse Jackson Phenomenon: The Crisis of Purpose in Afro-American Politics.* New Haven: Yale University Press, 1986. A critical examination of the development and accomplishments of the 1984 Jackson presidential campaign including commentary on the perception of the black politician among voters, the role of the black church in black politics, and the influence of the media in portraying black politicians.

1863

JAN 1
President Abraham Lincoln issues Emancipation Proclamation, freeing "all slaves in areas still in rebellion" with exception of 13 parishes and the border states.

1865

JAN 31
Congress passes the 13th Amendment, abolishing slavery in America beginning Dec 18, 1865.

MAR 3
Congress establishes the Bureau of Refugees, Freedmen, and Abandoned Lands (Freedmen's Bureau) to aid former slaves and white refugees.

APR 14–15
President Lincoln is shot and killed at Ford's Theater in Washington, DC. Andrew Johnson becomes President.

DEC 28
Ku Klux Klan (KKK) is established in Giles County, TN.

1866

APR 9
Civil Rights Bill gives citizenship to all native-born Americans except Indians.

JUN 13
House passes 14th Amendment, providing equal protection under the law to all citizens.

1867

MAY 1
Reconstruction period begins. Arkansas and Louisiana start to register voters, followed soon by other states. By the end of October, 1,363,000 southern citizens are registered, including 700,000 blacks. Black voters constitute a majority in Alabama, Florida, Louisiana, Mississippi, and South Carolina.

AUG 1
Blacks vote for the first time in a southern state election, contributing to a Republican sweep of Tennessee.

NOV 5
First Reconstruction Constitutional Convention opens in Montgomery, AL; 18 blacks and 90 whites attend.

1868

NOV 3
First successful black congressional candidate, John W. Menard, defeats a white candidate 5107 to 2833 in Louisiana. [In 1869 he is denied the opportunity to fill an unexpired seat in the 40th Congress because of his race.]

Ulysses S. Grant is elected President; black voters in the south provide the decisive margin.

1869

APR 6
Ebenezer Don Carlos Bassett, principal of the Institute for Colored Youth in Philadelphia, PA, is named minister to Haiti and becomes first black diplomat and the first American black to receive a major diplomatic appointment.

1870

JAN 20   Hiram R. Revels is elected to the U.S. Senate from Mississippi to fill the unexpired term of Jefferson Davis; he is the first black to serve in Congress.

MAR 30   The 15th Amendment is ratified by Congress, protecting the right to vote from state action or interference.

DEC 12   South Carolinian Joseph H. Rainey, first black in the House of Representatives, is sworn in.

1872
DEC 9   In Louisiana, after racial and voter violence and the impeachment of the former official, P.B.S. Pinchback becomes the first black governor.

1874
AUG 30   More than 60 blacks are killed by white Democrats in the Coushatta Massacre in Louisiana.

1875
MAR 1   Congress enacts the Civil Rights Act giving equal rights and access to blacks and other citizens to public accommodations and places of public amusement, as well as jury duty.

SEP 8   Mississippi governor requests federal troops to protect black voters. U.S. Atty. Gen. Edward Pierrepont refuses request.

1881
DEC   Tennessee enacts first Jim Crow law, segregating railroad coaches in a separate-but-equal manner. The rest of the south soon follows this model.

1882
Tuskegee Institute begins organized collection of records of lynching in the U.S. [Between 1882 and 1955, about 5000 lynchings occur in racially motivated incidents, about 95 percent of them directed against black men, women, and children.]

1883
OCT 15   U.S. Supreme Court declares the Civil Rights Act of 1875 unconstitutional on the grounds that individual business rights to choose their own clientele are violated by giving blacks equal access.

1884
NOV 15   Berlin Conference brings together 14 European nations to partition Africa into colonial territories.

1890
JAN 25   National Afro-American League, pioneer black protest organization, is founded in Chicago.

1895
SEP 18   Booker T. Washington gains national attention from his "Atlanta Compromise" address when he articulates his philosophy of accommodation and industrial education for blacks.

MAY 18   U.S. Supreme Court decides constitutionality of separate-but-equal doctrine in *Plessy* v. *Ferguson*, upholding a Louisiana law segregating railroad cars.

JUL 21   National Association of Colored Women is founded in Washington, DC.

1898
SEP 15   National Afro-American Council is established in Rochester, NY.

1900
JUL   First Pan-African Congress meets in London. Among its leaders are H. Sylvester Williams, a West Indian lawyer with a London practice, W.E.B. DuBois, and Bishop Alexander Walters.

1903   The publication of W.E.B. DuBois' *The Souls of Black Folk* foreshadows the use of patriotic, nonviolent activism by black Americans to bring about social reforms.

1905
JUL   Black intellectuals and activists organize the Niagara Movement at meeting near Niagara Falls, NY. Led by W.E.B. DuBois and Monroe Trotter, delegates demand abolition of all laws resulting in racial distinctions.

1908
AUG 14–15 Race riot erupts in Springfield, IL after large influx of black migrants creates economic pressure. Incensed by a rumor that a black man had raped a white woman, whites rampage in black areas killing eight people and causing 2000 to flee before the state militia stops the violence.

1909
MAY 30   National Association for the Advancement of Colored People (NAACP) holds first conference.

1911   The National Urban League (NUL) is founded in New York to improve conditions of urban blacks through negotiation and gradualism.

1913
APR 11   President Woodrow Wilson issues executive order that segregates work areas, eating facilities, and bathrooms in government departments in Washington, DC.

1914
JUN 28   Archduke Franz Ferdinand of Austria is assassinated in Sarajavo, Serbia, initiating WW I.

1915   Black Americans migrate from south to north in great numbers to escape Mississippi and Alabama floods and to seek opportunities in the expanding northern war industry.

Fellowship of Reconciliation (FOR) is founded by white liberal pacifists.

JUN 21	U.S. Supreme Court rules in *Ginn* v. *United States* that "grandfather clauses" disfranchising black citizens in Maryland and Oklahoma constitutions violate the 15th Amendment.

1917
APR 6	America enters WWI. Blacks are segregated in armed forces and assigned menial work. First black officers are commissioned in October after protests by students and the NAACP. By armistice there are 370,000 black troops and 1400 officers, with more than half serving in the European theater where blacks are not segregated by law.
JUL 1–3	A major race riot in East St. Louis leaves at least 39 blacks and eight whites dead, with hundreds of blacks wounded or maimed; martial law is declared.
AUG 23	Fighting breaks out between white and black soldiers of the 24th Infantry Regiment after two local blacks are beaten. Two blacks and 18 whites are killed. On September 3, 19 soldiers are hanged, and 45 are sent to prison for their alleged involvement.
NOV 15	U.S. Supreme Court in *Buchanan* v. *Worley* strikes down a Louisville, KY restrictive covenant requiring blacks and whites to live in separate areas.

1919
Summer	Major race riots around the nation give this period the designation, "Red Summer of 1919."

1920
AUG 1	The Universal Negro Improvement Association (UNIA), founded by Marcus Garvey in 1914 to foster a program of black pride and awareness and a return of black Americans to Africa, holds its first national convention. [In 1923, Garvey is sentenced to five years in prison for mail fraud. Following a commutation of his sentence, Garvey is deported to his native Jamaica on Dec 4, 1927.]
1920s	The "Harlem Renaissance," a literary and artistic movement, champions black pride and cultural integrity.

1925
AUG 25	Brotherhood of Sleeping Car Porters (BSCP) is organized at mass meeting at Elks Hall in Harlem, NY. A. Philip Randolph is elected president.

1927
MAR 7	U.S. Supreme Court in *Nixon* v. *Herndon* strikes down a Texas law barring blacks from voting in the Democratic party's so-called "white primary."

1931

APR 6   Trial begins of nine Scottsboro, AL black youths accused of raping two
               white women on a freight train. The boys are represented by the
               International Labor Defense, a communist-controlled group rather than
               by the NAACP. [The case, which continues for twenty years, stimulates
               two major decisions: *Powell* v. *Alabama* (1932) which says blacks
               accused of capital crimes have the right to legal council and *Norris* v.
               Alabama (1935) which says that systematic exclusion of blacks from a
               trial with black defendants is unconstitutional, underscoring the right
               to trial by a jury of one's peers.]

1933
MAR 15   The NAACP begins legal attack on segregation and discrimination, filing
               suit against the University of North Carolina for refusing admission to
               black student Thomas Hocutt. Case is dropped after a black college
               refused to certify the records of the plaintiff.

1935
NOV 5   Maryland Court of Appeals orders the University of Maryland to admit
               Donald Murray, a black student previously refused admission on the
               basis of race.

1936
JUN 24   Mary McLeod Bethune, founder-president of Bethune-Cookman Col-
               lege, is named Director of Negro Affairs of the National Youth Adminis-
               tration (NYA), the first black woman to receive a major federal
               appointment.

AUG 9   Jesse Owens wins four gold medals at the Berlin Olympics.

NOV   Black voters shift political affiliation from traditional Republican sup-
               port to overwhelming support of the Democratic party.

DEC 8   NAACP files first suit in process to equalize the salaries of black and
               white teachers.

1938
DEC 12   U.S. Supreme Court rules in *Missouri ex rel Gaines* v. *Canada* that a
               state must provide equal educational facilities for blacks. The plantiff,
               Lloyd Gaines, who is enrolled at the University of Michigan, disappears
               after the decision and is never heard from again.

1939
SEP 27   Black leaders protest discrimination in the armed forces and war indus-
               tries in a White House meeting with President Roosevelt.

1941
APR 28   U.S. Supreme Court rules in complaint brought by Congressman Arthur
               Mitchell (IL) that separate railroad facilities for blacks and whites must
               be "substantially equal."

MAY 1   A. Philip Randolph calls for 100,000 blacks to march on Washington, DC
               to protest discrimination in the armed forces and in employment in war
               industries with government contracts.

JUN 25   President Franklin D. Roosevelt issues executive order forbidding racial and religious discrimination in war industries and government. Fair Employment Practices Committee is set up. March on Washington is cancelled.

DEC 7   Japan attacks Pearl Harbor; America enters WW II. A total of 1,154,720 blacks are inducted or drafted into the U.S. armed forces, with 7768 commissioned officers, 3902 black women in the Women's Army Auxilliary Corps, and 68 black women in the Navy auxilliary.

1942
NOV 3   Black and white advocates of direct, nonviolent action organize the Congress of Racial Equality (CORE) in Chicago. A group of members initiate sit-ins at Stoner's Restaurant.

1943
JUN 5–8   "Zoot suit" riots occur in Los Angeles as mobs attack anyone with a dark skin following a minor fight between sailors and Mexicans dressed in the fashionable suits of the period.

JUN 20–21   Race riot breaks out in Detroit; 25 blacks and nine whites are killed, 700 wounded. Federal troops are called in to maintain order.

1944
APR 3   U.S. Supreme Court in *Smith* v. *Allwright* rules that political party primary elections that exclude blacks from voting are unconstitutional.

JUL 8   U.S. War Department bans segregation in recreational and transport facilities; protests and clashes break out at several forts.

1945
APR 12   President Roosevelt dies during fourth term; Harry S Truman becomes president.

APR 25   The United Nations (UN) is formed in San Francisco.

SEP 18   One thousand white students walk out of three Gary, IN schools to protest integration. Similar disturbances occur in Chicago, IL and other northern and western urban areas.

1946
JUN 3   U.S. Supreme Court rules in *Irene Morgan* v. *Commonwealth of Virginia* that segregation on interstate buses and in terminals is unconstitutional.

DEC 5   President Truman creates the Committee on Civil Rights.

1947
APR 9   CORE and FOR send 28 riders on a "Journey of Reconciliation" (early freedom ride) through the upper south to test compliance with the Morgan decision.

APR 10   Jackie Robinson joins the Brooklyn Dodgers and becomes the first black in baseball major leagues in modern times.

OCT 23   NAACP petition on racism, "An Appeal to the World," is presented to the United Nations.

OCT 29	President Truman's Committee on Civil Rights condemns racial injustice in America.

1948

JAN 12	U.S. Supreme Court rules in *Sipuel* v. *Oklahoma State Board of Regents* that black students have the right to have "an opportunity to commence the study of law at state institutions at the same time as [other] students."
MAR 16	Levi Patterson sues Clarendon County, SC claiming that his children are suffering "irreparable damage" because the county pays to bus white children, but not black children, to school. In June, the case is thrown out of court on a technicality.
MAY 3	U.S. Supreme Court rules in *Shelley* v. *Kraemer* that federal and state courts cannot enforce restrictive covenants which bar persons from owning or occupying property because of their race.
JUL 26	President Truman issues executive order directing "equality of treatment and opportunity" in the armed forces.
	University of Arkansas Fayetteville Law School, Medical School, and Graduate School desegregate.

1949

	CORE begins sit-ins in downtown facilities in St. Louis, MO which continue until 1953.

1950

JUN 5	U.S. Supreme Court decisions begin to undermine the legal foundations of segregation in three landmark cases, *Sweatt* v. *Painter*, *McLaurin* v. *Oklahoma State Regents*, and *Henderson* v. *United States*, all filed by NAACP Legal Defense and Educational Fund. The *Sweatt* case involves the equality of a black Texas law school as compared to a white one. The *McLaurin* case involves racial separation at Oklahoma State Graduate School. The *Henderson* case upholds the end of segregation in interstate travel on the same basis as the earlier *Morgan* decision.
JUL 22	Ralph J. Bunche, former professor of political science at Howard University, becomes first black to receive a Nobel Peace Prize for his work as UN mediator in Palestine.

1951

MAY 24	Washington, DC's Municipal Court of Appeals rules that racial segregation in restaurants is illegal.
JUN	The NAACP begins to attack segregation in elementary and high schools before three-judge federal courts in South Carolina and Kansas. In *Briggs* v. *Elliott* the South Carolina court holds that segregation is not discrimination. The Kansas court rules that the separate facilities can be equal, but that segregation has an adverse effect on black children.
JUL 12	Gov. Adlai Stevenson calls out the National Guard after rioting in Cicero, IL when 3500 whites try to prevent a black family from moving into the all-white city.

JAN 12	The University of Tennessee admits first black student.
Fall	*Briggs* v. *Elliott* is added to similar cases of black school children from Kansas, Delaware, Virginia, and Washington, DC. Because the Kansas case is listed first, it gives its name to the historic litigation: *Oliver Brown* et al. v. *Board of Education of Topeka, Kansas.*
DEC 30	Tuskegee Institute reports that 1952 is the first year in 71 years of tabulation that no lynchings were reported in America.

1953

FEB	CORE begins sit-ins in Baltimore, MD.
JUN 19	The black community of Baton Rouge, LA begins a mass boycott of segregated buses after many drivers refuse to comply with a city ordinance which allows blacks to be seated on a first-come-first-served basis. The boycott is led by Rev. T.J. Jemison of the Mt. Zion Baptist Church. Mass meetings are held and a car pool is organized.
SEP 30	Earl B. Warren, Republican governor of California and former state attorney general, is appointed U.S. Supreme Court chief justice after sudden death of Chief Justice Frederick Vinson.

1954

MAY 17	In *Brown* v. *Board of Education*, U.S. Supreme Court rules that separate-but-equal segregated schools violate the 14th Amendment and are unconstitutional.
MAY 18	Little Rock, AR School Board votes to develop a plan consistent with the Brown decision.
JUL 11	First white Citizens' Council is organized in Indianola, MS.
SEP 7–8	Public school integration begins in Washington, DC and Baltimore, MD.

1955

MAR 24	Mississippi legislature amends the state constitution to require voters to pass a reading and writing test in order to register.
MAY 7	Rev. George Lee is killed in Belzoni, MS after refusing to remove his name from a voters' list.
MAY 31	U.S. Supreme Court, rules that school desegregation must take place "with all deliberate speed" in *Brown II* decision.
JUL 11	Hoxie, AR school integration begins peacefully but problems soon become sufficiently difficult that the Hoxie School Board starts harvest recess two weeks early.
AUG 13	Black voter Lamar Smith, who had voted in the state primary, is killed in Brookhaven, MS in front of the courthouse at noon; no indictments are made.
AUG 28	Emmett L. Till is kidnapped and lynched in Money, MS, after being accused of insulting a white woman.

SEP 21–23	Till's Uncle Moses Wright identifies the men who took Till away, becoming the first black to testify against a white in a murder trial in Mississippi. An all-white jury finds Roy Bryant and J.W. Milam not guilty. [Several months later, Bryant and Milam attempt to justify their actions.]
OCT 24	Hoxie, AR schools reopen as planned, integrated.
NOV 7	Baltimore, MD Supreme Court bans segregation in public recreational facilities.
DEC 1	Rosa Parks is arrested for refusing to give up her bus seat in Montgomery, AL.
DEC 5	Montgomery bus boycott begins. Rev. Martin L. King, Jr. is elected to head the Montgomery Improvement Association (MIA).
DEC 8	MIA organizes a citywide car pool.

1956

JAN 28	Black children are refused registration at Mann HS in Little Rock, AR.
JAN 30	King's house is bombed in Montgomery, AL.
FEB 1	Montgomery, AL activist E.D. Nixon's house is bombed.
FEB 3–MAR 7	Autherine J. Lucy becomes first black student to attend University of Alabama, Tuscaloosa. Rioting students protest her presence, and she is suspended by the Board of Trustees "for her own safety." A U.S. District Court orders Lucy readmitted, but after accusing university officials of cooperating with white mob, Lucy is expelled.
FEB 8	The NAACP files *Aaron v. Cooper* to force the integration of Mann HS in Little Rock, AR and to challenge that city's gradual integration plan.
FEB 21	King and some 90 Montgomery colleagues are indicted by a grand jury; the leaders turn themselves in and attract national attention to the situation. King is convicted on charges of conspiring to conduct an illegal boycott.
MAR 12	The Southern Manifesto ("Declaration of Constitutional Principles"), denouncing the U.S. Supreme Court ruling on segregation in public schools, is issued by 19 southern senators and 82 members of the House of Representatives.
MAY 30	Following Montgomery model, bus boycott is started in Tallahassee, FL.
JUN 5	Federal court rules that racial segregation on Montgomery city buses is unconstitutional.
JUN 11	Alabama outlaws the NAACP. Birmingham's black community forms the Alabama Christian Movement for Human Rights (ACMHR); Rev. Fred Shuttlesworth is elected president.
AUG 28	Federal Judge John E. Miller decides in *Aaron v. Cooper* that Little Rock's integration plan does not violate the *Brown* ruling, allowing the state to delay integration.
AUG 30	White mob prevents the enrollment of black students at Mansfield HS, Mansfield, TX.
SEP	A program of massive resistance to integration in public schools is put into law in Richmond, VA.

NOV 6 — In Arkansas, the Interposition Amendment, which encourages opposition to desegration by every means available, is passed by the state legislature.

NOV 13–
DEC 20 — U.S. Supreme Court unanimously reaffirms lower court decision banning segregation in Montgomery, AL. Federal injunctions prohibiting segregation on Montgomery buses are served to city, state, and bus company officials.

DEC 21 — Montgomery, AL buses are integrated.

DEC 25 — Shuttlesworth's home is bombed in Birmingham, AL.

DEC 26 — Birmingham blacks begin mass defiance of Jim Crow bus laws.

1957
JAN 10–11 — Southern Christian Leadership Conference (SCLC) is organized in Atlanta; King is elected president.

MAR — Ghana becomes an independent state.

MAY 17 — The Prayer Pilgrimage, biggest civil rights demonstration to date, is held in Washington, DC.

AUG 27–30 — A temporary injunction against integration is granted to the Mothers League for Central HS, a segregationist organization in Little Rock. The School Board gets a stay of the injunction.

AUG 29 — Congress passes the Civil Rights Act of 1957, the first federal civil rights legislation since 1875, establishing a civil rights commission and a civil rights division in the Justice Department and giving the Justice Department authority to seek injunctions against voting rights infractions.

SEP 2–4 — Arkansas Gov. Orval Faubus announces the National Guard will surround Central High to prevent black students from enrolling because the climate is too dangerous. NAACP and school officials decide to keep the nine black students away from Central HS on opening day, Sep 3. Federal Judge Ronald N. Davies orders implementation of the desegregation plan "forthwith" but the National Guard blocks black students' admission.

SEP 9 — Davies directs U.S. Justice Dept. to file for an injunction against Faubus to force immediate compliance with the desegregation order.

Nashville, TN's Hattie Cotton Elementary School with one black and 388 whites is destroyed by dynamite blast.

Shuttlesworth is attacked and beaten by mob when he attempts to enroll his daughters in a "white" Birmingham, AL school.

SEP 10–20 — Faubus accepts summons for trial on Sep 20, but refuses to remove National Guard from Central HS. Trial ends with an injunction against Faubus, who then complies and withdraws National Guard from Central HS.

SEP 23–25 — Black students are admitted to Central HS but are withdrawn following riots after only a few hours. President Dwight D. Eisenhower sends National Guard to Central HS. Soldiers escort nine black students to Central HS.

1958

AUG	NAACP Youth Council supervises sit-ins at Wichita, KS lunch counters which result in desegregation at Kress Co. and Katz Drug Stores.
SEP 12–27	U.S. Supreme Court rejects lower court's suspension of Little Rock's integration plan; Faubus wins vote to shut down Little Rock's public high schools on Sep 27.
SEP 20	King is stabbed in chest by a deranged black woman during a book signing session in Harlem, NY.
SEP 29	U.S. Supreme Court, in *Cooper* v. *Aaron*, denies Faubus' "claim that state officials have no duty to obey federal court," thus rejecting the interposition argument.
OCT 25	Ten thousand students, led by Jackie Robinson, Harry Belafonte, and A. Philip Randolph, participate in the Youth March for Integrated Schools in Washington, DC.
NOV 10–12	U.S. Court of Appeals overrules lease of Little Rock public schools to private corporation and orders school board to carry out integration; schools remain closed. Little Rock School Board resigns.

1959

JAN	Courts overrule closing of Virginia schools. Virginia Gov. J. Lindsay Almond, Jr. reopens schools. Prince Edward County, VA Board of Supervisors abandons school system; it stays closed until 1963.
APR 18	Approximately 25,000 high school and college students take part in second Youth March for Integrated Schools, held in Washington, DC.
APR–SEP	CORE sponsors sit-ins and interracial nonviolence workshops in Miami, FL.
JUN 18	Federal court decides that Arkansas laws permitting the leasing of public schools to private corporations are unconstitutional.
NOV–DEC	Nashville, TN Christian Leadership Conference holds test sit-ins at department stores.

1960

FEB 1	Four black North Carolina A and T students sit-in at Woolworth's lunch counter in Greensboro, NC. Within two weeks, the sit-ins spread to 11 cities in five southern states. By the end of the month sit-ins are held in many cities in North Carolina, Virginia, and Alabama.
FEB 27–29	Four hundred Nashville students protest segregated stores; 81 are charged with disorderly conduct. Black community raises nearly $50,000 for bail but students choose "jail, no bail" strategy.
MAR	CORE and NAACP call for a nationwide boycott of Woolworth's.
	Nashville students boycott downtown merchants before Easter. Informal organizations to support southern sit-ins form in 21 northern schools, including Harvard, Yale, Princeton, City College of New York, University of Chicago, and University of California/Berkeley. Boycotts continue through Apr.
MAR 2	Sixty-three students are charged with "conspiracy to obstruct trade and commerce" at two bus stations in Nashville.

MAR 3	James Lawson is expelled from Vanderbilt University for conducting workshops on nonviolence.
	Nashville Mayor Benjamin West appoints a biracial committee to resolve the protests; students agree to halt sit-ins temporarily while solution is sought, but plan boycott.
MAR 16	Four blacks are served at Nashville's newly integrated Greyhound terminal but are badly beaten up; two bombs are found the next day at the terminal.
	San Antonio, TX is first large southern city to integrate lunch counters; schools, buses, parks, and pools had been previously integrated.
MAR 28–30	Sixteen students from Southern University in Baton Rouge, LA are arrested; 2500 SU students march to capitol to protest arrests; University expels 17.
APR 5	Nashville biracial committee recommends a blacks-only counter, a whites-only counter, and an integrated counter; proposal is rejected by both students and merchants.
APR 15–17	Student Nonviolent Coordinating Committee (SNCC) is formed at Shaw University, Raleigh, NC.
APR 19	Black lawyer Alexander Looby's Nashville home is bombed; 3000 join protest march to courthouse; Mayor West admits that refusal of service to blacks is immoral.
MAY 10	Six Nashville stores desegregate lunch counters.
SUMMER	Dahomey, Niger, Upper Volta, Ivory Coast, Chad, Congo Brazzaville, Gabon, Senegal, Somalia, and Zaire become independent nations.
JUN 23	Hot Shoppes, Arlington, VA becomes first national chain to desegregate.
JUL 25	Greensboro, NC lunch counters are desegregated.
AUG 27	Race riots erupt in Jacksonville, FL after 10 days of sit-ins; 50 are reported injured.
FALL	Mali and Nigeria become independent.
OCT 17	Four national chain stores report that lunch counters in 112 southern towns have been integrated.
OCT 22–25	Mass sit-in is held in Atlanta; King is one of 80 people arrested and is sentenced to four months of hard labor.
OCT 26	Presidential candidate John F. Kennedy calls Mrs. King to express sympathy; Robert Kennedy calls judge in King case to protest. Judge, in response to renewed request by King's attorney, allows King's release. Kennedy campaign gets increased black support.
NOV 8	John F. Kennedy wins presidential election by narrow margin. Black vote contributes heavily to his win.
DEC 5	U.S. Supreme Court determines that segregated bus terminals are unconstitutional.

JAN–APR	CORE leaders develop idea for freedom rides.
MAY 1–13	Freedom ride workshops begin in Washington, DC with seven blacks and six whites. CORE freedom ride leaves Washington, DC on May 4; riders are arrested and assaulted in North and South Carolina on May 8–10 and arrive in Atlanta on May 13.
MAY 14–15	One Greyhound and one Trailways bus leave Atlanta. Greyhound bus is ambushed and bombed outside Anniston, AL. Thugs board Trailways bus and assault riders. In Birmingham, Trailways riders are beaten by waiting mob and bus drivers refuse to continue. [In 1975, Gary T. Rowe an FBI informant in the Klan, admits that Birmingham police promised the KKK 15 minutes free reign without intervention.]
MAY 17–20	CORE riders fly to New Orleans, LA. Ten Nashville students—eight black, two white—decide to continue the rides via Greyhound from Birmingham to Montgomery, AL accompanied by state patrol. No police are visible in Montgomery when crowd attacks riders. Robert Kennedy sends 600 federal marshals to Montgomery.
MAY 22	Governor John Patterson (AL) declares martial law and deploys National Guard to disperse mob and escort 1500 people home from church meeting.
MAY 23	SNCC, SCLC, and CORE leaders decide to continue rides despite violence and federal pressure for "cooling off" period.
MAY 24–26	A new group of 27 freedom riders leave Montgomery for Jackson, MS with press and Alabama National Guard aboard. They are met by Mississippi National Guard as they enter the state but are arrested at the Jackson Greyhound terminal on May 25. The next day 27 freedom riders are convicted in Jackson and sent to Parchman State Penitentiary.
MAY 31	NAACP lawyers sue for admission of James Meredith to University of Mississippi Law School; the case is initially dismissed but is appealed.
AUG	A SNCC national conference targets Albany, GA and surrounding counties for a voter registration drive.
AUG 14	Freedom riders' trials begin in Jackson. Courts levy stiff fines, nearly bankrupting CORE. NAACP provides lawyers and helps defray CORE's expenses. Trials continue through June 1962. [Convictions are overturned in 1965].
NOV 1	Interstate Commerce Commission (ICC) implements ban on segregated travel facilities. Air and train facilities are integrated by federal authorities over next few years. In SNCC test of ICC ruling in Albany, GA nine are ordered out of white waiting room. SNCC notifies U.S. Justice Department but receives no response.
NOV 17	Several black improvement organizations in Albany, GA form the Albany Movement.
NOV 22	Several students, including three from the NAACP Youth Council and two from SNCC, are arrested at Albany Trailways bus station in separate protests.
DEC 10	Eleven freedom riders are arrested at Albany, GA railroad station and charged with disorderly conduct.

DEC 11–14	The first stage of the Albany Movement begins with a series of mass meetings and marches involving hundreds of Albany blacks. By Dec 14 nearly 500 people are in jail. Albany Movement president Dr. William Anderson calls King for assistance.
DEC 15	King arrives in Albany with Rev. Ralph Abernathy and Rev. Wyatt T. Walker to speak at a rally.
DEC 16	King, Abernathy, and Anderson lead 250 people to city hall and are arrested for parading without a permit. King vows to stay in jail until city desegregates.
DEC 18	Albany Movement leaders and city representatives reach verbal agreement to desegregate terminal facilities, and King leaves jail. In ensuing days, city denies agreement.
1962	Council of Federated Organizations (COFO) is formed in Mississippi to coordinate manpower and resources of civil rights organizations.
JAN 16	Law suit charges New York City Board of Education with the use of "racial quotas."
FEB 5	Suit seeking to bar Englewood, NJ from maintaining "racially segregated" elementary schools is filed in U.S. District Court.
MAY 28	NAACP files suit alleging segregation in Rochester, NY schools.
JUN 25	Fifth Circuit Court of Appeals supports James Meredith's right to admission to "Ole Miss."
JUL 10–11	King and Abernathy are convicted of leading Albany's Dec 16, 1961 march. Albany Movement organizes a march and rally to show support for King and Abernathy; 32 people are arrested.
JUL 20–24	Federal district judge enjoins King and other leaders from participating in any further demonstrations; appeals court judge sets aside the injunction. That evening a large number of blacks, including many teenagers, battle police with rocks and bottles.
JUL 25	King calls for a Day of Penance to atone for violent behavior. He visits throughout community to encourage people to be nonviolent.
AUG 10	King leaves Albany for Atlanta.
AUG 15	The Albany City Commission refuses to meet any of the demands of the Albany Movement.
SEP 10	U.S. Supreme Court vacates a lower court ruling and decides that the University of Mississippi has to admit James H. Meredith.
SEP 13	Mississippi Gov. Ross R. Barnett says he will interpose state authority between the University of MS and the federal judges who ordered the admission of Meredith; he promises to go to jail if necessary to prevent integration at the state university.
SEP 20	Gov. Barnett is made registrar of the University of MS by the Board of Trustees and flies from Jackson to Oxford to personally block Meredith's first attempt to enroll.
SEP 24	U.S. Circuit Court of Appeals orders MS Board of Higher Education to admit Meredith to the University or be held in contempt.

SEP 26   Mississippi bars Meredith for a third time, as Lt. Gov. Paul Johnson and a state patrol blockade turn back Meredith and federal marshals.

SEP 28–29   Barnett and Johnson are found guilty of civil contempt.

SEP 30   Large force of federal marshals escort Meredith to the University. President Kennedy federalizes the Mississippi National Guard and appears on Mississippi television to urge Mississippians to accept the court orders. A riot ensues that results in two deaths.

OCT 1   Meredith registers at the University of MS.

1963
APR 3–6   The first phase of the SCLC's Birmingham campaign begins with a series of sit-ins. On Apr 6, about 45 demonstrators march to city hall in silence and are arrested.

APR 10   A state court enjoins King and other Birmingham leaders from leading demonstrations.

APR 12   King decides to lead a march of 50 volunteers in spite of concern that his arrest will seriously hinder needed fundraising; King and Abernathy are surprised when they are placed in solitary confinement.

APR 14   Coretta S. King places call on Easter Sunday to President Kennedy to have him intercede in the release of her husband; U.S. Atty. Gen. Robert Kennedy returns call for the President.

APR 26   Rather than being convicted for violating the Apr 10 injunction, King and Abernathy are convicted on the lesser charge of criminal contempt of court and fined because Birmingham officials do not want the pair in jail.

MAY 2   A new stage of protest is launched in Birmingham as hundreds of school children join the SCLC's demonstrations; 959 children are arrested.

MAY 3   Bull Connor's restraint ends as Birmingham police use dogs and high-pressure water hoses on demonstrators; black onlookers throw rocks and bottles; the violence attracts wide media coverage.

MAY 4   U.S. Justice Department official Burke Marshall goes to Birmingham to encourage negotiations.

MAY 7   ACMHR head Shuttlesworth is hospitalized as a result of violence that erupts in Birmingham streets; SCLC agrees to a 24-hour truce; Connor enlists Alabama Gov. George C. Wallace's support and 500 state troopers are sent to the area, 250 to the city itself.

MAY 10   The SCLC and ACMHR reach agreement with Birmingham leaders on limited desegregation changes in hiring practices in return for an end to mass demonstrations.

JUN 11   Under guard of federal troops, Vivian Malone and James Hood enter the University of Alabama at Tuscaloosa after Wallace stands in the schoolhouse door. In a nationally televised speech President Kennedy tells nation that segregation is morally wrong and that it is time for action.

JUN 12   Medgar Evers, NAACP field secretary, is assassinated in front of his Jackson home.

JUN 20 President Kennedy meets with national civil rights leaders and reluctantly agrees to March on Washington demonstration.

JUL 17 President Kennedy states that Aug 28 March on Washington will be "in the great tradition of peaceful assembly for the redress of grievance."

AUG 18 James Meredith becomes the first black graduate of Ole Miss.

AUG 28 More than 250,000 persons participate in the March on Washington; King delivers his "I Have A Dream" speech at the Lincoln Memorial.

SEP 9 Tuskegee, AL schools open late, as Gov. Wallace tries to fight desegregation order.

SEP 10 President Kennedy federalizes the Alabama National Guard to enable blacks to enter the school system.

SEP 15 Four black girls are killed in bombing of Sixteenth Street Baptist Church in Birmingham.

NOV 22 President Kennedy is assassinated in Dallas, TX; Lyndon B. Johnson becomes President.

1964
JAN 8 Johnson's State of the Union address calls passage of a Civil Rights Act essential to "increased opportunity" for all.

FEB Forty-five percent of students stay home in elementary school strike to protest segregated and unequal facilities in New York, NY; other school strikes take place in Cleveland, Chicago, Boston, and Cincinnati.

FEB 7 The Jackson, MS trial of Byron de la Beckwith for Medgar Evers' murder ends with a hung jury.

MAR 12 Malcolm X leaves the Nation of Islam and founds the Muslim Mosque, Inc.

APR 26 SNCC members organize the Mississippi Freedom Democratic Party (MFDP).

JUN Mississippi Freedom Summer Project (MFSP) launches voter registration campaigns; "freedom schools" offer developmental education to local people; four MFDP congressional candidates qualify for the Democratic party primary.

JUN 21–25 Three civil rights workers—Michael Schwerner, James Chaney, and Andrew Goodman—are reported missing. U.S. Atty. Gen. Robert Kennedy orders full-scale FBI search for missing men. On Jun 25, President Johnson authorizes the use of 200 Navy men in the search.

JUN 28 Organization for Afro-American Unity is founded in New York by Malcolm X.

JUL 2 Civil Rights Act of 1964, banning discrimination in voting and public accommodations and requiring fair employment practices, is passed.

SUMMER Riots occur in Harlem and Rochester, NY; Paterson and Elizabeth, NJ; Dixmoor, IL; and Philadelphia, PA.

AUG 4 The bodies of Schwerner, Chaney, and Goodman are found buried near Philadelphia, MS.

AUG 6–12	The MFDP state convention is attended by some 2500 supporters; 68 delegates, including four whites, are selected for the Democratic National Convention.
AUG 20	The Economic Opportunity Act creates the Office of Economic Opportunity (OEO) to develop and administer antipoverty programs.
AUG 22–26	MFDP asks to be seated at the Democratic National Convention. Fannie Lou Hamer tells of being beaten in jail by black prisoners on orders from white state patrolmen. Although a Johnson press conference pulls away television coverage before she is finished, the speech has a moving effect on the convention. Johnson forces try to arrange a compromise that allows MFDP delegates the right to participate in the convention but not to vote. A second compromise offers two MFDP delegates at-large seats at the convention, with the other delegates accepted as "guests." In addition, the convention adopts a rule for 1968 that bars any state delegation that discriminates against blacks. The MFDP delegates support a proposal to seat all delegates—regular and MFDP—who sign a loyalty pledge and then divide the Mississippi vote among them. They vote overwhelmingly to reject the administration's compromise.
SEP 8	Prince Edward County, VA public schools reopen after five years and enroll seven whites and 1400 blacks.
NOV 3	President Johnson is reelected in a landslide. The black vote is estimated at 85–97 percent Democratic, with 75 percent of registered blacks voting.
DEC 4	Johnson issues an executive order which bars discrimination in federal aid programs.
	FBI charges 20 men with conspiracy in connection with the July murders of Schwerner, Chaney, and Goodman. [In 1967, seven are convicted.]
DEC 10	King is awarded the Nobel Peace Prize.

1965

JAN 4	U.S. Justice Department files school desegregation suits in Louisiana and Tennessee, the first filed under the 1964 Civil Rights Act.
JAN 18–19	King leads voter registration march to Selma, AL courthouse; 67 demonstrators are arrested.
JAN 23	Federal judge issues a temporary restraining order prohibiting Selma and Dallas County officials from interfering with voter registration efforts.
FEB 1–2	Mass marches are held in Selma; more than 700 demonstrators are arrested, many of them teenagers; in accordance with SCLC strategy, King and Abernathy are arrested to stir protest; they refuse bond.
FEB 4	Federal judge bans the use of a complex voter registration test in Selma and requires the Selma registration board to process at least 100 voter applications per day.
FEB 7	Cabinet-level Council on Equal Opportunity is created to coordinate all federal civil rights activities.

FEB 8	A small group of protestors goes to Selma's voter registration office and demands to be registered immediately; the whole group is arrested. Two hundred students march to the courthouse to protest the arrests, but are dispersed peacefully.
FEB 10	Selma sheriff James Clark arrests 165 teenagers and forces them to march into the countryside, using cattleprods and nightsticks to keep them moving.
FEB 11–18	Marches, confrontations, and registration efforts continue in Selma. On Feb 18 in nearby Marion, AL, movement marcher Jimmie Lee Jackson is shot in the stomach and killed while trying to protect his mother from a state trooper's attack.
FEB 21	Malcolm X is assassinated during a rally of the Organization of Afro-American Unity at the Audubon Ballroom in New York City.
MAR 7	While King preaches in Atlanta, 600 marchers set out for Montgomery from Selma's Brown Chapel, led by the SCLC's Hosea Williams and SNCC's John Lewis. East of downtown Selma, at the Pettus Bridge, marchers are halted by state troopers in riot gear and Sheriff Clark's possemen. The troopers attack the marchers with nightsticks and tear gas, injuring more than 50. Outrage is expressed around the nation. In Atlanta, King announces a second march for Mar 9. The SCLC petitions federal judge Frank M. Johnson, Jr. for an order allowing a march to Montgomery without state interference.
MAR 9	King leads a group of marchers to the edge of a state trooper barricade on the outskirts of Selma. After a prayer, King turns the marchers around and returns to Selma. Later, local whites attack three white Unitarian ministers who participated in the protests, seriously injuring Rev. James J. Reeb.
MAR 11–14	Reeb's death on Mar 11 stimulates demonstrations in many northern cities for federal intervention and voting rights legislation.
MAR 16	SNCC march in Montgomery is attacked by mounted police using cattle prods.
MAR 17	Federal judge Johnson decides to allow the Selma-to-Montgomery march to take place.
MAR 20	President Johnson federalizes Alabama National Guard to protect demonstrators.
MAR 21–25	Thousands of demonstrators, led by King, undertake and complete the five-day march. March ends at the Alabama state capitol, where King addresses a rally of about 50,000 people. After the rally, Mrs. Viola Liuzzo, a white housewife and activist from Detroit, is shot to death. [Three Klansmen are later convicted of the crime.]
AUG 6	President Johnson signs the Voting Rights Act of 1965, eliminating literacy and other voter examinations and allowing federal examiners to register black voters in many southern counties.
AUG 11–16	Insurrection in the predominantly black Watts section of Los Angeles is the worst race riot in U.S. history.

JAN	King opens a SCLC campaign in Chicago, IL joining the Coordinating Council of Community Organizations (CCCO) and other local organizations to protest segregation in public schools and to seek improved housing and job opportunities for the city's black residents. On Jan 22, King moves into a slum tenement in Chicago as part of drive to force slumlords to clean up their properties.
JAN 6	SNCC issues a policy statement condemning American involvement in Vietnam, referring to the murder of Samuel Younge, Jr., a student leader from Tuskegee Institute who was killed by a gas station attendant for using a "white only" restroom, as analogous to the killing of Vietnamese peasants.
JAN 10	Julian Bond, SNCC communications director, is denied a seat in the Georgia House of Representatives because of his opposition to the Vietnam conflict.
APR 13	King publicly denounces the Vietnam conflict as "rapidly degenerating into a sordid military adventure."
MAY 16	Stokely Carmichael is named chairman of SNCC, replacing John Lewis.
JUN 1–2	Approximately 2400 persons attend the White House Conference on Civil Rights.
JUN 6–26	James Meredith is wounded by a white sniper near Hernando, MS on the second day of 220-mile March Against Fear from Memphis, TN to Jackson, MS. The march is continued on June 7 by King, CORE director Floyd McKissick, Carmichael, and other activists. It ends on June 26 with a rally of some 30,000 people at the Mississippi state capital. During this march, the slogan *black power* is first used by Stokely Carmichael to articulate a growing feeling of racial pride and independence.
JUL 2–5	CORE national convention adopts a statement in support of the black power concept.
JUL 4–9	NAACP national convention disassociates itself from the black power concept.
JUL 10–11	King speaks at Chicago's Soldier Field rally on the SCLC's "freedom Sunday." He then leads a march of 30,000 people to Chicago's City Hall where he calls on city officials to end discriminatory real estate practices, increase black employment, end police brutality, and create a police department civilian review board. Chicago Mayor Richard M. Daley claims that the city already has a "massive antislum program." King warns that he will lead large-scale acts of civil disobedience.
JUL 12–15	Riot breaks out in Chicago, IL as blacks using fire hydrants to stay cool are harassed by police; nine people are injured; 24 are jailed. King and his aides travel throughout the city urging calm and ask the city government to provide swimming facilities for the west side. Riots resume on July 14, leaving two people dead, 56 injured, and 282 in jail. On the 15th, Gov. Otto Kerner orders 4000 National Guardsmen into the city. King negotiates with Daley again and receives portable swimming pools and a citizen's committee to study the police department. He then meets with leaders of the Blackstone Rangers, a local gang, who are confronting police, and gets them to commit to nonviolence.

JUL 19	Ohio Gov. James A. Rhodes declares state of emergency in Cleveland and dispatches troops to riot-torn Hough district.
AUG 5	King leads an integrated march to Chicago's Marquette Park area where he is met by a crowd of whites who jeer and throw bricks and bottles at the demonstrators.
AUG 7	Race riot occurs in Lansing, MI.
AUG 12	Philadelphia police, led by Acting Police Commissioner Frank Rizzo, raid local SNCC offices; four people are arrested for possession of deadly weapons after dynamite is allegedly discovered in one of the offices.
AUG 26	King and Chicago leaders negotiate an agreement with Daley for improved attention to black housing needs and fair bank loan policies for blacks. The Leadership Council for Metropolitan Housing is established to implement the accord.
AUG 27	Race riot occurs in Waukegan, IL.
AUG 30	Constance Baker Motley is confirmed as a U.S. District Court judge, becoming the first black woman on the federal bench.
SEP 4	King announces that jobs are now the main priority in Chicago and will be pursued by the SCLC's Operation Breadbasket, headed by Jesse Jackson.
OCT	The Black Panther Party (BPP) is founded in Oakland, CA by Huey Newton and Bobby Seale.
NOV 7–8	A preelection mass meeting is held at the Mount Moriah Baptist Church by the Lowndes County (AL) Freedom Organization (LCFO), a SNCC-established voting rights organization; Stokely Carmichael speaks. On Nov 8, all seven LCFO candidates are defeated in Lowndes County election following all-out effort by whites to defeat them, allegedly including fraud and coercion.
NOV 8	Edward W. Brooke (Republican, MA) is elected to U.S. Senate, the first black senator since Reconstruction and the first black senator elected by popular vote.
DEC	SNCC decides to exclude whites from membership but allows them to be involved in projects.

1967

JAN 9	Harlem, NY Rep. Adam Clayton Powell, Jr. is ousted as chairman of the House Education and Welfare Committee on a charge of wrongfully appropriating congressional funds; Powell accuses his critics of racism.
	Bowing to legal decisions, the Georgia legislature seats Julian Bond.
JAN 16	Lucius D. Amerson is sworn in as sheriff of Tuskegee (Macon County), AL, the first southern black sheriff of the 20th century.
MAR 1	U.S. House of Representatives expels Powell by a vote of 307 to 116.
APR 11	Harlem voters reelect Powell.

APR 28　　World Boxing Association and New York State Athletic Commission withdraw recognition of Muhammad Ali as world heavyweight boxing champion because of his refusal to serve in the U.S. armed forces. [Ali is later convicted in federal court of violating the Selective Service Act.]

MAY 12　　H. Rap Brown replaces Carmichael as SNCC chairman.

JUN　　　Race riots occur in Roxbury section of Boston, MA; Tampa, FL; Cincinnati, OH; and Buffalo, NY.

JUN 12　　U.S. Supreme Court rules in *Loving* v. *Virginia* that a law banning miscegenation is unconstitutional.

JUN 13　　U.S. solicitor general Thurgood Marshall is named to the Supreme Court by President Johnson, becoming the first black Supreme Court justice.

JUL　　　Race riots occur in Cairo, IL; Durham, NC; Memphis, TN; Cambridge, MD; and Milwaukee, WI.

JUL 12–17　　Twenty-three are killed in Newark, NJ rebellion. The racial uprising spreads through ten of the city's 23 square miles. More than 1500 persons are injured and 1300 arrested. Police report 300 fires. The Newark rebellion, the worst since the 1965 Watts riot, spreads to other New Jersey communities, including New Brunswick, Englewood, Paterson, Elizabeth, Palmyra, Passaic, and Plainfield.

JUL 20–23　　More than 1000 persons attend the first Black Power Conference in Newark, NJ.

JUL 23–30　　Forty-three persons are killed in Detroit riots, the largest racial rebellion in a U.S. city in the 20th century. Federal troops are called out for the first time since a Detroit riot of 1943. More than 2000 persons are injured and some 5000 are arrested. Police report 1442 fires. Rioting spreads to other Michigan cities.

AUG 14　　SNCC publishes a memo denouncing Zionism, declaring support for the Palestine Liberation Organization (PLO), and accusing Israel of practicing segregation and of assigning second-class status to darker-skinned Jews.

　　　　　SNCC chairman Brown is indicted in Dorchester County, MD for inciting a riot, committing arson, and disturbing the peace in connection with the July 24–26 riots in Cambridge, MD.

AUG 25　　FBI Director J. Edgar Hoover orders the FBI's Counterintelligence Program (COINTELPRO) to begin a new effort to "expose, disrupt, misdirect, discredit, or otherwise neutralize the activities of black nationalist, hate-type organizations and groupings, their leadership, spokesmen, membership, and supporters, and to counter their propensity for violence and civil disorder."

SEP 6　　President Johnson names Walter E. Washington commissioner and "unofficial" mayor of Washington, DC.

NOV 7–13　　Carl B. Stokes is elected mayor of Cleveland, OH and Richard G. Hatcher is elected mayor of Gary, IN. Stokes becomes the first black to serve as mayor of a major American city.

DEC	The Senate Permanent Investigating Committee reports 75 major riots occurred in 1967, compared with 21 in 1966; 83 persons were killed in the 1967 riots, compared with 11 in 1966 and 36 in 1965.
DEC 4	King announces plans to lead an army of poor whites, poor blacks, and Hispanics to Washington, DC in April 1968 to demonstrate for jobs and income for all Americans.

1968

JAN 9	The Black United Front (BUF) is formed in Washington, DC by Stokely Carmichael and other black community leaders.
FEB 8	Police kill three students who were protesting segregation at a bowling alley during demonstrations near the campus of South Carolina State in Orangeburg.
FEB 17	A major rally is held at The Oakland Auditorium on the birthday of Huey Newton to express support for the jailed Black Panther leader. The Black Panther party announces it will merge with SNCC; Stokely Carmichael is to be prime minister; H. Rap Brown, minister of justice; James Forman, minister of foreign affairs; and Eldridge Cleaver, master of ceremonies.
FEB 20	State troopers use tear gas to stop demonstrations at Alcorn A & M College in Mississippi.
FEB 29	President Johnson's National Advisory Commission on Civil Disorders, set up in July 1967, issues its report, warning that the nation "is moving toward two societies, one black, one white—separate and unequal" and recommends sweeping reforms in federal and local law enforcement, welfare, employment, housing, and education.
MAR 19–21	In Washington, DC, Howard University students seize administration building and demand campus reform and a black-oriented curriculum.
MAR 22–24	State troopers are mobilized to put down student rebellion at Cheyney State College in Pennsylvania.
MAR 29	Students seize building at Bowie State College in Maryland.
APR	Three hundred students hold 12 school trustees captive for 12 hours demanding campus reforms at Tuskegee Institute in Alabama. Black students occupy administration building at Boston University and demand an increase in black student admissions and Afro-American history courses. Columbia University, in New York City, ends semester early when an integrated group of students seize five buildings on campus. Students seize administration building at Ohio State University.
APR 4	The Rev. Martin L. King, Jr. is assassinated by a white sniper while standing on the balcony of the Lorraine Motel in Memphis, TN. The assassination precipitates a national crisis and riots in more than 100 cities. Forty-six persons are killed in major rebellions in Washington, DC, Chicago, and other cities. Twenty thousand federal troops and 34,000 National Guardsmen are mobilized to quell disturbances. Memorial marches and rallies are held throughout the country. Many public school systems close and the opening of the major league baseball season is postponed. President Johnson declares Sunday, April 6, a national day of mourning.

APR 9 — Abernathy becomes president of SCLC.

APR 11 — President Johnson signs a civil rights bill that bans racial discrimination in the sale or rental of about 80 percent of the nation's housing and makes it a crime to interfere with civil rights workers or to cross state lines to incite a riot.

APR 29–MAY 11 — Poor People's Campaign begins when Abernathy leads a delegation of leaders representing poor whites, blacks, Indians, and Hispanics to Washington, DC for conferences with cabinet members and congressional leaders. Nine caravans of poor people arrive in Washington and erect a camp called Resurrection City on a 16-acre site near the Lincoln Memorial.

JUN 5 — Senator Robert F. Kennedy is assassinated in Los Angeles, CA moments after addressing a rally celebrating a victory in the California primary in his quest for the U.S. presidency.

JUN 8 — James Earl Ray, alleged assassin of Martin L. King, Jr., is captured at a London airport.

JUN 18 — U.S. Supreme Court bans racial discrimination in the sale and rental of housing.

JUN 19 — Fifty thousand demonstrators participate in Poor People's Campaign Solidarity Day March.

JUN 24 — Resurrection City is closed. More than 100 residents are arrested by DC police when they refuse to leave the site. Other residents, including Abernathy, are arrested during a demonstration at the U.S. Capitol. The National Guard is mobilized later in the day to stop disturbances.

JUL — Race riots occur in Cleveland, OH and Gary, IN.

AUG 1 — President Johnson signs the Housing and Urban Development Act of 1968, authorizing more than five billion dollars for a three-year program aimed at providing 1.7 million units of housing for low-income families and subsidies for construction and ownership of these units.

AUG 8 — Race riot breaks out in Miami, FL while the Republican party is holding its national convention; National Guard is mobilized.

SEP 8–27 — Black Panther Supreme Commander Huey Newton is convicted of manslaughter in the October 28, 1967 fatal shooting of a white policeman. [Three weeks later, he is sentenced to 2–15 years imprisonment.] Protests are held daily by the Black Panther party outside the courthouse. The extensive media coverage brings many Americans their first glimpse of the group, whose black leather uniforms and military-like organization create a powerful symbol of emerging black militancy.

SEP 17–24 — The University of CA, Berkeley asks Eldridge Cleaver, Black Panther minister of information, to give a series of lectures on race relations and touches off a battle between militant student supporters and conservatives who denounce Cleaver as "an advocate of racism and violence."

NOV 5   A record number of black congressmen and the first black woman representative are elected to Congress. The woman, Shirley Chisholm of the Bedford-Stuyvesant section of Brooklyn, NY, defeats former CORE director James Farmer. Harlem voters reelect Adam Clayton Powell, Jr. in spite of his expulsion from Congress the previous year. Other black incumbents reelected are: William L. Dawson (IL), Charles C. Diggs (MI), Augustus Hawkins (CL), Robert N.C. Nix (PA), and John Conyers (MI). Newly elected to Congress in addition to Mrs. Chisholm are Louis Stokes (OH) and William L. Clay (MO). The nine black representatives and one senator, Edward W. Brooke (MA) top the previous high of eight blacks in the Reconstruction congress of 1875–77.

Richard M. Nixon wins the 1968 presidential election, defeating Hubert H. Humphrey in a close race.

DEC 14   Classes at San Francisco State University are suspended after demonstrations by the Black Student Union and the Third World Liberation Front.

1969
JAN 3   Rep. Adam Clayton Powell, Jr. is again seated by Congress.

MAR 10   James Earl Ray pleads guilty to King's murder and is sentenced to 99 years in prison. [The House Select Committee on Assassinations later states that Ray fired the shot that killed King but reflected a broader conspiracy against King and his movement.]

MAR 27   Black Academy of Arts and Letters is founded in Boston, MA.

APR–MAY   In New York City, student Afro-American Society seizes Columbia University admissions office and demands a special admissions board and staff. One hundred black students armed with rifles and shotguns seize the student union building at Cornell University, Ithaca, NY to protest university racism. Police and National Guardsmen fire on demonstrators at North Carolina A & T College in Greensboro; one student is killed, five policemen are injured.

JUN 16   U.S. Supreme Court rules that the House of Representatives 1967 expulsion of Adam Clayton Powell, Jr. was unconstitutional.

AUG 23   U.S. Justice Department reports that rioting in urban areas in 1969 was down at least 50 percent from 1968 and concludes that the period of the worst large-scale racial rebellions is over.

OCT 17   Dr. Clifton R. Wharton, Jr. is named president of Michigan State University, the first black to head a major, predominantly white university.

OCT 29   U.S. Supreme Court rules in *Alexander* v. *Holmes County Board of Education* that school systems must end segregation "at once" rather than "with all deliberate speed" and must "operate now and hereafter only unitary schools."

DEC 4   Two Black Panther leaders—Fred Hampton and Mark Clark—are killed in Chicago police raid. Civil rights leaders charge that the two men were murdered in their beds and that excessive violence was used.

JAN 3	U.S. Department of Health, Education, and Welfare (HEW) reports that 61 percent of the nation's black students and 65.6 percent of its white students were attending segregated schools as of 1968.
JAN 10–23	Governors of Georgia, Alabama, Louisiana, and Florida promise to reject all busing plans designed for their states by the federal government or the courts.
FEB 28	Presidential domestic advisor Daniel P. Moynihan counsels Richard Nixon that "the time may have come when the issue of race could benefit from a period of 'benign neglect.'"
MAR 20	University of Michigan students strike demanding increased black enrollment. The strike ends on April 2 after the school administration agrees to meet their demands.
MAR 24	President Nixon affirms that the 1954 *Brown* decision is right "in both constitutional and moral terms," but rejects busing as the best vehicle for change.
APR 8	U.S. Senate rejects Supreme Court nominee G. Harrold Carswell, after strong opposition by liberals and civil rights organizations to his segregationist views.
MAY	Two students are killed by police officers in a major racial disturbance at Jackson State University, MS. National Guard is mobilized to quell disturbances at Ohio State University when black and white students demand the admission of additional black students and an end to ROTC programs.
MAY 29	California Court of Appeals overturns the manslaughter conviction of Huey Newton, finding that procedural errors had deprived the Black Panther leader of a fair trial.
JUN 22	Nixon signs a bill extending the Voting Rights Act of 1965 to 1975.
JUN 23	Charles Rangel defeats Adam Clayton Powell, Jr. in the Democratic primary in Harlem, NY, ending the political career of one of the major black political figures of the post-WWII period.
AUG 3–7	Two thousand delegates and observers attend the Congress of African Peoples convention in Atlanta, GA.
AUG 7	Four persons, including presiding Judge Harold Haley, are killed in a dramatic courthouse shootout in San Rafael, CA. Police charge UCLA instructor and activist Angela Davis with allegedly helping to provide the weapons used by the attackers and issue a nationwide warrant for her arrest.
AUG 29–31	One policeman is killed and six wounded in a confrontation between police and Black Panther activists in Philadelphia, PA. In New Haven, CT, Lonnie McLucas, a Black Panther activist, is convicted of conspiracy in the murder of Alex Rackley, a suspected FBI informant.
SEP 12	California Gov. Ronald W. Reagan signs a bill forbidding busing of school children without the written consent of a parent or guardian.

OCT 13 Angela Davis is arrested in New York City and charged with unlawful flight to avoid prosecution for her alleged role in the California courthouse shootout.

OCT 19 The government dismisses conspiracy charges against Black Panther leader Bobby Seale in connection with the Chicago riot of 1968, but Seale must still face a four-year prison term for contempt of court, kidnapping, and murder charges in connection with the Connecticut slaying of Alex Rackley.

 The NAACP sues HEW for general and calculated default in enforcement of desegregation guidelines.

1971
JAN 16 Preliminary 1970 census figures indicate that since 1960, the black urban population increased 3 million and the white urban population decreased about 2.5 million. Reports also indicate that 1.4 million blacks emigrated from the south in the 1960s and nearly half of these settled in New York or California. Since 1940, the percentage of black Americans living in the south declined from 77 percent to 53 percent.

JAN–FEB Twelve black congressmen boycott Nixon's State of the Union address because of his "consistent refusal" to respond to petitions of black Americans. Nixon meets with members of the Congressional Black Caucus and appoints a White House panel to study a list of recommendations made by the group.

MAR 1 U.S. Defense Dept. limits electronic surveillance after disclosure of a "civil disturbance information collection plan" which directs the gathering of information on civil rights groups.

MAR 23 Rev. Walter Fauntroy, a former King aide, becomes the first nonvoting congressional delegate from the District of Columbia since the Reconstruction period.

APR 20 U.S. Supreme Court rules unanimously in *Swann* v. *Charlotte-Mecklenburg Board of Education* that busing is a constitutionally acceptable method of integrating public schools where *de jure* segregation has existed.

MAY 13 Thirteen Black Panthers are acquitted on all 156 counts of bombing police stations and department stores in New York, NY.

MAY 18 Nixon rejects the 60 demands of the Congressional Black Caucus.

MAY 20 A Pentagon report shows that blacks constitute 11 percent of U.S. soldiers fighting in Southeast Asia and that 12.5 percent of all soldiers killed in Vietnam since 1961 are black.

JUN 14 U.S. Justice Department files suit against the St. Louis suburb of Black Jack, charging the illegal use of municipal procedures to block an integrated housing development.

JUN 15 Vernon E. Jordan, Jr., former executive director of the United Negro College Fund, is appointed executive director of the NUL.

JUN 28 U.S. Supreme Court unanimously overturns the draft evasion conviction of boxing champion Muhammad Ali.

AUG 18   One white policemen is killed during a joint FBI/Mississippi police raid on the headquarters of the Republic of New Africa in Jackson, MS. A black nationalist, separatist organization, the Republic of New Africa calls for an independent black nation within America, to be composed of five southern states. Imari Obadele (Richard Henry), provisional president of the organization, and 10 of his followers are arrested.

AUG 21   George Jackson, one of three convicts known as the Soledad Brothers, is killed in an alleged escape attempt from the California prison at San Quentin.

SEP 9–13   Inmates seize Attica State Correctional Facility in Attica, NY and hold several guards hostage demanding coverage by the state's minimum wage law, better food, and no reprisals against inmates involved; on Sep 13, 1500 troopers and officers storm the prison; 32 convicts and 10 guards are killed; an investigation later shows that nine of the 10 guards were killed by the storming party.

SEP 20   The National Urban Coalition's Committee on Cities reports that present trends indicate the majority of American cities will be predominantly black, brown, and bankrupt by 1980, that cities have become more polarized, and that the commitment of the federal government to correcting urban problems has decreased.

DEC 6   Lewis F. Powell and William H. Rehnquist are confirmed as Supreme Court justices despite opposition to their racial records by civil rights organizations.

DEC 18   People United to Save Humanity (PUSH) is founded in Chicago, IL by Rev. Jesse Jackson.

1972
JAN 25   Rep. Shirley Chisholm opens her campaign for President of the United States, the first black American to run for the presidency.

MAR 10–12   In Gary, IN, 3000 delegates and 5000 observers attend the first National Black Political Convention; they approve a "black agenda," which calls for reparations, proportional Congressional representation for blacks, an increase in federal spending to control drug traffic, reduction of the military budget, and a guaranteed annual income of $6500 a year for a family of four, to adjust with inflation; the NAACP and several other groups withdraw from the convention after the adoption of resolutions critical of busing and the state of Israel.

MAR 27   Two surviving Soledad Brothers are acquitted by an all-white jury of charges that they killed a white guard at Soledad Prison in 1970.

APR   National Education Association (NEA) study reveals that blacks have lost 30,000 teaching jobs in 17 southern and border states since 1954 because of discrimination and desegregation.

JUN 4   Angela Davis is acquitted by an all-white jury in San Jose, CA of charges stemming from a 1970 courtroom shootout.

JUN 30   The NAACP reports that the unemployment of "urban blacks in 1971 was worse than at any time since the great depression of the thirties" and that more school desegregation occurred in 1971 than in any other year since the 1954 *Brown* decision.

JUL 10	Democratic National Convention in Miami Beach, FL nominates Sen. George S. McGovern for president, although black Rep. Shirley Chisholm (NY) receives 151.95 of the 2000-plus ballots on the first roll call; blacks constitute 15 percent of the delegates.
JUL 13	U.S. Census Bureau reports that black unemployment averaged 9.9 percent in 1971, compared with 5.4 percent rate for whites.
AUG 21–22	Republican National Convention opens in Miami Beach, FL with 56 black delegates, 4.2 percent of the total; Richard Nixon is renominated.
SEP 13	Two blacks, Johnny Ford of Tuskegee and A.J. Cooper of Prichard, are elected mayors in Alabama.
OCT 12–13	Forty-six black and white sailors are injured in a race riot on board the aircraft carrier *Kitty Hawk* off North Vietnam.
NOV 16	In Baton Rouge, LA National Guard is called and the campus is closed after local police officers kill two students during Southern University demonstrations calling for the resignation of university president Dr. G. Leon Netterville because he is thought to have arbitrarily dismissed any professor he regarded as militant.
NOV 17	President Nixon is reelected, carrying 49 of the 50 states, despite massive black vote for Sen. George McGovern; 16 blacks are elected to Congress, including Andrew Young of Atlanta who becomes the first black elected to Congress from the deep south since the Reconstruction era; also elected for the first time are Barbara Jordan (TX) and Yvonne B. Burke (CA); Republican Sen. Edward W. Brooke (MA) is overwhelmingly endorsed for a second term.
DEC	Rev. W. Sterling Cary, former administrator of the United Church of Christ's Greater New York District, is elected the first black president of the National Council of Churches.

1973

APR	Black Panther leader Bobby Seale runs for mayor of Oakland, CA on the democratic ticket; he comes in second with 49 percent of the vote.
MAY 29	Thomas Bradley is elected mayor of Los Angeles, CA.
JUN 5	Cardiss R. Collins of Chicago is elected to Congress to succeed her late husband.
OCT 16	Maynard Jackson is elected mayor of Atlanta, GA.
NOV 6	Coleman Young is elected mayor of Detroit, MI.

1974

MAR	The Second National Black Political Convention meets in Little Rock, AR. Mayors Richard Hatcher of Gary, IN and Maynard Jackson of Atlanta, GA, and Amiri Baraka are major participants, but many prominent black leaders are absent, including Rep. Charles Diggs, who resigned as cochairman following the first conference.

APR — The Joint Center for Political Studies reports that 2991 blacks hold elective offices in 45 states and the District of Columbia, compared with 2621 in 1973 and 1185 in 1969.

U.S. Department of Justice releases memos confirming that in the 1960s and early 1970s the FBI had waged a campaign designed to disrupt, discredit, and neutralize black nationalist groups, including the Black Panthers.

MAY 9 — House Judiciary Committee opens hearings to decide whether to recommend the impeachment of President Richard M. Nixon in the Watergate conspiracy. Two blacks, Rep. John Conyers of Michigan and Rep. Barbara Jordan of Texas, are members of the committee.

MAY 19–27 — Approximately 500 delegates and observers, almost half of them Afro-Americans, attend the Sixth Pan-African Congress in Dar es Salaam, Tanzania.

JUN 30 — A black man kills Mrs. Martin L. King, Sr. and deacon Edward Boykin during church services at Ebenezer Baptist Church, Atlanta, GA. [The assailant, Marcus Chennault of Dayton, OH, is later convicted.]

JUL — U.S. Supreme Court rules in *Milliken* v. *Bradley* that interdistrict busing between Detroit, MI and its suburbs is not an appropriate means to integrate city schools.

AUG 9 — President Nixon resigns as a result of the Watergate scandal and is succeeded by Vice President Gerald R. Ford.

OCT 3 — Frank Robinson is named manager of the Cleveland Indians and becomes the first black manager in major league baseball.

NOV 5 — State Sen. Mervyn M. Dymally is elected Lt. Gov. of California. State Sen. George L. Brown is elected Lt. Gov. of Colorado. Walter E. Washington becomes the first elected mayor of Washington, DC. Harold Ford of Memphis, TN is elected to the U.S. House of Representatives.

1975

FEB 25 — Elijah Muhammad, leader of the Nation of Islam, dies in Chicago, IL and is succeeded by his son, Wallace D. Muhammad, who later opens the nation to people of all races.

JUN 25 — Mozambique proclaims independence.

JUL 5 — Arthur Ashe defeats Jimmy Connors to win the men's singles championship at Wimbledon, the first black to win a major singles tennis title.

AUG 15 — Joanne Little is acquitted of murder charges in the August 27, 1974 killing of a white police jailer. She had stabbed the jailer with an ice pick after she had been allegedly forced into sexual relations with him.

NOV 11 — Angola proclaims independence.

1976

APR 5 — FBI documents, released in response to a freedom of information suit, reveal details about the government's intensive campaign against SNCC and the SCLC in the 1960s.

JUL 1 — Kenneth Gibson, mayor of Newark, NJ, becomes the first black president of the U.S. Conference of Mayors.

OCT 25	Alabama Gov. George Wallace grants a full pardon to Clarence ("Willie") Norris, the last known survivor of the nine "Scottsboro Boys," who were convicted in 1931.
NOV 2	Jimmy Carter, former governor of Georgia, is elected 39th President of the United States with strong support from black voters.
NOV 6	Benjamin Hooks, Federal Communications Commission member, succeeds Roy Wilkins as NAACP executive director.
DEC 16	Rep. Andrew Young (GA) is named ambassador and chief delegate to the UN.
DEC 21	Patricia R. Harris is named secretary of the U.S. Department of Housing and Urban Development (HUD).

1977

JAN 15	Second World Festival of Black and African Art (FesTac) occurs in Lagos, Nigeria, attended by a large black American delegation.
JAN 23–30	Some 130 million viewers watch televised production of *Roots*, an Afro-American biography by Alex Haley, during its eight-night presentation.
FEB 11	Clifford Alexander, Jr. is confirmed as the first black secretary of the U.S. Army.
MAR 8	Henry L. Marsh III is elected mayor of Richmond, VA.
SEP 24	John T. Walker is installed as bishop of the Episcopal diocese of Washington, DC.
OCT 27	Dr. Clifton R. Wharton, president of Michigan State University, is appointed chancellor of the State University of New York, the nation's largest state university.
NOV 12	Ernest N. Morial is elected mayor of New Orleans, LA.
NOV 19	Robert E. Chambliss, a former KKK member, is convicted of first-degree murder in the 1963 bombing of the Sixteenth Street Baptist Church where four black girls were killed and is sentenced to life imprisonment.

1978

JAN 16	National Aeronautics and Space Administration (NASA) names three black astronauts—Maj. Frederick D. Gregory, Maj. Guion S. Bluford, and Dr. Ronald E. McNair.
JUN 28	U.S. Supreme Court rules in *University of California Regents* v. *Bakke* that the University of California Medical School at Davis' refusal to admit Allan P. Bakke constitutes reverse discrimination.
NOV 4	William Howard, Jr. is elected president of the National Council of Churches.
NOV 7	Five blacks are elected to Congress for the first time: William Gray III (PA), Bennett Stewart (IL), Melvin Evans (Virgin Islands), Julian Dixon (CA), and George Leland (TX).
NOV 18	More than 900 persons, most of them black Americans, perish with leader Jim Jones in mass murder and suicide pact in Jonestown, Guyana.

JAN 30	Franklin A. Thomas is named president of the Ford Foundation, the first black to head a major American foundation.
FEB 23	Frank E. Petersen, Jr. is named the first black general in the U.S. Marine Corps.
FEB 27	HUD announces it will foreclose the financially troubled Soul City, a new town in rural North Carolina that is run by blacks, but open to all.
MAY 31	Zimbabwe proclaims independence.
JUN 19	U.S. Census Bureau announces that black Americans still remain far behind white Americans in employment, income, health, housing, political power, and other measures of social well-being.
JUL 19	Patricia Harris, secretary of the U.S. Department of Housing and Urban Development (HUD), is named secretary of the U.S. Department of Health, Education, and Welfare (HEW).
AUG 15–31	Andrew Young resigns under pressure as UN ambassador after an unauthorized meeting with representatives of the Palestinian Liberation Organization (PLO); black leaders express support for Young and demand that blacks be given a voice in shaping American foreign policy; Donald McHenry is named to succeed Young.
OCT 3	City Councilman Richard Arrington is elected the first black mayor of Birmingham, AL.
NOV 15	B'nai B'rith Anti-Defamation League study reports a sharp rise in KKK activity: membership in 22 states has risen from 8000 to 10,000 in a 20-month period ending in November 1979 and the number of sympathizers has grown from 30,000 to 100,000.
DEC	The U.S. Bureau of Labor Statistics (BLS) reports that since 1970 one-parent households in the general population increased 79 percent, affecting nearly 6 million of 30.4 million families. Among black Americans, the proportion of one-parent households increased to 49 percent.

1980

MAY 17–19	Major race riot occurs in Miami, FL.
MAY 29	Vernon E. Jordan, Jr., president of the NUL, is critically wounded in an attempted assassination in Fort Wayne, IN.
OCT 13	Unprovoked slayings of six blacks in Buffalo, NY triggers demands for a national investigation.
NOV 4	Ronald W. Reagan wins the presidential election in a landslide victory over incumbent Jimmy Carter.
NOV 23	About 1,000 people from 25 states attend a convention in Philadelphia, PA and form the National Black Independent Political Party.
DEC	The BLS reports that in 1980, 10 percent of black families had a high standard of living, defined as an income of $30,317 for a family of four, 26 percent had a minimum standard of $20,517 for a family of four, but 46 percent were at the low end of the economic spectrum with an income of $13,000 or less.

Aid to Families with Dependent Children (AFDC) reports that 700,000 poor families, half of them black, received no welfare aid at all, and that 70 percent of all unemployed blacks never received jobless benefits. About 34 percent of all food stamp participants are black, AFDC reports, but 40 perent of poor black families receive no food stamps at all.

1981

JAN 9   Labor Department reports that black unemployment is 14 percent compared with 7.8 percent for whites.

JAN 14   James Frank, president of Lincoln University (MO), is installed as first black president of the National Collegiate Athletic Association (NCAA).

JAN 22   Samuel Pierce is named secretary of HUD by President Reagan.

MAR 5   The federal government grants Atlanta, GA $1 million to finance mental health and social programs in the wake of a series of abductions and bizarre slayings involving at least 27 black youth.

JUL 17   Fulton County (Atlanta), GA grand jury indicts Wayne B. Williams, a 23-year-old photographer, for the murder of two of the 28 black youths killed in a series of disappearances and slayings in Atlanta; Williams is convicted in February 1982.

JUL 31   Attorney Arnette R. Hubbard is installed as the first woman president of the National Bar Association, an organization of black lawyers.

AUG 10   The Coca-Cola Bottling Company agrees to put $34 million into black businesses and the black community, ending a national boycott called by PUSH.

SEP 9   Vernon E. Jordan resigns as NUL president and is succeeded by executive vice president John E. Jacob.

SEP 19   More than 300,000 demonstrators from labor and civil rights organizations protest the social policies of the Reagan administration in Solidarity Day march in Washington, DC.

SEP 28   Avowed racist Joseph P. Franklin is sentenced to life imprisonment for killing two black joggers in Salt Lake City, UT.

OCT 29   Andrew Young is elected mayor of Atlanta, GA to succeed Maynard Jackson.

NOV 3   Coleman Young is reelected mayor of Detroit, MI. Thurman L. Milner is elected mayor of Hartford, CT. James Chase is elected mayor of Spokane, WA.

NOV 28   Clarence M. Pendleton, president of the Urban League of San Diego who has promoted private industry efforts to solve black economic problems and expressed opposition to affirmative action and busing programs, is nominated to be chairman of the U.S. Commission on Civil Rights by President Reagan.

NOV 30   Four additional blacks are elected to Congress: Mervyn Dymally (CA), Augustus Savage (IL), Harold Washington (IL), and George W. Crockett, Jr. (MI).

DEC 8   William B. Reynolds, Asst. Atty. Gen. of the Justice Department's civil rights division, announces plans to seek a reversal of the Supreme Court's decision in 1979 in *Weber* v. *Kaiser Aluminum and Chemical Corporation*, which upheld the legality of the company's affirmative action hiring and promotion practices.

1982
FEB 5   Mayor Ernest N. "Dutch" Morial, the first black to be elected mayor of New Orleans, wins reelection.

FEB 6   A small band of southern civil rights workers, followed by 300 sympathizers, starts a 140-mile march from Carrollton, AL to Montgomery, AL in support of the Federal Voting Rights Act and in protest against the vote fraud conviction of two black political activists.

FEB 9   NUL president John E. Jacob announces five priority issues: black teenage pregnancy; the plight of the poor; female-headed households; crime in black neighborhoods; and voter registration and education.

FEB 10   Rep. Shirley Chisholm, a Democrat from New York who has served the Brooklyn communities of Bedford-Stuyvesant and Bushwick since 1968 and the first black woman to win a seat in Congress, announces that she will not seek another term.

FEB 11   U.S. Justice Department proposes that the city of Chicago, IL be allowed to desegregate its schools through voluntary student transfers rather than mandatory busing.

FEB 12   Bowing to opposition from civil rights groups and several Democratic senators, President Reagan withdraws the nomination of William M. Bell as chairman of the Equal Employment Opportunity Commission and announces the nomination of Clarence Thomas, an assistant secretary for civil rights in the U.S. Department of Education.

FEB 14   Hundreds of voting rights marchers going from Carrollton to Montgomery, AL march peacefully across the four-lane Edmund Pettus Bridge, where police had violently attacked the 1965 march.

APR 4   U.S. Census Bureau reports that the 1980 census missed counting 1.3 million or 4.8 percent of the nation's 28 million blacks and that the 1970 census missed 1.9 million or 7.7 percent of 24.4 million blacks.

APR 18   A study of national test results shows that black children improved on educational achievement tests during the 1970s.

JUN 18–23   The Senate and House approve the extension of the Voting Rights Act of 1965 for 25 years.

JUL 19   The Census Bureau reports a poverty rate of 14 percent, the highest since 1967, and a 7.4 percent increase over 1980. For blacks, however, the poverty rate is 36 percent.

NOV 5   U.S. Department of Labor reports the highest unemployment rate in U.S. since 1940 at 10.8 percent overall, with 20.2 percent black unemployment.

| JAN 23 | In a statement by the U.S. Commission on Civil Rights which is opposed by Chairman Clarence Pendleton, a majority of the commissioners state that various stands taken by the U.S. Justice Department could result in continued discrimination against minorities and women. |

JAN 23   In a statement by the U.S. Commission on Civil Rights which is opposed by Chairman Clarence Pendleton, a majority of the commissioners state that various stands taken by the U.S. Justice Department could result in continued discrimination against minorities and women.

APR 13   Rep. Harold Washington is elected as mayor of Chicago, IL becoming the first black to hold that office.

APR 19   The Leadership Conference on Civil Rights challenges changes in the enforcement of an executive order which prohibits federal contractors from discriminating and requires affirmative action programs, stating that the Reagan administration's proposals will dismantle the equal employment opportunity requirements for federal contractors and have a devastating impact on employment opportunities for minorities and women.

APR 26   The National Commission on Excellence in Education labels U.S. elementary and secondary education "mediocre" and recommends that schools put more emphasis on English, math, social studies, and computer science, that teachers be rewarded on merit, and that college admissions standards be raised.

MAY 18   W. Wilson Goode is elected mayor of Philadelphia, PA.

JUN 15   U.S. Commission on Civil Rights criticizes the Reagan administration for failing to appoint more women and minorities to high-level positions in the federal government.

AUG 28   Commemorating the 20th anniversary of the historic March on Washington, 250,000 people call for jobs, peace, and freedom.

AUG 31   District of Columbia Delegate Walter E. Fauntroy announces that congressional efforts to make Martin Luther King, Jr.'s birthday a national holiday will intensify.

NOV 3   Rev. Jesse Jackson, head of Operation PUSH, announces plans to run for the 1984 Democratic Presidential nomination.

NOV 22   A U.S. Commission on Civil Rights report charges the Reagan administration with weakening civil rights enforcement efforts by underfunding several key agencies.

DEC 4   During an antiterrorist operation in southern Lebanon, a navy plane is shot down by ground fire. One of the fliers is killed; the other, a black American named Robert Goodman, is captured and held by Syrian forces.

1984
JAN 3   After the personal intervention of Jackson, Syria frees Goodman.

JUN 4–6   At the Democratic Presidential Convention Jackson seeks changes in rules for primary elections and an end to gerrymandering and run-off elections in congressional, state, and local elections. Walter Mondale is nominated.

MAR 15	Several public opinion polls show a huge increase in black voter turnout, particularly in the south, as a result of the presidential candidacy of Jesse Jackson, who runs on the Independent ticket. Record averages of black statewide turnout are cited in Georgia and Alabama, where Jackson captures significant margins of voters.
MAY 2–7	Jackson scores his first major campaign victory by winning the District of Columbia primary with 70 percent of the vote. On May 7, black voters in Louisiana give Jackson his first state win in the primary elections with 43 percent of the vote.
JUN 13	U.S. Supreme Court rules in *Memphis Firefighters* v. *Stotts* that white workers with seniority may not be laid off their jobs to preserve the jobs of recently-hired blacks or affirmative action gains when company layoffs become necessary.
JUN 14	Asst. Atty. Gen. William B. Reynolds announces that the U.S. Justice Dept. will begin to reexamine all federal antidiscrimination settlements, and that the Equal Employment Opportunity Commission and other agencies will be authorized not to negotiate any new agreements using numerical quotas.
AUG 3	U.S. Census Bureau reports that despite improvements in the economy, the national poverty rate increased to 15.2 percent in 1983 from 15 percent in 1982, the highest in 18 years. In its annual report, the Census Bureau says that the ranks of the poor include 5.3 million children and that blacks comprise 28 percent of the 34 million Americans living in poverty.

TELECOURSE STAFF

The EYES ON THE PRIZE telecourse and telecourse materials were developed for Blackside, Inc. by Toby Levine Communications, a research and consulting firm established in 1984 to improve the use of media in education. Prior to establishing this firm, Toby Levine was director of educational activities at WETA/Washington, D.C., where she served as curriculum director of *From Jumpstreet: A Story of Black Music* and project manager of *Congress: We The People,* in addition to managing a telecourse programming service for local colleges and a marketing/distribution service for WETA-produced programs. She has also served as telecourse director and print managing editor for *The Africans,* a prime-time PBS series and telecourse funded by The Annenberg/CPB Project.

Senior Advisors and General Editors of Text

Clayborne Carson is Associate Professor of History at Stanford University. He was active in the civil rights movement and has written extensively about modern black protest movements. His first book, *In Struggle: SNCC and the Black Awakening of the 1960s* (Harvard University Press, 1981) won the Frederick Jackson Turner Prize of the Organization of American Historians. He currently is Director of the Martin Luther King, Jr. Papers Project which will edit and publish 12 volumes of King's letters, speeches, and other writings.

David J. Garrow is Associate Professor of Political Science at City College of New York and the City University Graduate School. He is the author of *Protest at Selma* (Yale University Press, 1978), *The FBI and Martin Luther King* (W.W. Norton, 1981), and *Bearing the Cross: Martin Luther King and the Southern Christian Leadership Conference* (William Morrow & Company, 1986).

Vincent Harding is currently Lang Visiting Professor at Swarthmore College in Pennsylvania and is on leave from the Iliff School of Theology in Denver where he is a Professor of Religion and Social Transformation. Professor Harding's two most recent books are *The Other American Revolution* (UCLA/CAAS) and *There Is a River* (Vintage), histories of the black struggle for freedom, justice, and transformation in which he has been an active participant.

Darlene Clark Hine is Vice Provost and Professor of History at Purdue University. She is the editor of *The State of Afro-American History: Past, Present and Future* (LSU Press, 1986) and the author of *Black Victory: The Rise and Fall of the Texas White Primary* (KTO Press, 1979). Dr. Hine is currently working on *Black Women in White: A History of Black Women in the Nursing Profession* to be published by the University of Illinois Press.

Telecourse Director/Managing Editor
Toby Kleban Levine

Research Coordinator
Raynard T. Davis

Copy Editor
Eleanor A. Gavin

Editorial Assistant
Ann Chervinsky

Research Assistant
Kevin Bohn

Manuscript Preparation
Judith Pickford-Barse

Design
DRPollard and Associates, Inc.,
Washington, DC

Composition
Carver Photocomposition, Inc.,
Arlington, VA

Special thanks to Ethelbert Miller, Founders Library, Howard University; Walter W. Morrison, NAACP; Arybie Rose; and the Staff of Moorland Spingarn Research Center, Howard University.

EYES ON THE PRIZE was developed by Blackside, Inc., a Boston-based independent film company founded in 1968 that has produced more than 40 major film and media projects. Among the previous production credits of its executive producer, Henry Hampton, president and founder of Blackside, Inc., are *Kinfolks,* a documentary examining the state of the black family (selected for a 1979 CEBA Award as the best long-form documentary on minority Americans), and *Voices of a Divided City,* a nationally broadcast PBS documentary about the aftermath of the desegregation of Boston's public schools. Hampton also was project manager of *The Black Chronicle,* a print-based educational package for secondary schools, published in association with Holt, Rinehart & Winston.

Executive Producer
Henry Hampton

Series Senior Producer
Judith Vecchione

Series Producer
Jon Else

*Series Consulting
Executive Producer*
Michael Ambrosino

Producers
Judith Vecchione
Orlando Bagwell
Callie Crossley
James A. DeVinney

Associate Producers
Llewellyn Smith
Prudence Arndt

Series Writer
Steve Fayer

Senior Researcher
Laurie Kahn-Leavitt

Series Research Consultant
Judy Richardson

Editors
Daniel Eisenberg
Jeanne Jordan
Charles Scott

Assistant Editors
Victoria Garvin
MJ Doherty
Ann Bartholomew

*Stock Footage
Coordinator*
Kenn Rabin

Production Manager
Jo Ann Mathieu

Production Assistant
Peter Montgomery

Editing Room Assistants
Elizabeth Carver
Meredith Woods
Eliza Gagnon

Production Interns
Renee Bovelle
Charisse Chavious
Gordon Eriksen
Theresa Garofalo
Rosiland Jordan
Ismael Ramirez
Joseph Rogers

Ruth Shupp
Lisa Silvera
Dawne Simon
Alfonzo Smith
Matthew Sucherman
Peter Vrooman

Director of Publishing
Robert Lavelle

Trade Book Author
Juan Williams

Publishing Associates
Frances Norris
Bennett Singer

Accountant
Lorraine Flynn

Business Manager
J. Benjamin Harris

Project Administrator
Inez Robinson

Production Secretaries
Sara Chazen
Karen Chase

NATIONAL ADVISORY BOARD

FUNDERS

EYES ON THE PRIZE is funded by public television stations, the Corporation for Public Broadcasting and by major grants from The Ford Foundation, Lotus Development Corporation, and The Lilly Endowment. Additional funding has been provided by Abelard Foundation, Ruth Batson Educational Foundation, Bay Packaging & Converting Co., Inc., Bird Companies Charitable Foundation, The Boston Foundation, The Boston Globe Foundation, The Columbia Foundation, Cummins Engine Company, Inc., The Freed Foundation, Freedom House, Friedman Family Foundation, The Wallace Alexander Gerbode Foundation, Richard and Rhoda Goldman Fund, The Irving I. Goldstein Foundation, The Edward W. Hazen Foundation, Hillsdale Fund Inc., The Charles Evans Hughes Foundation, Joint Foundation Support, Inc., The Kraft Foundation, Metropolitan Foundation of Atlanta, The New York Community Trust, The Philadelphia Foundation, Polaroid Foundation, The Mary Norris Preyer Fund, Raytheon Company, The San Francisco Foundation, The Sapelo Island Research Foundation, Sun Company, The Tides Foundation, and The Villers Foundation.

Special thanks to the Charles H. Revson Foundation for its support.

University of Alabama, 103, 119–120
University of California, Davis Medical
      School, 252–258
University of Chicago, 89
University of Mississippi, 55, 136, 180
University of Missouri, 54
University of Oklahoma, 54
University of Texas, 54
University of Wisconsin, 209
Urban Renewal, 205
USSR, 17, 22, 30

Van Alstyne, William, 258–262
Vanderbilt University, 78
   Divinity School, 86
Vanik, Charles, 206
Vietnam, 201–204, 235–237
Vietnamese War, 180, 181, 182, 191,
      201, 205, 291, 235–236
Violence, 14, 21, 31, 32, 35, 50, 80,
      110, 111, 115, 134, 135, 136,
      138, 140, 154, 155, 160, 162,
      190, 217, 237
Virginia
   Petersburg, 105
   Prince Edward County, 55, 58, 63
   Richmond, 105
Voter Education, 153, 154–155, 156,
      157–158, 159, 170–171
Voter Registration, 39–40, 102, 105,
      126–149, 156, 157, 168, 194,
      198, 207
Voting, 23, 34, 35, 120, 126, 156,
      207–208, 244, 249, 264
Voting Rights, 11, 22, 79, 85, 153, 154,
      155, 270, 292
Voting Rights Act of 1965, 155, 167,
      180, 244, 294

Walker, Rosa, 110
Walker, Wyatt T., 113
Wallace, George C., 55, 103, 119–120,
      123
Walls, Carlotta, 68
War on Poverty, 201, 216, 271
Warren, Earl B., 56–58, 66–67
Washington, Seattle, 73
Washington, Booker T., 4, 10–11, 298

Washington, George, 62
Washington, DC, see District of
      Columbia
Watergate, 225
Watts, 180, 198, 219
Wayne State University, 230
Wells-Barnett, Ida B., 5–7, 9, 12, 183
White Backlash, 181, 215, 225, 299
White Citizens' Council, see Citizens'
      Councils
White Moderates, 117, 165–166. See
      also Black-white Alliance
White Philanthropy, 7, 12
White Religious Leadership, 117
White Supremacy, 4, 7, 10, 12, 16, 22
Wilkins, Roy, 39, 104, 176, 193
Williams, Hosea, 154, 164
Williams, Robert F., 29, 80–81, 96
Williamson, Rev. Cecil
Willie, Charles, 74
Wilson, William, 281–282
Wilson, Woodrow, 13
Wisconsin, 110–111
Wise, Stanley, 192
Women's Political Council (WPC),
      39–42
Women's Rights, 263, 264, 265, 267,
      283–285, 294, 299
Women's Suffrage, 7
Woolworth's, 83, 84, 90. See also Sit-ins
World War I, 12–15
World War II, 17, 20–22
Wretched of the Earth, 198
Wright, Mose, 35
Wright, Richard, 16–17

Yale University, 126
Young, Andrew, 164
Young, Whitney, 104, 193
Young Negroes' Cooperative League, 87
Young Womens' Christian Association
      (YWCA), 87
Youth March for Integration, 89

Zellner, Robert, 93–95, 132, 139

355

Concept of complementarity on
multiple fronts

grassroots but organized
specific action coupled with multiple   boycott
                                            or writ or
                                            legal
                               Strategies   action

Collective + individual leadership.

widespread support < Black
                          +
                        White .